Advanced Structural Equation Modeling

Issues and Techniques

Advanced Structural Equation Modeling

Issues and Techniques

Edited by

George A. Marcoulides
California State University, Fullerton

Randall E. Schumacker
University of North Texas

LEA LAWRENCE ERLBAUM ASSOCIATES, PUBLISHERS
1996 Mahwah, New Jersey

Lawrence Erlbaum Associates, Inc., Publishers
10 Industrial Avenue
Mahwah, New Jersey 07430-2262

Cover design by Gail Silverman

Library of Congress Cataloging-in-Publication Data

Advanced structural equation modeling : issues and techniques / edited by George A. Marcoulides, Randall E. Schumacker.
    p.   cm.
Includes bibliographical references and index.
ISBN 0-8058-1819-7
1. Multivariate analysis. 2. Social sciences—Statistical methods. I. Marcoulides, George A. II. Schumacker, Randall E.
QA278.A27 1996
519.5′35—dc20   95-34310
                                                                    CIP

Books published by Lawrence Erlbaum Associates are printed on acid-free paper, and their bindings are chosen for strength and durability.

Printed in the United States of America
10 9 8 7 6 5 4 3 2 1

Contents

Acknowledgments

We would like to thank all of the contributors for their time and effort in preparing chapters for this volume. They all provided excellent chapters and the authors worked diligently with us through the various stages of the publication process. Without them, this volume would not exist. We would also like to thank Larry Erlbaum, Judith Amsel, Kathleen Dolan, Kathryn Scornavacca, and the rest of the editorial staff at Lawrence Erlbaum Associates for their assistance and support in putting together this volume. Finally, we thank our families for their love and for enduring yet another project.

—*George A. Marcoulides*
—*Randall E. Schumacker*

CHAPTER ONE

Introduction

George A. Marcoulides
California State University, Fullerton

Randall E. Schumacker
University of North Texas

Structural equation models (SEMs) are used by biologists, educational researchers, market researchers, medical researchers, psychologists, social scientists, and others who traditionally deal with nonexperimental and quasi-experimental data. One reason for the pervasive use in almost every scientific field of study is that SEMs provide researchers with a comprehensive method for the quantification and testing of theories. In fact, it has been suggested that the development of SEM is perhaps the most important and influential statistical revolution to have recently occurred in the scientific arena (Cliff, 1983).

SEM techniques are accepted today as a major component of applied multivariate analysis. The use of the term *structural equation modeling* is broadly defined to accomodate models that include latent variables, measurement errors in both dependent and independent variables, multiple indicators, reciprocal causation, simultaneity, and interdependence. As implemented in most commercial computer packages (e.g., Amos, EQS, LISREL, LISCOMP, Mx, SAS PROC-CALIS, STATISTICA-SEPATH), the method includes as special cases such procedures as confirmatory factor analysis, multiple regression, path analysis, models for time-dependent data, recursive and nonrecursive models for cross-sectional and longitutinal data, and covariance structure analysis.

The purpose of this volume is to introduce the latest issues and developments in SEM techniques. The goal is to provide an understanding and working knowledge of advanced SEM techniques with a minimum of

1

mathematical derivations. The strategy is to focus primarily on the application of SEM techniques in example cases and situations. We believe that by using this didactic approach, readers will better understand the underlying logic of advanced SEM techniques and, thereby, assess the suitability of the method for their own research. As such, the volume is targeted to a broad audience across multiple disciplines. It is assumed that the reader has mastered the equivalent of a graduate-level multivariate statistics course that included coverage of introductory SEM techniques.

The chapters in this volume provide a timely contribution to the literature on SEM. The theoretical developments and applications of SEMs are burgeoning, and so this volume could have easily become several volumes. Unfortunately, within the limitations of a single volume, only a limited number of topics could be addressed. Each chapter included in this volume was selected to address what we believe are currently the most important issues and developments in SEM. The topics selected include models for multitrait–multimethod (MTMM) matrix analysis, nonlinear structural equation models, multilevel models, cross-domain analyses of change over time, structural time series models, bootstrapping techniques in the analysis of mean and covariance structure, limited information estimators, dealing with incomplete data, problems with equivalent models, and an evaluation of incremental fit indices.

OVERVIEW OF THE VOLUME

Some 35 years ago, Campbell and Fiske (1959) presented the MTMM matrix as a device to assess convergent and divergent validity. Although the qualitative criteria that Campbell and Fiske proposed to judge convergent and divergent validity are quite well known, what is the best method to evaluate quantitatively these two validities is not yet known. In chapter 2, Wothke concentrates on three quantitative approaches to MTMM analysis: confirmatory factor analysis, covariance component analysis, and the direct product model. The three approaches are presented in formal notation and illustrated with worked examples. In addition, model specifications of the worked examples for the Amos (Arbuckle, 1995), LISREL (Jöreskog & Sörbom, 1993), and Mx (Neale, 1994) programs are provided in an appendix. It is shown that covariance component analysis and the direct product model can yield simultaneous estimates of method and trait components. However, there are many cases where these two approaches provide inadmissible solutions or very poor fit. In contrast, the confirmatory factor-analytic approach generally provides admissible solutions but does not yield reliable results when both correlated trait and method factors are included in a measurement design. The chapter concludes by emphasizing the importance of carefully conceptualized MTMM measurement designs.

Models with interaction and nonlinear effects are often encountered in the social and behavioral sciences. In SEM, estimating the interaction effects of latent variables is made possible by using nonlinear and product indicators. In chapter 3, Jöreskog and Yang investigate the interaction effects model proposed by Kenny and Judd (1984) as a general model with nonlinear relationships between latent variables. Using both articificial and empirical data from example cases that involve interactions among latent variables, the authors demonstrate how nonlinear models can be estimated. Model specifications and output using the LISREL program are provided throughout the chapter. The chapter concludes by providing some general guidelines researchers must consider before attempting to model nonlinear relationships among latent variables.

In chapter 4, McArdle and Hamagami present an overview of the multilevel modeling approach from a multiple group SEM perspective. Multilevel models (also referred to as random coefficient, variance components, or hierarchical linear models; Bryk & Raudenbush, 1992) have recently become popular because they permit researchers to deal with estimation problems in complex nested data collection designs. The authors examine the major models of multilevel analysis (i.e., the variance components model, the random coefficients model, the logit model, longitudinal growth models, and multilevel factor models) and attempt to relate these models to standard SEMs for multiple groups. Using examples of multilevel models from their own work on individual differences in human cognitive abilities, the authors illustrate some of the benefits and limitations of the multilevel approach.

In chapter 5, Willett and Sayer demonstrate how the methods of individual growth modeling and covariance structure analysis can be integrated to investigate interindividual differences in change over time. The individual growth-modeling approach uses a pair of hierarchical statistical models to represent two distinct models: (a) individual status as a function of time (the so-called "Level 1" model), and (b) interindividual differences in true change (the so-called "Level 2" model). In the covariance structure approach, these two models can be reformatted as the "measurement" and "structural" components of the general LISREL model with mean structures, and their parameter estimates can be determined. Using longitudinal data drawn from the National Child Development Study (a longitudinal study of all children born in Britain between March 3–9, 1958), Willett and Sayer explain and demonstrate how the new approach can be used to investigate the interrelationships among simultaneous individual changes in two domains (reading and mathematics achievement) over the entire school career, for both healthy children and children with chronic illness. Generalizations of the approach to more than two domains are also discussed, and sample LISREL programs (Jöreskog & Sörbom, 1993) are provided in an appendix.

4   MARCOULIDES AND SCHUMACKER

Time series models attempt to describe the behavior of a process across multiple occasions (Harvey, 1981). To date, time series models have not received extensive usage in the social and behavioral sciences. The most cited reasons for this neglect have been the need to collect data across numerous occasions, and the mathematical complexity of the models (Schmitz, 1990). In chapter 6, Hershberger, Molenaar, and Corneal describe how various time series models can be analyzed using an SEM approach. For each time series model presented, the authors provide a basic description of the model, how the model is analyzed in SEM, and the results of fitting the model to an example data set. In addition, LISREL instructions and model specifications of the example data sets are provided in an appendix.

In chapter 7, Yung and Bentler focus on the application of bootstrapping techniques to covariance structure analysis, of which exploratory and confirmatory factor analysis are considered the leading cases. In general, bootstrapping techniques involve the drawing of random subsamples from an original sample and estimating various parameters from each subsample for the purpose of studying some characteristic of the distribution of these parameter estimates (Efron & Tibshirani, 1993). Using real data, the authors examine the application of bootstrap methods suitable for covariance structure analysis and determine whether the bootstrap "works" for the given situations. The authors also present two new applications of the bootstrap approach to mean and covariance structures.

Estimators for SEMs fall into two classes: full-information and limited-information estimators. Full-information estimators attempt to derive parameter estimates in a model by using all information in the sets of equations simultaneously (e.g., maximum likelihood, generalized least squares, weighted least squares). Limited-information estimators attempt to derive parameter estimates in a model, one equation at a time. Unfortunately, a critical drawback with full-information estimators is that any specification error in the set of equations can bias the estimates throughout the system. In contrast, the use of limited-information estimators results in the bias sometimes being isolated to either one equation or just part of the system. In chapter 8, Bollen presents a two-stage least squares (2SLS) limited-information estimator for structural equation models with latent variables. Using example data, Bollen explains and demonstrates how the proposed 2SLS estimator can be used in various SEMs, including those with heteroscedastic errors.

In chapter 9, Arbuckle discusses the application of maximum likelihood (ML) estimation as an alternative method for handling missing data. Incomplete or missing data are routinely encountered in structural equation modeling, and are even a byproduct from the use of certain designs (e.g., Balanced Incomplete Block, Spiraling Designs; Brown, 1994). To date, a considerable number of approaches for dealing with missing data have been proposed in the literature (Little & Rubin, 1989). The most common approaches are ad hoc adjustments to the data that attempt to remedy the problem either by removal or replacement of values. SEMs are built on the assumption that the covariance matrix follows a Wishart distribution (Brown, 1994; Jöreskog, 1969). As such, complete data are required for the probability density function estimation, and ad hoc adjustments must be made to the data set when there are missing values. Current practice in the handling of missing data for SEMs appears to be dominated by the methods sometimes known as "pairwise deletion" and "listwise deletion." In Arbuckle's chapter, two simulations are presented in which the performance of a full-information ML estimation method is compared to the performance of competing missing data techniques. The results demonstrate both the efficiency and the reduced bias of ML estimates. It appears that ML estimation with incomplete data should be the preferred method of treating missing data when the alternatives are pairwise deletion and listwise deletion.

The problem of equivalent models has been known since the earliest developmental stages of SEM. Equivalent models are those that provide identical statistical fit to the data as the hypothesized model but may imply very different substantive interpretations of the data. In chapter 10, Williams, Bozdogan, and Aiman-Smith provide an overview of problems associated with testing equivalent models and propose the use of a novel information complexity approach to assess model fit for equivalent models. Using results of analyses from both simulated and real sample data, the authors demonstrate how to assess model fit among the equivalent models and how substantive conclusions about relationships in models can be impacted when selecting one model from among a set of equivalent models.

In order to assess the goodness of fit of SEMs, researchers generally rely on subjective indices of fit (Bentler, 1990). Although different types of indices have been proposed in the literature, no concensus has been reached as to which are the best (Tanaka, 1993). Currently, the most popular indices are from the family of incremental fit indices (Bollen & Long, 1993). The final chapter by Marsh, Balla, and Hau, examines seven incremental fit indices in relation to their mathematical and empirical properties in a large Monte Carlo study. These seven incremental fit indices are provided as standard output in most commercially available SEM computer packages. The authors recommend that the nonnormed fit index (or its normed counterpart the normed Tucker–Lewis index), and the relative noncentrality index (or its normed counterpart the comparative fit index) should be preferred when evaluating goodness of fit of SEMs. The normed fit index, the incremental fit index, and the relative fit index are not recommended because they are systematically biased by sample size and can inappropriately penalize model complexity.

6 MARCOULIDES AND SCHUMACKER

REFERENCES

Arbuckle, J. L. (1995). *Amos for Windows. Analysis of moment structures (Version 3.5)*. Chicago, IL: Smallwaters.

Bentler, P. M. (1990). Comparative fit indices in structural models. *Psychological Bulletin, 107,* 238–246.

Bollen, K. A., & Long, J. S. (1993). Introduction. In K. A. Bollen & J. S. Long (Eds.), *Testing structural equation models*. Newbury Park, CA: Sage.

Brown, R. L. (1994). Efficacy of the indirect approach for estimating structural equation models with missing data: A comparison of five methods. *Structural Equation Modeling, 1,* 287–316.

Bryk, A. S., & Raudenbush, S. W. (1992). *Hierarchical linear models: Applications and data analysis methods*. Newbury Park, CA: Sage.

Campbell, D. T., & Fiske, D. W. (1959). Convergent and discriminant validation by the multitrait-multimethod matrix. *Psychological Bulletin, 56,* 81–105.

Cliff, N. (1983). Some cautions concerning the application of causal modeling methods. *Multivariate Behavioral Research, 18,* 115–126.

Efron, B., & Tibshirani, R. J. (1993). *An introduction to the bootstrap*. New York: Chapman & Hall.

Harvey, A. C. (1981). *Time-series models*. Oxford: Philip Alan.

Jöreskog, K. G. (1969). A general approach to confirmatory maximum likelihood factor analysis. *Psychometrika, 34,* 183–202.

Jöreskog, K. G., & Sörbom, D. (1993). *LISREL 8. Structural equation modeling with the SIMPLIS command language*. Chicago, IL: Scientific Software International.

Kenny, D. A., & Judd, C. M. (1984). Estimating the nonlinear and interactive effects of latent variables. *Psychological Bulletin, 96,* 201–210.

Little, R. J. A., & Rubin, D. B. (1989). The analysis of social science data with missing values. *Sociological Methods and Research, 18,* 292–326.

Neale, M. C. (1994). *Mx: Statistical modeling* (2nd ed.). Richmond, VA: Author.

Schmitz, B. (1990). Univariate and multivariate time-series models: The analysis of intra-individual variability and interindividual relationships. In A. Von Eye (Ed.), *Statistical methods in longitudinal research* (Vol. 2). New York: Academic Press.

Tanaka, J. S. (1993). Multifaceted conceptions of fit in structural equation models. In K. A. Bollen & J. S. Long (Eds.), *Testing structural equation models*. Newbury Park, CA: Sage.

CHAPTER TWO

Models for Multitrait–Multimethod Matrix Analysis

Werner Wothke
SmallWaters Corporation, Chicago

The well-known contribution by Campbell and Fiske (1959) presented the multitrait–multimethod (MTMM) matrix format as a device to study trait validity across different assessment methods. The crossed measurement design in the MTMM matrix derives from a simple rationale: Traits are universal, manifest over a variety of situations and detectable with a variety of methods. Most importantly, the magnitude of a trait should not change just because different assessment methods are used.

This chapter discusses several multivariate statistical models for analyzing the MTMM matrix. Throughout the following, the terms *trait* and *measure* will frequently appear. The *trait* concept is always used in psychometric terms, as a "latent" variable (Lord & Novick, 1968, p. 530). Its use does not imply the presence of an enduring personality disposition. As used here, the term *trait* could be applied equally to magnitude perceptions or attitudes. The other term, *measure*, designates an observed variable like a test score, rating, and the like. A *measure* is directly observed and is usually subject to measurement error. This is in contrast to *traits*, which are free of error but not directly observable.

Ideally, if a MTMM covariance matrix contains m equivalent sets of measures of t traits, each utilizing a different method of assessment, it will have the structure

$$\Sigma_{(mt \times mt)} = (1_m 1'_m) \otimes \Sigma_{\tau(t \times t)} + \text{diag}(\theta_{(1,1)}, \theta_{(1,2)},..., \theta_{(m,t)})_{(mt \times mt)}$$

$$= \begin{pmatrix} \Sigma_\tau & \cdots & \Sigma_\tau \\ \vdots & \ddots & \vdots \\ \Sigma_\tau & \cdots & \Sigma_\tau \end{pmatrix} + \text{diag}(\theta_{(1,1)}, \theta_{(1,2)}, \ldots, \theta_{(m,t)})_{(mt \times mt)}, \qquad (1)$$

where

Σ is the $mt \times mt$ covariance matrix among all measures,

1 is an $m \times 1$ vector of unit values,

$\otimes$ symbolizes the (right) Kronecker product operator (cf. Bock, 1975),

Σ_τ is the $t \times t$ covariance matrix among trait measures within each method, and

$\text{diag}(\theta_{(1,1)}, \theta_{(1,2)}, \ldots, \theta_{(m,t)})$ is the diagonal matrix of uncorrelated uniqueness components of the mt measures.

A trivial implication of model Equation 1 is that all measurements must be on a comparable scale. This is the same as the psychometric concept of τ-equivalent measurement (Jöreskog, 1971; Lord & Novick, 1968). In the behavioral and social sciences, where such diverse methods as test scores, behavioral observations, and one-item ratings are often being compared, strong scale assumptions are not usually warranted. These fields have typically regarded scale information as arbitrary or of little interest and, since Spearman's days, have had a tradition of analyzing *correlation* matrices, thereby neglecting any information due to the original scale of measurement.

Following the scale-free tradition, Campbell and Fiske (1959) avoided the strict terminology of Equation 1 and proposed, instead, several qualitative criteria to judge convergent and discriminant validity (more recently reviewed by Schmitt & Stults, 1986). These criteria are based on direct comparisons among correlation coefficients, appear to be rigorous, and do not require complicated statistical computation. Yet, while the Campbell and Fiske criteria will often detect method effects, they can be equally violated in the absence of method effects when measures merely differ in reliability (Wothke, 1984). The Campbell and Fiske criteria can therefore be unnecessarily restrictive compared to the more recent psychometric concepts of τ-equivalent and congeneric measurement (Jöreskog, 1971). Also, because of their lack of a statistical basis, the Campbell and Fiske criteria should be replaced by quantitative rules that are sensitive to sampling error (see, e.g., Althauser, 1974; Althauser & Heberlein, 1970; Althauser, Heberlein, & Scott, 1971).

This chapter concentrates on three quantitative approaches that easily lend themselves to MTMM analysis: *confirmatory factor analysis* (CFA;

Jöreskog, 1966, 1971, 1974, 1978), *covariance component analysis* (CCA; Bock, 1960; Bock & Bargmann, 1966; Wiley, Schmidt, & Bramble, 1973), and the *direct product model* (DPM; Browne, 1984a; Cudeck, 1988; Wothke & Browne, 1990). CFA and CCA are immediate realizations of the multivariate linear model. The DPM, while having a distinctly nonlinear appearance, can, nevertheless, be expressed as a constrained version of second-order factor analysis (Wothke & Browne, 1990). All three approaches are therefore instances of the linear model and its host of statistical theory, but they are structurally distinct and derive from different statistical traditions: CFA is rooted in the psychometric tradition of validity theory, as outlined by Lord and Novick (1968); CCA is a multivariate generalization of random effects analysis of variance, based on R. A. Fisher's work; and the DPM is a new animal altogether.

The remainder of the chapter is organized as follows: The next section describes two commonly used factor models for the MTMM matrix; one having only trait factors, the other including additional method factors. It illustrates their application with worked examples and discusses frequently occurring identification problems of the second model. I then present a structural modeling framework for covariance component analysis, state identification conditions for its fixed-scale and scale-free variants, and illustrate the application of the scale-free version with two worked examples. A distinction is made between planned comparisons of traits and methods and arbitrarily chosen contrasts. To aid interpretation in the latter case, it is shown how to transform the estimates to simple structure using blockwise principal components decomposition and varimax rotation methods. The next section gives the specifications and identification conditions for the DPM. A worked example of the direct product model is interpreted from both multiplicative and linear viewpoints. The final section develops a common framework for all three models, discusses how they are nested within each other, and relates them to the Campbell and Fiske validity criteria. Model specifications of the worked examples, for the Amos (Arbuckle, 1995), LISREL (Jöreskog & Sörbom, 1993) and Mx (Neale, 1994) programs, are given in the appendix.

CONFIRMATORY FACTOR ANALYSIS

Among the several competing multivariate models for MTMM matrix analysis reviewed by Schmitt and Stults (1986) and by Millsap (1995), virtually only the CFA approach has maintained an appreciable following in the literature. In this section, two prominent types of factor models are evaluated: the *trait-only* model, outlined by Jöreskog (1966, 1971), which expresses the observed variables in terms of t nonoverlapping, oblique trait factors, and the *trait-method* factor model (cf. Althauser & Heberlein, 1970; Jöreskog, 1971, 1978; Werts & Linn, 1970), which contains *m* additional method factors to absorb method components of measurement. Instructions for specifying the two MTMM factor model structures have long been available (e.g., Jöreskog, 1971, 1978). These apply equally to the several available statistical estimation methods, such as normal-theory maximum likelihood (ML), asymptotically distribution-free (Browne, 1984b), and others that are nowadays available in commercially distributed statistical software.

Exemplary analyses in this and the following sections are worked out with the Amos (Arbuckle, 1995) and LISREL (Jöreskog & Sörbom, 1993) programs, with program input displayed in the appendix. All examples use the common normal-theory ML estimation method, and fit is evaluated by the G^2 statistic,[1] computed as

$$G^2 = (n-1) \ [\ln |\hat{\Sigma}| - \ln|S| + \text{trace}(S\hat{\Sigma}^{-1}) - mt],$$ (2)

where *n* is the sample size. Under multivariate normality, given the population covariance structure Σ, G^2 is asymptotically χ^2-distributed with

$$df = \frac{mt(mt+1)}{2} - q,$$ (3)

where *q* is the number of independently estimated model parameters.

Factor analysis decomposes the $n \times p$ data matrix **X** of *p* measures on *n* units into an $n \times k$ matrix Ξ of a lesser number *k* of latent factors:

$$X = \Xi \Lambda' + E,$$ (4)

where Λ is the $p \times k$ matrix of partial regression coefficients of observed measures regressed onto the latent factors and **E** is the matrix of unique components assumed to be uncorrelated with each other and with the factor scores in Ξ. Expressing the population covariance matrices of **X**, Ξ and **E** as Σ_x, Φ, and Θ, respectively, Equation 4 implies the covariance representation

$$\Sigma_x = \Lambda \Phi \Lambda' + \Theta.$$ (5)

Factor models with correlated uniqueness coefficients have also been proposed (e.g., Browne, 1980; Kenny & Kashy, 1992; Marsh, 1989; Marsh & Bailey, 1991; Stacy, Widaman, Hays, & DiMatteo, 1985), but these are

---

[1]Alternative fit indices are discussed by Bozdogan (1987); Cudeck and Henley (1991); Marsh, Balla, and McDonald (1988); and McDonald and Marsh (1990).

not considered here because they violate the postulate of conditional independence (Bartholomew, 1987) and hence prevent one from concluding that the factors account for all systematic covariation among the observed variables. In the following, CFA models of the MTMM matrix are described by the particular restrictions they impose on the Λ and Φ matrices. Θ is always estimated as a diagonal matrix.

Trait-Only Factor Analysis

A simple form of factor-analytic models for MTMM matrices takes the view that all common variation of the observed measures is accounted by latent trait factors and none of the variance can be attributed to methods. The different traits may be correlated (or oblique). Each measure assesses exactly one trait factor. Such a trait-only model (Jöreskog, 1971, 1978; Schmitt, 1978; Werts, Jöreskog, & Linn, 1972; Werts & Linn, 1970) shows the properties of *congeneric* measurement. When traits are ordered within methods, the factor loading matrix for a 3×3 MTMM design has the form

$$\Lambda_\tau = \begin{pmatrix} \lambda_{1,\tau_1} & 0 & 0 \\ 0 & \lambda_{2,\tau_2} & 0 \\ 0 & 0 & \lambda_{3,\tau_3} \\ \lambda_{4,\tau_1} & 0 & 0 \\ 0 & \lambda_{5,\tau_2} & 0 \\ 0 & 0 & \lambda_{6,\tau_3} \\ \lambda_{7,\tau_1} & 0 & 0 \\ 0 & \lambda_{8,\tau_2} & 0 \\ 0 & 0 & \lambda_{9,\tau_3} \end{pmatrix} \qquad (6)$$

and the matrix of factor intercorrelations is

$$\Phi_\tau = \begin{pmatrix} 1.0 & \text{(symm.)} & \\ \phi_{\tau_2,\tau_1} & 1.0 & \\ \phi_{\tau_3,\tau_1} & \phi_{\tau_3,\tau_2} & 1.0 \end{pmatrix}, \qquad (7)$$

whereby the subscript τ in Λ_τ and Φ_τ indicates that only trait factors are included. All zero entries in Λ_τ and all diagonal entries in Φ_τ are fixed (predetermined) parameters, the nine parameters $\lambda_{i,\tau j}$ and the three parameters $\phi_{\tau j,\tau j'}$ are estimated from the data. Also estimated are the nine uniqueness coefficients in the diagonal of Θ.

The worked example uses a MTMM matrix from Flamer (1983), reproduced in Table 2.1. The traits are *Attitude toward Discipline in Children* (ADC), *Attitude toward Mathematics* (AM), and *Attitude toward the Law* (AL). All assessment methods are paper-and-pencil, but comprise different item types and response formats: dichotomous Likert scales, Thurstone scales, and the semantic differential (SD) technique. Relatively large entries in the validity diagonals suggest convergent trait validation. Similar patterns of relatively small correlations in the monomethod triangles and in the heterotrait–heteromethod blocks suggest stability across the three scaling methods.

Table 2.2 shows the parameter estimates for the trait-only factor model of the Flamer data. The solution is admissible and the ML G^2-statistic indicates acceptable model fit. One can also see that *Attitude toward Mathematics* measures have consistently higher factor loadings than those for *Attitude toward the Law*. Somewhat puzzling is the loading pattern for measures of *Attitude toward Discipline in Children* which shows appreciable variation in the size of its factor loadings. The heterogeneity of the factor loadings is marginally significant: Tested against a model with equal factor loading for each trait, the fit increases by Diff-$G^2 = 15.1$ ($df = 6$, $P = 0.020$).

Correlations of the (disattenuated) traits are estimated in matrix Φ_τ. Evidently, *Attitude toward Mathematics* is virtually unrelated with the other two traits, whereas the disattenuated correlation coefficient of $\hat{\phi}_{\tau_3 \tau_1} = .39$ shows a mild association between the attitudes toward the law and toward discipline in children.

Trait-Method Factor Analysis

Measures may not only be correlated because they reflect the same trait but also because they share the same assessment method. Several authors have therefore suggested to expand the factor model by including method factors (Althauser, 1974; Althauser & Heberlein, 1970; Althauser et al., 1971; Jöreskog, 1971; Kalleberg & Kluegel, 1975; Schmitt, 1978; Werts et al., 1972; Werts & Linn, 1970; Werts, Linn, & Jöreskog, 1971). The rationale was to provide a trait-method factor model as a less restrictive alternative, permitting systematic variation due to both shared traits and shared methods.

TABLE 2.1
Flamer (1983) Attitude Data, Sample A ($N = 105$)

	ADC_L	AM_L	AL_L	ADC_Th	AM_Th	AL_Th	ADC_SD	AM_SD	AL_SD
ADC_L	1.00								
AM_L	-.15	1.00							
AL_L	.19	-.12	1.00						
ADC_Th	**.72**	-.11	.19	1.00					
AM_Th	-.01	**.61**	-.03	-.02	1.00				
AL_Th	.26	-.04	**.34**	.27	.01	1.00			
ADC_SD	**.42**	-.15	.21	**.40**	.01	.34	1.00		
AM_SD	-.06	**.72**	-.05	-.03	**.75**	-.03	.00	1.00	
AL_SD	.13	-.12	**.46**	.17	-.01	**.44**	.33	.00	1.00

TABLE 2.2
Trait-Only Factor Analysis of the Flamer A Data

Factor loading matrix $\hat{\Lambda}_\tau$

Method	Trait	Trait factors ADC	AM	AL	Uniqueness Estimates θ
Likert	ADC	.85	.00	.00	.28
	AM	.00	.77	.00	.41
	AL	.00	.00	.61	.63
Thurstone	ADC	.84	.00	.00	.29
	AM	.00	.80	.00	.36
	AL	.00	.00	.62	.62
SD	ADC	.50	.00	.00	.75
	AM	.00	.94	.00	.12
	AL	.00	.00	.71	.50

Factor correlations $\hat{\Phi}_\tau$

	ADC	AM	AL
ADC	1.0		
AM	-.07	1.0	
AL	.39	-.05	1.0

$G^2 = 23.28$	$P = 0.503$
$df = 24$	$N = 105$

For a 3-trait × 3-method measurement design, the factor loading matrix $\Lambda_{\tau,\mu}$ of the trait-method factor model is simply constructed by augmenting Λ_τ from Equation 6 with additional columns for three method factors μ_1, μ_2, and μ_3:

$$\Lambda_{\tau\mu} = \begin{pmatrix} \lambda_{1,\tau_1} & 0 & 0 & \lambda_{1,\mu_1} & 0 & 0 \\ 0 & \lambda_{2,\tau_2} & 0 & \lambda_{2,\mu_1} & 0 & 0 \\ 0 & 0 & \lambda_{3,\tau_3} & \lambda_{3,\mu_1} & 0 & 0 \\ \lambda_{4,\tau_1} & 0 & 0 & 0 & \lambda_{4,\mu_2} & 0 \\ 0 & \lambda_{5,\tau_2} & 0 & 0 & \lambda_{5,\mu_2} & 0 \\ 0 & 0 & \lambda_{6,\tau_3} & 0 & \lambda_{6,\mu_2} & 0 \\ \lambda_{7,\tau_1} & 0 & 0 & 0 & 0 & \lambda_{7,\mu_3} \\ 0 & \lambda_{8,\tau_2} & 0 & 0 & 0 & \lambda_{8,\mu_3} \\ 0 & 0 & \lambda_{9,\tau_3} & 0 & 0 & \lambda_{9,\mu_3} \end{pmatrix} \tag{8}$$

Different forms of the factor correlation matrix $\Phi_{\tau\mu}$ avail themselves, at least in theory, for model comparisons (Widaman, 1985). Because it implies linear independence between trait and method factors, a particularly interesting form is the block-diagonal model, obtained by restricting the factor correlations to

$$
\Phi_{\tau\mu} = \left(
\begin{array}{ccc|ccc}
1.0 & \phi_{\tau_1,\tau_2} & \phi_{\tau_1,\tau_3} & 0 & 0 & 0 \\
\phi_{\tau_2,\tau_1} & 1.0 & \phi_{\tau_2,\tau_3} & 0 & 0 & 0 \\
\phi_{\tau_3,\tau_1} & \phi_{\tau_3,\tau_2} & 1.0 & 0 & 0 & 0 \\
\hline
0 & 0 & 0 & 1.0 & \phi_{\mu_1,\mu_2} & \phi_{\mu_1,\mu_3} \\
0 & 0 & 0 & \phi_{\mu_2,\mu_1} & 1.0 & \phi_{\mu_2,\mu_3} \\
0 & 0 & 0 & \phi_{\mu_3,\mu_1} & \phi_{\mu_3,\mu_2} & 1.0
\end{array}
\right) \tag{9}
$$

The covariance matrix Θ of unique components is diagonal.

Although the specifications of the trait-method model appear attractive at first, applications to empirical (and simulated) data have been plagued by unidentified and/or inadmissible parameter estimates. For demonstration purposes, I use the Kelly and Fiske (1951) clinical assessment data. This data set comprises measurements of 124 trainees with respect to personality characteristics *Assertive, Cheerful, Serious, Unshakable Poise,* and *Broad Interests* as traits, using *Staff ratings, Teammate ratings,* and *Self-ratings* as assessment methods. Teammate and staff ratings each comprise median values from panels of three judges and should be more reliable than self-ratings. The correlation matrix is well known in the psychometric literature and is not reproduced here. It can be found, for instance, in Browne (1984a), Campbell and Fiske (1959), Jöreskog (1974), and Jöreskog and Sörbom (1979).

The results of fitting the trait-method factor model are given in Table 2.3. Note that the estimated correlation between staff and self-rating factors is −2.34. This parameter estimate is clearly outside its admissible range. Earlier analyses of this well-known data set have occasionally concluded that the staff and self-rating method factors should be combined because their correlation was so excessive (Jöreskog, 1971). Such a decision would suppose that the inadmissible estimates are merely a consequence of problems in the sample correlation matrix.

Recent work on the trait-method factor model suggests, however, that the block-diagonal trait-method factor model seems to be inherently flawed. Brannick and Spector (1990), Marsh and Bailey (1991), and Wothke (1987) find inadmissible or unidentified model solutions occurring at high frequency in simulation studies and/or reanalyses of published MTMM data. In addition, Kenny and Kashy (1992), Millsap (1992), and Wothke (1984) formally demonstrate identification problems of the trait-method factor model. Consider, for instance, a somewhat simplified, but important factor-loading structure that restricts the nonzero loadings within each column of Equation 8 to be equal to each other:

TABLE 2.3
Trait-Method Factor Analysis of the Kelly and Fiske (1951) Assessment Data

Factor loading matrix $\hat{\Lambda}_{\tau\mu}$

Method	Trait	Trait factors					Method factors			Uniqueness
		A	C	S	P	I	Staff	Mate	Self	Estimates θ
	A	.86	.00	.00	.00	.00	-.07	.00	.00	.26
Staff	C	.00	.83	.00	.00	.00	-.05	.00	.00	.31
Ratings	S	.00	.00	.60	.00	.00	.09	.00	.00	.62
	P	.00	.00	.00	.89	.00	.14	.00	.00	.20
	I	.00	.00	.00	.00	.72	.15	.00	.00	.45
	A	.84	.00	.00	.00	.00	.00	.13	.00	.29
Teammate	C	.00	.83	.00	.00	.00	.00	.28	.00	.47
Ratings	S	.00	.00	.68	.00	.00	.00	.35	.00	.41
	P	.00	.00	.00	.18	.00	.00	.58	.00	.65
	I	.00	.00	.00	.00	.57	.00	.50	.00	.43
	A	.56	.00	.00	.00	.00	.00	.00	.16	.68
Self-	C	.00	.45	.00	.00	.00	.00	.00	.24	.76
Ratings	S	.00	.00	.44	.00	.00	.00	.00	.28	.74
	P	.00	.00	.00	.43	.00	.00	.00	.41	.66
	I	.00	.00	.00	.00	.67	.00	.00	.57	.28

Factor correlations $\hat{\Phi}_\tau$

	A	C	S	P	I	Staff	Mate	Self
A	1.00							
C	.56	1.00						
S	-.39	-.43	1.00					
P	.33	.62	-.07	1.00				
I	.54	.30	-.03	.46	1.00			
Staff	.00	.00	.00	.00	.00	1.00		
Mate	.00	.00	.00	.00	.00	.88	1.00	
Self	.00	.00	.00	.00	.00	-2.34	-.01	1.0

$G^2 = n/a$	$P = n/a$
$df = 62$	$N = 105$

$$\Lambda_{\tau\mu}^{(e)} = (\mathbf{1}_\mu \otimes \mathbf{I}_\tau | \mathbf{I}_\mu \otimes \mathbf{1}_\tau)\, \mathbf{D}_\xi, \tag{10}$$

where $\mathbf{D}_\xi$ is a diagonal matrix of $t + m$ column scale parameters. Wothke (1984) shows that, under restriction (Equation 10), the block-diagonal factor model is always underidentified by exactly one parameter. Kenny and Kashy (1992) describe a proof showing that the same loading model (Equation 10) remains underidentified even when the factor correlation matrix is unconstrained (i.e., trait factors are correlated with method factors). Both results generalize to any loading structure with *proportional* nonzero entries in rows *and* columns (Grayson & Marsh, 1994, Theorems 2 and 3):

$$\Lambda_{\tau\mu}^{(p)} = \mathbf{D}_x\, (\mathbf{1}_\mu \otimes \mathbf{I}_\tau | \mathbf{I}_\mu \otimes \mathbf{1}_\tau)\, \mathbf{D}_\xi, \tag{11}$$

where $\mathbf{D}_x$ is a diagonal matrix of mt nonzero scale parameters for the rows of $\Lambda_{\tau\mu}$, up to $mt - 1$ of which may be freely estimated.

At the present time, identification conditions for the general form of the trait-method model are not completely known. Although the identification and admissibility problems seem to be the rule with empirical data, one can construct correlation matrices for which the block-diagonal trait-method model will actually yield an identified solution, but their factor loading estimates must necessarily be different from Equation 10 and Equation 11. However, the more the estimated loadings differ from Equation 11, the harder it is to interpret the factors and, consequently, to evaluate trait validity issues. Estimation itself can also be difficult: The usually iterative estimation process often approaches an intermediate solution of the form (Equation 11) and cannot continue because the matrix of second derivatives of the fit function becomes rank-deficient at that point. This is a serious practical problem because condition Equation 11 is so general that it "slices" the identified solution space into many disjoint subregions, so that the model estimates can become extremely sensitive to the choice of start values. Kenny and Kashy (1992) state that "estimation problems increase as the factor loadings become increasingly similar."

Conclusions Regarding Factor Analysis

Trait-only factor analysis and the block-diagonal trait-method factor model are prominent confirmatory factor models for MTMM correlation analysis.

The trait-only model is a simple model with $2mt + t(t-1)/2$ free parameters; it employs the assumptions that the assignment of measures to traits is empirically correct and that the t trait factors yield a fully sufficient description of the correlation structure of the MTMM matrix (i.e., no method factors are needed). Trait-only factor analysis is the simplest and most powerful model discussed in this chapter, but the model fits only a few published empirical MTMM matrices (Wothke, 1987). Trait-only factor analysis is apparently too restrictive for many empirical datasets.

The trait-method factor model has been proposed as a more general model for MTMM matrices. It incorporates factors for traits as well as for methods. When trait factors are uncorrelated with method factors, the trait-method model has $3mt + t(t-1)/2 + m(m-1)/2$ free parameters. The added parameters allow for method components in the MTMM correlation structure, and one would suppose that the model should fit better. However, the model's performance with both empirical and simulated data has been disappointing. The seemingly sensible joint estimation of trait and method factors does not produce very useful results.

The reason for the poor performance of the trait-method factor analysis is related to a conceptual deficiency of the model. While the set of trait factors is orthogonal to the set of method factors, the relative orientation of the two sets of factors is usually not unique. Orientation of the factor sets depends on how the average value of correlations of the MTMM matrix is being modeled, and its assignment during the iterative estimation process tends to oscillate between the trait and method components. It is possible to demonstrate this underidentification algebraically for a large class of simple-structured submodels of trait-method factor analysis (Grayson & Marsh, 1994; Kenny & Kashy, 1990; Millsap, 1992; Wothke, 1984).

While identification of the trait-method factor model fails with the majority of empirical data sets, this does not have to be the case. For instance, Bollen (1989) reports an MTMM matrix for which the trait-method factor model yields admissible estimates. Furthermore, a model with a factor-loading structure different from Equation 11 may be identified in the population. Even in this case, however, Monte-Carlo results suggest that sample sizes in excess of 1,000 cases and large measurement designs may be needed to establish model identification with sample data (Marsh & Bailey, 1991). These inordinate data requirements render block-diagonal trait-method factor analysis virtually useless.

COVARIANCE COMPONENT ANALYSIS

CCA was proposed by Bock (1960) and Bock and Bargmann (1966) as a multivariate random model for factorial measurement designs. Although the name of the method was originally *covariance structure analysis*, this term is avoided here because it has since become synonymous with a much more general class of structural equation models (SEMs). A successful application by Bock, Dicken, and Van Pelt (1969) investigated effects of content-acquiescence interaction in MMPI scales.

Much of the early treatment of CCA concerned the derivation of numeric algorithms for parameter estimation as well as the discussion of identification problems. In doing so, strict assumptions about the scale of measurement and the size of error variance were employed, rendering the first CCA models unsuitable for correlation matrix analysis. This section first reviews the structural characteristics of fixed-scale CCA and then expand on a scale-free generalization of the model. The discussion is limited to structural characteristics of CCA. The worked examples in this section employ normal theory ML estimation, as did the CFA examples.

Covariance Component Structures
with Fixed Scale Factors

CCA describes measurements on a facet-structure of $m \times t$ observed variables as linear functions of separate latent variates for the general level of performance on all measures, for trait-specific characteristics, and for method-specific components (Bock & Bargmann, 1966). Let the observed measurements be arranged in an $n \times mt$ matrix $\mathbf{X}$ with rows corresponding to individuals and columns corresponding to measures. By convention, columns are ordered by trait within method blocks. Similarly, the latent variate parameters for a person i are arranged in a $1 \times (1 + t + m)$ row vector

$$\xi_i = (\xi_{ig}, \underbrace{\xi_{i\tau_1}, \ldots, \xi_{i\tau_t}}_{t\ \text{traits}}, \underbrace{\xi_{i\mu_1}, \ldots, \xi_{i\mu_m}}_{m\ \text{methods}}), \tag{12}$$

with the following terms:

ξ_{ig} denotes a *general* variate, indicating the individual's disposition to excel on, or to show deficiency in, *all* measures in the study. ξ_{ig} absorbs variation that cannot be unambiguously assigned either to traits or to methods. No substantive relation to Spearman's (1904) factor terminology is intended.

$\xi_{i\tau_j}$ expresses the individual's specific tendency to excel on measures of trait τ_j over and above the contribution of the general variate.

$\xi_{i\mu_k}$ describes method bias or, in other words, the individual's relative disposition toward advantageous, or disadvantageous, measurements when method μ_k is used.

For n individuals i, the parameter vectors ξ_i are collected in the $n \times (1 + t + m)$ matrix Ξ.

Given these stipulations, the set of measures X has the latent structure decomposition

$$\mathbf{X}_{(n \times mt)} = \Xi_{n \times (1+t+m)} \mathbf{A}'_{(1+t+m) \times mt} + \mathbf{E}_{(n \times mt)}, \tag{13}$$

with a known structural coefficient matrix $\mathbf{A}$ and a matrix $\mathbf{E}$ of uncorrelated error components. For three traits and three methods, for example, $\mathbf{A}$ will take the form

$$\mathbf{A} = \begin{pmatrix} 1 & 1 & 0 & 0 & 1 & 0 & 0 \\ 1 & 0 & 1 & 0 & 1 & 0 & 0 \\ 1 & 0 & 0 & 1 & 1 & 0 & 0 \\ 1 & 1 & 0 & 0 & 0 & 1 & 0 \\ 1 & 0 & 1 & 0 & 0 & 1 & 0 \\ 1 & 0 & 0 & 1 & 0 & 1 & 0 \\ 1 & 1 & 0 & 0 & 0 & 0 & 1 \\ 1 & 0 & 1 & 0 & 0 & 0 & 1 \\ 1 & 0 & 0 & 1 & 0 & 0 & 1 \\ g & & \text{traits} & & \text{methods} & & \end{pmatrix} \tag{14}$$

Under multivariate normality, the expectation of the sample covariance matrix S_x is

$$\Sigma_x = \mathcal{E}(S_x) = A\Phi A' + \Theta, \tag{15}$$

with Φ as the covariance matrix of the latent variates Ξ and Θ as a diagonal covariance matrix of unique and error components. The matrix Φ was specified as diagonal in Bock and Bargmann (1966), but, as such an assumption is unnecessarily restrictive in many applied settings, Wiley et al. (1973) and Jöreskog (1978) have since extended the model to include correlated latent structures.

Model Identification. Since A in Equation 13 is not of full rank, not all parameters in Φ and Θ can be estimated (Graybill, 1961, pp. 228–229). In order to estimate at least the *essential* variance components, the model must be reparameterized. This can be accomplished by selecting two matrices K and L with

$$A = K \cdot L, \tag{16}$$

so that K is a matrix of $m + t - 1$ orthonormal column contrasts in A and L is a matrix of $m + t - 1$ orthogonal row contrasts in A with

$$L = (K'K)^{-1}K'A = K'A. \tag{17}$$

Let $\Xi^* = \Xi \cdot L'$ be the matrix of rank-reduced orthogonal transforms of Ξ. Then, X can be expressed in terms of a reduced $n \times (t + m - 1)$ parameter matrix $\Xi^* = \Xi \cdot L'$ as

$$X_{(n \times mt)} = \Xi^* K' + E \tag{18}$$

$$= \Xi L' K' + E. \tag{19}$$

Clearly, Equations 13 and 18 are equivalent representations of X. It is therefore sufficient to estimate $\Phi^* = L\Phi L'$, the covariance matrix of $\xi^* = \xi \cdot L$, as given in the covariance equation

$$\Sigma_x = \mathcal{E}(S_x) = K\Phi^* K' + \Theta. \tag{20}$$

Due to the removal of redundant parameters, Φ^* has two fewer rows and columns than Φ. Yet, Equations 15 and 20 are equivalent—Φ^* merely omits the terms that could not be estimated in the first place.

Typology of Covariance Structures. Model interpretation should distinguish entries in Φ^* with respect to three groups of transformed variates:

1	variate for the general level of covariation,
$t - 1$	variates (or profiles) describing differences in covariation due to traits, and
$m - 1$	variates (or profiles) to expressing differential variation due to methods.

In a 3 traits × 3 methods measurement design, the contrast matrix $\mathbf{K}$ may be chosen as

$$
\mathbf{K} = \begin{pmatrix}
1/3 & \sqrt{2}/3 & 0 & \sqrt{2}/3 & 0 \\
1/3 & -1/\sqrt{18} & 1/\sqrt{6} & \sqrt{2}/3 & 0 \\
1/3 & -1/\sqrt{18} & -1/\sqrt{6} & \sqrt{2}/3 & 0 \\
1/3 & \sqrt{2}/3 & 0 & -1/\sqrt{18} & 1/\sqrt{6} \\
1/3 & -1/\sqrt{18} & 1/\sqrt{6} & -1/\sqrt{18} & 1/\sqrt{6} \\
1/3 & -1/\sqrt{18} & -1/\sqrt{6} & -1/\sqrt{18} & 1/\sqrt{6} \\
1/3 & \sqrt{2}/3 & 0 & -1/\sqrt{18} & -1/\sqrt{6} \\
1/3 & -1/\sqrt{18} & 1/\sqrt{6} & -1/\sqrt{18} & -1/\sqrt{6} \\
1/3 & -1/\sqrt{18} & -1/\sqrt{6} & -1/\sqrt{18} & -1/\sqrt{6}
\end{pmatrix} \qquad (21)
$$

$$\qquad g \qquad\qquad\quad \textit{traits} \qquad\qquad \textit{methods}$$

$\mathbf{K}$ is columnwise orthonormal (i.e., $\mathbf{K'K} = \mathbf{I}$). The first column, labeled g, shows the general variate entering each measure with a constant weight (1/3), the second column (or first *trait* contrast) represents individual differences between Trait 1 and Traits 2 and 3, and the second trait contrast compares individual differences between Traits 2 and 3. Correspondingly, the two *method* contrasts address individual differences in method-specific variance.

The amount of observed variation attributable to these latent differences is estimated by $\hat{\Phi}^*$. Trait validation or general method effects can be established to the degree that diagonal entries of $\hat{\Phi}^*$ have large positive values. Conversely, when the estimated variance of a trait contrast is zero, the involved traits cannot be discriminated on empirical grounds. In analogy, measurement methods can be said to be equivalent to each other when the associated method contrasts have zero variance.

Interpretation of covariance component estimates can be simplified by choosing $\mathbf{K}$ to be *orthonormal*, $\mathbf{K'K} = \mathbf{I}$. Then, because the columns of $\mathbf{K}$ are orthogonal, correlations derived from Φ^* can be interpreted directly and, consequently, independence between trait and method components can be easily tested. Second, because the columns of an orthonormal $\mathbf{K}$ are also normed to unit length, all parameters in $\mathbf{\Phi}^*$ are estimated on the same scale, allowing direct comparisons of the resulting variance component estimates.

Several types of covariance component models may be distinguished, defined by restrictions of the matrix $\mathbf{\Phi}^*$.

Fully correlated $\mathbf{\Phi}^*$: The observed covariance matrix can be expressed as a compound of trait and method variance components:

$$\mathbf{\Phi}^* = \begin{pmatrix} \sigma_g^{*2} & (\text{symm.}) & \\ \sigma_{g\tau}^* & \mathbf{\Phi}_{\tau\tau}^* & \\ \sigma_{g\mu}^* & \mathbf{\Phi}_{\mu\tau}^* & \mathbf{\Phi}_{\mu\mu}^* \end{pmatrix} \tag{22}$$

General, trait, and method variates sufficiently describe the covariance structure of the measured variables but are correlated with each other.

Independent-common-variation: The first row and column show zero entries in the off-diagonal elements:

$$\mathbf{\Phi}^* = \begin{pmatrix} \sigma_g^{*2} & (\text{symm.}) & \\ 0 & \mathbf{\Phi}_{\tau\tau}^* & \\ 0 & \mathbf{\Phi}_{\mu\tau}^* & \mathbf{\Phi}_{\mu\mu}^* \end{pmatrix} \tag{23}$$

Trait variation and method variation are independent of the general variate, while trait contrast may still correlate with method contrasts.

Block-diagonal $\mathbf{\Phi}^*$: Trait contrasts are uncorrelated with method contrasts and, in addition, the general variate is independent of both trait and method contrasts.

$$\mathbf{\Phi}^* = \begin{pmatrix} \sigma_g^{*2} & (\text{symm.}) & \\ 0 & \mathbf{\Phi}_{\tau\tau}^* & \\ 0 & 0 & \mathbf{\Phi}_{\mu\mu}^* \end{pmatrix} \tag{24}$$

For block-diagonal covariance component structures, the following conclusions are legitimate: (a) patterns of individual differences in traits do not predict individual differences in response to methods, (b) differential response to method does not predict an individual's average level on all measures, and (c) trait contrasts do not predict the individual's relative standing on the general variate.

Diagonal $\mathbf{\Phi}^*$: All (reparameterized) variates are uncorrelated. Diagonality is postulated *by design* only in the case of 2^n measurement designs. When trait or method facets contain more than two elements, diagonality will depend on the particular choice of contrasts. In these cases, contrast selection must be guided by substantive theory, because the diagonal solution is more parsimonious than the block-diagonal CCA model, and its interpretation transcends the simpler question whether trait and method components are independent.

CCA With Unknown Scale Factors

MTMM studies are frequently conducted in settings where the scale of measurement is not available, of little interest, lost due to standardization, or not even conceptually meaningful. Any such scenario violates the assumptions implicit to the fixed-scale CCA model of Equation 20. In order to obtain relative covariance component estimates in similar settings, Wiley et al. (1973) introduced a class of scale-free generalizations by including a diagonal matrix $\mathbf{D}_x$ of scale parameters:

$$\Sigma_x = \mathbf{D}_x\mathbf{K}\Phi^*\mathbf{K}'\mathbf{D}_x + \Theta. \tag{25}$$

$\mathbf{D}_x$ will absorb scale differences among the observed measures and should be interpreted accordingly. Wiley et al. (p. 317) state that:

> The major utility of . . . [$\mathbf{D}_x$] is for dealing with those situations in which the observed variables are measured in different metrics. For such cases the introduction of . . . [$\mathbf{D}_x$] whose elements do not have to be related to the variances of the variables allows for optimal rescaling.

Model Identification. In addition to identification problems discussed in the earlier section on identification in the fixed-scale model, scale-free CCA is subject to two further identification conditions. First, there is a trivial scale trade-off between $\mathbf{D}_x$ and Φ^* in the sense that any solution can be rescaled by an arbitrary positive constant a without changing Σ_x:

$$\mathbf{D}_x\mathbf{K}\Phi^*\mathbf{K}'\mathbf{D}_x = (\tfrac{1}{a}\mathbf{D}_x)\mathbf{K}(a^2\Phi^*)\mathbf{K}'(\tfrac{1}{a}\mathbf{D}_x)$$

$$= \tilde{\mathbf{D}}_x\mathbf{K}\tilde{\Phi}^*\mathbf{K}'\tilde{\mathbf{D}}_x.$$

To resolve this underidentification, a single nonzero equality constraint must be introduced; the illustrative analyses presented here use the identity

$$\sigma_g^{*2} = 1, \tag{26}$$

restricting the variance of the general variate to unity. Variance component estimates for trait and method contrasts have to be evaluated relative to the variance of the general variate.

A second, less overt identification problem arises with the fully correlated CCA model. Generally, there are $m + t - 2$ unidentified parameters in $\mathbf{D}_x$, $\sigma^*_{g\tau}$ and $\sigma^*_{g\mu}$ (Wothke, 1988). Identification can be established by imposing zero constraints on the $m + t - 2$ parameters $\sigma^*_{g\tau_j}$ and $\sigma^*_{g\mu_k}$, effectively fixing all covariance components involving the general variate (Wothke, 1988). Scale-free versions of diagonal, block-diagonal, and independent-common-variation CCA models can be identified, while the scale-free version of the fully correlated model is not. This latter finding contradicts some of the claims by Wiley et al. (1973). In other words, scale factors must be known beforehand in order to estimate correlations involving the common variate. Alternatively, if scale factors are to be estimated, strict assumptions must be imposed regarding the correlation structure of the common variate g.

Examples

This section demonstrates the interpretation of covariance component estimates with two worked examples. In the first case, using a data set from Dickinson and Tice (1973), planned contrasts offer a meaningful direct interpretation of diagonal (co)variance component estimates. In the second case, which uses the well-known clinical assessment data from Campbell and Fiske (1959), contrasts are chosen arbitrarily and no meaningful profiles are implied. Here, the solution must be interpreted more cautiously, aided by traditional techniques of exploratory data analysis. In both examples, some knowledge in the application of contrasts is assumed; the textbooks by Bock (1975), Finn (1974), and Graybill (1961) provide advantageous terminology.

Planned Contrasts. The correlation matrix of the Dickinson and Tice (1973) job behavior ratings is reproduced in Table 2.4. Three traits (*Getting along with others* [G], *Dedication* [D], and *ability to apply Learning* [L]) are assessed by three methods (*Peer Nominations* [PN], *Peer Checklist ratings* [PC], and *Supervisor Checklist ratings* [SC]). The entries in the validity diagonals (bold) are small, and it seems questionable whether the trait concepts generalize across assessment methods. Several heterotrait–heteromethod

TABLE 2.4
Dickinson and Tice (1973) Job Behavior Data ($N = 149$)

	G_PN	D_PN	L_PN	G_PC	D_PC	L_SC	G_SC	D_SC	L_SC
G_PN	1.000								
D_PN	.524	1.000							
L_PN	.241	.403	1.000						
G_PC	**.071**	.102	-.018	1.000					
D_PC	.022	**.096**	.018	.435	1.000				
L_PC	.076	.102	**.100**	.342	.347	1.000			
G_SC	**.136**	.132	.061	**.243**	.203	.100	1.000		
D_SC	-.028	**.168**	.135	.093	**.209**	.042	.461	1.000	
L_SC	-.054	.162	**.252**	.053	.108	**.108**	.294	.280	1.000

correlations are of similar magnitude as the corresponding entries on the validity diagonals, further weakening validity considerations about the traits. On the other hand, some, albeit weak, support for trait validation derives from the similarity between correlation patterns in the method blocks, with noticeably raised coefficients between G and D measures. The generally larger entries in the monomethod blocks, however, indicate considerable method variance, implying that all or most individual measures have poor convergent validity. No single measure would probably be very useful in applied settings, but the matrix as a whole might still yield information about the validity of the postulated latent trait model.

Table 2.5 reproduces the contrast matrix and the estimates for the diagonal CCA model. Contrasts are identical to those in Equation 21; six-digit precision was used in computations. The contrast δ_{τ_1} describes a profile between social skills (*Getting along with others*) and the less tangible motivation/ability trait complex (*Dedication* and *Learning Ability*), which is then further differentiated by δ_{τ_2}. Method comparisons are ordered in similar step-down fashion: δ_{μ_1} defines the difference between the nomination approach and the two (peer and supervisor) checklist rating methods, δ_{μ_2} compares peer ratings against supervisor ratings.

With this parameterization, the diagonal CCA model fits the data well ($G^2 = 19.5$, $df = 23$). Neither the block-diagonal model ($G^2 = 16.3$, $df = 21$) nor the independent-common-variation structure ($G^2 = 14.0$, $df = 17$) show significant fit improvement. It is safe to conclude that the contrast

TABLE 2.5
Diagonal CCA Solution for the Job Behavior Data

Variable	Scale $\mathbf{D}_x$	\multicolumn{5}{c}{Fixed contrast matrix $\mathbf{K}$}	Uniqueness $\hat{\Theta}$
		δ_g	δ_{τ_1}	δ_{τ_2}	δ_{μ_1}	δ_{μ_2}	
G_PN	1.256	.333	.471	0.0	.471	0.0	.568
D_PN	1.811	.333	-.236	.408	.471	0.0	.141
L_PN	.946	.333	-.236	-.408	.471	0.0	.760
G_PC	1.376	.333	.471	0.0	-.236	.408	.526
D_PC	1.416	.333	-.236	.408	-.236	.408	.515
L_PC	1.149	.333	-.236	-.408	-.236	.408	.681
G_SC	1.932	.333	.471	0.0	-.236	-.408	.116
D_SC	1.238	.333	-.236	.408	-.236	-.408	.635
L_SC	1.129	.333	-.236	-.408	-.236	-.408	.700
	\multicolumn{6}{c}{Covariance components $\hat{\Phi}^*$}	
		$1^\dagger$	$0^\dagger$	$0^\dagger$	$0^\dagger$	$0^\dagger$	
		$0^\dagger$	.134	$0^\dagger$	$0^\dagger$	$0^\dagger$	
		$0^\dagger$	$0^\dagger$	.075	$0^\dagger$	$0^\dagger$	
		$0^\dagger$	$0^\dagger$	$0^\dagger$	.601	$0^\dagger$	
		$0^\dagger$	$0^\dagger$	$0^\dagger$	$0^\dagger$	.437	

$G^2 = 19.54$	$df = 23$	$P = 0.669$

† Fixed parameter.

matrix **K** describes individual-difference profiles that are essentially uncorrelated.

The estimated scale factors vary within reasonable limits (from 0.95 to 1.93); and the uniqueness coefficients $\hat{\theta}_{ij}$, which correspond to $1 - \rho_{ii}^2$ (1 minus reliability) in correlation matrix analysis, vary correspondingly from 0.75 to 0.12. Measures of *Getting along with others* and *Dedication* have consistently higher scale factors (and smaller uniqueness components) than measures of *Learning ability*. The difference in reliability partly accounts for the observed correlation pattern in the monomethod and heteromethod blocks.

The (relative) variances of the trait and method profiles in Table 2.5, with respective estimates of .134, .075, .601, and .437, each remain small relative to the variance of the general variate δ_g, fixed at unity. δ_g reflects individual differences that are common in all observed variables, comprising general trait-related components (like overall work performance) as well as method-related ones (like overall halo effects). The general variate is thus a catchall and usually requires further external validation before it can be interpreted. In the Dickinson and Tice (1973) data, the effects of trait differences on the correlation structure appear marginal at best. The variance of δ_{τ_1} is estimated at $\hat{\phi}_{\tau_1\tau_1} = 0.134$ with a standard error of 0.047. This effect is small, but significant, and indicates that the trait *Getting along with others* is consistently differentiated from the two motivation/ability measures. The effect of the second trait contrast is negligible: there is no support in the Dickinson and Tice data that *Dedication* and *Learning Ability* establish distinct traits. In comparison, method contrasts have sizable variance components, practically occluding any trait components in the observed variables.

It is apparent that fit of the model assures neither convergent nor discriminant validity. The model fits well, but convergent and discriminant validation would require large variance components associated with trait profiles and small variance components associated with method profiles. This would be the exact opposite of the current results. Neither convergent nor discriminant validity can be asserted with the job behavior data.

Arbitrary Contrasts. The Kelly and Fiske clinical assessment data are used for this example. The choice of contrast matrix is somewhat arbitrary, since the five personality traits do not naturally lend themselves to planned comparisons. Any set of $t + m - 1$ linear independent contrasts may be used that contain a general variate and spans separate $t - 1$ and $m - 1$ dimensional subspaces for trait and method profiles. Table 2.6 shows a technically convenient choice of orthonormal Helmert contrasts **K** at three-digit precision. For actual calculations, all contrasts were entered at six-digit precision.

Fit of the block-diagonal CCA model is marginally significant ($G^2 = 104.7$, $df = 77$) and can be considered satisfactory, given that the raw data are rating

TABLE 2.6
Contrast Matrix **K** for the Kelly and Fiske Assessment Data

Method	Trait	δ_g	δ_{τ_1}	δ_{τ_2}	δ_{τ_3}	δ_{τ_4}	δ_{μ_1}	δ_{μ_2}
Staff	Assertive	.258	.516	0.0	0.0	0.0	.365	0.0
Ratings	Cheerful	.258	-.129	.5	0.0	0.0	.365	0.0
	Serious	.258	-.129	-.167	.471	0.0	.365	0.0
	Poise	.258	-.129	-.167	-.236	.408	.365	0.0
	Interests	.258	-.129	-.167	-.236	-.408	.365	0.0
Team-	Assertive	.258	.516	0.0	0.0	0.0	-.182	.316
mate	Cheerful	.258	-.129	.5	0.0	0.0	-.182	.316
Ratings	Serious	.258	-.129	-.167	.471	0.0	-.182	.316
	Poise	.258	-.129	-.167	-.236	.408	-.182	.316
	Interests	.258	-.129	-.167	-.236	-.408	-.182	.316
Self-	Assertive	.258	.516	0.0	0.0	0.0	-.182	-.316
Ratings	Cheerful	.258	-.129	.5	0.0	0.0	-.182	-.316
	Serious	.258	-.129	-.167	.471	0.0	-.182	-.316
	Poise	.258	-.129	-.167	-.236	.408	-.182	-.316
	Interests	.258	-.129	-.167	-.236	-.408	-.182	-.316

scale responses and may have been nonnormal. Model estimates are displayed in Tables 2.7 and 2.8. The uniqueness coefficients $(\hat{\Theta})_{ii}$ in Table 2.7 are interpreted as in factor analysis: self-ratings of *Assertiveness*, *Cheerfulness*, and *Seriousness* have considerably larger uniqueness components than the corresponding teammate or staff ratings; this difference reflects both the increase in reliability due to using group averages of the staff and teammate ratings and the higher degree of specificity that is to be expected in self-rating

TABLE 2.7
Scale Factor and Uniqueness Estimates $\hat{\mathbf{D}}_x$ and $\hat{\Theta}$

Method	Trait	Scale Factors $(\hat{\mathbf{D}}_x)_{ii}$	Uniqueness Coeffs. $(\hat{\Theta})_{ii}$
Staff	Assertive	1.628	.250
Ratings	Cheerful	1.650	.330
	Serious	.774	.639
	Poise	2.253	.425
	Interests	1.836	.533
Team-	Assertive	1.616	.255
mate	Cheerful	1.468	.478
Ratings	Serious	.956	.404
	Poise	1.126	.837
	Interests	1.907	.418
Self-	Assertive	.925	.714
Ratings	Cheerful	.987	.709
	Serious	.557	.811
	Poise	1.725	.569
	Interests	1.975	.367

TABLE 2.8
Covariance Component Estimates Φ

	δ_g	δ_{T_1}	δ_{T_2}	δ_{T_3}	δ_{T_4}	δ_{μ_1}	δ_{μ_2}
δ_g	1.0†						
δ_{T_1}	0.0†	.670			(symmetric)		
δ_{T_2}	0.0†	.387	.793				
δ_{T_3}	0.0†	-.639	-.821	1.284			
δ_{T_4}	0.0†	-.087	.107	.020	.169		
δ_{μ_1}	0.0†	0.0†	0.0†	0.0†	0.0†	.126	
δ_{μ_2}	0.0†	0.0†	0.0†	0.0†	0.0†	.100	.360

† Fixed Parameter.

data. Teammate and staff ratings differ most noticeably for *Unshakable Poise*, the unique component being twice as large for the teammate data.

The scale factor estimates $(\hat{\mathbf{D}}_x)_{ii}$ in Table 2.7 manifest "true score" scale differences among observed measures. For analyses based on *covariance* matrices, larger scale factors identify measures that discriminate on a relatively larger scale, over and above systematic variance explained by the covariance component matrix $\mathbf{K}\Phi^*\mathbf{K}'$. With *correlation* matrix analysis, on the other hand, scale factor estimates are also dependent on the unique variances of the original (unstandardized) measures complicating substantive interpretations of $\mathbf{D}_x$. In either case, the diagonal of $\hat{\mathbf{D}}_x$ contains the factors needed to optimally rescale the original variables as $\mathbf{Y} = \mathbf{X}\mathbf{D}_x^{-1}$, transforming Equation 25 to

$$\Sigma_y = \mathbf{D}_x^{-1}\Sigma_x\mathbf{D}_x^{-1} \tag{27}$$

$$= \mathbf{D}_x^{-1}(\mathbf{D}_x\mathbf{K}\Phi^*\mathbf{K}'\mathbf{D}_x + \Theta)\mathbf{D}_x^{-1} \tag{28}$$

$$= \mathbf{K}\Phi^*\mathbf{K}' + \mathbf{D}_x^{-1}\Theta\mathbf{D}_x^{-1} \tag{29}$$

All three ratings of *Broad Interests* show comparable scale factors. *Assertiveness*, *Cheerfulness*, and *Seriousness* have similar scale factors for staff and teammate rating methods, whereas self-rating factors are substantially smaller. Self-ratings of these personality characteristics are hardly equivalent to ratings made by others.

Interpretation of Φ^* in Table 2.8 is similar to describing a "normal" covariance matrix. The diagonal entries are relative variance components estimated under constraint (26). The off-diagonal elements are covariances between individual-difference profiles and can be standardized into correlation coefficients.

Because Φ^* is block-diagonal, the trait profiles are independent of method differences (cf. section on typology of covariance structures), and, consequently, any further exploratory treatment can be carried out independently within each block. The toolbox of multivariate statistics offers several exploratory methods suitable for transforming block-diagonal CCA solutions; among these, *principal axes decomposition* of the covariance component blocks and *varimax rotation* are well known and yield easily interpretable results.

Blockwise Principal Axes Decomposition. This section proposes the principal axes decomposition to transform the submatrices $\Phi_{\tau\tau}^*$ and $\Phi_{\mu\mu}^*$ into diagonal form and, by producing orthogonal variates in the process, to simplify the interpretation of model estimates. The principal axes method was successfully introduced to the factor analytic field by Hotelling (1933).

Eigenvalues λ_ℓ and the corresponding (nonzero) eigenvectors q_ℓ of a symmetric matrix A are defined as the roots of

$$Aq_\ell = q_\ell \lambda_\ell. \tag{30}$$

For a $p \times p$ matrix, there will be up to p distinct eigenvalues. Solutions of Equation 30 can be obtained by various numerical methods, many of which are implemented in commercially maintained software libraries, for example, IMSL (IMSL, Inc., 1980), LAPACK (E. Anderson et al., 1992) and the NAG library (Numerical Algorithms Group, Ltd., 1987), or in mathematical programs such as SAS/IML (SAS Institute, 1985) and Mathcad (Mathsoft, 1992).

For symmetric matrices, eigenvectors associated with different eigenvalues are orthogonal. All eigenvectors of A may be scaled to unit-length and assembled in the columns of the matrix Q, so that $Q'Q = I$. By collecting the associated eigenvalues in the same order in the diagonal matrix D_λ, Equation 30 can be written more compactly as

$$AQ = QD_\lambda, \tag{31}$$

implying the canonical decomposition

$$A = QD_\lambda Q'. \tag{32}$$

It has become customary in principal component analysis to rescale the normed eigenvectors Q of a correlation or covariance matrix into so-called principal axes coefficients $P = QD_\lambda^{1/2}$ (Harman, 1967; Hotelling, 1933). Clearly, $PIP' = QD_\lambda Q' = A$ (i.e., the P_ℓ are rescaled so that their underlying components have unit variance, while the components underlying the q_ℓ have variance λ_ℓ).

In covariance components models, computation of principal axis components is applied to the product $K\Phi^*K'$ and yields invariant results for full-rank choices of trait and method contrasts in the $(tm) \times (1 + (t-1) + (m-1))$ matrix K. When the estimate of Φ^* is block-diagonal, the covariance components can be partitioned into additive general, trait, and method components as:

$$\mathbf{K\Phi^*K'} = (\mathbf{K}_g | \mathbf{K}_\tau | \mathbf{K}_\mu) \begin{pmatrix} \sigma_g^{*2} & (\text{symm.}) & \\ \hline 0 & \Phi_{\tau\tau}^* & \\ \hline 0 & 0 & \Phi_{\mu\mu}^* \end{pmatrix} \begin{pmatrix} \mathbf{K}'_g \\ \mathbf{K}'_\tau \\ \mathbf{K}'_\mu \end{pmatrix} \qquad (33)$$

$$= \mathbf{K}_g \sigma_g^{*2} \mathbf{K}'_g + \mathbf{K}_\tau \Phi_{\tau\tau}^* \mathbf{K}'_\tau + \mathbf{K}_\mu \Phi_{\mu\mu}^* \mathbf{K}'_\mu, \qquad (34)$$

where the subscripts g, τ and μ refer to the general, trait, and method parts of the model, respectively. Separate eigenstructures have to be computed for the trait component $\mathbf{K}_\tau \Phi_{\tau\tau}^* \mathbf{K}'_\tau$ and the method component $\mathbf{K}_\mu \Phi_{\mu\mu}^* \mathbf{K}'_\mu$.

Blockwise Varimax Rotation. Analytic rotation of the principal axes coefficient blocks $\mathbf{P}_\tau$ and $\mathbf{P}_\mu$ may be employed to rotate the estimates to simple structure. A rotated solution comprises the same numeric information as an unrotated principal axes representation, and thereby, as the original covariance component solution (Equation 33). Let $\mathbf{T}$ be an orthogonal rotation matrix, with $\mathbf{TT'} = \mathbf{I}$, and $\mathbf{L}_\tau = \mathbf{P}_\tau \mathbf{T}$ be a rotated matrix. Any such $\mathbf{L}_\tau$ is equivalent to $\mathbf{P}_\tau$ as a decomposition of $\mathbf{K}_\tau \Phi_{\tau\tau}^* \mathbf{K}'_\tau$, since

$$\mathbf{K}_\tau \Phi_{\tau\tau}^* \mathbf{K}'_\tau = \mathbf{P}_\tau \mathbf{P}'_\tau \qquad (35)$$

$$= \mathbf{P}_\tau \mathbf{TT'} \mathbf{P}'_\tau \qquad (36)$$

$$= \mathbf{L}_\tau \mathbf{L}'_\tau. \qquad (37)$$

Methods to obtain simple structure rotations have long been available, for example, Kaiser's (1958) varimax criterion. Researchers familiar with factor analysis will find it easy to interpret simple structure solutions derived from covariance component models.

Table 2.9 shows the simple structure solution after separate varimax rotation of trait and method blocks. This solution suggests four uncorrelated "simple" trait contrasts between *Seriousness* and each of the other traits: p_{τ_1} is clearly defined as a contrast between *Seriousness* and *Assertiveness*, p_{τ_2} mostly describes the difference between *Seriousness* and *Cheerfulness*, and so on. The size of the variance explained by the rotated components suggests a clear discrimination between the traits *Seriousness*, *Assertiveness*, and *Cheerfulness*, while the concepts *Broad Interests* and *Unshakable Poise* do not seem to differ appreciably from *Seriousness*. Rotated method components also appear as simple contrasts: p_{μ_1} shows a difference between *self* ratings and *teammate* ratings; p_{μ_2} describes the difference between *self* ratings and *staff* ratings. Both rotated method components are independent. Their size is comparable to the two minor trait components p_{τ_3} and p_{τ_4}.

TABLE 2.9
Rotated Principal Axes Coefficients **P** of the Kelly and Fiske Data

Method	Trait	δ_g	p_{τ_1}	p_{τ_2}	p_{τ_3}	p_{τ_4}	p_{μ_1}	p_{μ_2}
Staff	Assertive	.258	-.407	-.078	-.030	.076	-.014	-.129
Ratings	Cheerful	.258	-.084	-.374	.064	-.086	-.014	-.129
	Serious	.258	.500	.481	.176	.171	-.014	-.129
	Poise	.258	.018	-.043	.019	-.185	-.014	-.129
	Interests	.258	-.025	.016	-.231	.022	-.014	-.129
Team-	Assertive	.258	-.407	-.078	-.030	.076	-.170	-.004
mate	Cheerful	.258	-.084	-.374	.064	-.086	-.170	-.004
Ratings	Serious	.258	.500	.481	.176	.171	-.170	-.004
	Poise	.258	.018	-.043	.019	-.185	-.170	-.004
	Interests	.258	-.025	.016	-.231	.022	-.170	-.004
Self-	Assertive	.258	-.407	-.078	-.030	.076	.184	.134
Ratings	Cheerful	.258	-.084	-.374	.064	-.086	.184	.134
	Serious	.258	.500	.481	.176	.171	.184	.134
	Poise	.258	.018	-.043	.019	-.185	.184	.134
	Interests	.258	-.025	.016	-.231	.022	.184	.134
Explained variance		1.0	1.271	1.138	.269	.231	.315	.173

Guidelines for Interpretation

The following rules were applied, interpreting the scale-free CCA examples in the preceding sections:

- The general variate δ_g must be interpreted separately from trait and method contrasts. Variation explained by δ_g may address both trait and method domains. This acknowledges the fact that general variation due to traits is indistinguishable (in the MTMM measurement design) from general variation due to methods. Knowledge from sources beyond the MTMM matrix is needed to discern these general components.

- The variance of δ_g is standardized. All other parameter estimates are relative to σ_g^2.

- When planned trait and method contrasts are employed (as in the Dickinson and Tice example), the elements of $\hat{\Phi}^*$ are the corresponding variance and covariance components. The solution can be interpreted directly, especially when the estimate of Φ^* is diagonal or block-diagonal.

- When arbitrary contrasts are used (as with the Kelly and Fiske data), direct interpretation of individual elements of $\hat{\Phi}^*$ is hardly possible. Resulting CCA solutions are generally oblique, and the orientation of the latent variates depends on the particular choice of contrasts. Analytical methods like principal axes decomposition and blockwise varimax rotation can be employed to erase the effects of arbitrary contrast selection.

CCA is fully confirmatory when planned contrasts are used. In this case, all individual parameter estimates and fit statistics are instantly meaningful. In many MTMM studies, however, the main interest lies in the question of whether the traits manifest themselves independently of the measurement methods used. In these cases, confirmatory procedures should be limited to fit considerations and to the Difference-G^2 test between block-diagonal and independent-common-variation models. Selecting a contrast matrix is then merely a technical issue and the interpretation of parameter estimates has to follow the exploratory tradition.

Conclusions Regarding CCA

CCA employs MANOVA terminology to analyze factorial measurement designs. The method uses an additive multivariate random effects model, which decomposes an individual's measurements into a general component, trait profiles, and method profiles. CCA is most rigorous when the contrasts (or profiles) are specified a priori as planned comparisons. Then, testing and interpretation of covariance components are straightforward just as they would be with successive tests of 1-df treatment contrasts in an ANOVA application.

When planned comparisons of traits and methods cannot be established beforehand, an arbitrary full-rank set of contrasts may be used to obtain the G^2 fit statistic of the entire model. Further interpretation of specific trait or method effects can often be aided by transforming the CCA model estimates with exploratory methods, such as principal components decomposition and varimax rotation techniques. While changes of the coordinate system by these exploratory methods tend to obscure confidence intervals of individual parameter estimates, the transformed point estimates can still be useful. Exact confidence regions for unrotated principal components can be evaluated with some computational effort from the asymptotic covariance matrix of $\mathbf{K\Phi^*K'}$, applying Section 11.6 of T. Anderson (1984).

MTMM *correlation* matrix analysis requires a scale-free extension of the traditional CCA model, demonstrated by the earlier examples. Even though the original fixed-scale formulation of CCA is still more parsimonious and usually more powerful when scales of measurement are meaningful and a covariance matrix is being analyzed, the introduction of scale-factor estimates makes correlation matrix analysis possible.

It may seem peculiar that CCA's general variate is neutral with respect to trait or method contributions. However, this indeterminacy is fully intended and in the following sense correct: Every measure in the MTMM matrix is doubly classified into a trait and a method. Suppose that all traits in the matrix share some common variance, that is, they are correlated at some degree. Denote this variance component by $\tilde{\sigma}_\tau^2$, say. Suppose further that all methods also share some common variance, $\widetilde{\sigma}_{\mu}^{2}$, say. Because of the double classification into traits and methods, each measure receives both common variance components, $\widetilde{\sigma}_{\tau}^{2}$ and $\widetilde{\sigma}_{\mu}^{2}$. The problem is that, under these conditions, every element of the resulting MTMM covariance matrix contains the sum of the two variance components, $\widetilde{\sigma}_{o}^{2} = \widetilde{\sigma}_{\tau}^{2} + \widetilde{\sigma}_{\mu}^{2}$; and no element of the matrix reflects the two terms in a different proportion. Hence, estimates of the individual $\widetilde{\sigma}_{\tau}^{2}$ and $\widetilde{\sigma}_{\mu}^{2}$ components are not identified.

The MTMM matrix provides information about the size of variance component $\widetilde{\sigma}_{o}^{2}$. However, although the crossed measurement design permits investigating many aspects of trait and method concepts, estimating the relative sizes of any underlying $\widetilde{\sigma}_{\tau}^{2}$ and $\widetilde{\sigma}_{\mu}^{2}$ is not possible. This indeterminacy was already recognized by Campbell and Fiske (1959), who wrote that "perhaps all that can be hoped for is evidence for relative validity" (p. 84). Accordingly, CCA uses the general variate, δ_{g}, as a neutral concept to model a generic common variance term. The substantive interpretation of the δ_{g} estimates requires evidence other than the MTMM matrix itself, such as comparison with outside validity criteria, strong theory, and so on.

DIRECT PRODUCT MODEL

The DPM, initiated by Campbell and O'Connell (1967, 1982) and Swain (1975) and related to Tucker's three-modal factor analysis (Bloxom, 1968; Tucker, 1966), describes the MTMM correlation matrix in a multiplicative fashion. Its complete form, with scale factors and error terms, was proposed by Browne (1984a, 1992) and Cudeck (1988) as

$$\Sigma = D_{x}(\Pi_{\mu} \otimes \Pi_{\tau} + E)D_{x}, \tag{38}$$

where Π_{μ} and Π_{τ} are the symmetric nonnegative definite matrices of multiplicative factors, D_{x} is a diagonal matrix of scale constants, E a diagonal matrix of nonnegative uniqueness coefficients, and "$\otimes$" is the right direct (Kronecker) product of two matrices. Maximum likelihood and generalized least squares estimation procedures were provided by Browne (1980).

Parameters in Equation 38 can be easily restricted to suitable submodels. Two versions of the model are distinguished here, the more general *heteroscedastic error* model given in Equation 38 and a *composite error* model, defined by the additional restriction

$$E = E_{\mu} \otimes E_{\tau}, \tag{39}$$

with E_{μ} and E_{τ} diagonal.

Equation (38) can also be expressed as a quadratic form (Wothke & Browne, 1990), allowing parameter estimation by standard computer programs such as LISREL (Jöreskog & Sörbom, 1993):

$$\Sigma = \mathbf{D}_x[(\mathbf{C}_\mu \otimes \mathbf{I}_\tau)(\mathbf{I}_\mu \otimes \mathbf{\Pi}_\tau)(\mathbf{C}_\mu \otimes \mathbf{I}_\tau)' + \mathbf{E}]\mathbf{D}_x, \qquad (40)$$

where $\mathbf{C}_\mu$ is an $m \times m$ lower triangular matrix of method components, with $\mathbf{\Pi}_\mu = \mathbf{C}_\mu \mathbf{C}'_\mu$, and $\mathbf{I}_\tau$ and $\mathbf{I}_\mu$ are identity matrices of order t and m, respectively.

The model with *heteroscedastic* error terms, that is, Equation 38, therefore has an expression as a second-order factor model

$$\Sigma = \mathbf{\Lambda}\mathbf{\Gamma}\mathbf{\Phi}\mathbf{\Gamma}'\mathbf{\Lambda}' \qquad (41)$$

where $\mathbf{\Lambda} = \mathbf{D}_x$, $\mathbf{\Gamma}$ is the partitioned matrix

$$\begin{aligned}\mathbf{\Gamma} &= (\mathbf{C}_\mu \otimes \mathbf{I}_\tau | \mathbf{I}_{\mu\tau}) \\ &= (\, \mathbf{\Gamma}_1 \quad |\mathbf{\Gamma}_2\,)\end{aligned} \qquad (42)$$

and $\mathbf{\Phi}$ is the partitioned matrix

$$\begin{aligned}\mathbf{\Phi} &= \left(\begin{array}{c|c} \mathbf{I}_\mu \otimes \mathbf{\Pi}_\tau & \mathbf{0} \\ \hline \mathbf{0} & \mathbf{E} \end{array} \right) \\[2mm] &= \left(\begin{array}{c|c} \mathbf{\Phi}_1 & \mathbf{0} \\ \hline \mathbf{0} & \mathbf{\Phi}_2 \end{array} \right)\end{aligned} \qquad (43)$$

Reparameterization of the *composite* error model (see Equation 39) uses the additional restrictions:

$$\mathbf{E} = \mathbf{E}_\mu \otimes \mathbf{E}_\tau \qquad (44)$$

$$= (\mathbf{E}_\mu^{1/2} \otimes \mathbf{I}_\tau)(\mathbf{I}_\mu \otimes \mathbf{E}_\tau)(\mathbf{E}_\mu^{1/2} \otimes \mathbf{I}_\tau)' \qquad (45)$$

$$= \mathbf{\Gamma}_2 \mathbf{\Phi}_2 \mathbf{\Gamma}_2', \qquad (46)$$

requiring the two modifications $\mathbf{\Gamma}_2 = \mathbf{E}_\mu^{1/2} \otimes \mathbf{I}_\tau$ and $\mathbf{\Phi}_2 = \mathbf{I}_\mu \otimes \mathbf{E}_\tau$.

Versatile computer programs like Amos (Arbuckle, 1995) or LISREL (Jöreskog & Sörbom, 1993) permit the restricted estimation of either Equation 38 or Equation 41 by means of simple equality constraints.[2]

---

[2]An alternative, noniterative estimation method was proposed recently by Browne and Strydom (in press).

Model Identification

One equality restriction per method component is needed to identify the scale of the estimates. For example, one may select one trait and set all its scale factors (corresponding elements of $\mathbf{D}_x = \mathbf{\Lambda}$) equal to 1. Alternatively, all diagonal elements of $\mathbf{C}_\mu$ could be fixed at unity. The two types of restriction may also be suitably combined.

The composite error model requires a second identification condition. Since $\mathbf{E}_\mu \otimes \mathbf{E}_\tau = (a \cdot \mathbf{E}_\mu) \otimes (b \cdot \mathbf{E}_\tau)$ for any $a = 1/b$, the scale of the error components must be identified. Constraining one element in either $\mathbf{E}_\mu$ or $\mathbf{E}_\tau$ to unity will fix the scale of the uniqueness components.

The estimate $\hat{\mathbf{\Pi}}_\mu$ is obtained by rescaling $\hat{\mathbf{C}}_\mu\hat{\mathbf{C}}_\mu'$ into a correlation matrix. Although standard errors of elements of $\hat{\mathbf{\Pi}}_\tau$ will be available, those of $\hat{\mathbf{\Pi}}_\mu$ will not. It seems worth mentioning that these may be obtained from an alternative parameterization similar to Equation 41 but with

$$\mathbf{\Gamma} = (\mathbf{I}_\mu \otimes \mathbf{C}_\tau | \mathbf{I}_\mu \otimes \mathbf{E}_\tau^{1/2})$$

and

$$\mathbf{\Phi} = \left(\begin{array}{c|c} \mathbf{\Pi}_\mu \otimes \mathbf{I}_\tau & 0 \\ \hline 0 & \mathbf{E}_\mu \otimes \mathbf{I}_\tau \end{array} \right)$$

Worked Example

Lawler's (1967) MTMM matrix of managerial job performance is used as an example. The sample correlation matrix is given in Table 2.10. Three traits are postulated: *quality* of job performance, *ability* to perform on the job, and *effort* put forth on the job; each trait is assessed with *superior, peer,* and *self*-rating methods.

Convergent validity among ratings by superiors and peers is shown by large entries in the first validity diagonal and by similar correlation patterns in the heterotrait triangles. Self-ratings, on the other hand, do not converge with ratings made by others—entries in the related validity diagonals are small and sometimes exceeded by correlations in the same heteromethod block.[3] It appears that discriminant validity of the measures is not clearly established: Sizable entries in all monomethod blocks suggest the presence of method variance.

---

[3]Lack of convergence between self-ratings and ratings by others has also been observed in other studies; a well-known example is the Kelly and Fiske assessment data discussed previously.

TABLE 2.10
Lawler's (1967) Managerial Job Performance Data ($N = 113$)

	Su_Q	Su_A	Su_E	P_Q	P_A	P_E	Se_Q	Se_A	Se_E
QualSupe	1.00								
AbilSupe	.53	1.00							
EfftSupe	.56	.44	1.00						
QualPeer	**.65**	.38	.40	1.00					
AbilPeer	.42	**.52**	.30	.56	1.00				
EfftPeer	.40	.31	**.53**	.56	.40	1.00			
QualSelf	**.01**	.01	.09	**.01**	.17	.10	1.00		
AbilSelf	.03	**.13**	.03	.04	**.09**	.02	.43	1.00	
EfftSelf	.06	.01	**.30**	.02	.01	**.30**	.40	.14	1.00

Note. Reprinted with permission.

Maximum likelihood estimates for the direct-product model (see Equation 40) with composite errors are displayed in Table 2.11. Identification conditions are satisfied using the four equality constraints $(\mathbf{C}_\mu)_{1,1} = (\mathbf{E}_\mu)_{1,1} = 1$ and $(\mathbf{D}_x)_{1,1} = (\mathbf{D}_x)_{4,4} = (\mathbf{D}_x)_{7,7}$. The diagonal entries of $\mathbf{\Pi}_\tau$ are fixed to unity. These restrictions are indicated in Table 2.11 by boldface type. All zero entries in the table were also fixed, as required by the direct product expressions involving identity matrices. Model fit is satisfactory ($G^2 = 28.9$, $df = 25$).

An instructive result of the analysis is that the unique variance components of *self*-ratings are at least twice as large as those of ratings by others. The larger unique variance may be a consequence of higher specificity of self-ratings, rather than a reduction in reliability. Similar heterogeneity of unique variances is associated with traits: *Quality* of job performance has the smallest error component, uniqueness for ratings of *effort* put forth on the job is about 2.5 times as large, and ratings of *ability* to perform have unique components 3.4 times as large.

Interpretation of scale factors and structural parameters depends on whether it is made from a multiplicative or from a linear modeling framework. From the multiplicative point of view, the correlation "factors" $\mathbf{\Pi}_\mu$ and $\mathbf{\Pi}_\tau$ are interpreted like complementary sources of similarity among measured variables. No conceptual ordering of the two matrices needs to be adopted. The linear model interpretation, on the other hand, requires a conceptual ordering of trait and method components. In the present context, $\mathbf{\Pi}_\tau$ expresses multiplicative correlation components between trait factors, and the coefficients $\mathbf{C}_\mu$ may be interpreted as factor loadings or partial regression coefficients moderating the effect of each method. Factors may be rotated to assist the interpretation.

Multiplicative Interpretation. The two structural components $\hat{\mathbf{\Pi}}_\tau$ and $\hat{\mathbf{\Pi}}_\mu$ are easily retrieved from the form (Equation 40) estimates in Table 2.11 as

$$\hat{\Pi}_\mu = \begin{pmatrix} 1.00 & \text{(symm.)} & \\ .72 & 1.00 & \\ .21 & .20 & 1.00 \end{pmatrix}$$

and

$$\hat{\Pi}_\tau = \begin{pmatrix} 1.00 & \text{(symm.)} & \\ .69 & 1.00 & \\ .66 & .51 & 1.00 \end{pmatrix}.$$

TABLE 2.11
Estimates for the Lawler Job Performance Data

	$\hat{D}_x$	$\hat{E}_\mu \otimes I_\tau$	$I_\mu \otimes \hat{E}_\tau$
QualSupe	.94	1.00	.12
AbilSupe	.84	1.00	.41
EfftSupe	.87	1.00	.31
QualPeer	.94	.94	.12
AbilPeer	.85	.94	.41
EfftPeer	.88	.94	.31
QualSelf	.94	2.26	.12
AbilSelf	.75	2.26	.41
EfftSelf	.79	2.26	.31

	$\hat{C}_\mu \otimes I_\tau$								
QualSupe	1.00	.00	.00	.00	.00	.00	.00	.00	.00
AbilSupe	.00	1.00	.00	.00	.00	.00	.00	.00	.00
EfftSupe	.00	.00	1.00	.00	.00	.00	.00	.00	.00
QualPeer	.71	.00	.00	.70	.00	.00	.00	.00	.00
AbilPeer	.00	.71	.00	.00	.70	.00	.00	.00	.00
EfftPeer	.00	.00	.71	.00	.00	.70	.00	.00	.00
QualSelf	.20	.00	.00	.06	.00	.00	.92	.00	.00
AbilSelf	.00	.20	.00	.00	.06	.00	.00	.92	.00
EfftSelf	.00	.00	.20	.00	.00	.06	.00	.00	.92

	$I_\mu \otimes \hat{\Pi}_\tau$								
QualSupe	1.00								
AbilSupe	.69	1.00							
EfftSupe	.66	.51	1.00		(symmetric)				
QualPeer	.00	.00	.00	1.00					
AbilPeer	.00	.00	.00	.69	1.00				
EfftPeer	.00	.00	.00	.66	.51	1.00			
QualSelf	.00	.00	.00	.00	.00	.00	1.00		
AbilSelf	.00	.00	.00	.00	.00	.00	.69	1.00	
EfftSelf	.00	.00	.00	.00	.00	.00	.66	.51	1.00

All off-diagonal entries in these component matrices have t values larger than 2.

The elements of Π_μ and Π_τ are the multiplicative components of correlation coefficients corrected for attenuation and are consequently larger than the correlation coefficients in Table 2.10. The two matrices clearly reflect trends in the sample correlations. Off-diagonal entries in Π_μ indicate changes in MTMM matrix patterns relative to the monomethod blocks. For instance, the value of .72 in Π_μ signifies a 28% drop in the size of correlation coefficients when one trait is measured by supervisor ratings and the other by peer ratings. The numbers .21 and .20 in Π_μ similarly indicate that correlations are reduced by 79% or 80% when supervisor or peer ratings are compared to self-ratings.

Off-diagonal entries in Π_τ express magnitude changes relative to validity diagonal entries. The value of .69 describes the average disattenuated correlation between *quality* and *ability* ratings as 31% smaller than the (disattenuated) diagonal entries. Correspondingly, the correlation between *quality* and *effort* is 34% smaller, and the correlation between *ability* and *effort* is 49% smaller.

Just as in the case with the CCA model, the *fit* of the DPM assures neither *convergent* nor *discriminant* validity. Convergent and discriminant validation require an asymmetric evaluation of the two structural matrices: Π_μ should approach a matrix of unit entries while the off-diagonal elements in Π_τ should approximate zero. This is not the case with the Lawler data: The average off-diagonal entry is .38 in $\hat{\Pi}_\mu$ and .62 in $\hat{\Pi}_\tau$; these two figures point in the exact opposite direction from where they should be, suggesting poor discriminant validity.

Linear Interpretation. The linear parameterization (see Equation 40) of the DPM provides a matrix of disattenuated correlation components among traits (Π_τ) and a matrix (C_μ) of method-specific weight factors. While interpretation of Π_τ remains the same as in the previous section, entries in C_μ are order-dependent. Analytic rotation methods such as Kaiser's (1958) varimax rotation criterion may again be employed to obtain an order-independent solution, and the rotated method component loadings can be interpreted as regression coefficients of observed variables onto orthogonal latent variates similar to traditional exploratory factor analysis.

Varimax rotated method loadings for the Lawler (1967) job performance data are given in Table 2.12. The factor structure shows three components, the first of which affects *superior* ratings, the second *peer* ratings, and the third *self*-ratings. All three methods lead to fairly specific measurements, most of all the self-ratings method. *Superior* and *peer* rating measures do not draw information from the third factor, but share a moderate amount of common variance with each other, indicated by the two factor loadings of 0.38.

TABLE 2.12
Varimax Rotated Method Components for Lawler Data

	$\hat{\mathbf{L}}_\mu$		
Superior	.92	.38	.10
Peer	.38	.92	.09
Self	.08	.07	.94

The structure of the rotated loading matrix $\mathbf{L}_\mu$ corresponds closely to the substance of the Campbell and Fiske criteria. If trait measurement is virtually independent of the methods used, only one column of $\mathbf{L}_\mu$ (or $\mathbf{C}_\mu$) should show large entries, and the estimates in all other columns should vanish. Such a solution implies a congeneric measurement model (Jöreskog, 1966, 1971), as discussed elsewhere. Conversely, large entries in any additional column of $\mathbf{L}_\mu$ indicate independent sources of method variation that would likely lead to considerable violations of the Campbell and Fiske criteria. In the case of the Lawler data, all three methods show a substantial degree of independent variation; *self*-ratings are found to have the smallest overlap with the other methods.

Conclusions Regarding the DPM

The DPM (Browne, 1984a; Cudeck, 1988) presents a relatively novel, multiplicative model for MTMM correlation matrices. The modeling principle of the direct product approach is that crossing two different methods a and b will attenuate the trait correlation pattern $\mathbf{\Pi}_\tau$ by a constant factor $\pi_{\mu(a),\mu(b)}$, $[0 \le \pi_{\mu(a),\mu(b)} \le 1]$, relative to the monomethod correlations. Correlation patterns in the different heteromethod blocks must therefore be proportional to each other. Results may differ from covariance component and factor-analytic approaches that represent method effects by *adding* constant terms to the covariance patterns in the heteromethod blocks.

Under the DPM, scale factors and error terms of the observed variables may be fixed, free, or restricted to suitable patterns. Browne's (1984a) formulation suggests that individual scale factors are estimated for all trait-method units. This ensures that model estimates are scale-free, applying equally to covariance or correlation matrices. The variances of measurement errors may either be generally heteroscedastic, leaving the uniqueness coefficients essentially unconstrained, or follow a composite error model, reflecting trait and method components in the product $\hat{\mathbf{E}} = \mathbf{E}_\mu \otimes \mathbf{E}_\tau$ (Browne, 1984a).

Wothke and Browne's (1990) reparameterization relates the DPM to second-order factor analysis. The resulting linear (re)formulation of the DPM permits interpretation of the same model parameters from linear as well as multiplicative modeling viewpoints. Although the multiplicative framework focuses on the relative attenuation of correlation structures across traits or methods, a linear viewpoint may likewise be entertained, interpreting the estimates in terms of factorial components that reflect independent sources of variation. Both linear and multiplicative approaches to MTMM analysis are not only accommodated under the DPM, but there is also a one-to-one translation between the respective sets of estimates. The difference between these two modeling approaches is therefore merely a matter of conceptual style.

DISCUSSION

Because different structural assumptions for the MTMM matrix are incorporated in the factor-analytic, as well as CCA and direct product models, the question often arises which of these is best. Some comparative remarks are therefore in order.

When selecting a formal model for empirical data, or a larger theory for that matter, consideration should to be given to aspects of model parsimony, statistical fit, statistical power, and conceptual meaningfulness of model parameters. The next section discusses model parsimony and the known conceptual relationships among the different models. Exact statistical power analysis of multivariate models is a somewhat more complicated issue, and is not addressed in this chapter. As a general rule, however, more parsimonious models also tend to be more powerful. Conversely, models usually lose statistical power when many additional parameters are included. Since loss of power implies higher costs in terms of increased sample size requirements and/or higher Type II error rates, it is advantageous to keep the number of conceptually uninteresting (or nuisance) parameters small.

Fit statistics and parameter estimates of the models can be interpreted informally, as demonstrated by worked examples in the preceding sections, or a more formal interpretation in terms of validity criteria may be attempted. The later part of this section outlines the ways in which the models generalize the Campbell and Fiske criteria.

Relation Between Factor Analysis, CCA, and DPMs

The parameter counts for standard versions of the MTMM models, and for two special models with additional constraints, are shown in Table 2.13. Among the standard models, trait-only factor analysis has the least number of parameters, whereas the block-diagonal trait-method factor model has the most parameters, with $mt + m(m-1)/2$ additional terms for the method factor structure. Between these two extremes are the block-diagonal CCA and the DPM (with unconstrained error terms) approaches, both of which

40

TABLE 2.13
Parameter Counts of Scale-Free MTMM Models

Model	Number of parameters
a. Standard models	
Trait-only factor analysis	$2mt + t(t-1)/2$
Block-diagonal CCA	$2mt + t(t-1)/2 + m(m-1)/2$
DPM with unconstrained errors	$2mt + t(t-1)/2 + m(m-1)/2$
Block-diagonal trait-method FA	$3mt + t(t-1)/2 + m(m-1)/2$
b. Models with additional constraints	
Diagonal CCA	$2mt + t + m - 2$
DPM with composite errors	$mt + t(t+1)/2 + m(m+1)/2 - 1$

have $m(m-1)/2$ more parameters than the trait-only factor model and mt fewer parameters than block-diagonal trait-method factor analysis. The nesting relationships among these four standard models will be discussed.

The two models with additional constraints establish interesting variants of scale-free MTMM models, but are singled out in Table 2.13 because they clearly do not form a hierarchical relation with the factor-analytic approaches. Diagonal CCA (illustrated earlier) contains the same $2mt$ parameters for scale factors and error variances as block-diagonal CCA, but $(m-1)(m-2)/2 + (t-1)(t-2)/2$ covariance components are fixed at zero so that only the $m + t - 2$ *variance* components of the trait and method profiles have to be estimated. The DPM with composite errors (demonstrated earlier) uses only $t + m - 1$ parameters to describe the unique variance components instead of the mt parameters used by the unconstrained error model.

Further constraints are possible. Especially when strict assumptions about the scale of measurement and/or the size of error variance can be entertained, then some or all of the mt scale parameters can be fixed. A worthwhile advantage of using fixed-scale models would be model parsimony as well as their considerably higher statistical power compared to scale-free models. However, scale constraints can only be applied to *covariance* matrices; they cannot be used to model correlation matrices that have traditionally been studied with MTMM designs.

Relation Between Factor Analysis and CCA. Trait-only factor analysis is a more restricted form of CCA. Specifically, the trait-only factor model is equivalent to a (scale-free) block-diagonal CCA model with the $m(m-1)/2$ parameter method covariance block $\Phi_{\mu\mu}^*$ fixed at zero.

The equivalence can be demonstrated by a one-to-one mapping of the model parameters. Note that, with $\Phi_{\mu\mu}^* = 0$, both models have $2mt + t(t-1)/2$ parameters. The mt uniqueness parameters in the two models are already mapped one-to-one. It only needs to be shown that the $mt + t(t-1)/2$ parameters for factor loading and factor correlation parameters generate the same covariance structure as the mt scale factors and $t(t-1)/2$ elements of $\Phi_{\mu\mu}^*$ in the CCA model.

Consider the trait-only factor contributions defined by Equations 6 and 7. Since the factor loadings in Λ_τ are nonoverlapping, the matrix can be expressed as

$$\Lambda_\tau = D_x(1_\mu \otimes I_\tau). \tag{47}$$

Define $K = 1_\mu \otimes C_\tau$ as a rank t contrast matrix for the t traits in the model, including one general variate and $t - 1$ trait profile comparisons. C_τ has full rank. Hence, the relation between factor covariances Φ_τ and covariance components Φ_τ^* can be written as

$$\Phi_\tau = C_\tau \Phi_\tau^* C_\tau'. \tag{48}$$

Then, by repeated application of the elementary matrix identity $AB \otimes CD = (A \otimes C)(B \otimes D)$, the covariance matrix of the factor model is

$$\Sigma = \Lambda_\tau \Phi_\tau \Lambda_\tau + \Theta \tag{49}$$

$$= D_x(1_\mu \otimes I_\tau)\Phi_\tau(1'_\mu \otimes I_\tau)D_x + \Theta \tag{50}$$

$$= D_x(1_\mu 1'_\mu \otimes \Phi_\tau)D_x + \Theta \tag{51}$$

$$= D_x(1_\mu 1'_\mu \otimes C_\tau \Phi_\tau^* C'_\tau)D_x + \Theta \tag{52}$$

$$= D_x(1_\mu \otimes C_\tau)\Phi_\tau^*(1'_\mu \otimes C'_\tau)D_x + \Theta \tag{53}$$

$$= D_x K_\tau \Phi_\tau^* K'_\tau D_x + \Theta, \tag{54}$$

yielding a covariance components formulation. Identification rules for scale-free CCA (discussed previously) require that the first row and column of Φ_τ^* be fixed at suitable values (e.g., $\psi_{1,1} = 1$ and $\psi_{i,1} = \psi_{1,i} = 0$ for $i \neq 1$). Thus, parameterization (see Equation 54) is the block-diagonal scale-free covariance components model, omitting all terms for method covariance structures.

The trait-method factor model is more general than the scale-free block-diagonal CCA. This can be shown by equating the CCA model with the following restricted version of trait-method factor analysis: As discussed earlier, the trait-method factor is generally underidentified when the loading matrix has the proportional structure (see Equation 11)

$$\Lambda_{\tau\mu}^{(p)} = D_x(1_\mu \otimes I_\tau | I_\mu \otimes 1_\tau)D_\xi$$

$$= D_x A_{\tau\mu}^* D_\xi, \tag{55}$$

using the $mt \times (m + t)$ design matrix $\mathbf{A}_{\tau\mu}^*$. Defining $\mathbf{\Psi} = \mathbf{D}_\xi\mathbf{\Phi}\mathbf{D}_\xi$ yields the covariance structure

$$\mathbf{\Sigma} = \mathbf{D}_x\mathbf{A}_{\tau\mu}^*\mathbf{D}_\xi\mathbf{\Phi}\mathbf{D}_\xi\mathbf{A}_{\tau\mu}^{*\prime}\mathbf{D}_x + \mathbf{\Theta} \qquad (56)$$

$$= \mathbf{D}_x\mathbf{A}_{\tau\mu}^*\mathbf{\Psi}\mathbf{A}_{\tau\mu}^{*\prime}\mathbf{D}_x + \mathbf{\Theta}. \qquad (57)$$

The apparent problem is that $\mathbf{A}_{\tau\mu}^*$ has only column rank $m + t - 1$ so that the parameters in $\mathbf{\Psi}$ cannot all be uniquely estimated. To resolve the identification problem, select an $mt \times (m + t - 1)$ matrix $\mathbf{K}_{\tau\mu}$ of column contrasts of $\mathbf{A}_{\tau\mu}^*$, so that $\mathbf{A}_{\tau\mu}^* = \mathbf{K}_{\tau\mu}\mathbf{L}_{\tau\mu}$. Define $\mathbf{\Psi}^* = \mathbf{L}_{\tau\mu}\mathbf{\Psi}\mathbf{L}_{\tau\mu}$ and apply the identifying constraints of the section on model identification for CCA to $\mathbf{\Psi}^*$, yielding the constrained covariance component matrix $\mathbf{\Phi}^*$. Hence, the model covariance matrix represented by the trait-method factor model with proportional loadings (see Equation 11) is:

$$\mathbf{\Sigma} = \mathbf{D}_x\mathbf{K}_{\tau\mu}\mathbf{\Phi}^*\mathbf{K}_{\tau\mu}'\mathbf{D}_x + \mathbf{\Theta}, \qquad (58)$$

again, a CCA formulation. Identification conditions for scale-free CCA estimation require that the first row and column of $\mathbf{\Phi}^*$ have fixed values, such as $\phi_{1,1}^* = 1$ and zeros in the other fields. Furthermore, because the original factor covariance matrix $\mathbf{\Phi}$ was block-diagonal, the submatrix $\mathbf{\Phi}_{\mu\tau}^*$ will also be zero. Thus, parameterization (see Equation 58) is the scale-free block-diagonal CCA model.

Not only is Equation 58 an identified parameterization of an entire class of otherwise unidentified trait-method factor models, it also relinquishes mt factor loading parameters that would frequently be of no substantive interest.

Relation Between Factor Analysis and DPM. Trait-only factor analysis is equivalent to the DPM with no method effects except, maybe, a simple change in reliability of measurement. In such a case, the DPM's method factor $\mathbf{\Pi}_\mu$ has unit entries throughout:

$$\mathbf{\Pi}_\mu = \mathbf{1}_\mu\mathbf{1}'_\mu. \qquad (59)$$

Defining $\mathbf{\Theta} = \mathbf{D}_x\mathbf{E}\mathbf{D}_x$, the DPM without method effects derives from Equation 38 as

$$\mathbf{\Sigma} = \mathbf{D}_x(\mathbf{1}_\mu\mathbf{1}'_\mu \otimes \mathbf{\Pi}_\tau)\mathbf{D}_x + \mathbf{\Theta}, \qquad (60)$$

which is identical to form Equation 51 of the trait-only factor model.

Not much is currently known about the relation of block-diagonal trait-method factor analysis to the DPM. Even though Wothke and Browne

(1990) reparameterize the DPM in terms of second-order factor analysis, their work probably does not extend to the trait-method factor model. As far as is known, the DPM and the trait-method factor model are different generalizations of trait-only factor analysis.

Relation Between CCA and the DPM. Because the scale-free versions of block-diagonal CCA and the DPM have exactly the same number of degrees of freedom, it is worthwhile considering whether the two models are, or are not, equivalent to each other.

Browne (1989) presents an approximation suggesting that CCA and DPM produce nearly identical model covariance matrices. My own experience in analyzing MTMM matrices is that differences between the two models can be negligible in the presence of sampling variation, especially when the MTMM matrix has all positive entries. A case in point are the nearly identical fit statistics for the Lawler data of Table 2.10: $G^2 = 29.2$ for CCA and $G^2 = 28.8$ for the DPM with heteroscedastic errors.

Browne's approximation between the two models tends to break down, however, with MTMM matrices containing both positive and negative correlations. Because CCA adds or subtracts constant method effects, its heterotrait–heteromethod patterns can range from completely positive, over mixed, to completely negative. DPM, on the other hand, only changes the absolute values of the correlation patterns, but leaves the signs of individual entries in the heterotrait–heteromethod blocks unaffected. Differences between the models may be occluded by sign changes in the scale factor coefficients, but counterexamples to Browne's approximation do exist. For instance, using the Kelly and Fiske assessment data discussed earlier, DPM has a G^2 of 115.6 at 77 degrees of freedom, while CCA fits marginally better with a G^2 of 104.7.

It is safe to conclude that CCA and the DPM are differing models. They are neither equivalent nor nested. The fact that the two models have the same degrees of freedom is merely coincidental.

Relation of the Models to Campbell and Fiske Criteria

It appears that Campbell and Fiske (1959) had in mind a model similar to trait-only factor analysis when they proposed their well-known qualitative criteria of convergent and discriminant validation:

CF1 (convergent validity): . . . the entries in the validity diagonal should be significantly different from zero and sufficiently large . . . (p. 82)

CF2 (discriminant validity): . . . a validity diagonal value should be higher than the values lying in its column and row in the heterotrait–heteromethod triangles. (p. 82)

CF3 (discriminant validity): . . . a variable correlate higher with an independent effort to measure the same trait than with measures designed to get at different traits which happen to employ the same method. (p. 83)

CF4 (discriminant validity): . . . the same pattern of trait interrelationship be shown in all of the heterotrait triangles of both the monomethod and heteromethod blocks. (p. 83)

Convergent validity assures that measures of the same trait are statistically related to each other and that their error and unique components are relatively small. Discriminant validity postulates that a purported measure of one trait is not too highly correlated with measures of different traits, and particularly not because these measures were taken with the same assessment method (monomethod bias).

These criteria apply to the trait-only factor model in the following sense: Assuming that the term *large* in CF1 implies positive, then convergent validity is established by the trait-only factor model when the nonzero loadings λ_{i,τ_k} in Equation 6 are all large and of the same sign (Wothke, 1984, p. 29). When factor loadings are all positive, CF2 implies that the trait factor correlations be restricted to their usual admissible range of $-1 < \phi_{\tau_k\tau_l} < 1$ (Wothke, 1984, p. 31); yet, CF3 translates into a somewhat peculiar trade-off between free factor loadings and factor correlations (Wothke, 1984, pp. 32–35):

$$|\phi_{\tau_k\tau_l}| < \lambda_{i,\tau_k}/\lambda_{j,\tau_l} < |1/\phi_{\tau_k\tau_l}| \tag{61}$$

and

$$\max_{\substack{k \\ k\neq l}}(\phi_{\tau_k\tau_l}^2) < \min_i(\lambda_{i,\tau_l})/\max_i(\lambda_{i,\tau_l}) \leq 1. \tag{62}$$

The meaning of CF4 is imprecise because the terms *same, pattern,* and *interrelationship* were left undefined by Campbell and Fiske (1959). A more useful requirement would be that any two heterotrait triangles have *proportional* entries. This proportionality rule imposes $(m-1)(t-1)$ restrictions on the factor loading coefficients in Equation 47 in the form of $\mathbf{D}_\lambda = \mathbf{D}_\mu \otimes \mathbf{D}_\tau$ (Wothke, 1984, pp. 35–39).

All four validity criteria by Campbell and Fiske will usually only be met when the factor loadings in Equation 6 are fairly large and similar in size. If Campbell and Fiske actually did develop the validity criteria for the MTMM matrix with a trait-only factor model in mind, they apparently also assumed that all observed variables have equal communalities.

Conversely, because the trait-only factor model incorporates the general notion of varying reliabilities between measures, its fit to an MTMM correlation matrix does not, by itself, establish convergent or discriminant validation in the sense of Campbell and Fiske. The trait-only model rather comprises a generalization of the Campbell–Fiske criteria with explicit adjustments for heterogeneous scales or reliabilities. Convergent and discriminant validation is still established, but in a different sense from Campbell and Fiske. Validation by the trait-only factor model is convergent because each trait (factor) accounts for the entire systematic variance of its measures. Validation of the measured variables is also discriminant because the correlation between measures of different traits is only a function of the correlation between the two hypothesized traits and the communalities of the measures—there are no contributions by other trait factors, and no method factors are needed.

Experience with applying the trait-only factor model to psychological data has not been very promising. Of the 23 published MTMM data sets analyzed by Wothke (1984, 1987), admissible solutions were obtained for 13, but only 2 of these showed acceptable model fit. It appears that most empirical data sets do not support the strict notion of convergent and discriminant validity. In the 2 cases where the trait-only model shows a good fit, assessment methods differ only in paper-and-pencil formats. These studies add important information to the attitude assessment field, but cannot claim to establish strong tests of method independence.

Different approaches to validity are needed for the *covariance component analysis* and *direct product* models. Discriminant validity is lost in these models because, in order to achieve fit, method components have been added to describe the impact of assessment methods on the correlation structure of the observed measures. Both CCA and DPM, therefore, violate the central idea of discriminant validation that "(tests) can be invalidated by too high correlations with other tests from which they are intended to differ" (Campbell & Fiske, 1959, p. 81). And when the CCA or DPM extensions of the trait-only factor model are needed, elevated correlations are often found in the monomethod blocks.

The CCA and DPM approaches are definitely weaker models than the Campbell and Fiske criteria, because they allow both trait and method effects in measurement. CCA and DPM are important generalized models that permit researchers to decompose and quantify the relative variance components of trait and method contributions in the MTMM matrix. When DPM or CCA show a substantial improvement in fit over the trait-only factor model, then the previous trait concepts are pretty much drawn into question and further conceptual elaboration of the measurement process is required. Such theoretical development will be easier when CCA or DPM themselves fit the data well. In this case, instead of haphazard deviations from the trait-only factor model, a regular decomposition of variance components into trait and method facets has been found, adding justification to further systematic study of these method effects and/or to further refinement of measurement procedures.

Applications of CCA and DPM to published empirical MTMM data sets
(Wothke, 1987) tend to fit the data considerably better than the trait-only
factor model. This reflects the prevalence of method effects in these types
of data. In roughly one quarter of the cases, block-diagonal CCA and/or
DPM have a satisfactory overall fit to the data, suggesting that the correlation
structure is dependent only on the trait and method facets. However, many
cases remain where CCA and DPM still show inadmissible solutions or very
poor fit. These problems may be due to a variety of causes, ranging from
small sample size and choice of unreliable indicators over ordinal measurement, outliers and non-normality issues to misspecification of the model
itself (Wothke, 1993). These points must be attended to because many data
sets labeled as MTMM matrices suffer from them. It is very important that
the MTMM study be designed carefully and knowledgeably. Although the
methods discussed in this chapter are important statistical tools for evaluating MTMM measurement designs, they cannot serve as statistical panaceas
for inaccurate ideas of trait generality and method independence.

APPENDIX: MODEL SPECIFICATION
OF WORKED EXAMPLES

Program scripts for the three MTMM models of this chapter appear here,
using the SEM programs Amos (Arbuckle, 1995), LISREL (Jöreskog &
Sörbom, 1993), and/or Mx (Neale, 1994). The programs differ in suitability
for particular problems and in the ease with which they can be used. Amos
is the most graphics-oriented program; its model input consists of drawing
a path diagram on the screen. Amos input is given for the factor analysis
and CCA models. LISREL, having been around longer, is the most widely
known program. In LISREL (version 8), authors have made the transition
from a fixed matrix-oriented language to an equation-oriented syntax (using the SIMPLIS language). Specifications of all three models are shown
for the LISREL program, although the DPM turns out to be quite lengthy.
The Mx program, in contrast to the Amos and LISREL, is an advanced
matrix-oriented package with extremely flexible matrix functions. It rec-
ognizes the Kronecker product as a modeling operation, so that the DPM
can be specified in its original form (see Equation 38).

The Amos and LISREL programs are distributed commercially. At the
time of this writing, the Mx program is distributed as *freeware*, which can be
downloaded by anonymous ftp from `sapphire.gen.vcu.edu` on the
Internet.

Due to space limitations, the example setups do not include sample
data. Conventions for reading correlation matrices differ somewhat between the three programs, but are easily figured out. The sample MTMM
matrices are already given in Tables 2.1, 2.4, and 2.10.

Trait-Only Factor Model of Flamer's Attitude Data

This confirmatory factor model is shown in Amos 3.5 and LISREL (SIM-PLIS) notation. The two programs employ different default scale con-straints for the latent variables: Amos fixes one of the factor loadings to unity (1.0) for each factor, whereas the LISREL input file sets the factor variances to unity. However, the two programs will provide the same stand-ardized solution, when requested (e.g., LISREL OUTPUT: SS).

Both Amos and LISREL run into minor technical hitches, which may require work-around solutions: Amos expects *covariance* matrix input, yet Flamer's MTMM matrix contains only correlations. To persuade Amos into analyzing correlations, one has to relabel the correlation matrix as a co-variance matrix. Because the factor model is scale-free, and ML estimation is used, the standardized parameter estimates and the G^2-statistic will not be affected by this "trick" (Jöreskog & Sörbom, 1989). LISREL, on the other hand, is not as strict about analyzing correlation matrices and usually proceeds as if a covariance matrix had been supplied.

In LISREL 8, the factor model may run afoul of the program's internal admissibility checks of intermediate parameter estimates or not reach con-vergence within the default number of iterations. It is not clear whether this behavior is due to a bug or is merely an odd feature of the program. Nevertheless, turning off the admissibility check and increasing the number of iterations will often produce the ML solution.

Model Input With Amos 3.5

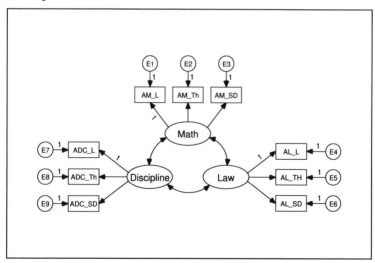

FIG. A.1. Flamer (1983) attitude data, Sample A. Model with three trait factors. Specification in Amos Graphics.

Model Input With LISREL 8

```
Three-trait factor model of Flamer's attitude data
   . . . (Supply input data, sample size and variable labels here)
Latent variables:
      Math Law Discipline     ! Set number of factors and their names


Relationships:


      AM_L    = Math         ! 1. Math
      AM_TH   = Math         !    factor
      AM_SD   = Math         !    structure
      AL_L    = Law          ! 2. Law
      AL_TH   = Law          !    factor
      AL_SD   = Law          !    structure
      ADC_L   = Discipline   ! 3. Discipline
      ADC_TH  = Discipline   !    factor
      ADC_SD  = Discipline   !    structure


Set the variances of Math - Discipline to 1.0 ! Standardize factors
Set the covariances of Math - Discipline free ! Let factors correlate
Options: AD=OFF IT=100 ! No admissibility check, up to 100 iterations
```

Covariance Components Model of the Dickinson and Tice Work-Related Attitudes Data

The scale-free covariance components model is shown in Amos 3.5 and LISREL 8 (matrix) notation. Both programs employ the identical model structure: Five uncorrelated covariance components are related (by fixed contrasts) to nine phantom (Rindskopf, 1984) variables each of which, in turn, is attached to a single observed variable by a scale factor. To establish scale identification, the variance of the *General* component is fixed to unity (1.0), and its correlation with the other latent variates is set to zero (0.0). The variances of the remaining four covariance components is estimated, but their correlations are set to zero as a substantive model constraint.

Note: Before calculating the estimates, Amos requires the user's confirmation that the models are indeed meant to have (a) uncorrelated latent factors, and (b) endogenous variables without residual terms. The program regards such models as nonstandard.

Model Input With Amos 3.5

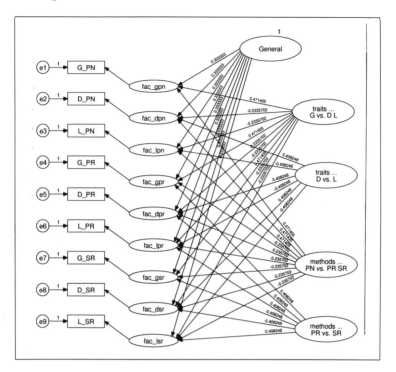

FIG. A.2. Dickinson and Tice (1973) work-related attributes. Scale-free
CCA, uncorrelated components. Specification in Amos Graphics.

Model Input With LISREL 8

```
Scale-free CCA of Dickinson and Tice MTMM matrix, diagonal covariance structure:
!
DAtaparameters . . . (Supply input data, sample size and variable labels here)
!
! Structural model specifications:
!
MOdelspecs NY=9 NEta=9 NKsi=5 PSi=ZEro,FIxed  Continue
   LY=DIag,FRee GAmma=FUll,FIxed PH=DIag,FRee
!
MAtrix GAmma                                     ! Contrasts go into GAmma
    0.333333        0.471405            0        0.471405            0
    0.333333       -0.235702     0.408248        0.471405            0
    0.333333       -0.235702    -0.408248        0.471405            0
    0.333333        0.471405            0       -0.235702     0.408248
```

0.333333	−0.235702	−0.408248	−0.235702	0.408248
0.333333	−0.235702	−0.408248	−0.235702	0.408248
0.333333	0.471405	0	−0.235702	−0.408248
0.333333	−0.235702	0.408248	−0.235702	−0.408248
0.333333	−0.235702	−0.408248	−0.235702	−0.408248

```
!
VAlue 1.0 LY 1 - LY 9 PHi 1 - PHi 5   ! Start values for LY and PH
VAlue 0.5 TE 1 - TE 9                  ! Start values for TE
!
FIx PHi 1                              ! Identification constraint
!
! Estimation and output options:
!                                      ! Use specified start values,
!                                      ! print iteration history
OU NS PT RS ND=5                       ! and residual statistics.
```

DPM of Lawler's Job Performance Data

The scale-free DPM is shown in Mx 1.1 and LISREL 8 (matrix) notation. In Mx, the DPM can be entered in Browne's (1984a) formulation, using Equations 38 and 39. The LISREL 8 specification is equivalent to that model, but written in the second-order factor form of Equations 40 and 41.

Note: At least with Lawler's data, the DPM appears to have multiple local minima, for the estimates are quite sensitive to the choice of start values. I found several model solutions for this DPM, but the one with the lowest G^2-statistic of 28.9 appears to be unique.

Model Input With Mx 1.1

```
Direct product model of Lawler's Job performance data.
!
DAta . . . (Supply input data, sample size and variable labels here)
!
Matrices          ! Declare matrices used in model:
  D DIAGonal       9 9 /   ! Diagonal matrix of scale factors (D)
  E DIAGonal       3 3 /   ! Diagonal matrix of method errors (E_M)
  F DIAGonal       3 3 /   ! Diagonal matrix of trait errors (E_T)
  M STANdardized   3 3 /   ! Standardized method 'RHO' matrix (P_M)
  T STANdardized   3 3 /   ! Standardized trait 'RHO' matrix (P_T)
!
MOdel             ! Sigma = DPM model; symbol '@' used for
  D * ( M @ T + E @ F ) * D /        ! Kronecker product
!
FREE D(1,1) TO D(9,9)              ! Declare
FREE E(1,1) TO E(3,3)             ! various
```

```
FREE F(1,1) TO F(3,3)           ! parameters
FREE M(2,1) TO M(3,2)           ! to be
FREE T(2,1) TO T(3,2)           ! free.
!
START 1.0 D(1,1) TO D(9,9)      ! Reasonably
START 1.0 E(1,1) TO E(3,3)      ! close
START 1.0 F(1,1) TO F(3,3)      ! start values
START 0.5 M(2,1) TO M(3,2)      ! must be
START 0.5 T(2,1) TO T(3,2)      ! supplied.
!
FIX E(1,1) ! Necessary scale constraint
!
OUTPUT ML SE ! Maximum likelihood estimates, s.e.'s
```

Model Input With LISREL 8

```
TItle Lawler (1967) managerial job performance
!
! Specifications use the second-order factor analysis
! form of the DPM.
!
DAtaparameters . . . (Supply input data, sample size and variable labels here)
! MOdelspecs NY=9 NE=9 NK=18 LY=DI,FR GA=FU,FR PH=SY,FR PS=ZE BE=ZE TE=ZE
STartvalues .5 LY 1 - LY 9        ! Matrix of scale factors
EQuality        LY 1 LY 4 LY 7    ! Scale constraints
MAtrix GAmma                      ! Gamma is the partitioned matrix
*                                 ! ( C_M @ I_T | sqrt(E_M) @ I_T )
1 0 0 0 0 0 0 0 0 1 0 0 0 0 0 0 0 0
0 1 0 0 0 0 0 0 0 0 1 0 0 0 0 0 0 0
0 0 1 0 0 0 0 0 0 0 0 1 0 0 0 0 0 0
1 0 0 1 0 0 0 0 0 0 0 0 1 0 0 0 0 0
0 1 0 0 1 0 0 0 0 0 0 0 0 1 0 0 0 0
0 0 1 0 0 1 0 0 0 0 0 0 0 0 1 0 0 0
1 0 0 1 0 0 1 0 0 0 0 0 0 0 0 1 0 0
0 1 0 0 1 0 0 1 0 0 0 0 0 0 0 0 1 0
0 0 1 0 0 1 0 0 1 0 0 0 0 0 0 0 0 1
PAttern GAmma
*
0 0 0 0 0 0 0 0 0 1 0 0 0 0 0 0 0 0    ! Implied value
0 0 0 0 0 0 0 0 0 0 1 0 0 0 0 0 0 0    ! constraints for
0 0 0 0 0 0 0 0 0 0 0 1 0 0 0 0 0 0    ! (1,1), (2,2) and (3,3)
1 0 0 1 0 0 0 0 0 0 0 0 1 0 0 0 0 0
0 1 0 0 1 0 0 0 0 0 0 0 0 1 0 0 0 0
0 0 1 0 0 1 0 0 0 0 0 0 0 0 1 0 0 0
1 0 0 1 0 0 1 0 0 0 0 0 0 0 0 1 0 0
0 1 0 0 1 0 0 1 0 0 0 0 0 0 0 0 1 0
0 0 1 0 0 1 0 0 1 0 0 0 0 0 0 0 0 1
```

```
EQuality GA 4 1 GA 5 2 GA 6 3          ! Equality
EQuality GA 4 4 GA 5 5 GA 6 6          ! constraints
EQuality GA 7 1 GA 8 2 GA 9 3          ! to simulate
EQuality GA 7 4 GA 8 5 GA 9 6          ! C_M @ I_T
EQuality GA 7 7 GA 8 8 GA 9 9
FIx       GA 1 10 GA 2 11 GA 3 12      ! More scale constraints
EQuality GA 4 13 GA 5 14 GA 6 15
EQuality GA 7 16 GA 8 17 GA 9 18
PAttern PHi                            ! PHi is the partitioned
*                                      ! matrix:
0                                      ! ( I_M @ P_T | 0 )
1 0                                    ! (- - - - - - - - - -+- - - - - - - - - -)
1 1 0                                  ! (    0     | I_M @ E_T )
0 0 0 0
0 0 0 1 0
0 0 0 1 1 0
0 0 0 0 0 0
0 0 0 0 0 0 1 0
0 0 0 0 0 0 1 1 0
0 0 0 0 0 0 0 0 0 1
0 0 0 0 0 0 0 0 0 0 1
0 0 0 0 0 0 0 0 0 0 0 1
0 0 0 0 0 0 0 0 0 0 0 0 1
0 0 0 0 0 0 0 0 0 0 0 0 0 1
0 0 0 0 0 0 0 0 0 0 0 0 0 0 1
0 0 0 0 0 0 0 0 0 0 0 0 0 0 0 1
0 0 0 0 0 0 0 0 0 0 0 0 0 0 0 0 1
0 0 0 0 0 0 0 0 0 0 0 0 0 0 0 0 0 1
MAtrix PHi
*
1
.5 1
.5 .5 1
0 0 0 1
0 0 0 .5 1
0 0 0 .5 .5 1
0 0 0 0 0 0 1
0 0 0 0 0 0 .5 1
0 0 0 0 0 0 .5 .5 1
0 0 0 0 0 0 0 0 0 .2
0 0 0 0 0 0 0 0 0 0 .2
0 0 0 0 0 0 0 0 0 0 0 .2
0 0 0 0 0 0 0 0 0 0 0 0 .2
0 0 0 0 0 0 0 0 0 0 0 0 0 .2
0 0 0 0 0 0 0 0 0 0 0 0 0 0 .2
0 0 0 0 0 0 0 0 0 0 0 0 0 0 0 .2
0 0 0 0 0 0 0 0 0 0 0 0 0 0 0 0 .2
```

```
0 0 0 0 0 0 0 0 0 0 0 0 0 0 0 0 0 .2
EQuality PH 2 1 PH 5 4 PH 8 7
EQuality PH 3 1 PH 6 4 PH 9 7
EQuality PH 3 2 PH 6 5 PH 9 8
EQuality PH 10 10 PH 13 13 PH 16 16
EQuality PH 11 11 PH 14 14 PH 17 17
EQuality PH 12 12 PH 15 15 PH 18 18
OU NS SS PT TV RS ND=4 AD=5000
```

REFERENCES

Althauser, R. P. (1974). Inferring validity from the multitrait–multimethod matrix: Another assessment. In H. L. Costner (Ed.), *Sociological methodology 1973–1974*. San Francisco: Jossey-Bass.

Althauser, R. P., & Heberlein, T. A. (1970). Validity and the multitrait–multimethod matrix. In E. F. Borgatta (Ed.), *Sociological methodology 1970*. San Francisco: Jossey-Bass.

Althauser, R. P., Heberlein, T. A., & Scott, R. A. (1971). A causal assessment of validity: The augmented multitrait–multimethod matrix. In H. M. Blalock (Ed.), *Causal models in the social sciences*. Chicago: Aldine.

Anderson, E., Bai, Z., Bischof, C., Demmel, J., Dongarra, J., Du Croz, J., Greenbaum, A., Hamarling, S., McKenney, A., Ostrouchov, S., & Sorensen, D. (1992). *LAPACK users' guide*. Philadelphia, PA: SIAM.

Anderson, T. W. (1984). *An introduction to multivariate statistical analysis* (2nd ed.). New York: Wiley.

Arbuckle, J. L. (1995). *Amos for Windows. Analysis of moment structures (Version 3.5)*. Chicago, IL: SmallWaters.

Bartholomew, D. J. (1987). *Latent variables models and factor analysis*. New York: Oxford University Press.

Bloxom, B. (1968). A note on invariance in three-mode factor analysis. *Psychometrika, 33*(3), 347–350.

Bock, R. D. (1960). Components of variance analysis as a structural and discriminal analysis of psychological tests. *The British Journal of Statistical Psychology, 13*(2), 151–163.

Bock, R. D. (1975). *Multivariate statistical methods in behavioral research*. New York: McGraw-Hill.

Bock, R. D., & Bargmann, R. E. (1966). Analysis of covariance structures. *Psychometrika, 31*(4), 507–534.

Bock, R. D., Dicken, C., & Van Pelt, J. (1969). Methodological implications of content-acquiescence correlation in the MMPI. *Psychological Bulletin, 71*(2), 127–139.

Bollen, K. A. (1989). *Structural equations with latent variables*. New York: Wiley.

Bozdogan, H. (1987). Model selection and Akaike's information criterion (AIC): The general theory and its analytical extensions. *Psychometrika, 52*(2), 345–370.

Brannick, M. T., & Spector, P. E. (1990). Estimation problems in the block-diagonal model of the multitrait-multimethod matrix. *Applied Psychological Measurement, 14*(4), 325–339.

Browne, M. W. (1980). Factor analysis of multiple batteries by maximum likelihood. *British Journal of Mathematical and Statistical Psychology, 33*, 184–199.

Browne, M. W. (1984a). The decomposition of multitrait-multimethod matrices. *British Journal of Mathematical and Statistical Psychology, 37*, 1–21.

Browne, M. W. (1984b). Asymptotically distribution-free methods for the analysis of covariance structures. *British Journal of Mathematical and Statistical Psychology, 37*, 62–83.

Browne, M. W. (1989). Relationships between an additive model and a multiplicative model for multitrait-multimethod matrices. In R. Coppi & S. Bolasco (Eds.), *Analysis of multiway data matrices*. Amsterdam: Elsevier.

Browne, M. W. (1992). Models for multitrait–multimethod matrices. In R. Steyer, K. F. Wender, & K. F. Widaman (Eds.), *Proceedings of the 7th European Meeting of the Psychometric Society in Trier*. Stuttgart: Gustav Fischer.

Browne, M. W., & Strydom, H. F. (in press). Noniterative fitting of the direct product model for multitrait–multimethod matrices. In M. Berkane (Ed.), *Latent variable modeling with applications to causality*. New York: Springer.

Campbell, D. T., & Fiske, D. W. (1959). Convergent and discriminant validation by the multitrait–multimethod matrix. *Psychological Bulletin, 56*, 81–105.

Campbell, D. T., & O'Connell, E. J. (1967). Method factors in multitrait-multimethod matrices: Multiplicative rather than additive? *Multivariate Behavioral Research, 2*, 409–426.

Campbell, D. T., & O'Connell, E. J. (1982). Methods as diluting trait relationships rather than adding irrelevant systematic variance. In D. Brinberg & L. H. Kidder (Eds.), *Forms of validity in research. New Directions for Methodology of Social and Behavioral Science* (Vol. 12). San Francisco: Jossey-Bass.

Cudeck, R. (1988). Multiplicative models and MTMM matrices. *Journal of Educational Statistics, 13*(2), 131–147.

Cudeck, R., & Henley, S. J. (1991). Model selection in covariance structure analysis and the "problem" of sample size: A clarification. *Psychological Bulletin, 109*(3), 509–512.

Dickinson, T. L., & Tice, T. E. (1973). A multitrait–multimethod analysis of scales developed by retranslation. *Organizational Behavior and Human Performance, 9*, 421–438.

Finn, J. D. (1974). *A general model for multivariate data analysis*. New York: Holt, Rinehart & Winston.

Flamer, S. (1983). Assessment of the multitrait–multimethod matrix validity of Likert scales via confirmatory factor analysis. *Multivariate Behavioral Research, 18*, 275–308.

Graybill, F. A. (1961). *An introduction to linear statistical models* (Vol. 1). New York: McGraw-Hill.

Grayson, D., & Marsh, H. W. (1994). Identification with deficient rank loading matrices in confirmatory analysis: Multitrait-multimethod models. *Psychometrika, 59*(1), 121–134.

Harman, H. H. (1967). *Modern factor analysis* (2nd ed.). Chicago: University of Chicago Press.

Hotelling, H. (1933). Analysis of a complex of statistical variables into principal components. *Journal of Educational Psychology, 24*, 417–441, 498–520.

IMSL, Inc. (1980). *The IMSL library* (Edition 8). Houston, TX: Author.

Jöreskog, K. G. (1966). Testing a simple structure hypothesis in factor analysis. *Psychometrika, 31*, 165–178.

Jöreskog, K. G. (1971). Statistical analysis of sets of congeneric tests. *Psychometrika, 36*(2), 109–133.

Jöreskog, K. G. (1974). Analyzing psychological data by structural analysis of covariance matrices. In D. H. Krantz, R. C. Atkinson, R. D. Luce, & P. Suppes (Eds.), *Contemporary developments in mathematical psychology* (Vol. 2). San Francisco: Freeman.

Jöreskog, K. G. (1978). Structural analysis of covariance and correlation matrices. *Psychometrika, 43*(4), 443–477.

Jöreskog, K. G., & Sörbom, D. (1979). *Advances in factor analysis and structural equation models*. Cambridge, MA: Abt Books.

Jöreskog, K. G., & Sörbom, D. (1989). *LISREL 7. A guide to the program and applications* (2nd ed.). Chicago, IL: SPSS.

Jöreskog, K. G., & Sörbom, D. (1993). *LISREL 8. Structural equation modeling with the Simplis command language*. Chicago, IL: Scientific Software International.

Kaiser, H. F. (1958). The varimax criterion for analytic rotation in factor analysis. *Psychometrika, 23*, 187–200.

Kalleberg, A. L., & Kluegel, J. R. (1975). Analysis of the multitrait–multimethod matrix: Some limitations and an alternative. *Journal of Applied Psychology, 60*(1), 1–9.

Kelly, E. L., & Fiske, D. W. (1951). *The prediction of performance in clinical psychology.* Ann Arbor: University of Michigan Press.

Kenny, D. A., & Kashy, D. A. (1992). Analysis of the multitrait–multimethod matrix by confirmatory factor analysis. *Psychological Bulletin, 112*(1), 165–172.

Lawler, E. E., III. (1967). The multitrait–multimethod approach to measuring managerial job performance. *Journal of Applied Psychology, 51*(5), 369–381.

Lord, F. M., & Novick, M. R. (1968). *Statistical theories of mental test scores.* Reading, MA: Addison-Wesley.

Marsh, H. W. (1989). Confirmatory factor analyses of multitrait–multimethod data: Many problems and a few solutions. *Applied Psychological Measurement, 13*(4), 335–361.

Marsh, H. W., & Bailey, M. (1991). Confirmatory factor analyses of multitrait–multimethod data: A comparison of alternative models. *Applied Psychological Measurement, 15*(1), 47–70.

Marsh, H. W., Balla, J. R., & McDonald, R. P. (1988). Goodness-of-fit indexes in confirmatory factor analysis: The effect of sample size. *Psychological Bulletin, 103*(3), 391–410.

Mathsoft, Inc. (1992). *Mathcad 3.1. User's guide.* Cambridge, MA: Author.

McDonald, R. P., & Marsh, H. W. (1990). Choosing a multivariate model: Noncentrality and goodness of fit. *Psychological Bulletin, 107*(2), 247–255.

Millsap, R. E. (1992). Sufficient conditions for rotational uniqueness in the additive MTMM model. *British Journal of Mathematical and Statistical Psychology, 45*, 125–138.

Millsap, R. E. (1995). The statistical analysis of method effects in multitrait-multimethod data: A review. In P. E. Shrout & S. T. Fiske (Eds.), *Personality research, methods, and theory: A festschrift honoring Donald W. Fiske.* Hillsdale, NJ: Lawrence Erlbaum Associates.

Neale, M. C. (1994). *Mx: Statistical modeling* (2nd ed.). Richmond, VA: Author.

Numerical Algorithms Group, Ltd. (1987). *NAG FORTRAN libraries Mark 12.* Oxford, GB: Author.

Rindskopf, D. M. (1984). Using phantom and imaginary latent variables to parameterize constraints in linear structural models. *Psychometrika, 49*, 109–119.

SAS Institute Inc. (1985). *SAS/IML, user's guide for personal computers* (Version 6). Cary, NC: Author.

Schmitt, N. (1978). Path analysis of multitrait–multimethod matrices. *Applied Psychological Measurement, 2*(2), 157–173.

Schmitt, N., & Stults, D. M. (1986). Methodology review: Analysis of multitrait–multimethod matrices. *Applied Psychological Measurement, 13.*

Spearman, C. (1904). General intelligence, objectively determined and measured. *American Journal of Psychology, 15*, 201–293.

Stacy, A. W., Widaman, K. F., Hays, R., & DiMatteo, M. R. (1985). Validity of self-reports of alcohol and other drug use: A multitrait–multimethod assessment. *Journal of Personality and Social Psychology, 49*(1), 219–232.

Swain, A. J. (1975). *Analysis of parametric structures for variance matrices.* Unpublished doctoral thesis. University of Adelaide, Adelaide, Australia.

Tucker, L. R. (1966). Some mathematical notes on three-mode factor analysis. *Psychometrika, 31*(3), 279–311.

Werts, C. E., Jöreskog, K. G., & Linn, R. L. (1972). A multitrait–multimethod model for studying growth. *Educational and Psychological Measurement, 32*, 655–678.

Werts, C. E., & Linn, R. L. (1970). Path analysis. Psychological examples. *Psychological Bulletin, 74*(3), 193–212.

Werts, C. E., Linn, R. L., & Jöreskog, K. G. (1971). Estimating the parameters of path models involving unmeasured variables. In H. M. Blalock (Ed.), *Causal models in the social sciences.* Chicago: Aldine.

Widaman, K. F. (1985). Hierarchically nested covariance structure models for multitrait–multimethod data. *Applied Psychological Measurement, 9*(1), 1–26.

Wiley, D., Schmidt, W. H., & Bramble, W. J. (1973). Studies of a class of covariance structure models. *Journal of the American Statistical Association, 68*(342), 317–323.

Wothke, W. (1984). *The estimation of trait and method components in multitrait–multimethod measurement.* Unpublished doctoral dissertation, Department of Behavioral Science, University of Chicago, Chicago.

Wothke, W. (1987, April). *Multivariate linear models of the multitrait–multimethod matrix.* Paper presented at the meeting of the American Educational Research Association, Washington, DC.

Wothke, W. (1988, June). *Identification conditions for scale-free covariance components models.* Paper presented at the annual meeting of the Psychometric Society, Los Angeles.

Wothke, W. (1993). Nonpositive definite matrices in structural modeling. In K. A. Bollen & S. Long (Eds.), *Testing structural equation models.* Newbury Park, CA: Sage.

Wothke, W., & Browne, M. W. (1990). The direct product model for the MTMM matrix parameterized as a second order factor analysis model. *Psychometrika, 55*(2), 255–262.

CHAPTER THREE

Nonlinear Structural Equation Models: The Kenny–Judd Model With Interaction Effects

Karl G. Jöreskog
Fan Yang
Uppsala University, Sweden

Kenny and Judd (1984) formulated a model with interaction effects of two latent variables and suggested using product variables to estimate the model. This model and the implications of using products of latent and observed variables is investigated.

In this chapter, we use the Kenny–Judd model as an example of a general model with nonlinear relationships between latent variables. Most of the arguments presented apply more generally than just to the Kenny–Judd model.

The Kenny–Judd model is formulated in the next section. In the third section, it is shown that the model cannot be estimated without the use of products of observed variables. Kenny and Judd suggested using four product variables, but, in fact, only one product variable is necessary for identification, so this case is considered first. The case of four product variables is considered later.

The implications of using product variables are non-normality and constraints on the mean vector as well as on the covariance matrix. A number of alternative ways of estimating the model are discussed and evaluated.

THE KENNY–JUDD MODEL

Kenny and Judd (1984) formulated a nonlinear regression equation:

$$y = \alpha + \gamma_1 \xi_1 + \gamma_2 \xi_2 + \gamma_3 \xi_1 \xi_2 + \zeta, \tag{1}$$

with the idea that there is an interactive effect of ξ_1 and ξ_2 on y, in addition to the direct effects of ξ_1 and ξ_2 alone, and this interactive effect is manifesting itself in terms of an effect of the product of ξ_1 and ξ_2.

The variables ξ_1 and ξ_2 are latent variables that are not directly observable. Kenny and Judd considered the case when there are two observable indicators x_1 and x_2 of ξ_1 and two observable indicators x_3 and x_4 of ξ_2, such that

$$\begin{pmatrix} x_1 \\ x_2 \\ x_3 \\ x_4 \end{pmatrix} = \begin{pmatrix} \tau_1 \\ \tau_2 \\ \tau_3 \\ \tau_4 \end{pmatrix} + \begin{pmatrix} \lambda_1 & 0 \\ \lambda_2 & 0 \\ 0 & \lambda_3 \\ 0 & \lambda_4 \end{pmatrix} \begin{pmatrix} \xi_1 \\ \xi_2 \end{pmatrix} + \begin{pmatrix} \delta_1 \\ \delta_2 \\ \delta_3 \\ \delta_4 \end{pmatrix}. \tag{2}$$

Kenny and Judd did not include the constant intercept terms α and τ_i in Equations 1 and 2. The usual argument for leaving these out—that one can work with the observed variables in deviation scores from their means—is not valid here. The point is that even if $y, \xi_1, \xi_2,$ and ζ in (1) all have zero means, α will still be nonzero. As is seen later, the means of the observed variables are functions of other parameters in the model and therefore the intercept terms have to be estimated jointly with all the other parameters.

To begin with, we make the following assumptions

1. ξ_1 and ξ_2 are bivariate normal with zero means
2. $\zeta \sim N(0,\psi)$
3. $\delta_i \sim N(0,\theta_i)$, $i = 1,\ldots, 4$
4. δ_i is independent of δ_j for $i \neq j$
5. δ_i is independent of ξ_j for $i = 1,\ldots, 4$ and $j = 1,2$
6. ζ is independent of δ_i and ξ_j for $i = 1,\ldots, 4$ and $j = 1,2$

Of these, Assumptions 4–6 are crucial and untestable, whereas Assumptions 1–3 are not essential and testable, see section on testing normality assumptions, later.

Assumptions 1–6 can be summarized by saying that $(\xi_1, \xi_2, \delta_1, \delta_2, \delta_3, \delta_4, \zeta)$ has a multivariate normal distribution with zero mean vector and covariance matrix

$$\begin{pmatrix} \phi_{11} & & & & & & \\ \phi_{21} & \phi_{22} & & & & & \\ 0 & 0 & \theta_1 & & & & \\ 0 & 0 & 0 & \theta_2 & & & \\ 0 & 0 & 0 & 0 & \theta_3 & & \\ 0 & 0 & 0 & 0 & 0 & \theta_4 & \\ 0 & 0 & 0 & 0 & 0 & 0 & \psi \end{pmatrix},$$

where $\phi_{ij} = Cov(\xi_i, \xi_j)$, $i,j = 1,2$.

IDENTIFICATION

The consequences of product variables in the model are

- y is not normal even though ξ_1 and ξ_2 are. The joint distribution of (y,x_1,x_2,x_3,x_4) is not multivariate normal even though that of (x_1,x_2,x_3, x_4) is.

- The mean of y is $\mu_y = \alpha + \gamma_3\phi_{21}$. So the mean vector of (y,x_1,x_2,x_3,x_4) is a function not only of $(\alpha,\tau_1,\tau_2,\tau_3,\tau_4)$ but also of γ_3 and ϕ_{21}. So both the mean vector and the covariance matrix of the observed variables should be used to estimate the model.

- Kenny and Judd (1984) suggested using product variables $x_1x_3, x_1x_4,$ x_2x_3, x_2x_4 together with (y,x_1,x_2,x_3,x_4) to estimate the model. This implies still more non-normality and even more complicated constraints on both the mean vector and the covariance matrix of the observed variables.

In this section, we show that the model cannot be estimated without product variables. But one product variable is sufficient to identify the model in terms of first and second moments of the observed variables. Note that this implies using third- and fourth-order moments of the variables forming the product variable.

In the following, we set $\lambda_1 = 1$ and $\lambda_3 = 1$ to define the scales for ξ_1 and ξ_2. Alternatively, one can leave λ_1 and λ_3 free and assume that ξ_1 and ξ_2 are standardized (i.e., set $\phi_{11} = 1$ and $\phi_{22} = 1$).

The mean vector and covariance matrix of (y,x_1,x_2,x_3,x_4) are

$$\mu' = (\alpha + \gamma_3\phi_{21},\tau_1,\tau_2,\tau_3,\tau_4), \tag{3}$$

where

$$\Sigma = \begin{pmatrix} \sigma_{yy} & & & & \\ \gamma_1\phi_{11} + \gamma_2\phi_{21} & \phi_{11} + \theta_1 & & & \\ \gamma_1\lambda_2\phi_{11} + \gamma_2\lambda_2\phi_{21} & \lambda_2\phi_{11} & \lambda_2^2\phi_{11} + \theta_2 & & \\ \gamma_1\phi_{21} + \gamma_2\phi_{22} & \phi_{21} & \lambda_2\phi_{21} & \phi_{22} + \theta_3 & \\ \gamma_1\lambda_4\phi_{21} + \gamma_2\lambda_4\phi_{22} & \lambda_4\phi_{21} & \lambda_4\lambda_2\phi_{21} & \lambda_4\phi_{22} & \lambda_4^2\phi_{22} + \theta_4 \end{pmatrix}, \tag{4}$$

$$\sigma_{yy} = \gamma_1^2\phi_{11} + \gamma_2^2\phi_{22} + 2\gamma_1\gamma_2\phi_{21} + \gamma_3^2(\phi_{11}\phi_{22} + \phi_{21}^2) + \psi. \tag{5}$$

The fourth term in Equation 5 follows from the fact, if ξ_1 and ξ_2 are bivariate normal, then

$$Var(\xi_1\xi_2) = E(\xi_1^2\xi_2^2) - [E(\xi_1\xi_2)]^2 = \phi_{11}\phi_{22} + 2\phi_{21}^2 - \phi_{21}^2 = \phi_{11}\phi_{22} + \phi_{21}^2$$

(see e.g., Anderson, 1984, p. 49, Equation 26).

It is well-known (see, e.g., Jöreskog & Sörbom, 1989) that the parameters $\tau_1,\tau_2,\tau_3,\tau_4,\lambda_2,\lambda_4,\phi_{11},\phi_{21},\phi_{22},\theta_1,\theta_2,\theta_3,\theta_4$ are identified by the mean vector and covariance matrix of x_1,x_2,x_3,x_4. If $\lambda_2 \neq 0$, the equations for σ_{21} and σ_{31} are linearly dependent. Similarly, if $\lambda_4 \neq 0$, the equations for σ_{41} and σ_{51} are linearly dependent. The equations for σ_{21} and σ_{41} determine γ_1 and γ_2, unless ξ_1 and ξ_2 are collinear. For given $\tau_1,\tau_2,\tau_3,\tau_4,\lambda_2,\lambda_4,\phi_{11},\phi_{21},\phi_{22},\theta_1,\theta_2,\theta_3,\theta_4,\gamma_1,\gamma_2$, the remaining two equations for μ_1 and σ_{11} are functions of the three parameters α,γ_3, and ψ, so obviously these parameters are not identified. It may be tempting to set α to zero but there is no way of knowing whether α is zero and, in fact, any chosen value of α is arbitrary and will affect the values of γ_3 and ψ.

If we add the product variable

$$x_5 = x_1 x_3 = (\tau_1 + \xi_1 + \delta_1)(\tau_3 + \xi_2 + \delta_3)$$

$$= \tau_1\tau_3 + \tau_3\xi_1 + \tau_1\xi_2 + \xi_1\xi_2 + \delta_5, \tag{6}$$

where

$$\delta_5 = \tau_1\delta_3 + \tau_3\delta_1 + \xi_1\delta_3 + \xi_2\delta_1 + \delta_1\delta_3. \tag{7}$$

to the variables we already have, we get seven additional manifest parameters namely the mean and variance of x_5 and the covariances between x_5 and the other variables.

The mean vector and covariance matrix of (y,x_1,x_2,x_3,x_4,x_5) are

$$\boldsymbol{\mu}' = (\alpha + \gamma_3\phi_{21},\tau_1,\tau_2,\tau_3,\tau_4,\tau_1\tau_3 + \phi_{21}), \tag{8}$$

$$\Sigma = \begin{pmatrix} \sigma_{yy} & & & & & \\ \gamma_1\phi_{11} + \gamma_2\phi_{21} & \phi_{11} + \theta_1 & & & & \\ \gamma_1\lambda_2\phi_{11} + \gamma_2\lambda_2\phi_{21} & \lambda_2\phi_{11} & \lambda_2^2\phi_{11} + \theta_2 & & & \\ \gamma_1\phi_{21} + \gamma_2\phi_{22} & \phi_{21} & \lambda_2\phi_{21} & \phi_{22} + \theta_3 & & \\ \gamma_1\lambda_4\phi_{21} + \gamma_2\lambda_4\phi_{22} & \lambda_4\phi_{21} & \lambda_4\lambda_2\phi_{21} & \lambda_4\phi_{22} & \lambda_4^2\phi_{22} + \theta_4 & \\ \sigma_{61} & \sigma_{62} & \sigma_{63} & \sigma_{64} & \sigma_{65} & \sigma_{66} \end{pmatrix}, \tag{9}$$

where

$$\sigma_{61} = \tau_3\gamma_1\phi_{11} + \tau_3\gamma_2\phi_{21} + \tau_1\gamma_1\phi_{21} + \tau_1\gamma_2\phi_{22} + \gamma_3(\phi_{21}^2 + \phi_{11}\phi_{22}), \tag{10}$$

$$\sigma_{62} = \tau_3\phi_{11} + \tau_1\phi_{21} + \tau_3\theta_1, \tag{11}$$

$$\sigma_{63} = \tau_3\lambda_2\phi_{11} + \tau_1\lambda_2\phi_{21}, \tag{12}$$

$$\sigma_{64} = \tau_3\phi_{21} + \tau_1\phi_{22} + \tau_1\theta_3, \tag{13}$$

$$\sigma_{65} = \tau_3\lambda_4\phi_{21} + \tau_1\lambda_4\phi_{22}, \tag{14}$$

$$\sigma_{66} = \tau_3^2\phi_{11} + \tau_1^2\phi_{22} + \phi_{12}^2 + \phi_{11}\phi_{22} + \tau_1^2\theta_3 + \tau_3^2\theta_1 + \phi_{11}\theta_3 + \phi_{22}\theta_1 + \theta_1\theta_3. \quad (15)$$

Only Equation 10 gives any information about γ_3. The other equations are functions of already identified parameters. Since the coefficient of γ_3 in Equation 10 is nonzero, this can be solved for γ_3 in terms of σ_{61} and other already identified parameters. Then, with γ_3 identified, ψ can be obtained from σ_{yy} in Equation 5 and α from μ_1 in Equation 3. So the model with one product variable is identified. The model has nine degrees of freedom. This is obtained as the number of elements in μ (6) plus the number of distinct elements in Σ (21) minus the number of parameters in θ (18). Because of rank deficiency in the weight matrix, this is not necessarily the degrees of freedom for the chi-square test of the model, see later section on rank deficiency.

ESTIMATION

Let z_1, z_2,. . ., z_N be N independent observations of the random vector

$$z = (y, x_1, x_2, x_3, x_4, x_5),$$

and let $\bar{z}$ and S be the sample mean vector and covariance matrix. Let μ and Σ be the corresponding population mean vector and covariance matrix. These are functions of the parameter vector

$$\theta = (\alpha, \gamma_1, \gamma_2, \gamma_3, \psi, \tau_1, \tau_2, \tau_3, \tau_4, \lambda_2, \lambda_4, \phi_{11}, \phi_{21}, \phi_{22}, \theta_1, \theta_2, \theta_3, \theta_4).$$

To estimate the model we fit $\mu(\theta)$ and $\Sigma(\theta)$ to $\bar{z}$ and S simultaneously. In this section, we consider three approaches to estimation. Each approach is based on a fit function

$$F(\theta) = F(\bar{z}, S, \mu(\theta), \Sigma(\theta)),$$

which is to be minimized with respect to θ, where $F(\theta)$ is non-negative and zero if and only if there is a perfect fit, in which case $\bar{z} = \mu(\theta)$ and $S = \Sigma(\theta)$ for some θ. The value of θ which minimizes $F(\theta)$ for given $\bar{z}$ and S is denoted $\hat{\theta}$.

Maximum Likelihood

The maximum likelihood (ML) approach will estimate θ by minimizing the fit function

$$F(\theta) = \log||\Sigma|| + \text{tr}(S\Sigma^{-1}) - \log||S|| - k + (\bar{z} - \mu)'\Sigma^{-1}(\bar{z} - \mu). \quad (16)$$

where k is the number of variables in $\mathbf{z}$ (here $k=6$). This fit function is derived from the ML principle based on the assumption that the observed variables $\mathbf{z}$ have a multinormal distribution (see, e.g., Anderson, 1984, for a derivation of the multinormal likelihood). Because of the product variables, this assumption does not hold for the Kenny–Judd model. As stated previously, the random vector $\mathbf{z}$ is not multivariate normal. Nevertheless, the maximum likelihood approach is worth consideration because it may be robust against the kind of non-normality generated by the Kenny–Judd model.

Weighted Least Squares

The weighted least squares (WLS) approach will estimate θ by minimizing the fit function

$$F(\theta) = (\mathbf{s} - \sigma)'W^{-1}(\mathbf{s} - \sigma) + (\bar{z} - \mu)'S^{-1}(\bar{z} - \mu), \quad (17)$$

where

$$\mathbf{s}' = (s_{11}, s_{21}, s_{22}, s_{31}, ..., s_{kk}),$$

is a vector of the non-duplicated elements in $\mathbf{S}$,

$$\sigma' = (\sigma_{11}, \sigma_{21}, \sigma_{22}, \sigma_{31}, ..., \sigma_{kk}),$$

is the vector of corresponding elements of $\Sigma(\theta)$ reproduced from the model parameters θ, and $\mathbf{W}$ is a symmetric positive definite matrix. The usual way of choosing $\mathbf{W}$ in WLS is to let $\mathbf{W}$ be a consistent estimate of the asymptotic covariance matrix of $\mathbf{s}$. In the general case when the observed variables are continuous and have a multivariate distribution satisfying very mild assumptions, the covariance matrix of $\mathbf{s}$ has a typical element (see Browne, 1984)

$$\omega_{gh,ij} = Cov(s_{gh}, s_{ij}) = \mu_{ghij} - \sigma_{gh}\sigma_{ij}, \quad (18)$$

where μ_{ghij} is a fourth-order central moment. This can be estimated as

$$w_{gh,ij} = m_{ghij} - s_{gh}s_{ij}, \quad (19)$$

where

$$m_{ghij} = (1/N) \sum_{a=1}^{N} (z_{ag} - \bar{z}_g)(z_{ah} - \bar{z}_h)(z_{ai} - \bar{z}_i)(z_{aj} - \bar{z}_j) \quad (20)$$

is a fourth-order central sample moment. Using such a **W** in Equation 17 gives what Browne (1984) called "asymptotically distribution free best GLS estimators" for which correct asymptotic chi-squares and standard errors may be obtained under non-normality.

WLS does not assume multivariate normality of **z** but it does assume that $\bar{z}$ and **S** are asymptotically independent, an assumption that does not hold in this case. Another disadvantage with WLS is that the matrix **W** must be estimated from the data and is therefore subject to sampling fluctuations that may affect the parameter estimates. To avoid severe effects of this kind, **W** must be estimated from a large sample.

WLS Based on Augmented Moment Matrix

One way to avoid the problems associated with ML and WLS, is to use the augmented moment matrix

$$\mathbf{A} = (1/N) \sum_{c=1}^{N} \binom{\mathbf{z}_c}{1} (\mathbf{z}'_c \ 1) = \begin{pmatrix} \mathbf{S} + \overline{\mathbf{z}}\overline{\mathbf{z}}' \\ \overline{\mathbf{z}}' \end{pmatrix} \begin{matrix} \\ 1 \end{matrix}. \tag{21}$$

This is the matrix of sample moments about zero for the vector **z** augmented with a variable which is constant equal to one for every case. The corresponding population matrix is

$$(\alpha_{ij}) = E\binom{\mathbf{z}}{1} (\mathbf{z}' \ 1) = \begin{pmatrix} \mathbf{\Sigma} + \boldsymbol{\mu}\boldsymbol{\mu}' \\ \boldsymbol{\mu}' \end{pmatrix} \begin{matrix} \\ 1 \end{matrix}. \tag{22}$$

Note that the last element in these matrices is a fixed constant equal to 1. Let

$$\mathbf{a}' = (a_{11}, a_{21}, a_{22}, a_{31}, ..., a_{k+1,k}, 1),$$

be a vector of the nonduplicated elements of **A**, and let

$$\boldsymbol{\alpha}' = (\alpha_{11}, \alpha_{21}, \alpha_{22}, \alpha_{31}, ..., \alpha_{k+1,k}, 1),$$

be a vector of the corresponding population moments. We can then form another WLS fit function (WLSA):

$$F(\boldsymbol{\theta}) = (\mathbf{a} - \boldsymbol{\alpha})' \mathbf{W}_a^- (\mathbf{a} - \boldsymbol{\alpha}), \tag{23}$$

where $\mathbf{W}_a$ is a consistent estimate of the covariance matrix of **a** and $\mathbf{W}_a^-$ is a Moore–Penrose generalized inverse of $\mathbf{W}_a$. See, for example, Graybill (1969, chapter 6) for definition of generalized inverse and Satorra (1989) and Koning, Neudecker, and Wansbeek (1993) for its use in covariance structure analysis.

64   JÖRESKOG AND YANG

The covariance matrix of **a** has a typical element

$$\omega_{gh,ij} = Cov(a_{gh}, a_{ij}) = v_{ghij} - \alpha_{gh}\alpha_{ij}, \qquad (24)$$

where v_{ghij} is a fourth-order moment about zero. This can be estimated as

$$w_{gh,ij} = n_{ghij} - a_{gh}a_{ij}, \qquad (25)$$

where

$$n_{ghij} = (1/N)\sum_{a=1}^{N} z_{ag}z_{ah}z_{ai}z_{aj} \qquad (26)$$

is a fourth-order sample moment about zero. Note that since the last element in **a** is a fixed constant, the last row of W_a is zero. Hence, W_a is singular. Its rank is even further reduced, however, as shown in Section 5. This is the reason for using a generalized inverse in Equation 23.

Standard Errors and Chi-Squares

Any one of the three methods described in the previous sections gives consistent estimates of the parameters. For further inference about the model, one also needs standard errors of parameter estimates and a chi-square goodness-of-fit statistic for each model. Traditionally, the standard errors are obtained from the information matrix and the chi-square is obtained as $N - 1$ times the minimum value of the fit function (see, e.g., Jöreskog & Sörbom, 1989). Because of non-normality, standard errors and chi-squares for the ML method are not asymptotically correct. Conditions for asymptotically correct standard errors and chi-square goodness-of-fit statistics are given by Browne (1987), Anderson and Amemiya (1988), Amemiya and Anderson (1990), and Satorra (1992). Because of the constraints on the covariance matrix $(\xi_1, \xi_2, \xi_1\xi_2)$, none of these conditions are satisfied. Nevertheless, it may turn out that standard errors and chi-squares for ML are sufficiently close for most practical purposes. This is investigated in a forthcoming dissertation of Yang (in prep.).

Standard errors and chi-square values for WLS are also incorrect because WLS uses an incorrect weight matrix. Recall that the sample mean vector and covariance matrix are not asymptotically uncorrelated. Again, it is an open question how much this means in practice and under what circumstances WLS is better than ML.

Standard errors and chi-squares for WLSA are asymptotically correct because W_a^- is a correct weight matrix. This matrix satisfies Assumption 6 in Satorra (1989), so all asymptotic results of that paper apply (W_a^- is

Satorra's V). The degrees of freedom for chi-square equals the rank of W_a^- minus the number of independent parameters in θ.

RANK DEFICIENCY

Consider the sample moment matrix of the vector $(x_1, x_2, x_1 x_2, 1)$:

$$A = \begin{pmatrix} 11 & & & \\ \mathbf{12} & 22 & & \\ 112 & 122 & 1122 & \\ 1 & 2 & \mathbf{12} & 1 \end{pmatrix}$$

Here we have used the notation

$$g = (1/N)\sum_{c=1}^{N} z_{cg},$$

$$gh = (1/N)\sum_{c=1}^{N} z_{cg}z_{ch},$$

$$ghi = (1/N)\sum_{c=1}^{N} z_{cg}z_{ch}z_{ci},$$

$$ghij = (1/N)\sum_{c=1}^{N} z_{cg}z_{ch}z_{ci}z_{cj},$$

where z_{cg} is the observed value on variable g for case c. Obviously, in every sample we will have $a_{21} = a_{43}$. This is noted in the matrix by boldfacing the elements that are equal. Obviously, the covariance matrix of

$$a' = (11,\mathbf{12},22,112,122,1122,1,2,\mathbf{12},1)$$

is singular and of rank 8.

For the Kenny–Judd model with one product variable, the sample moment matrix of the vector $(x_1, x_2, x_3, x_4, x_1 x_3, 1)$ is:

$$A = \begin{pmatrix} 11 & & & & & \\ 12 & 22 & & & & \\ \mathbf{13} & 23 & 33 & & & \\ 14 & 24 & 34 & 44 & & \\ 113 & 123 & 133 & 134 & 1133 & \\ 1 & 2 & 3 & 4 & \mathbf{13} & 1 \end{pmatrix}$$

The corresponding W_a is of order 21×21 and of rank 19. With the y-variable included, W_a is of order 28×28 and of rank 26.

With four product variables the rank deficiency is much greater. The sample moment matrix of the vector $(x_1, x_2, x_3, x_4, x_1 x_3, x_1 x_4, x_2 x_3, x_2 x_4, 1)$ is:

$$
\mathbf{A} = \begin{pmatrix}
11 & & & & & & & & \\
12 & 22 & & & & & & & \\
13 & \mathbf{23} & 33 & & & & & & \\
14 & \mathbf{24} & 34 & 44 & & & & & \\
113 & \mathbf{123} & 133 & \mathbf{134} & 1133 & & & & \\
114 & \mathbf{124} & \mathbf{134} & 144 & \mathbf{1134} & 1144 & & & \\
\mathbf{123} & 223 & 233 & \mathbf{234} & 1233 & \mathbf{1234} & 2233 & & \\
\mathbf{124} & 224 & \mathbf{234} & 244 & \mathbf{1234} & 1244 & 2234 & 2244 & \\
1 & 2 & 3 & 4 & \mathbf{13} & 14 & 23 & 24 & 1
\end{pmatrix}
$$

As shown in boldface characters there are nine pairs of equal values. Hence, $\mathbf{W}_a$ is of order 45×45 and of rank 35. With the y-variable included, $\mathbf{W}_a$ is of order 55×55 and of rank 45.

LISREL IMPLEMENTATION

The Kenny–Judd model is easily estimated with LISREL 8 using nonlinear constraints, see Jöreskog and Sörbom (1993b). We write the model as a LISREL Submodel 1 with mean structure, see Jöreskog and Sörbom (1989, chapter 10):

$$
\begin{pmatrix} y \\ x_1 \\ x_2 \\ x_3 \\ x_4 \\ x_5 \end{pmatrix} = \begin{pmatrix} \alpha \\ \tau_1 \\ \tau_2 \\ \tau_3 \\ \tau_4 \\ \tau_1 \tau_3 \end{pmatrix} + \begin{pmatrix} \gamma_1 & \gamma_2 & \gamma_3 \\ 1 & 0 & 0 \\ \lambda_2 & 0 & 0 \\ 0 & 1 & 0 \\ 0 & \lambda_4 & 0 \\ \tau_3 & \tau_1 & 1 \end{pmatrix} \begin{pmatrix} \xi_1 \\ \xi_2 \\ \xi_1 \xi_2 \end{pmatrix} + \begin{pmatrix} \zeta \\ \delta_1 \\ \delta_2 \\ \delta_3 \\ \delta_4 \\ \delta_5 \end{pmatrix}.
\tag{27}
$$

In LISREL, this equation corresponds to

$$
\mathbf{x} = \boldsymbol{\tau}_x + \boldsymbol{\Lambda}_x \boldsymbol{\xi} + \boldsymbol{\delta}.
$$

The mean vector and covariance matrix of $(\xi_1, \xi_2, \xi_1 \xi_2)$ are

$$
\boldsymbol{\kappa} = \begin{pmatrix} 0 \\ 0 \\ \phi_{21} \end{pmatrix} \quad \boldsymbol{\Phi} = \begin{pmatrix} \phi_{11} & & \\ \phi_{21} & \phi_{22} & \\ 0 & 0 & \phi_{11}\phi_{22} + \phi_{21}^2 \end{pmatrix},
\tag{28}
$$

and the covariance matrix of $(\zeta,\delta_1,\delta_2,\delta_3,\delta_4,\delta_5)$ is

$$
\Theta_\delta = \begin{pmatrix}
\psi & & & & & \\
0 & \theta_1 & & & & \\
0 & 0 & \theta_2 & & & \\
0 & 0 & 0 & \theta_3 & & \\
0 & 0 & 0 & 0 & \theta_4 & \\
0 & \tau_3\theta_1 & 0 & \tau_1\theta_3 & 0 & \theta_5
\end{pmatrix}, \tag{29}
$$

where

$$
\theta_5 = \tau_1^2\theta_3 + \tau_3^2\theta_1 + \phi_{11}\theta_3 + \phi_{22}\theta_1 + \theta_1\theta_3. \tag{30}
$$

The last row of Equation 29 follows by multiplying δ_5 in (7) by $\delta_1,\delta_2,\delta_3,\delta_4$, and δ_5, in turn, and taking expectation using the fact that the ξ's and δ's have a joint multinormal distribution.

The key point in the estimation of the model is to express the elements $\tau_6^{(x)},\phi_{33},\theta_{6,2}^{(\delta)},\theta_{6,4}^{(\delta)},\theta_{6,6}^{(\delta)}$ as nonlinear functions of the free parameters.

To estimate the model by ML, the following command file for LISREL 8 may be used

```
Fitting Kenny-Judd Model by ML
DA NI=6 NO=800
LA
Y X1 X2 X3 X4 X1X3
ME=KJ1.ME
CM=KJ1.CM
MO NX=6 NK=3 TD=SY TX=FR KA=FR
FR LX(1,1) LX(1,2) LX(1,3) LX(3,1) LX(5,2)
FR PH(1,1)-PH(2,2)
FI PH(3,1) PH(3,2)
VA 1 LX(2,1) LX(4,2) LX(6,3)
FI KA(1) KA(2)
CO LX(6,1)=TX(4)
CO LX(6,2)=TX(2)
CO PH(3,3)=PH(1,1)*PH(2,2)+PH(2,1)**2
CO TD(6,2)=TX(4)*TD(2,2)
CO TD(6,4)=TX(2)*TD(4,4)
CO TD(6,6)=TX(2)**2*TD(4,4)+TX(4)**2*TD(2,2) +C
    PH(1,1)*TD(4,4)+PH(2,2)*TD(2,2)+TD(2,2)*TD(4,4)
CO KA(3)=PH(2,1)
CO TX(6)=TX(2)*TX(5)
OU
```

where it is assumed that the sample covariance matrix **S** and the sample mean vector $\bar{z}$ are in the files KJ1.CM and KJ1.ME, respectively. To estimate the model by WLS, add the line

AC=KJ1.ACC

after the line

CM=KJ1.CM

The file KJ1.ACC contains the estimated asymptotic covariance matrix **W** in Equation 17. This is a binary file that is produced by PRELIS 2 (see Jöreskog & Sörbom, 1993a).

To use WLSA, one must write the model in a different way:

$$
\begin{pmatrix} y \\ x_1 \\ x_2 \\ x_3 \\ x_4 \\ x_5 \end{pmatrix} = \begin{pmatrix} \gamma_1 & \gamma_2 & \gamma_3 & \alpha \\ 1 & 0 & 0 & \tau_1 \\ \lambda_2 & 0 & 0 & \tau_2 \\ 0 & 1 & 0 & \tau_3 \\ 0 & \lambda_4 & 0 & \tau_4 \\ \tau_3 & \tau_1 & 1 & \tau_1\tau_3 \end{pmatrix} \begin{pmatrix} \xi_1 \\ \xi_2 \\ \xi_1\xi_2 \\ 1 \end{pmatrix} + \begin{pmatrix} \zeta \\ \delta_1 \\ \delta_2 \\ \delta_3 \\ \delta_4 \\ \delta_5 \end{pmatrix}.
\tag{31}
$$

In LISREL, this corresponds to

$$ y = \Lambda_y \eta + \varepsilon. $$

Furthermore,

$$
\begin{pmatrix} \xi_1 \\ \xi_2 \\ \xi_1\xi_2 \\ 1 \end{pmatrix} = \begin{pmatrix} 0 \\ 0 \\ \phi_{21} \\ 1 \end{pmatrix} 1 + \begin{pmatrix} \xi_1 \\ \xi_2 \\ \xi_1\xi_2 - \phi_{21} \\ 0 \end{pmatrix},
$$

which corresponds to the structural equation part of LISREL

$$ \eta = \Gamma x + \zeta. $$

There is one single x-variable in the model, namely the fixed variable 1. The parameter matrices Ψ and Θ_ε are

$$\Psi = \begin{pmatrix} \phi_{11} & & & \\ \phi_{21} & \phi_{22} & & \\ 0 & 0 & \phi_{11}\phi_{22} + \phi_{21}^2 & \\ 0 & 0 & 0 & 0 \end{pmatrix} \tag{32}$$

$$\Theta_\varepsilon = \begin{pmatrix} \psi & & & & & \\ 0 & \theta_1 & & & & \\ 0 & 0 & \theta_2 & & & \\ 0 & 0 & 0 & \theta_3 & & \\ 0 & 0 & 0 & 0 & \theta_4 & \\ 0 & \tau_3\theta_1 & 0 & \tau_1\theta_3 & 0 & \theta_5 \end{pmatrix}, \tag{33}$$

where

$$\theta_5 = \tau_1^2\theta_3 + \tau_3^2\theta_1 + \phi_{11}\theta_3 + \phi_{22}\theta_1 + \theta_1\theta_3 .$$

It may be verified that $E(\mathbf{zz'}) = (\alpha_{ij})$ where $\mathbf{z}$ is the vector on the left in Equation 31 augmented with the constant 1 and (α_{ij}) is the population augmented moment matrix in Equation 22.

To estimate the model by WLSA, one must first estimate the asymptotic covariance matrix $\mathbf{W}_a$ using PRELIS 2, and then use the program GINV to compute its generalized inverse $\mathbf{W}_a^-$. This is then read by LISREL 8 by the command line (see Jöreskog & Sörbom, 1993a).

```
WM=KJ1.WMA
```

The LISREL command file for WLSA is

```
Fitting Kenny-Judd Model by WLSA
DA NI=7 NO=800
LA
Y X1 X2 X3 X4 X1X3 CONST
CM=KJ1.AM
WM=KJ1.WMA
MO NY=6 NE=4 NX=1 GA=FI TE=SY PS=SY,FI FI
FR LY(1,1) LY(1,2) LY(1,3) LY(3,1) LY(5,2)
FR PS(1,1)-PS(2,2)
FR LY(1,4) LY(2,4) LY(3,4) LY(4,4) LY(5,4)
VA 1 LY(2,1) LY(4,2) LY(6,3) GA(4)
CO LY(6,1)=LY(4,4)
CO LY(6,2)=LY(2,4)
CO LY(6,4)=LY(2,4)*LY(4,4)
CO PS(3,3)=PS(1,1)*PS(2,2)+PS(2,1)**2
```

```
CO TE(6,2)=LY(4,4)*TE(2,2)
CO TE(6,4)=LY(2,4)*TE(4,4)
CO TE(6,6)=LY(2,4)**2*TE(4,4)+LY(4,4)**2*TE(2,2) +C
   PS(1,1)*TE(4,4)+PS(2,2)*TE(2,2)+TE(2,2)*TE(4,4)
CO GA(3)=PS(2,1)
ST .5 ALL
ST 0 LY(2,4) LY(3,4) LY(4,4) LY(5,4)
ST 1 LY(1,4)
OU SO NS AD=OFF DF=-1
```

Since Ψ is singular, one must put AD=OFF on the OU line. There is no reference variable for the fourth factor, so starting values must be provided and NS must be specified on the OU line. It is also a good idea to put SO on the OU line to tell LISREL not to check the scales for the factors. Because of the fixed variable 1, LISREL automatically reduces the degrees of freedom by one. The DF=-1 on the OU line reduces the degrees of freedom further by one as required since the rank of $\mathbf{W}_a$ is 8.

THE KENNY–JUDD MODEL
WITH FOUR PRODUCT VARIABLES

Kenny and Judd (1984) suggested using four product variables instead of only one. As stated previously, this is not necessary because the model is identified with just one product variable. The addition of three more product variables just adds many more manifest parameters without adding any new parameters to estimate. So it would seem that one gains degrees of freedom and that the model therefore is more parsimonious. However, there is a price paid for this. First, the augmented moment matrix $\mathbf{A}$ is now of order 10×10 and the corresponding estimated asymptotic covariance matrix $\mathbf{W}_a$ of $\mathbf{a}$ has a rank deficiency of 10 rather than 2. Second, the more product variables used, the larger $\mathbf{A}$ will be and the larger the sample size required to estimate $\mathbf{W}_a$ with sufficient precision in terms of statistical sampling error. Recall that $\mathbf{W}_a$ contains several moments of eighth order of the original variables. It is also more difficult to compute $\mathbf{W}_a^-$ accurately for large $\mathbf{A}$ matrices. Third, using highly singular weight matrices in LISREL increases the possibilities of multiple local minima of the fit function.

Also WLS is more problematic with four product variables for it turns out that, with four product variables, $\mathbf{W}$ in Equation 19 is singular with a rank deficiency of 1. It is a conjecture that this holds generally when there are four product variables. We have found this to be the case in all matrices $\mathbf{W}$ we have examined. If $\mathbf{W}$ is singular, one must replace $\mathbf{W}^{-1}$ in Equation 17 by the Moore–Penrose generalized inverse $\mathbf{W}^-$.

With four product variables, the LISREL implementation of ML and WLS uses the following specification:

$$
\begin{pmatrix} y \\ x_1 \\ x_2 \\ x_3 \\ x_4 \\ x_1x_3 \\ x_1x_4 \\ x_2x_3 \\ x_2x_4 \end{pmatrix}
=
\begin{pmatrix} \alpha \\ \tau_1 \\ \tau_2 \\ \tau_3 \\ \tau_4 \\ \tau_1\tau_3 \\ \tau_1\tau_4 \\ \tau_2\tau_3 \\ \tau_2\tau_4 \end{pmatrix}
+
\begin{pmatrix}
\gamma_1 & \gamma_2 & \gamma_3 \\
1 & 0 & 0 \\
\lambda_2 & 0 & 0 \\
0 & 1 & 0 \\
0 & \lambda_4 & 0 \\
\tau_3 & \tau_1 & 1 \\
\tau_4 & \tau_1\lambda_4 & \lambda_4 \\
\tau_3\lambda_2 & \tau_2 & \lambda_2 \\
\tau_4\lambda_2 & \tau_2\lambda_4 & \lambda_2\lambda_4
\end{pmatrix}
\begin{pmatrix} \xi_1 \\ \xi_2 \\ \xi_1\xi_2 \end{pmatrix}
+
\begin{pmatrix} \zeta \\ \delta_1 \\ \delta_2 \\ \delta_3 \\ \delta_4 \\ \delta_5 \\ \delta_6 \\ \delta_7 \\ \delta_8 \end{pmatrix},
$$

$$
\Theta_\delta =
\begin{pmatrix}
\psi & & & & & & & & \\
0 & \theta_1 & & & & & & & \\
0 & 0 & \theta_2 & & & & & & \\
0 & 0 & 0 & \theta_3 & & & & & \\
0 & 0 & 0 & 0 & \theta_4 & & & & \\
0 & \tau_3\theta_1 & 0 & \tau_1\theta_3 & 0 & \theta_5 & & & \\
0 & \tau_4\theta_1 & 0 & 0 & \tau_1\theta_4 & \theta_{65} & \theta_6 & & \\
0 & 0 & \tau_3\theta_2 & \tau_2\theta_3 & 0 & \theta_{75} & 0 & \theta_7 & \\
0 & 0 & \tau_4\theta_2 & 0 & \tau_2\theta_4 & 0 & \theta_{86} & \theta_{87} & \theta_8
\end{pmatrix},
\tag{34}
$$

where

$$\theta_{65} = \tau_3\tau_4\theta_1 + \lambda_4\phi_{22}\theta_1 \,,$$

$$\theta_{75} = \tau_1\tau_2\theta_3 + \lambda_2\phi_{11}\theta_3 \,,$$

$$\theta_{86} = \tau_1\tau_2\theta_4 + \lambda_2\phi_{11}\theta_4 \,,$$

$$\theta_{87} = \tau_3\tau_4\theta_2 + \lambda_4\phi_{22}\theta_2 \,,$$

$$\theta_5 = \tau_1^2\theta_3 + \tau_3^2\theta_1 + \phi_{11}\theta_3 + \phi_{22}\theta_1 + \theta_1\theta_3 \,,$$

$$\theta_6 = \tau_1^2\theta_4 + \tau_4^2\theta_1 + \phi_{11}\theta_4 + \lambda_4^2\phi_{22}\theta_1 + \theta_1\theta_4 \,,$$

$$\theta_7 = \tau_2^2\theta_3 + \tau_3^2\theta_2 + \lambda_2^2\phi_{11}\theta_3 + \phi_{22}\theta_2 + \theta_2\theta_3 \,,$$

$$\theta_8 = \tau_2^2\theta_4 + \tau_4^2\theta_2 + \lambda_2^2\phi_{11}\theta_4 + \lambda_4^2\phi_{22}\theta_2 + \theta_2\theta_4 \,.$$

The parameter matrices κ and Φ are the same as in Equation 28. The corresponding LISREL input file is given in Appendix A.

For WLSA, the LISREL specification is

$$
\begin{pmatrix} y \\ x_1 \\ x_2 \\ x_3 \\ x_4 \\ x_1 x_3 \\ x_1 x_4 \\ x_2 x_3 \\ x_2 x_4 \end{pmatrix} = \begin{pmatrix} \gamma_1 & \gamma_2 & \gamma_3 & \alpha \\ 1 & 0 & 0 & \tau_1 \\ \lambda_2 & 0 & 0 & \tau_2 \\ 0 & 1 & 0 & \tau_3 \\ 0 & \lambda_4 & 0 & \tau_4 \\ \tau_3 & \tau_1 & 1 & \tau_1 \tau_3 \\ \tau_4 & \tau_1 \lambda_4 & \lambda_4 & \tau_1 \tau_4 \\ \tau_3 \lambda_2 & \tau_2 & \lambda_2 & \tau_2 \tau_3 \\ \tau_4 \lambda_2 & \tau_2 \lambda_4 & \lambda_2 \lambda_4 & \tau_2 \tau_4 \end{pmatrix} \begin{pmatrix} \xi_1 \\ \xi_2 \\ \xi_1 \xi_2 \\ 1 \end{pmatrix} + \begin{pmatrix} \zeta \\ \delta_1 \\ \delta_2 \\ \delta_3 \\ \delta_4 \\ \delta_5 \\ \delta_6 \\ \delta_7 \\ \delta_8 \end{pmatrix},
$$

$$
\begin{pmatrix} \xi_1 \\ \xi_2 \\ \xi_1 \xi_2 \\ 1 \end{pmatrix} = \begin{pmatrix} 0 \\ 0 \\ \phi_{21} \\ 1 \end{pmatrix} 1 + \begin{pmatrix} \xi_1 \\ \xi_2 \\ \xi_1 \xi_2 - \phi_{21} \\ 0 \end{pmatrix},
$$

The last two equations correspond to

$$\mathbf{y} = \mathbf{\Lambda}_y \boldsymbol{\eta} + \boldsymbol{\varepsilon},$$

$$\boldsymbol{\eta} = \mathbf{\Gamma} \mathbf{x} + \boldsymbol{\zeta},$$

in LISREL. The parameter matrices $\mathbf{\Psi}$ and $\mathbf{\Theta}_\varepsilon$ in LISREL are

$$
\mathbf{\Psi} = \begin{pmatrix} \phi_{11} & & & \\ \phi_{21} & \Phi_{22} & & \\ 0 & 0 & \phi_{11}\phi_{22} + \phi_{21}^2 & \\ 0 & 0 & 0 & 0 \end{pmatrix}, \tag{35}
$$

$$
\mathbf{\Theta}_\varepsilon = \begin{pmatrix}
\psi & & & & & & & & \\
0 & \theta_1 & & & & & & & \\
0 & 0 & \theta_2 & & & & & & \\
0 & 0 & 0 & \theta_3 & & & & & \\
0 & 0 & 0 & 0 & \theta_4 & & & & \\
0 & \tau_3\theta_1 & 0 & \tau_1\theta_3 & 0 & \theta_5 & & & \\
0 & \tau_4\theta_1 & 0 & 0 & \tau_1\theta_4 & \theta_{65} & \theta_6 & & \\
0 & 0 & \tau_3\theta_2 & \tau_2\theta_3 & 0 & \theta_{75} & 0 & \theta_7 & \\
0 & 0 & \tau_4\theta_2 & 0 & \tau_2\theta_4 & 0 & \theta_{86} & \theta_{87} & \theta_8
\end{pmatrix}, \tag{36}
$$

where $\theta_{65},\theta_{75},\theta_{86},\theta_{87},\theta_5,\theta_6,\theta_7,\theta_8$ are as before. The corresponding LISREL input file is given in Appendix B.

TESTING NORMALITY ASSUMPTIONS

In the preceeding sections we made the assumption that (ξ_1,ξ_2) and $(\delta_1,\delta_2,\delta_3,\delta_4)$ are independent and normally distributed. If the model holds and these assumptions hold, then x_1,x_2,x_3,x_4 should be normally distributed. A first test of this may be obtained by a PRELIS screening of the data on x_1,x_2,x_3,x_4, see discussion of Bagozzi's BEA data for an example. Further tests are also possible.

The normality assumption of (ξ_1,ξ_2) can be tested by relaxing the three constraints in the last row of Φ in Equation 28 (ML and WLS) or the constraints in the third row of Ψ in Equation 32 (WLSA). With four product variables one relaxes the corresponding elements in Equation 28 or 35. The difference between the chi-square for the model and the chi-square for the model where these $\phi_{31},\phi_{32},\phi_{33}$ are free parameters, can be used as chi-square with three degrees of freedom.

The normality assumption of $\delta_1,\delta_2,\delta_3,\delta_4$ can be tested by relaxing the constraint (see Equation 30) on θ_5 (one product variable). With four product variables, one must relax the constraints on $\theta_{65},\theta_{75},\theta_{86},\theta_{87},\theta_5,\theta_6,\theta_7,\theta_8$ in Equation 34 (ML and WLS) or in Equation 36 (WLSA). The difference between the chi-square for the model and the chi-square for the model where these θs are free parameters, can be used as a chi-square with eight degrees of freedom.

EXAMPLES

To illustrate the methodology described in the previous sections, we consider two examples, one based on artificial data and another based on empirical data.

Artificial Data

Artificial data $(y,x_1,x_2,x_3,x_4,x_1x_3,x_1x_4,x_2x_3,x_2x_4)$ satisfying the Kenny–Judd model can be generated directly by PRELIS 2 (see Jöreskog & Sörbom, 1994). The following command file:

```
Kenny-Judd Model 2
Generating Mean Vector and Covariance Matrix
DA NO=800
CO ALL
```

```
NE KSI1=.7*NRAND
NE KSI2=.48*KSI1+.726019*NRAND
NE Y=1+.2*KSI1+.4*KSI2+.7*KSI1*KSI2+.447214*NRAND
NE X1=KSI1+.7141428*NRAND
NE X2=.6*KSI1+.8*NRAND
NE X3=KSI2+.6*NRAND
NE X4=.7*KSI2+.7141428*NRAND
NE X1X3=X1*X3
NE X1X4=X1*X4
NE X2X3=X2*X3
NE X2X4=X2*X4
SD KSI1 KSI2
OU IX=123 MA=CM ME=KJ2.ME CM=KJ2.CM ACC=KJ2.ACC XM
```

generates data corresponding to the following parameter values:

$$\gamma_1 = 0.2 \; \gamma_2 = 0.4 \; \gamma_3 = 0.7 \; \lambda_2 = 0.6 \; \lambda_4 = 0.7$$

$$\phi_{11} = 0.49 \; \phi_{21} = 0.2352 \; \phi_{22} = 0.64 \; \psi = 0.20$$

$$\theta_1 = 0.51 \; \theta_2 = 0.64 \; \theta_3 = 0.36 \; \theta_4 = 0.51$$

$$\alpha = 1.00 \; \tau_i = 0.00, \; i = 1,2,3,4.$$

NRAND is a normal random deviate. IX is a seed for the random number generator. By putting RA=KJ2.RAW on the OU line, one can save the generated raw data on 800 cases. However, this is not necessary as one can compute and save the covariance matrix **S** directly, as done with this command file. The mean vector $\bar{z}$ and the asymptotic covariance matrix **W** can be obtained at the same time. To obtain the augmented moment matrix **A** and the corresponding asymptotic covariance matrix $\mathbf{W}_a$ instead, run the same command file again with the same seed and the following OU line:

```
OU IX=123 MA=AM AM=KJ2.AM AC=KJ2.ACA XM
```

The file KJ2.CM contains the covariance matrix **S** of order 9×9 and the file KJ2.ACC contains the corresponding asymptotic covariance matrix **W** of order 45×45. The file KJ2.AM contains the augmented moment matrix **A** of order 10×10 and the file KJ2.ACA contains the corresponding asymptotic covariance matrix $\mathbf{W}_a$ of order 55×55. These files all include four product variables. To analyze the model with only one product variable, include the lines:

```
SE
Y X1 X2 X3 X4 X1X3 /
```

in the input file for ML and WLS, and the lines

```
SE
Y X1 X2 X3 X4 X1X3 CONST /
```

in the input file for WLSA.

To obtain the generalized inverse $\mathbf{W}_a^-$, use the following command line:

```
GINV KJ2.ACA KJ2.WMA
```

$\mathbf{W}_a^-$ will be stored in the binary file KJ2.WMA. The 55 eigenvalues of $\mathbf{W}_a$ are given in the file OUTPUT produced by GINV as follows:

```
Eigenvalues of ACA Matrix:
             1            2            3            4            5            6
 0.319878D+02 0.217726D+02 0.123437D+02 0.667464D+01 0.514834D+01 0.421733D+01
             7            8            9           10           11           12
 0.389412D+01 0.305706D+01 0.250682D+01 0.243333D+01 0.236390D+01 0.190726D+01
            13           14           15           16           17           18
 0.177064D+01 0.168864D+01 0.158013D+01 0.135929D+01 0.134610D+01 0.118843D+01
            19           20           21           22           23           24
 0.107414D+01 0.847790D+00 0.776939D+00 0.769930D+00 0.713555D+00 0.615735D+00
            25           26           27           28           29           30
 0.546278D+00 0.474596D+00 0.453407D+00 0.406390D+00 0.377083D+00 0.327319D+00
            31           32           33           34           35           36
 0.286704D+00 0.279941D+00 0.240174D+00 0.221935D+00 0.197586D+00 0.162565D+00
            37           38           39           40           41           42
 0.134647D+00 0.113488D+00 0.991132D-01 0.789831D-01 0.616881D-01 0.548982D-01
            43           44           45           46           47           48
 0.406724D-01 0.349555D-01 0.277730D-01 0.224445D-15 0.192675D-15 0.996382D-16
            49           50           51           52           53           54
 0.915067D-16 0.520417D-17 0.000000D+00-0.514996D-16-0.100843D-15-0.105927D-15
            55
-0.307981D-15
45 out of 55 eigenvectors retained
```

Only 45 of the 55 eigenvalues are positive; the remaining are zero within machine capacity. This agrees with the statements made earlier in the discussion on rank deficiency.

The results using one and four product variables and the three different methods are given in Table 3.1. This shows that the methodology described in the previous sections work. Although only some of the parameters of the model are included in the table, all parameter estimates are very close to the true values. The model fits the data very well as judged by all the chi-squares presented. The standard errors are smaller for Model 2 than for Model 1, but they are very similar across methods. The table might suggest that chi-squares are underestimated particularly for methods ML and WLS. No such conclusion can be made on the basis of a single sample,

TABLE 3.1
Artificial Data ($N = 800$)
Model 1: One Product Variable

Parameter	True Value	ML	WLS	WLSA
α	1.0	1.02(.04)	1.02(.07)	.99(.04)
γ_1	.2	.22(.06)	.23(.07)	.17(.06)
γ_2	.4	.36(.05)	.36(.05)	.44(.05)
γ_3	.7	.66(.12)	.65(.12)	.72(.15)
ψ	.2	.20(.04)	.21(.04)	.17(.09)
λ_2	.6	.59(.09)	.60(.10)	.57(.10)
λ_4	.7	.72(.06)	.72(.06)	.74(.06)
χ^2	-	1.68	1.76	2.34
df	-	9	9	8
p	-	1.00	.99	.97

Model 2: Four Product Variables

Parameter	True Value	ML	WLS	WLSA
α	1.0	1.02(.03)	1.03(.06)	1.05(.03)
γ_1	.2	.22(.06)	.24(.06)	.19(.05)
γ_2	.4	.37(.04)	.36(.04)	.43(.04)
γ_3	.7	.64(.07)	.65(.08)	.63(.09)
ψ	.2	.21(.03)	.19(.05)	.18(.08)
λ_2	.6	.57(.05)	.59(.05)	.52(.07)
λ_4	.7	.71(.04)	.75(.05)	.78(.05)
χ^2	-	15.61	12.27	27.38
df	-	36	35	27
p	-	1.00	1.00	.44

however. Nor can anything be said about the accuracy of standard error estimates. Yang (in prep.) is investigating these questions in a forthcoming dissertation.

BAGOZZI'S BEA DATA

An example of a theory involving interactions among theoretical constructs is the theory of reasoned action in social psychology (Ajzen & Fishbein, 1980; Fishbein & Ajzen, 1975). See Bagozzi, Baumgartner, and Yi (1992) and references therein for its applications in consumer research. In essence, this theory states that beliefs and evaluations interact in determining attitudes.

Data for this model was kindly provided by Bagozzi. It consists of:

- two measures of beliefs that coupon use would lead to savings on the grocery bill: 7-point likely–unlikely scales

- two measures of evaluations of consequences of using coupons for shopping: 7-point good–bad scales
- three measures of overall attitude toward coupon use: 7-point favorable–unfavorable scales

The data comes from a survey of 253 female staff members at a large public university in United States. The questionnaire items are described in Bagozzi et al. (1992). We use the term *Bagozzi's BEA data* as a working name for this data (BEA = Beliefs, Evaluations, Attitudes).

Writing

$$\eta = at = attitude,$$

$$\xi_1 = be = belief$$

$$\xi_2 = vl = evaluation,$$

the expectancy value model is

$$at = \alpha + \gamma_1 be + \gamma_2 vl + \gamma_3 bevl + \zeta,$$

or in LISREL notation

$$\eta = \alpha + \gamma_1 \xi_1 + \gamma_2 \xi_2 + \gamma_3 \xi_1 \xi_2 + \zeta. \qquad (37)$$

There are three indicators *AA1*, *AA2*, *AA3* of *at*, two indicators *BE1* and *BE2* of *be*, and two indicators *VL1* and *VL2* of *vl*. In LISREL notation these correspond to $y_1, y_2, y_3, x_1, x_2, x_3, x_4$, respectively. The model will be estimated with one single product variable $BE1VL1 = x_1 x_3$ and with four product variables $BE1VL1 = x_1 x_3, BE1VL2 = x_1 x_4, BE2VL1 = x_2 x_3, BE2VL2 = x_2 x_4$. A path diagram is shown in Fig. 3.1. The model differs from the Kenny–Judd model only in that there are three y-variables rather than one.

For the model with four product variables, the LISREL specification for ML and WLS is:

$$\begin{pmatrix} y_1 \\ y_2 \\ y_3 \end{pmatrix} = \begin{pmatrix} \tau_1^{(y)} \\ \tau_2^{(y)} \\ \tau_3^{(y)} \end{pmatrix} + \begin{pmatrix} 1 \\ \lambda_2^{(y)} \\ \lambda_3^{(y)} \end{pmatrix} \eta + \begin{pmatrix} \varepsilon_1 \\ \varepsilon_2 \\ \varepsilon_3 \end{pmatrix}, \qquad (38)$$

$$\mathbf{y} = \boldsymbol{\tau}_y + \boldsymbol{\Lambda}_y \boldsymbol{\eta} + \boldsymbol{\varepsilon},$$

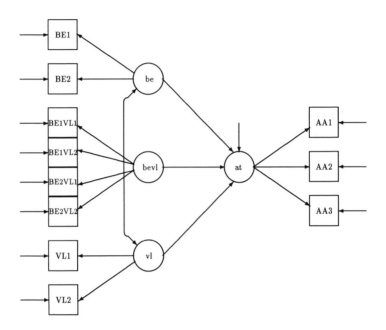

FIG. 3.1. Path diagram for Bagozzi's BEA data with four product variables.

$$\begin{pmatrix} x_1 \\ x_2 \\ x_3 \\ x_4 \\ x_1x_3 \\ x_1x_4 \\ x_2x_3 \\ x_2x_4 \end{pmatrix} = \begin{pmatrix} \tau_1 \\ \tau_2 \\ \tau_3 \\ \tau_4 \\ \tau_1\tau_3 \\ \tau_1\tau_4 \\ \tau_2\tau_3 \\ \tau_2\tau_4 \end{pmatrix} + \begin{pmatrix} 1 & 0 & 0 \\ \lambda_2 & 0 & 0 \\ 0 & 1 & 0 \\ 0 & \lambda_4 & 0 \\ \tau_3 & \tau_1 & 1 \\ \tau_4 & \tau_1\lambda_4 & \lambda_4 \\ \tau_3\lambda_2 & \tau_2 & \lambda_2 \\ \tau_4\lambda_2 & \tau_2\lambda_4 & \lambda_2\lambda_4 \end{pmatrix} \begin{pmatrix} \xi_1 \\ \xi_2 \\ \xi_1\xi_2 \end{pmatrix} + \begin{pmatrix} \delta_1 \\ \delta_2 \\ \delta_3 \\ \delta_4 \\ \delta_5 \\ \delta_6 \\ \delta_7 \\ \delta_8 \end{pmatrix},$$

$$\mathbf{x} = \tau_x + \Lambda_x\xi + \delta.$$

The parameter matrices κ and Φ are as in Equation 28 and

$$\Theta_\varepsilon = diag(\theta_1^{(\varepsilon)}, \theta_2^{(\varepsilon)}, \theta_3^{(\varepsilon)}),$$

$$\Theta_\delta = \begin{pmatrix}
\theta_1 & & & & & & & \\
0 & \theta_2 & & & & & & \\
0 & 0 & \theta_3 & & & & & \\
0 & 0 & 0 & \theta_4 & & & & \\
\tau_3\theta_1 & 0 & \tau_1\theta_3 & 0 & \theta_5 & & & \\
\tau_4\theta_1 & 0 & 0 & \tau_1\theta_4 & \theta_{65} & \theta_6 & & \\
0 & \tau_3\theta_2 & \tau_2\theta_3 & 0 & \theta_{75} & 0 & \theta_7 & \\
0 & \tau_4\theta_2 & 0 & \tau_2\theta_4 & 0 & \theta_{86} & \theta_{87} & \theta_8
\end{pmatrix},$$

where $\theta_{65},\theta_{75},\theta_{86},\theta_{87},\theta_5,\theta_6,\theta_7,\theta_8$ are as before.

The parameter α in Equation 37 and the three τs in Equation 38 are not identified. One can add a constant to the three τs and subtract the same constant from α without affecting the mean vector of **y**. (The α in Equation 1 is the sum of τ for y and α.) Hence, we may set $\alpha = 0$ in Equation 37 and estimate the τs in Equation 38. The estimates of the τs *will not* be equal to the means of the y-variables.

For WLSA, the corresponding **LISREL** specification is

$$\begin{pmatrix}
y_1 \\ y_2 \\ y_3 \\ x_1 \\ x_2 \\ x_3 \\ x_4 \\ x_1x_3 \\ x_1x_4 \\ x_2x_3 \\ x_2x_4
\end{pmatrix} = \begin{pmatrix}
1 & 0 & 0 & 0 & \tau_1^{(y)} \\
\lambda_2^{(y)} & 0 & 0 & 0 & \tau_2^{(y)} \\
\lambda_3^{(y)} & 0 & 0 & 0 & \tau_3^{(y)} \\
0 & 1 & 0 & 0 & \tau_1 \\
0 & \lambda_2 & 0 & 0 & \tau_2 \\
0 & 0 & 1 & 0 & \tau_3 \\
0 & 0 & \lambda_4 & 0 & \tau_4 \\
0 & \tau_3 & \tau_1 & 1 & \tau_1\tau_3 \\
0 & \tau_4 & \tau_1\lambda_4 & \lambda_4 & \tau_1\tau_4 \\
0 & \tau_3\lambda_2 & \tau_2 & \lambda_2 & \tau_2\tau_3 \\
0 & \tau_4\lambda_2 & \tau_2\lambda_4 & \lambda_2\lambda_4 & \tau_2\tau_4
\end{pmatrix} \begin{pmatrix}
\eta \\ \xi_1 \\ \xi_2 \\ \xi_1\xi_2 \\ 1
\end{pmatrix} + \begin{pmatrix}
\varepsilon_1 \\ \varepsilon_2 \\ \varepsilon_3 \\ \delta_1 \\ \delta_2 \\ \delta_3 \\ \delta_4 \\ \delta_5 \\ \delta_6 \\ \delta_7 \\ \delta_8
\end{pmatrix},$$

$$\mathbf{y} = \Lambda_y\boldsymbol{\eta} + \boldsymbol{\varepsilon},$$

$$\begin{pmatrix}
\eta \\ \xi_1 \\ \xi_2 \\ \xi_1\xi_2 \\ 1
\end{pmatrix} = \begin{pmatrix}
0 & \gamma_1 & \gamma_2 & \gamma_3 & 0 \\
0 & 0 & 0 & 0 & 0 \\
0 & 0 & 0 & 0 & 0 \\
0 & 0 & 0 & 0 & 0 \\
0 & 0 & 0 & 0 & 0
\end{pmatrix} \begin{pmatrix}
\eta \\ \xi_1 \\ \xi_2 \\ \xi_1\xi_2 \\ 1
\end{pmatrix} + \begin{pmatrix}
0 \\ 0 \\ 0 \\ \phi_{21} \\ 1
\end{pmatrix} 1 + \begin{pmatrix}
\zeta \\ \xi_1 \\ \xi_2 \\ \xi_1\xi_2 - \phi_{21} \\ 0
\end{pmatrix},$$

$$\eta = \mathbf{B}\eta + \mathbf{\Gamma}\mathbf{x} + \zeta,$$

with

$$\mathbf{\Psi} = \begin{pmatrix} \phi_{11} \\ \phi_{21} & \phi_{22} \\ 0 & 0 & \phi_{11}\phi_{22} + \phi_{21}^2 \\ 0 & 0 & 0 & 0 \\ 0 & 0 & 0 & 0 & 0 \end{pmatrix},$$

$$\mathbf{\Theta}_\varepsilon = \begin{pmatrix} \theta_1^{(y)} \\ 0 & \theta_2^{(y)} \\ 0 & 0 & \theta_3^{(y)} \\ 0 & 0 & 0 & \theta_1 \\ 0 & 0 & 0 & 0 & \theta_2 \\ 0 & 0 & 0 & 0 & 0 & \theta_3 \\ 0 & 0 & 0 & 0 & 0 & 0 & \theta_4 \\ 0 & 0 & 0 & \tau_3\theta_1 & 0 & \tau_1\theta_3 & 0 & \theta_5 \\ 0 & 0 & 0 & \tau_4\theta_1 & 0 & 0 & \tau_1\theta_4 & \theta_{65} & \theta_6 \\ 0 & 0 & 0 & 0 & \tau_3\theta_2 & \tau_2\theta_3 & 0 & \theta_{75} & 0 & \theta_7 \\ 0 & 0 & 0 & 0 & \tau_4\theta_2 & 0 & \tau_2\theta_4 & 0 & \theta_{86} & \theta_{87} & \theta_8 \end{pmatrix},$$

The data we obtained from Bagozzi were mean centered (i.e., the means of the x- and y-variables had been subtracted before the product variables were formed). This was probably done to avoid the τs in the model. However, the τs must nevertheless be estimated to get the correct degrees of freedom and their estimates will not necessarily be zero. Centering the data has the additional disadvantage that it makes the asymptotic covariance matrix $\mathbf{W}$ in WLS even more rank deficient. Fortunately, Bagozzi gave us the mean values, so we could reconstruct the original data, which are integer scores in the range from 1 to 7. The variables are actually ordinal. However, since the model requires data on interval scales, we ignore ordinality and treat scores 1 through 7 as coming from an interval scale. Since this limits variation, elements of $\mathbf{S}$ and $\mathbf{A}$ are underestimated and even more so for $\mathbf{W}$ and $\mathbf{W}_a$.

A simple data screening of the raw BEA data reveals the following information in the PRELIS output:

UNIVARIATE SUMMARY STATISTICS FOR CONTINUOUS VARIABLES

VARIABLE	MEAN	ST. DEV.	SKEWNESS	KURTOSIS	MINIMUM	FREQ.	MAXIMUM	FREQ.
AA1	4.514	1.359	−0.369	−0.109	1.000	6	7.000	14
AA2	5.036	1.307	−0.840	0.494	1.000	3	7.000	22
AA3	5.004	1.424	−0.838	0.157	1.000	4	7.000	27
BE1	5.115	1.327	−0.952	0.483	1.000	2	7.000	26
BE2	5.340	1.361	−1.339	1.860	1.000	7	7.000	38
VL1	5.814	0.909	−0.262	−0.667	3.000	1	7.000	66
VL2	5.723	0.931	−0.342	−0.593	3.000	1	7.000	54
BE1VL1	30.352	10.772	−0.141	−0.608	5.000	2	49.000	23
BE1VL2	29.755	10.392	−0.124	−0.544	5.000	2	49.000	17
BE2VL1	31.621	11.022	−0.285	−0.419	4.000	2	49.000	32
BE2VL2	31.229	10.920	−0.354	−0.309	4.000	5	49.000	26

TEST OF UNIVARIATE NORMALITY FOR CONTINUOUS VARIABLES

	SKEWNESS		KURTOSIS		SKEWNESS AND KURTOSIS	
	Z-SCORE	P-VALUE	Z-SCORE	P-VALUE	CHI-SQUARE	P-VALUE
AA1	−2.161	0.015	−0.169	0.433	4.700	0.095
AA2	−3.024	0.001	1.571	0.058	11.612	0.003
AA3	−3.022	0.001	0.705	0.240	9.630	0.008
BE1	−3.157	0.001	1.546	0.061	12.359	0.002
BE2	−3.520	0.000	3.727	0.000	26.283	0.000
VL1	−1.815	0.035	−3.072	0.001	12.733	0.002
VL2	−2.084	0.019	−2.555	0.005	10.874	0.004
BE1VL1	−1.230	0.109	−2.657	0.004	8.571	0.014
BE1VL2	−1.120	0.131	−2.236	0.013	6.253	0.044
BE2VL1	−1.897	0.029	−1.528	0.063	5.933	0.051
BE2VL2	−2.119	0.017	−0.989	0.161	5.468	0.065

It is seen that all the tests of normality of BE1, BE2, VL1, VL2 are significant at the 5% level. Hence, as pointed out earlier, the assumption that (ξ_1, ξ_2) and $(\delta_1, \delta_2, \delta_3, \delta_4)$ are independent and normally distributed is not likely to hold. We return to this question later.

For the raw BEA data, the augmented moment matrix **A** of order 12×12 is

AUGMENTED MOMENT MATRIX

	AA1	AA2	AA3	BE1	BE2	VL1
AA1	22.213					
AA2	23.917	27.059				
AA3	23.905	26.561	27.059			
BE1	23.573	26.423	26.304	27.913		
BE2	24.522	27.494	27.324	28.383	30.360	
VL1	26.858	29.933	29.842	30.352	31.621	34.628
VL2	26.300	29.387	29.182	29.755	31.229	33.822
BE1VL1	143.028	160.071	159.917	168.273	171.119	184.296
BE1VL2	139.739	156.676	155.984	164.458	168.364	179.411
BE2VL1	148.506	166.241	165.747	171.119	182.530	191.494
BE2VL2	146.146	163.968	162.960	168.364	180.289	187.893
CONST.	4.514	5.036	5.004	5.115	5.340	5.814

	VL2	BE1VL1	BE1VL2	BE2VL1	BE2VL2	CONST.
VL2	33.621					
BE1VL1	179.411	1036.810				
BE1VL2	177.518	1006.921	992.917			
BE2VL1	187.893	1053.727	1030.779	1120.870		
BE2VL2	186.953	1030.779	1021.336	1100.684	1094.051	
CONST.	5.723	30.352	29.755	31.621	31.229	1.000

The corresponding estimated asymptotic covariance matrix $\mathbf{W}_a$ is of order 78×78. The eigenvalues of $\mathbf{W}_a$ are

```
Eigenvalues of ACA Matrix :
        1            2            3            4            5            6
0.399789D+07 0.202917D+06 0.801046D+05 0.122443D+05 0.745755D+04 0.291676D+04
        7            8            9           10           11           12
0.257438D+04 0.212250D+04 0.138964D+04 0.801899D+03 0.616682D+03 0.401728D+03
       13           14           15           16           17           18
0.168772D+03 0.716356D+02 0.531332D+02 0.381141D+02 0.262670D+02 0.227560D+02
       19           20           21           22           23           24
0.207247D+02 0.153922D+02 0.136399D+02 0.815309D+01 0.752132D+01 0.645792D+01
       25           26           27           28           29           30
0.531786D+01 0.435327D+01 0.333554D+01 0.280914D+01 0.216030D+01 0.157503D+01
       31           32           33           34           35           36
0.111207D+01 0.965496D+00 0.746135D+00 0.677728D+00 0.626886D+00 0.514246D+00
       37           38           39           40           41           42
0.496423D+00 0.333297D+00 0.304961D+00 0.215930D+00 0.192858D+00 0.174372D+00
       43           44           45           46           47           48
0.148881D+00 0.139048D+00 0.109829D+00 0.104745D+00 0.936856D-01 0.448357D-01
       49           50           51           52           53           54
0.180818D-01 0.102172D-01 0.871979D-02 0.716253D-02 0.490175D-02 0.371843D-02
       55           56           57           58           59           60
0.304504D-02 0.215291D-02 0.162119D-02 0.100259D-02 0.934355D-03 0.448398D-03
       61           62           63           64           65           66
0.167989D-03 0.162696D-03 0.126967D-03 0.106424D-03 0.824996D-04 0.120282D-04
       67           68           69           70           71           72
0.584414D-05 0.378287D-05 0.139498D-12 0.327595D-13 0.671493D-14 0.000000D+00
       73           74           75           76           77           78
-0.417003D-13-0.188725D-12-0.381198D-12-0.571094D-12-0.978272D-12-0.117999D-11
68 out of 78 eigenvectors retained
```

So $\mathbf{W}_a^-$ is of order 78×78 and of rank 68. There is a rank deficiency of 10 for the same reason as stated in the rank deficiency section. The sample size 253 is too small for estimating the asymptotic covariance matrices $\mathbf{W}$ and $\mathbf{W}_a$. This results in inaccurate generalized inverses which in turn leads to serious convergence problems in LISREL 8. Solutions for ML, WLS, and WLSA were obtained using one product variable. But with four product variables both $\mathbf{W}^-$ and $\mathbf{W}_a^-$ are so bad that it was impossible to get any sensible solution for WLS and WLSA. In our analysis, we therefore added the value 1 to the diagonal elements of these matrices. This gives solutions which may be regarded as a mixture of ULS and WLS, here denoted UWLS and UWLSA, respectively. The chi-squares and standard errors reported should be regarded as very approximate.

The results are shown in Table 3.2 where only parameters of the structural relationship are included.

For the model with one product variable, all three solutions are rather close. Yet chi-square is much higher for ML than for WLS and WLSA. The estimate of γ_3 is not significant with any of the methods.

For the model with four product variables all three solutions are rather different. In particular, it seems that the ML solution is very different from the UWLS and UWLSA solutions that are more close. The t value for $\hat{\gamma}_3$ is significant at the 5% level for both UWLS and UWLSA, although the t value for UWLSA is a border line value. This is a reflection of the greater power obtained by using four product variables instead of one. The chi-squares differ considerably between methods. Pretending that the UWLSA chi-square value of 94.09 with 52 degrees of freedom is correct, this has a p value of 0.00032.

To test the normality of (ξ_1,ξ_2) we relax the constraints on $\psi_{42},\psi_{43},\psi_{44}$ in Equation 35 and reestimate the model. This gives $\chi^2 = 80.76$ with 49 degrees of freedom. The difference in chi-squares is 13.33 with three degrees of freedom, which is significant at the .5% level. Hence, the normality of (ξ_1,ξ_2) is rejected.

To test the normality of $(\delta_1,\delta_2,\delta_3,\delta_4)$ we relax the constraints on $\theta_5,\theta_{65},\theta_6$, $\theta_{75},\theta_7,\theta_{86},\theta_{87},\theta_8$ in Equation 36 and reestimate the model with $\psi_{42},\psi_{43},\psi_{44}$ free. This gives $\chi^2 = 55.00$ with 41 degrees of freedom. The difference in chi-squares is 25.76 with eight degrees of freedom, which is also significant at the .5% level. Hence, the normality assumption of $(\delta_1,\delta_2,\delta_3,\delta_4)$ is also rejected.

The chi-square of 55.00 with 41 degrees of freedom has a p value of 0.071. RMSEA is 0.037 with a 90% confidence interval from 0.00 to 0.06. This and other fit statistics given in the output suggests that the model represents a reasonable approximation to the population.

In the model where both normality assumptions are relaxed, the structural Equation 37 is estimated as

```
at = 0.09*be + 0.90*lv + 0.06*belv + z
    (0.08)     (0.12)     (0.10)
     1.12       7.33       0.61
```

Hence, neither *be* nor *belv* are significant in this equation. Much larger samples are needed to establish the existence of an interaction effect.

TABLE 3.2
Bagozzi's BEA Data ($N = 253$)
Model 1: One Product Variable

Parameter	ML	WLS	WLSA
$\hat{\gamma_1}$	−0.08	−0.04	−0.06
$s(\hat{\gamma_1})$	0.14	0.15	0.16
t-value	−0.58	−0.30	−0.36
$\hat{\gamma_2}$	1.06	1.01	1.01
$s(\hat{\gamma_2})$	0.20	0.17	0.17
t-value	5.38	5.80	6.13
$\hat{\gamma_3}$	0.02	0.12	0.15
$s(\hat{\gamma_3})$	0.09	0.08	0.10
t-value	0.23	1.42	1.53
$\hat{\psi}$	0.53	0.58	0.57
$s(\hat{\psi})$	0.10	0.09	0.10
t-value	5.56	6.12	5.98
R^2	0.51	0.50	0.51
χ^2	55.28	31.02	31.04
df	19	19	18

Model 2: Four Product Variables

Parameter	ML	UWLS	UWLSA
$\hat{\gamma_1}$	−1.10	0.13	0.05
$s(\hat{\gamma_1})$	1.06	0.07	0.10
t-value	−1.03	1.82	0.52
$\hat{\gamma_2}$	2.49	0.79	0.91
$s(\hat{\gamma_2})$	1.41	0.16	0.12
t-value	1.77	4.94	7.83
$\hat{\gamma_3}$	0.16	0.09	0.17
$s(\hat{\gamma_3})$	0.10	0.04	0.09
t-value	1.57	2.21	2.00
$\hat{\psi}$	0.27	0.55	0.59
$s\hat{\psi}$	0.25	0.09	0.09
t-value	1.08	6.45	6.74
R^2	0.74	0.46	0.47
χ^2	223.94	143.37	94.09
df	52	52	52

DISCUSSION

We have used the Kenny–Judd model Equation 1 to illustrate the problems that arise when trying to fit this model to data using existing software such as LISREL. Other nonlinear models can be handled in a similar way as long as the relationships are polynomials. For example, Equation 1 could be a more general form of a quadratic function:

$$y = \alpha + \gamma_1 \xi_1 + \gamma_2 \xi_2 + \gamma_{11} \xi_1^2 + \gamma_{22} \xi_2^2 + \gamma_{12} \xi_1 \xi_2 + \zeta. \tag{39}$$

The model then becomes more elaborate and complex. If the structural equation involves the square of a latent variable, as in Equation 39, one can use the squares of the indicators of that latent variable as indicators of the squared latent variable. It is probably not possible to use functional forms higher than the quadratic as this would require moments of higher order than eight which in turn would require huge samples.

The simple Kenny–Judd model is more problematic to estimate than most users of structural equation models might anticipate. In summary, these problems are:

- One must have a good theory that explains why the structural relationship must be nonlinear (or why there must be an interaction). It is not advisable to apply this technique routinely to just any data.
- Even with a good theory (e.g., Fishbein & Ajzen, 1975), one must have a very large sample to accurately estimate the asymptotic covariance matrix W_a, needed for WLSA.
- Of the three methods considered in this chapter, only WLSA gives correct chi-squares and consistent standard errors of parameter estimates. However, the disadvantage with WLSA is that the weight matrix W_a^- is rank deficient. This increases the risk of multiple solutions, nonconvergence, and other numerical problems, particularly if several product variables are used and if W_a is estimated from too small a sample.
- To estimate the model with LISREL, utmost care must be taken to specify the constraints in the model correctly. A single mistake may have severe consequences. As shown in Appendix B, these constraints are quite complex and it is easy to make a mistake.
- If one does not have a large sample, it is probably best to use the ML method as this does not require a weight matrix. But then chi-square should be used as a measure of fit rather than as a test statistic, as suggested elsewhere (Jöreskog, 1993; Jöreskog & Sörbom, 1989). Standard errors and t-values should not be taken as formal test statistics but rather be regarded as guidelines.

APPENDIX A: ARTIFICIAL DATA WITH FOUR
PRODUCT VARIABLES
LISREL 8 INPUT COMMAND FILE FOR ML AND WLS
UNDER NORMALITY ASSUMPTIONS

```
Kenny-Judd Model 2
Fitting Model to Mean Vector and Covariance Matrix by ML
DA NI=9 NO=800
LA
Y X1 X2 X3 X4 X1X3 X1X4 X2X3 X2X4
ME=KJ2.ME
CM=KJ2.CM
!WM=WM2.ACC
MO NX=9 NK=3 TD=SY TX=FR KA=FR
FR LX(1,1) LX(1,2) LX(1,3) LX(3,1) LX(5,2) PH(1,1)-PH(2,2)
FI PH(3,1) PH(3,2)
VA 1 LX(2,1) LX(4,2) LX(6,3)
FI KA(1) KA(2)
CO LX(6,1)=TX(4)
CO LX(6,2)=TX(2)
CO LX(7,1)=TX(5)
CO LX(7,2)=TX(2)*LX(5,2)
CO LX(7,3)=LX(5,2)
CO LX(8,1)=TX(4)*LX(3,1)
CO LX(8,2)=TX(3)
CO LX(8,3)=LX(3,1)
CO LX(9,1)=TX(5)*LX(3,1)
CO LX(9,2)=TX(3)*LX(5,2)
CO LX(9,3)=LX(3,1)*LX(5,2)
CO PH(3,3)=PH(1,1)*PH(2,2)+PH(2,1)**2
CO TD(6,2)=TX(4)*TD(2,2)
CO TD(6,4)=TX(2)*TD(4,4)
CO TD(6,6)=TX(2)**2*TD(4,4)+TX(4)**2*TD(2,2)+PH(1,1)*TD(4,4)+PH(2,2)*TD(2,2)+TD(2,2)*TD(4,4)
CO TD(7,2)=TX(5)*TD(2,2)
CO TD(7,5)=TX(2)*TD(5,5)
CO TD(7,6)=TX(4)*TX(5)*TD(2,2)+LX(5,2)*PH(2,2)*TD(2,2)
CO TD(7,7)=TX(2)**2*TD(5,5)+TX(5)**2*TD(2,2)+PH(1,1)*TD(5,5)+LX(5,2)**2*PH(2,2)*TD(2,2)+TD(2,2)*TD(5,5)
CO TD(8,3)=TX(4)*TD(3,3)
CO TD(8,4)=TX(3)*TD(4,4)
CO TD(8,6)=TX(2)*TX(3)*TD(4,4)+LX(3,1)*PH(1,1)*TD(4,4)
CO TD(8,8)=TX(3)**2*TD(4,4)+TX(4)**2*TD(3,3)+LX(3,1)**2*PH(1,1)*TD(4,4)+PH(2,2)*TD(3,3)+TD(3,3)*TD(4,4)
CO TD(9,3)=TX(5)*TD(3,3)
CO TD(9,5)=TX(3)*TD(5,5)
CO TD(9,7)=TX(2)*TX(3)*TD(5,5)+LX(3,1)*PH(1,1)*TD(5,5)
CO TD(9,8)=TX(4)*TX(5)*TD(3,3)+LX(5,2)*PH(2,2)*TD(3,3)
CO TD(9,9)=TX(3)**2*TD(5,5)+TX(5)**2*TD(3,3)+LX(3,1)**2*PH(1,1)*TD(5,5)+LX(5,2)**2*PH(2,2)*TD(3,3)+TD(3,3)*TD(5,5)
CO KA(3)=PH(2,1)
CO TX(6)=TX(2)*TX(4)
CO TX(7)=TX(2)*TX(5)
CO TX(8)=TX(3)*TX(4)
CO TX(9)=TX(3)*TX(5)
OU RS ND=4 AD=OFF XM WP
```

APPENDIX B: BAGOZZI'S BEA DATA WITH FOUR
PRODUCT VARIABLES
LISREL 8 INPUT COMMAND FILE FOR WLSA UNDER
NORMALITY ASSUMPTIONS

```
Kenny-Judd Model 2
Fitting Model to Mean Vector and Covariance Matrix by WLSA
DA NI=10 NO=800
LA
Y X1 X2 X3 X4 X1X3 X1X4 X2X3 X2X4 CONST
CM=KJ2.AM
WM=KJ2.WMA
MO NY=9 NE=4 NX=1 GA=FI TE=SY PS=SY,FI FI
FR LY(1,1) LY(1,2) LY(1,3) LY(3,1) LY(5,2) PS(1,1)-PS(2,2) LY(1,4) LY(2,4) LY(3,4) LY(4,4) LY(5,4)
FI PS(3,1) PS(3,2)
VA 1 LY(2,1) LY(4,2) LY(6,3) GA(4)
```

```
O LY(6,1)=LY(4,4)
O LY(6,2)=LY(2,4)
O LY(7,1)=LY(5,4)
O LY(7,2)=LY(2,4)*LY(5,2)
O LY(7,3)=LY(5,2)
O LY(8,1)=LY(4,4)*LY(3,1)
O LY(8,2)=LY(3,4)
O LY(8,3)=LY(3,1)
O LY(9,1)=LY(5,4)*LY(3,1)
O LY(9,2)=LY(3,4)*LY(5,2)
O LY(9,3)=LY(3,1)*LY(5,2)
O PS(3,3)=PS(1,1)*PS(2,2)+PS(2,1)**2
O TE(6,2)=LY(4,4)*TE(2,2)
O TE(6,4)=LY(2,4)*TE(4,4)
O TE(6,6)=LY(2,4)**2*TE(4,4)+LY(4,4)**2*TE(2,2)+PS(1,1)*TE(4,4)+PS(2,2)*TE(2,2)+TE(2,2)*TE(4,4)
O TE(7,2)=LY(5,4)*TE(2,2)
O TE(7,5)=LY(2,4)*TE(5,5)
O TE(7,6)=LY(4,4)*LY(5,4)*TE(2,2)+LY(5,2)*PS(2,2)*TE(2,2)
O TE(7,7)=LY(2,4)**2*TE(5,5)+LY(5,4)**2*TE(2,2)+PS(1,1)*TE(5,5)+LY(5,2)**2*PS(2,2)*TE(2,2)+TE(2,2)*TE(5,5)
O TE(8,3)=LY(4,4)*TE(3,3)
O TE(8,4)=LY(3,4)*TE(4,4)
O TE(8,6)=LY(2,4)*LY(3,4)*TE(4,4)+LY(3,1)*PS(1,1)*TE(4,4)
O TE(8,8)=LY(3,4)**2*TE(4,4)+LY(4,4)**2*TE(3,3)+LY(3,1)**2*PS(1,1)*TE(4,4)+PS(2,2)*TE(3,3)+TE(3,3)*TE(4,4)
O TE(9,3)=LY(5,4)*TE(3,3)
O TE(9,5)=LY(3,4)*TE(5,5)
O TE(9,7)=LY(2,4)*LY(3,4)*TE(5,5)+LY(3,1)*PS(1,1)*TE(5,5)
O TE(9,8)=LY(4,4)*LY(5,4)*TE(3,3)+LY(5,2)*PS(2,2)*TE(3,3) .
O TE(9,9)=LY(3,4)**2*TE(5,5)+LY(5,4)**2*TE(3,3)+LY(3,1)**2*PS(1,1)*TE(5,5)+LY(5,2)**2*PS(2,2)*TE(3,3)+TE(3,3)*TE(5,5)
O GA(3)=PS(2,1)
O LY(6,4)=LY(2,4)*LY(4,4)
O LY(7,4)=LY(2,4)*LY(5,4)
O LY(8,4)=LY(3,4)*LY(4,4)
O LY(9,4)=LY(3,4)*LY(5,4)
T .5 ALL
T O LY(2,4) LY(3,4) LY(4,4) LY(5,4)
T 1 LY(1,4)
U SO NS RS AD=OFF XM WP DF=-9
```

ACKNOWLEDGMENT

The research reported in this chapter has been supported by the Swedish Council for Research in the Humanities and Social Sciences (HSFR) under the program *Multivariate Statistical Analysis*.

REFERENCES

Ajzen, I., & Fishbein, M. (1980). *Understanding attitudes and predicting social behavior*. Englewood Cliffs, NJ: Prentice-Hall.

Amemiya, Y., & Anderson, T. W. (1990). Asymptotic chi-square tests for a large class of factor analysis models. *The Annals of Statistics, 3*, 1453–1463.

Anderson, T. W. (1984). *An introduction to multivariate statistical analysis* (2nd ed.). New York: Wiley.

Anderson, T. W., & Amemiya, Y. (1988). The asymptotic normal distribution of estimators in factor analysis under general conditions. *The Annals of Statistics, 16*, 759–771.

Bagozzi, R. P., Baumgartner, H., & Yi, Y. (1992). State versus action orientation and the theory of reasoned action: An application to coupon usage. *Journal of Consumer Research, 18*, 505–518.

Browne, M. W. (1984). Asymptotically distribution-free methods for the analysis of covariance structures. *British Journal of Mathematical and Statistical Psychology, 37*, 62–83.

Browne, M. W. (1987). Robustness of statistical inference in factor analysis and related models. *Biometrika*, 74, 375–384.

Fishbein, M., & Ajzen, I. (1975). *Belief, attitude, intention and behavior: An introduction to research.* Reading, MA: Addison-Wesley.

Graybill, F. A. (1969). *Introduction to matrices with applications in statistics.* Belmont, CA: Wadsworth.

Jöreskog, K. G. (1993). Testing structural equation models. In K. A. Bollen & J. S. Long (Eds.), *Testing structural equation models.* Beverly Hills, CA: Sage.

Jöreskog, K. G., & Sörbom, D. (1989). *LISREL 7—A guide to the program and applications* (2nd ed.). Chicago: SPSS Publications.

Jöreskog, K. G., & Sörbom, D. (1993a). *New features in PRELIS 2.* Chicago: Scientific Software.

Jöreskog, K. G., & Sörbom, D. (1993b). *New features in LISREL 8.* Chicago: Scientific Software.

Jöreskog, K. G., & Sörbom, D. (1994). *Simulation with PRELIS 2 and LISREL 8.* Chicago: Scientific Software.

Kenny, D. A., & Judd, C. M. (1984). Estimating the nonlinear and interactive effects of latent variables. *Psychological Bulletin*, 96, 201–210.

Koning, R., Neudecker, H., & Wansbeek, T. (1993). Imposed quasi-normality in covariance structure analysis. In K. Haagen, D. Bartholomew, & M. Deistler (Eds.), *Statistical modelling and latent variables* (pp. 191–202). Amsterdam: Elsevier Science.

Satorra, A. (1989). Alternative test criteria in covariance structure analysis: A unified approach. *Psychometrika*, 54, 131–151.

Satorra, A. (1992). Asymptotic robust inferences in the analysis of mean and covariance structures. In P. V. Marsden (Ed.), *Sociological methodology 1992* (pp. 249–278). Cambridge, MA: Basil Blackwell.

Yang, F. (in preparation). *Non-linear structural equation models: Simulation studies on the Kenny-Judd model.*

CHAPTER FOUR

Multilevel Models From a Multiple Group Structural Equation Perspective

John J. McArdle
Fumiaki Hamagami
University of Virginia

Whenever a promising new approach to data analysis becomes available many researchers are keen to try it out. In this chapter, we describe some of our attempts to use the new statistical models termed *random coefficient* or *hierarchical* or *multilevel structural models* (after Mason, Wong, & Entwisle, 1984). Of course, multilevel models are not really new models because they have been available for over two decades (e.g., Aitkin & Longford, 1986; Hartley & Rao, 1967; Harville, 1977; Jennrich & Sampson, 1976; Lindley & Smith, 1972; Novick, Jackson, Thayer, & Cole, 1972). However, several recent reviews show a surge of interest in multilevel models (see Bock, 1989; Bryk & Raudenbush, 1993; Goldstein, 1987; Hoc & Kreft, 1994; Longford, 1993; Muthen & Satorra, 1989; Raudenbush, 1988). These statistical models have become popular for a very good reason—multilevel models seem to provide a reasonable way to deal with the complex statistical and mathematical problems of "nested" or "clustered" data collection designs.

Much research on the multilevel model (ML) has focused on statistical and algorithmic issues in the efficient calculation of the fixed regression parameters and the random components in these models. Detailed treatments are presented by Bock (1989), Bryk and Raudenbush (1993), Longford (1993), and Kreft, DeLeeuw, and van de Leeden (1994). Most agree that Dempster, Laird, and Rubin (1977) provided a breakthrough in numerical efficiency for maximum likelihood estimation (MLE) of variance components with the EM algorithms. This method was used to estimate covariance structures for both "balanced" designs with equal numbers of observations per unit, and for "unbalanced" designs due to incomplete values (Dempster, Rubin, & Tsutakawa, 1981; Little & Rubin, 1987). In current work, other techniques and algorithms are being used and MLE of multilevel models with several levels of analysis can be fitted using several widely available computer programs (e.g., GENMOD by Wong & Mason, 1985; BMDP-5V by Jennrich & Schluchter, 1986; VARCL by Longford, 1987; Empirical Bayes models in Bock, 1989; ML3 by Prosser, Rabash, & Goldstein, 1991; HLM by Bryk & Raudenbush, 1993). Detailed comparisons of these programs are provided by Kreft, de Leeuw, and Kim (1990) and Kreft, de Leeuw, and van de Leeden (1994).

This chapter is not about these advances in computer programs but about the conceptual models underlying these developments. We explore some relationships between the "new" multilevel structural models (ML-SEM) and the "old" multiple groups structural equation models (MG-SEM). These questions were stimulated by work done by Goldstein and McDonald (1988), McDonald and Goldstein (1989), Muthen and Satorra (1989), and extended by McDonald (1994) and Muthen (1994). We extend this work in several different directions—we give a simple demonstration of the relationships between standard MG-SEMs to two basic models of multilevel analysis: (a) the variance components (ML-VC) model, and (b) the random coefficients (ML-RC) model. We do not elaborate on statistical or technical features, but we do discuss some of the available computer programs.

To further explore these issues, we present three applications of ML-SEM models on individual differences in human cognitive abilities. Each of these applications starts out with a substantive question that includes a nested data set and a model with some form of unobserved or latent variable. In some cases, these ML models will be considered as MG-SEM with large numbers of groups and additional parameter constraints. In other cases, these multilevel models will be considered as structural models for raw data with large amounts of incomplete scores (after Lange, Westlake, & Spence, 1976; Neale, 1993; McArdle, 1994). As it turns out, our ML-SEM representation does not lead to either improved statistical or algorithmic efficiency. But our work does show how to: (a) define the basic structural equation assumptions in ML models, (b) draw an *accurate path–graphic display* of ML models, and (c) add new *unobserved or latent variables* in ML models.

MULTILEVEL VARIANCE COMPONENTS (ML-VC) MODELS

Many data sets can be termed *multilevel* (ML) because they have some easy to identify levels of aggregation. The term *hierarchical* is an appropriate way to describe such data (but this should not be confused with hierarchically ordered set of regression equations). For example, we might be mainly interested in the behavior of students, and we might recognize that each student is a member of a specific classroom. To fully investigate the student's behaviors we might need to know about the overall behaviors of the classroom as well. We might even climb further up the scale of aggregation and recognize that each classroom also exists in a particular school, and each school is located in a certain district, and so on. When it is not possible for the same student to be in more than one class, and for the classroom to be in more than one school, we usually add the important statistical feature—the students are said to be "nested" within classrooms, and the classrooms are "nested" within schools (Aitkin & Longford, 1986; Cronbach, Gleser, Nanda, & Rajaratnam, 1972; Kreft, 1993).

In the models to follow, we write the outcome score $Y_{n,g}$ for the nth individual (of N_g) within the gth group (of G). These scores and groups are defined in each application, and we usually add general independence assumptions—the individual responses are independently sampled and the groups do not include any overlapping responses. In more advanced models, variables are measured or considered at higher levels of aggregation, and more complex forms of overlapping levels are possible. In this chapter we consider only the the simplest possible models for the analysis of such multilevel data.

Standard ANOVA as a Single Group Structural Equation Model (SEM)

A first multilevel model can be based on a comparison of means across groups. One standard approach to comparing group differences in means comes from the linear regression formulation of the well-known *analysis of variance* (ANOVA) model (Cohen & Cohen, 1985). Here we write

$$Y_{n,g} = \sum_{g=0}^{G-1} A_g * D_{n,g} + E_{n,g}, \tag{1}$$

where the G regression coefficients A_g are slopes associated with individual predictor variables D_g. As usually conceived, these D_g are categorical variables representing different contrasts among the G groups. For example, if the D_g are represented using "dummy codes," then an estimated A_0 intercept can be directly interpreted as the mean of the control group and the A_g in terms of mean differences from the control group. Alternatively, if the D_g are defined as "effect codes," then the estimated A_0 intercept can be directly interpreted as the grand mean of all groups and the A_g as mean differences from the grand mean. The E is an unobserved residual error term, and we usually assume that these scores are are normally distributed with mean zero and constant variance $[E_g \sim N(0, V_e)]$. Once the D_g are explicitly stated, we can obtain expectations and interpret the parameters A_g for each group G.

A structural path diagram of this standard ANOVA model is given in Fig. 4.1a. Observed variables (Y) are represented as squares and unobserved variables (E) are represented as circles. A triangle is used here to denote a constant or assigned variable (as suggested by McArdle & Boker, 1991). In this case, we use triangles to define all D_g group coded variables. This is a nontrivial graphic device only because it clarifies some important distinctions, which need to be made in more complex models. In each model here, the means, variances, and covariances of the D_g variables are a direct function of the coding scheme used.

ANOVA as a Multiple Group Structural Equation Model (MG-SEM)

The previous model can also be organized using the advanced techniques of multiple group (MG) SEMs (e.g., LISREL; Jöreskog & Sörbom, 1979, 1993). In one approach we write a specific model for each of the G groups as

$$Y_n^{(1)} = M^{(1)} + E_n^{(1)}, \tag{2}$$
$$Y_n^{(2)} = M^{(2)} + E_n^{(2)}, \; or \; generally,$$
$$Y_n^{(g)} = M^{(g)} + E_n^{(g)},$$

where, for the g-th group, the regression coefficient $M^{(g)}$ is the group mean, and the E_g is an unobserved residual or error term. As before, we assume that these residual scores are normally distributed with mean zero and constant variance within groups $[E^{(g)} \sim N(0, V_e^{(g)})]$.

The first step in a multiple group model for means and covariance is given in Fig. 4.1b. Here each separate group includes a single observed variable (square), a single error term (circle), and a single constant (triangle). Using widely available computer programs (e.g., LISREL), we can now set any or all coefficients to be *invariant* over groups, we can estimate the parameter values from the summary statistics [using MLE], and we can examine the goodness of fit of these restrictions [using χ^2]. For example, if set all of the error variances $[V_e^{(g)}]$ to be equal then we can test the hypothesis of "homogeneity of variance." In addition, we can set all of the means $[M^{(g)}]$ equal to test for the usual one-way ANOVA omnibus hypothesis of "equality of means." Specific hypotheses about equality of $(G–K)$ specific group means and variances can be tested by fitting separate models with different constraints across groups.

From this MG-SEM perspective, we can also more closely mimic the ANOVA model estimation for a particular coding scheme of interest. This can be done by writing a specific model for each for the G groups as

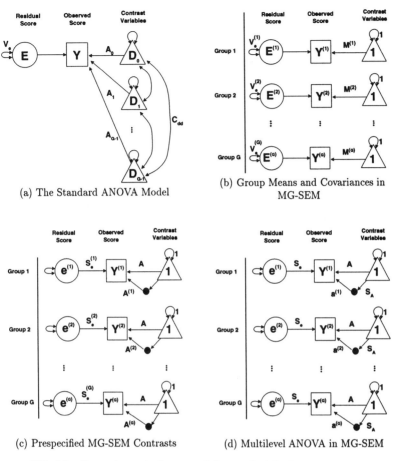

(a) The Standard ANOVA Model

(b) Group Means and Covariances in MG-SEM

(c) Prespecified MG-SEM Contrasts

(d) Multilevel ANOVA in MG-SEM

FIG. 4.1. Alternative path diagrams of the standard ANOVA model for G independent groups.

$$Y_n^{(1)} = A + A^{(1)} + E_n^{(1)},$$
$$Y_n^{(2)} = A + A^{(2)} + E_n^{(2)}, \ or$$
$$Y_n^{(g)} = A + A^{(g)} + E_n^{(g)}, \ where$$
$$\sum_{g=1}^{G} A^{(g)} = 0. \tag{3}$$

Here the regression coefficient A is the intercept term that is *invariant over all groups*, and the $G-1$ parameters $A^{(g)}$ are mean differences associated with differences over groups.

The restriction that the deviations $A^{(g)}$ from the grand mean A sum to zero must be added for proper estimation and interpretation. This kind of constraint over groups is not easy to implement in standard MG-SEM programs, but it is available a few current programs (i.e., LISREL-8, Mx). For example, using the LISREL-8 COnstraint command we write "CO

93

$BE(5,1,7) = - BE(1,1,7) - BE(2,1,7) - BE(3,1,7) - BE(4,1,7)$" so the parameters for $BE(1,7)$ sum to zero over 5 groups. A similar constraint can be introduced as a CALCulation group in the Mx program. More complex forms of these constraints will be needed in other models here.

A multiple group path diagram of these effect codes is given in Fig. 4.1c. This requires the decomposition of the intercept term from the constant to the observed variable into two parts. A first invariant parameter A is the value of the arrow which is pointed directly from the constant 1 to the observed variable Y. A second parameter $A^{(g)}$ connects the constant 1 to observed Y via a special kind of unobserved variable (labeled "•"). This additional unobserved variable has no variance and it acts only as a placeholder (augmenting the model matrices with an extra row and column). This kind of variable was originally used by Horn and McArdle (1980; termed a *node*) and by Rindskopf (1983; termed a *phantom variable*). This new unobserved variable adds no additional variance to the model equations and is included here simply to allow the standard linear model to easily include a complex path $A + A^{(g)}$.

We can also rewrite this model so that the variance terms are directly involved in the linear model expression. This can easily be done by writing the model for the g-th group as

$$Y_n^{(g)} = A + A^{(g)} + S_e^{(g)} * e_n^{(g)}, \ with$$
$$\sum_{g=1}^{G} e^{(g)} = 0, \sum_{g=1}^{G} e^{(g)^2} = 1, \sum_{g=1}^{G} A^{(g)} = 0 \tag{4}$$

where the lower case e terms represent "standardized" error scores with zero mean and unit variance. Although these constraints over groups are relatively simple, they require special MG-SEM programs and programming. This scaling allows us to reinterpret the regression coefficients $S^{(g)}$ as standard deviations of the within group differences over groups [$S^{(g)} = \sqrt{V_e}$]. These standard deviations are included in the path diagrams of Fig. 4.1c as the values of the arrow from the standardized error variables to the observed variables.

ANOVA as a Multilevel Variance Components (ML-VC) Model

One standard ML-ANOVA model has a strong similarity to the previous ANOVA model—the so-called *variance components* (VC) model. Rather than giving estimates for all separate group G mean differences $A^{(g)}$ (from the grand mean A), these multilevel models give a direct estimate of the variance V_a of these mean differences. In this standard multilevel model for the g-th group, we write the linear model and expectations [$\mathcal{E}$] as

$$Y_{n,g} = A_g^* * 1_{n,g} + E_{n,g}, \text{ with } V_e = \mathcal{E}(E_g^2) \text{ and}$$
$$A_g^* = A + A_g, \text{ with } V_a = \mathcal{E}(A_g^2) \tag{5}$$

where we usually assume that both scores A_g and E_g are normally distributed with mean zero and constant variances V_a and V_e (see Bock, 1989) and with no correlation among these group-level scores. The typical calculation of the "intraclass correlation" is now a direct function of the variance between groups V_a and within groups V_e [$R_{ic} = V_a/(V_a + V_e)$] (see Singer, 1987).

Using the MG-SEM notation set out earlier, we can rewrite this model for group g as

$$Y_n^{(g)} = A + S_a * a^{(g)} + S_e * e_n^{(g)}, \text{ with}$$
$$\sum_{g=1}^{G} e^{(g)} = 0 \text{ and } \sum_{g=1}^{G} e^{(g)^2} = 1 \tag{6}$$
$$\sum_{g=1}^{G} a^{(g)} = 0 \text{ and } \sum_{g=1}^{G} a^{(g)^2} = 1$$

so the $a^{(g)}$ are mean deviations standardized over all groups, and so the coefficient S_a represents the standard deviation of the mean differences over all groups [$S_a = \sqrt{V_a}$]. Further constraints on the $a^{(g)}$ terms are required to make their distribution be symmetric (e.g., no skew) or normal, but these constraints will not be discussed further here.

After including the standardization and independence constraints, these structural equations lead to the appropriate multilevel expectations for each group. To demonstrate this result here, we can expand the model expectations ($\mathcal{E}$) for the means of any group g as

$$\begin{aligned} M_y^{(g)} = C[y^{(g)}, 1^{(g)'}] &= \mathcal{E}([A + S_a * a^{(g)} + S_e * e^{(g)}][1]') \\ &= \mathcal{E}(A) + S_a * \mathcal{E}(a^{(g)}) + S_e * \mathcal{E}(e^{(g)}) \\ &= A + S_a * 0 + S_e * 0 \\ &= A, \end{aligned} \tag{7}$$

and for the variances of any group g as

$$\begin{aligned} V_y^{(g)} = C[y^{(g)} - M_y, y^{(g)} - M_y'] &= \mathcal{E}([A + S_a * a^{(g)} + S_e * e^{(g)}][A + S_a * a^{(g)} + S_e * e^{(g)}]') \\ &= \mathcal{E}(A^2) + \mathcal{E}(A * S_a * a^{(g)}) + \mathcal{E}(A * S_e * e^{(g)}) \\ &\quad + \mathcal{E}(S_a * a^{(g)} * A) + \mathcal{E}(S_a * a^{(g)^2}) \\ &\quad + \mathcal{E}(S_a * a^{(g)} * S_e * e^{(g)}) + \mathcal{E}(S_e * e^{(g)} * A) \\ &\quad + \mathcal{E}(S_e * e^{(g)} * S_a * a^{(g)}) + \mathcal{E}(S_e * e^{(g)^2}) \\ &= 0 + 0 + 0 + 0 + S_a^2 + 0 + 0 + 0 + S_e^2 \\ &= V_a + V_e \end{aligned} \tag{8}$$

These MG-SEM equations also allow us to draw a simple but accurate path diagram for an ML-ANOVA, shown here as Fig. 4.1d. The path diagram is unusual in several ways. First, it allows the tracing rules of path diagrams to provide the correct expectations for the group means and variances just given. Unfortunately, as drawn here, this model does not clearly show all the standardization (and possibly normalization) constraints required for the identification of the between groups standard deviation S_a term. These kinds of constraints can, in fact, be placed in a path diagram using additional nodes (as in Horn & McArdle, 1980), but this is neither efficient nor essential to the rest of our discussion. Needless to say, these constraints must be assumed or the multilevel model will not be properly fitted and represented in the expectations.

MULTILEVEL RANDOM COEFFICIENT (ML-RC) MODELS

More complex ML models are used to understand variation in the outcome variables $[Y_{n,g}]$ in terms of independent predictor variables $[X_{n,g}]$ measured on every individual within a group. In some of these models we will go further and try to understand group variation as a function of a set of group level predictor variables $[Z_g]$ (having only one value for all members of group g). The simplest cases of the kind of multilevel models will be considered in this section.

Standard ANCOVA Group Difference Models

Another important multilevel model is based on a comparison of regression coefficients across groups (i.e., random coefficient models). One standard approach to comparing group differences in equations comes from the well-known *analysis of covariance* (ANCOVA) model (Cohen & Cohen, 1985). In linear regression notation, we write

$$Y_{n,g} = A + B * X_{n,g} + Q * Z_g + P * (X_{n,g} * Z_g) + E_{n,g}, \qquad (9)$$

where the regression coefficient A is the intercept term (the expected score on Y when all predictors are zero), B is the slope for individual predictor X (the change in Y for a one-unit change in X holding Z constant), Q is the slope for group predictor Z (the change in the intercept for Y for a one-unit change in Z), and P is the slope for product variable $X * Z$ (the change in the X slope for Y for a one-unit change in $X * Z$). The E is an unobserved residual term with the usual assumptions $[E \sim N(0, V_e)]$. This standard ANCOVA model is drawn as a path diagram in Fig. 4.2a. From this model we can obtain expectations about the structure

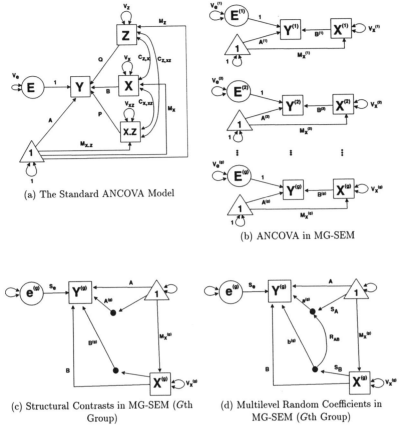

(a) The Standard ANCOVA Model

(b) ANCOVA in MG-SEM

(c) Structural Contrasts in MG-SEM (Gth Group)

(d) Multilevel Random Coefficients in MG-SEM (Gth Group)

FIG. 4.2. Alternative path diagrams of the ANOVA and variance components models for G independent groups.

of the means, variances, and covariances of our observed variables Y and X for each group G.

There are some advantages in writing this model as a MG-SEM (as in Sörbom, 1974, 1978). In our current notation, this can be done by writing

$$Y_n^{(g)} = A^{(g)} + B^{(g)} * X_n^{(g)} + E_n^{(g)}, \qquad (10)$$

leading to group expectations for the mean and variance of

$$M_y^{(g)} = \mathcal{E}(Y^g) = A^{(g)} + B^g * M_x^{(g)} \ \ and$$
$$V_y^{(g)} = \mathcal{E}([Y^g - M_y][Y^g - M_y]') = B^g * V_x^{(g)} * B^g + V_e^{(g)} \qquad (11)$$

where the expectations display the unstated independence assumptions.

This multiple group regression model is now redrawn as a path diagram in Fig. 4.2b. Using this MG-SEM, it is easy to see how $A^{(g)}$ intercepts or $B^{(g)}$ slope parameters can be constrained to form constraints represented by

97

the ANCOVA model just given. For example, the ANCOVA test of equal intercepts $[Q = 0]$ requires the constraint of invariance on all intercepts $[A^{(g)} = A]$. Alternatively, the ANCOVA test of equal slopes $[P = 0]$ requires the constraint of invariance on all slopes $[B^{(g)} = B]$. These tests are typically carried out under the assumption of equal error variance $[V_e^{(g)} = V_e]$, but this is a testable assumption in MG-SEM. It is also very easy to see how partial constraints may be placed on some groups and not others. Although possible, these constraints are more difficult to represent in the standard ANCOVA model.

In order to express some typical multilevel model constraints in this notation, it is useful to rewrite the previous multiple group regression model in terms of mean deviations

$$Y_n^{(g)} = A + A^{(g)} + (B + B^{(g)}) * X_n^{(g)} + Se^{(g)} * e_n^{(g)}, \text{ with}$$
$$\sum_{g=1}^{G} A^{(g)} = 0 \text{ and } \sum_{g=1}^{G} B^{(g)} = 0. \tag{12}$$

A path diagram for this kind of multiple group regression model is presented in Fig. 4.2c following the earlier conventions. Two separate nodes are used here to split the intercept and slope into group deviations. This model is only displayed here for a single group, but all scores and parameters with g superscripts are assumed to vary over groups $g = 1$ to G.

The ML-RC as a SEM Model

This multilevel model is routinely used as an enhancement of standard regression. Rather than giving estimates for all separate group G deviations in intercepts $A^{(g)}$ and slopes $B^{(g)}$ (from the grand means A and B), the multilevel model gives an estimate of the variances V_a and V_b of these mean differences. In this multilevel model we write

$$Y_{n,g} = A_g^* * 1_{n,g} + B_g^* * X_{n,g} + E_{n,g}, \text{ and } V_e = \mathcal{E}(E_g^2)$$
$$A_g^* = A + A_g, \text{ with } V_a = \mathcal{E}(A_g^2) \tag{13}$$
$$B_g^* = B + B_g, \text{ with } V_b = \mathcal{E}(B_g^2)$$

where we usually assume that A_g, B_g, and E_g are normally distributed with mean zero and constant variances V_a, V_b, and V_e over groups (see Bock, 1989).

Using the MG-SEM notation set out earlier we can now rewrite this model as

$$Y_n^{(g)} = A + S_a * a^{(g)} + (B + S_b * b^{(g)}) * X_n^{(g)} + S_e * e_n^{(g)}, \text{ with}$$
$$\sum_{g=1}^{G} e^{(g)} = 0 \text{ and } \sum_{g=1}^{G} e^{(g)^2} = 1, \tag{14}$$

$$\sum_{g=1}^{G} a^{(g)} = 0 \ \text{and} \sum_{g=1}^{G} a^{(g)^2} = 1,$$

$$\sum_{g=1}^{G} b^{(g)} = 0 \ \text{and} \sum_{g=1}^{G} b^{(g)^2} = 1, \ \text{and}$$

$$\sum_{g=1}^{G} (a^{(g)} b^{(g)}) = 0.$$

In this form the group scores $a^{(g)}$ and $b^{(g)}$ are standardized so the coefficients S_a and S_b represent the standard deviation of the mean differences over all groups. The assumption of zero sums-of-squares for these scores $[C_{a,b} = 0]$ will be relaxed in later models. Other constraints on the $a^{(g)}$ and $b^{(g)}$ scores are required to make their distribution symmetric (e.g., no skew) or normal.

Once again, we can demonstrate that the MG-SEM approach produces the standard multilevel expectations by using either standard algebra or path diagram tracing rules. In this case we can write the model expectations for the means and variances of any group as

$$\begin{aligned}
M_y^{(g)} &= \mathcal{E}(y^{(g)}, 1^{(g)\prime}) = A + B * M_x^{(g)}, \\
V_y^{(g)} &= \mathcal{E}(y^{(g)} - M_y^{(g)}, y^{(g)} - M_y^{(g)\prime}) = S_a^{(g)^2} + S_b^{(g)^2} * S_x^{(g)^2} + S_e^{(g)^2} \\
&= V_a^{(g)} + V_b^{(g)} * V_x^{(g)} + V_e^{(g)}, \\
C_{y,x}^{(g)} &= \mathcal{E}(y^{(g)} - M_y^{(g)}, x^{(g)} - M_x^{(g)\prime}) = B * V_x + B^{(g)} * V_x = (B + B^{(g)}) * V_x,
\end{aligned} \tag{15}$$

The constraint of equal error variance over all groups $[V_e^{(g)} = V_e]$ is typically added to form to the expectations of the ML model.

These MG-SEM equations allow us to draw an accurate representation of a path diagram for RC-ML regression, and this is included as Fig. 4.2d here. A complete path model for each group would require a very large and cluttered diagram, unless we introduced new graphic devices. Instead, (a) we only draw the model for the the g-th group, (b) we give values for the parameters that are invariant over groups (i.e., intercept A, between groups deviation S_a, and within groups deviation S_e), and (c) we do not fill in the score for the $a^{(g)}$ term because this varies over groups. This figure does not clearly show all the standardization (and possibly normalization) constraints required for the identification of the S_a and S_b standard deviation terms. However, and most importantly, this path diagram accurately displays the essential structure of the separate group means and covariances.

The ML model of Fig. 4.2c does not include a potential correlation $R_{a,b}$ among the random coefficients, and this is commonly included. The SEM approach used above creates some problems in including this correlation because the model represents deviations scores $a^{(g)}$ and $b^{(g)}$ as parameters in a group, and the usual correlation representation (a two-headed arrow) cannot be used. Among several possibilities, we can rewrite the covariance

$$C_{a,b} = \mathcal{E}(A^{(g)}B^{(g)}) = S_a^{(g)} * R_{a,b}^{(g)} * S_b^{(g)}, \text{ where}$$

$$R_{a,b} = \mathcal{E}(a^{(g)}b^{(g)}), \text{ so}$$

$$b^{(g)} = R_{a,b} * a^{(g)} + b^{*(2)}, \text{ where} \tag{16}$$

$$\sum_{g=1}^{G} b^{*(g)} = 0 \text{ and } \sum_{g=1}^{G} b^{*(g)^2} = 1 - R_{a,b}^2.$$

Here the correlation $R_{a,b}$ is expressed as a standardized regression parameter with a residual term $b^{*(g)}$. This correlation among group model parameters is now displayed directly in the diagram shown in Fig. 4.2d.

This kind of process would need to be repeated for any other correlation among parameters, so this may require extremely complex diagrams and programming. These additional constraints can be complex, and these MG-SEM models illustrate the basic structural complexity of even the simplest ML model. Rather than pursue more abstract MG-SEM models, a few actual ML applications are presented in the remainder of this chapter.

MODELING BINARY VARIABLES
WITH A MULTILEVEL LOGIT MODEL

In a first application from our own research, we examine the prediction of college graduation from the high school academic characteristics of students (see McArdle & Hamagami, 1994). This is a natural multilevel data set because the graduation rates of the students within a specific college are nested under the graduation rate for the college. This would be a standard multilevel analysis except the outcome variable of interest here is binary; a student either does or does not graduate. In this application, we illustrate the use of a multilevel model with a latent response (logit) variable.

The NCAA Student–Athlete Graduation Data

The data presented here were obtained from recent studies of the academic performance of student athletes by the *National Collegiate Athletic Association* (NCAA). This study was initially carried out for a stratified random sample of 1984 and 1985 freshman on full athletic scholarships ($N = 3,224$). College graduation (*GRADRATE*) five years later (by 1989–1990) was considered here as the primary outcome variable. We used high school core grade point average (*GPACORE*) based on the 11 high school "core courses" as one predictor. This sample of student athletes had a mean GPA = 2.87 (a B-minus average), which is just below the national average (*GPACORE* Z-score = −.357) Nationally standardized test scores were also used as predictor variables. We defined a variable labeled *ACTSAT* as a Z-score from either one or a combination of a national SAT or ACT test. This sample had a mean SAT = 879 or an ACT = 18.8, and this is just below the national averages for all college-bound students (*ACTSAT* Z-score = −.130).

Two college-level academic variables were also examined here. One variable termed *CGRAD* reflects the 6-year graduation rate of the overall student body at his or her specific college in 1990. A second variable termed *CACTSAT* is the pre-college average ACT or SAT score for the entering freshman class of the college of entry. (*CACTSAT* is defined as a Z-score using the same constants as the student *ACTSAT* just defined.) The college *CGRAD* and *CACTSAT* are strongly and positively correlated (Pearson r = .884) in these data. More complete details are available in the published report (McArdle & Hamagami, 1994).

A Multilevel Logit Model

In order to predict binary variables we initially use a *logistic* or *logit regression model* (see Hosmer & Lemeshow, 1989; McCullagh & Nelder, 1989) written as

$$Y_n = \pi_n + E_n, \ and$$
$$ln\left[\frac{\pi_n}{1 - \pi_n}\right] = \sum_{k=0}^{K} \beta_k * X_{k,n}, \tag{17}$$

where y is a binary variable, π is the predicted outcome based on some model, E is an unobserved error score assumed to follow a binomial distribution $[E \sim B(0, \pi[1-\pi])]$. The outcome parameters are the natural logarithm (ln) of the odds ratio $[\pi/1- \pi)]$ of the binary outcomes y_n, the X_k are observed scores on K independent variables, and the β_k are linear regression coefficients. We include the constant $X_{0,n} = 1_n$ so the β_0 is an intercept term. The parameters of the standard logit model can be interpreted directly or after transformation to an odds ratio $[e^{\beta k}]$, to a probability $[\pi]$, or to a difference in probability $[\Delta \pi]$ due to differences in X_k units. The overall likelihood $[L]$ is formed as a simple product of the individual likelihoods, and this rests on the assumption that the n observations are *independent*. In broad terms, this transformation of the Y scores by the logit expression means π parameters are unobserved or latent variables.

The standard logit model does not account for the nested structure of the students within schools, so we also use a *multilevel logit* model. This ML-logit model has been defined by Williams (1982) and Wong and Mason (1985), and used by Stiratelli, Laird, and Ware (1984), Wong and Mason (1991), and Longford (1987, 1993). We write this model as

$$ln\left[\frac{\pi_n}{1-\pi_n}\right] = \sum_{k=0}^{K} B_{k,c} * X_{k,g}, \ and$$

$$B_{k,c} = \sum_{j=0}^{J} G_{k,j} * Z_{j,c} + E_{k,c},$$

(18)

where $B_{k,c}$ is the kth first-level regression coefficient for college c, $Z_{j,c}$ is the jth predictor score for college c, and $G_{k,j}$ is the jth second-level regression coefficient for the linear prediction of the kth first level parameter. These G coefficients and the corresponding second-level error components $E_{k,c}$ reflect second level information about school differences in regression coefficients. In these models we will assume that the $E_{k,c}$ are normally distributed with mean zero and constant variance; i.e., $E_k \sim N(0, V e_{k,k})$ (see Bock, 1989).

The structure of this ML-logit model can be seen by rewriting the previous equation as

$$ln\left[\frac{\pi_n}{1-\pi_n}\right] = \sum_{k=0}^{K} (\sum_{j=0}^{J} G_{k,j} * Z_{j,c} + E_{k,c}) * X_{k,n},$$

$$= \sum_{k=0}^{K} ((\sum_{j=0}^{J} G_{k,j} * [Z_{j,c} * X_{k,n}]) + [E_{k,c} * X_{k,n}]).$$

(19)

The complexity of this structural model can be seen by rewriting the previous equation to include two independent product variables—the first product variable ($Z_{j,c} * X_{k,n}$) is observed, but the second product variable ($E_{k,c} * X_{k,n}$) is unobserved (because the second-level component $E_{k,c}$ is not observed). The inclusion of these interaction terms and this latent variable leads to a more complex set of structural expectations for the random components of the model.

Multilevel Logit Results on Graduation Rates

Some initial logit models were programmed using SAS-PROC LOGISTIC routine. These same models were then fitted using ML3, VARCL, and LIS-COMP (Muthén, 1988). The ML3 and VARCL programs (using only a first level model) produced identical results. The LISCOMP program required us to use a probit transformation, but these results were very similar also.

In Fig. 4.3a we present a graphic display of a first set of univariate logit equations (from McArdle & Hamagami, 1994). In this figure we display the overall relations between high school *GPACORE* on the X-axis and the probability of college graduation on the Y-axis. One striking feature of this

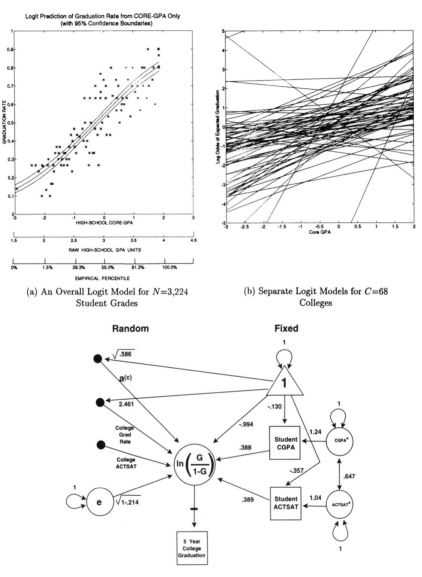

(a) An Overall Logit Model for $N=3{,}224$ Student Grades

(b) Separate Logit Models for $C=68$ Colleges

FIG. 4.3. Results from the NCAA Academic Performance Study of College Graduation.

plot is the increasing probability of college graduation for increasing high school *GPACORE* scores. This increase is linear in the log odds so it is slightly sigmoid shaped in terms of the probability. In Fig. 4.3b, we plot 68 logit regression lines for the individual *GPACORE* logits estimated separately for each college. For the most part, the lines tend upward showing positive effects of *GPACORE* on *GRADRATE* within each college, and a few outliers appear to be present.

TABLE 4.1
Multilevel Logit Model Results from the NCAA Academic Performance
Data (Table 8 from McArdle & Hamagami, 1994)

Variable	Model M_{23} Estimates			Model M_{24} Estimates		
	B_j	(se_B)	t-value	B_j	(se_B)	t-value
Student-Level Effects B						
Intercept	−.954			−.994		
GPACORE	.538 ★	(.134)	4.0	.388 ℗	(.044)	8.8
ACTSAT	.452 ★	(.168)	2.7	.389 ★	(.057)	6.8
College-Level Effects G						
CGRAD → Intercept	2.383 ★	(.527)	4.5	2.461 ★	(.522)	4.7
CACTSAT → Intercept	.115	(.185)	.6	.026	(.184)	.1
CGRAD → GPACORE	−.464	(.332)	1.4			
CACTSAT → GPACORE	.123	(.108)	1.1			
CGRAD → ACTSAT	−.193	(.425)	−.4			
CACTSAT → ACTSAT	.046	(.143)	.3			

Variances and Covariances C	C_B	(se_{CB})	t-value	C_B	(se_{CB})	t-value
Variance(Intercept)	.581 ★	(.069)	8.4	.586 ★	(.069)	8.5
Variance(GPACORE)	.133 ★	(.062)	2.1			
Variance(ACTSAT)	.135	(.082)	1.6			
Covariance(I,G)	−.002	(.031)	−.1			
Covariance(I,A)	−.041	(.039)	−1.0			
Covariance(G,A)	−.015	(.018)	−.8			

Notes.
(1) NCAA Data with N = 3,224 and Colleges = 68;
(2) Maximum-likelihood estimates from VARCL program;
(3) Model M_{23} obtains LRT = 964 and LIP = 21.6%;
(4) Model M_{24} obtains LRT = 958 and LIP = 21.4%.

The ML-logit model requires a specialized software to estimate the parameters (regressions B and G and variances and covariances C) of these models. We tried a variety of computer programs, including SAS-PROC MIXED, ML3, and VARCL, and LISCOMP. The VARCL program seemed most flexible, but the ML3 program produced virtually the same results for most models we tried. We attempted to use the LISCOMP programs with a probit option and 68 different groups, but models of this complexity with over 5 groups did not begin iterations (see Gibbons & Hedeker, 1994). These numerical results for two ML-logit models fitted by VARCL are presented in Table 4.1.

The first model (M_{23}) is a complete ML-logit model including student-level GPACORE and ACTSAT, college-level CGRAD and CACTSAT, and variances and covariances among the first-level residuals V_e terms. The other model listed (M_{24}) gives the results where we estimate only the strongest coefficients and the large *Intercept* variance term, and the resulting loss of fit is small ($dLRT = 6$).

This final summary model is drawn as an ML path diagram in Fig. 4.3c. Four additional latent nodes are required to create the necessary matrix placeholders for this model. As before, this is a diagram for only one group, but the group parameters (e.g., *CGRAD* and *CACTSAT*) are labeled on each path. We have also included the necessary constant, and the logit response function is included as a standard latent variable with an indicator of the functional form (the resistor symbol on the loading). The numerical values listed in Table 4.1 are placed in the appropriate location on this diagram, and here we use square root signs so we can include all variance terms from the table (and the usual program output). The main benefit of all these unusual graphic devices is that they now accurately display the structural expectation of the moments of any group *g*. Structural expectations can be formed for each group by substitution of the exact values of the second-level variables.

Only a few results are significant and noteworthy: (a) The student-level *GPACORE* and *ACTSAT* are both significant and approximately equal; (b) The *CGRAD* is a strong independent predictor of variability in the student-level *Intercept*, but it has no effect on the student-level slopes of *GPACORE* or *ACTSAT*; (c) The *CACTSAT* is not a significant predictor of any student-level coefficient, once the *CGRAD* is held constant; (d) The residual variance of the *Intercept* remains significant, but it has been reduced by approximately 28%; (e) The residual variance of the *GPACORE* is significant, and now it is larger than in earlier logit models; (f) The overall fit of the ML-logit ($LRT = 964$) is a large improvement compared to the previous logit model ($dLRT = 280$).

These ML-logit model results suggest the Intercepts of the college graduation vary a great deal, but the slopes of the *GPACORE* equation are largely parallel between each college. We conclude the colleges have different graduation rates for these student athletes, but the predictions from the average score within each college are similar. Also the college level variable *CGRAD* is found to be an important predictor of the within-college average *GRADRATE* (about 28% of the variance between colleges). After college level is taken into account, the *GPACORE* and *ACTSAT* differences within a college remain important, and they are equal in impact. This reflects a diminished influence of the *ACTSAT* (compared to a simple logit model) due to the strong positive correlations of variables at different levels. We have found that ML models which account for the nested structure of the data give a substantially different result from models that do not.

MODELING LONGITUDINAL GROWTH CURVES
FROM INCOMPLETE DATA

In a next application we use a ML model to examine group and individual differences in patterns of change over time. In this example we have measured several persons over different periods of time. The fact that the age at the time of measurement is not the same poses some interesting statistical issues. But even more interesting is the fact that these people were not measured on the same number of occasions, and there were several dropouts. We initially use the standard multilevel longitudinal models discussed by, among others, Jennrich and Schluchter (1986) and Bryk and Raudenbush (1993). We then extend these models by fitting a ML variation on the *latent growth curve model* (after Browne & DuToit, 1991; McArdle & Hamagami, 1992; Meredith & Tisak, 1990).

The Bradway Longitudinal Data

The data we used here come from one of the longest active longitudinal studies—the *Bradway longitudinal study* (see Bradway & Thompson, 1962; Kangas & Bradway, 1971). This study was started in 1931 when children ages 2–7 took part in original standardization of the Stanford-Binet (SB). About half of these children were retested at around age 14, again at age 30, and again at age 42 ($N = 111$). We added to these data by retesting about half ($N = 51$) of these same persons on similar instruments at ages 54 and again at age 64 ($N = 53$). These data are valuable because they include mental ability measures (SB and WAIS), family history, and personal health information on these subjects over a 60 year longitudinal time-lag (for more details, see McArdle & Hamagami, 1995).

In the plots of Fig. 4.4a and 4.4b, we display an individual growth curve for each person in the Bradway study. Here we have included the data from the early Stanford-Binet tests (the nonverbal items only) at average ages of 4, 14, 30, and 42, as well as the WAIS scores on Block Design at average ages 30, 42, 56, and at age 64. One complex aspect of this data collection is the increasingly varied pattern of incomplete data: Fig. 4.4a shows the $N_c = 29$ persons with complete data and Fig. 4.4b shows the $N_i = 82$ persons with some kind of incomplete data. More complete details on subject recruitment included: (a) $N = 51$ (46%) retested, (b) $N = 21$ (19%) not located, (c) $N = 20$ (18%) deceased, (d) $N = 12$ (10%) refused testing, and (e) $N = 7$ (6%) inaccessible. When examined over all age intervals, there are at least 9 different patterns of incomplete data with from 2 to 6 responses.

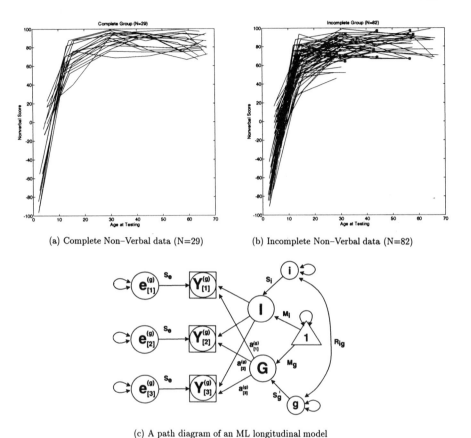

(a) Complete Non–Verbal data (N=29)   (b) Incomplete Non–Verbal data (N=82)

(c) A path diagram of an ML longitudinal model

FIG. 4.4.   Longitudinal data and models from the Bradway study.

A Multilevel Longitudinal Growth Model

It is now common in growth curve analysis to regard the growth parameters as random coefficients (following Bell, 1954; Rogosa & Willett, 1985; Vandenberg & Falkner, 1965; Wishart, 1931). This longitudinal growth model with incomplete data is another form of a random coefficient model where we write a linear model as

$$Y_{[t],n} = I_n + A_{[t]} * G_n + E_{[t],n} \tag{20}$$

where $Y_{[t],n}$ is the *observed or test* score at time $[t]$ for person n, I is a factor score representing an *initial level* at $t = 0$ with a constant impact over time, G is a factor score representing a *growth* or slope over time, and $E_{[t]} = error$ *of measurement* score at time t. In this standard linear model, the *basis* coefficients $A_{[t]}$ are assumed to be a fixed linear function of the age of the individual at each time point to test the hypothesis about linear growth. Other low order polynomial growth functions can be fitted as well by including other latent components with fixed coefficients [adding $A_{[t]}^2 \, G_{2,n}$, etc.]. These kinds of models can be fitted using a variety of standard "two-stage" regression techniques (Rogosa & Willett, 1985).

A ML approach to longitudinal analysis has been discussed by, among others, Strenio (1981), Jennrich and Schluchter (1986), and Bryk and Raudenbush (1993). Interesting examples of longitudinal ML models include Laird and Ware (1982), Liang and Zeger (1986), Goldstein (1987), and Bryk and Raudenbush (1987, 1993). In practical terms, the individual slopes are considered the regressions from a first stage analysis, and these random coefficients are then examined for variance and covariance at the second-level. The new ML computer programs (i.e., ML3, VARCL, HLM, etc.) permit a simultaneous estimation of these model parameters. Some statistical efficiency and precision are expected from this simultaneous approach, but these relative advantages are likely to differ with each problem.

Using the MG-SEM perspective, these models can be considered as special cases of factor analytic models with different patterns of incomplete data. Initially we write the structural expectations as

$$
\begin{aligned}
\mathcal{E}[Y_{[t]}] &= M_i + A_{[t]} * M_g \\
\mathcal{E}[Y_{[t]}, Y_{[t]}] &= V_i + A_{[t]} * V_g * A'_{[t]} + 2 * C_{i,g} * A'_{[t]} + V_e \text{ and} \\
\mathcal{E}[Y_{[t]}, Y_{[t-k]}] &= V_i + A_{[t]} * V_g * A'_{[t-k]} + A_{[t]} * C_{i,g} + C_{i,g} * A'_{[t-k]}.
\end{aligned}
\tag{21}
$$

From this point, we can follow previous work that shows how patterns of missing data can be *blocked* into submatrices and fitted with standard computer programs (e.g., Horn & McArdle, 1980; Marini, Olsen & Rubin, 1979; McArdle, 1994; McArdle & Hamagami, 1992; Meredith & Tisak, 1990). Likelihood based estimates are formed from the raw data vectors (Y_n), or from the incomplete block correlation matrices (R_g), standard deviations (D_g), and mean vectors (M_g).

One useful generalization of this approach is to consider each person with a specific set of observed variables as a separate group, and fit the model to the raw data directly. This kind of raw data procedure is available in the Mx computer program (Neale, 1993) based on the *unbalanced pedigree* approach in genetics (see Lange et al, 1976). In this approach, the number of variables measured is selected by an individual filter matrix (F_n) written as

$$
\begin{aligned}
Y_{[j],n} &= F_n Y_{n,[m]} = F_n * [I_n + A_{[m]} * G_n + E_{n,[m]}] \\
\mathcal{E}[Y_{[j]}] &= F_n \mathcal{E}[Y_{[m]}] = F_n * M_{y([m])} \text{ and} \\
\mathcal{E}[Y_{[j]}, Y_{[j-k]}] &= F_n * \mathcal{E}[Y_{[m]}, Y_{[m-k]}] = F'_n = F_n * C_{y_{[m,m-k]}} * F_n
\end{aligned}
\tag{22}
$$

where $F_n = [I_{[j](n)}, \; O_{[m-j]n}]$ = the n-th binary filter selecting j_n observed measures for individual n. These complex raw data procedures avoid the usual problems with the step-wise estimation of component scores, and the need to weight the further analyses (e.g., by different numbers of vectors T_n). In a general sense the standard likelihood function is adjusted to include only the available data. This raw data modeling approach allows different subjects to have different patterns of complete data on any of the T occasions of measurement.

We can draw a path diagram for every pattern of missing or incomplete data (as in McArdle & Hamagami, 1992), but this can be difficult with a large number of such patterns. The latent variable path diagram of Fig. 4.4c describes a filtering procedure for data with up to three observed variables at three specific time points. Here we use a new diagramming convention: The *circle inside a square* indicates a variable which may either be measured or not measured on a person (after McArdle, 1994). To accurately mimic the structural model, this diagram would need to include as many circle-in-a-square variables as the maximum number of measurements made on any single individual.

This MG-SEM perspective also allows us to examine alternative statistical models for these kinds of problems, such as a model where the age coefficients $A_{[t]}$ are not fixed but estimated as basis coefficients $B_{[t]}$ from the available data. These $B_{[t]}$ coefficients reflect a common factor of individual differences in the pattern of change over time. These are identical to estimating the factor loadings and have similar identification problems. Examples of this type of model are presented in Meredith and Tisak (1990), McArdle and Anderson (1990), McArdle and Hamagami (1992).

A variety of more complex nonlinear forms of growth are also possible. The *linear partial adjustment model* of a first order difference equation (see Arminger, 1986; Coleman, 1964) can be modeled by requiring $B_t = exp^{-(t-1)*\pi}$ (McArdle & Hamagami, 1995). This model allows for individual differences in the starting point and the slopes, and the basic rate parameter $[\pi]$ describes the way the group changes over time (also termed monomolecular). A more general approach to stochastic growth modeling has been introduced by Browne and DuToit (1991) who show how a *Gompertz-growth* model may be written using three components with restricted factor loadings $[B_{1,t} = 1, B_{2,t} = exp^{-(t-1)*\pi}, B_{3,t} = M_{2,g} * t * B_{2,t}]$. This model may be important because the third component allows for individual differences in rates (also termed autocatalytic). In general, these are all alternative forms of latent growth models and can be mixed with standard ML models of longitudinal data.

Results From Fitting Latent Growth Curves

The complete and incomplete six-occasion Bradway data (Fig 4.4a and 4.4b) have been fitted using a variety of computer programs for latent growth models. The standard HLM, ML3, VARCL, and Mx programs produced

TABLE 4.2
Longitudinal Multilevel Model Results
from the Bradway Longitudinal WAIS Data

		Latent Growth Model Estimates				
		Baseline	Linear	Latent	Partial	Stochas.
Parameter		M_0	M_1	M_2	M_3	M_4
Loadings	Time 1 B_4		=.0	=.0	3×10^4	-6×10^4
	Time 2 B_{14}		=.19	=.93	4×10^3	-8×10^3
	Time 3 B_{30}		=.49	1.01	199	−292
	Time 4 B_{42}		=.73	1.06	15	−19
	Time 5 B_{56}		=1.00	=1.00	=1.00	=1.00
	Time 6 B_{65}		=1.15	.97	.21	−.02
	Rate π				−.103	−.110
Means	Initial Level M_i	46.5	11.3	−36.7	75.6	74.0
	Growth M_g		77.4	108.6	−1.01	2.01
Covariances	Initial Level S_i		.01	30.7	10.6	11.0
	Growth S_g		.01	30.3	1.00	1.00
	Error S_e	49.8	39.4	10.0	11.2	11.0
	Correlation $R_{i,g}$		−.66	−.94	−.20	.24
Goodness-of-Fit	Likelihood $-2LL$	5134	4908	4014	4073	4059
	Parameters NP	3	6	10	7	11
	Like. Diff. LRT_0		226	1120	1061	1075
	Deg. Freedom DF		3	7	4	8

Notes.
(1) Bradway longitudinal data with $N = 111$ with incomplete data;
(2) Maximum-likelihood estimates from Mx-92 program;
(3) Equal sign indicates a fixed parameter;
(4) Alternative model equations follow:
M_0 Baseline based on $Y_{n,[t]} = I_n + E_{n,[t]}$;
M_1 Linear based on $Y_{n,[t]} = I_n + A_{[t]}G_n + E_{n,[t]}$;
M_2 Latent based on $Y_{n,[t]} = I_n + B_{[t]}G_n + E_{n,[t]}$;
M_3 Partial based on $Y_{n,[t]} = I_n + P_{[t]}G_n + E_{n,[t]}$ where $P_t = exp^{-(t-1)\pi}$ with rate π;
M_4 Stochastic based on $Y_{n,[t]} = I_n + P_{[t]}G_n + Q_tH_n + E_{n,[t]}$ where $Q_t = M_tP_t$.

similar results for models with a fixed basis. The models with estimated factor loadings [$B_{[t]}$] were fitted using the the general Mx unbalanced raw data with variable length (VL) approach. Some numerical results are listed in Table 4.2.

The first model listed [M_0] is a baseline model where only the initial level mean [M_i] and standard deviation [S_i] and the error deviation (S_e) were estimated. This fit yields a likelihood [$-2LL = 5134$] for 3 parameters. The linear model [M_1] adds a fixed basis coefficient $A_{[t]}$, growth mean [M_g] and standard deviation [S_g], and this yields a difference in likelihood of $LRT = 226$ for 3 degrees of freedom. The component means describe a function that starts low at at age 4 [$M_i = 11$] and increases rapidly between ages 4 and 56 [by $M_g = 77$]. The variance estimates of the intercept and growth parameters are too small to interpret [$D_g < .02$]. Quadratic and cubic polynomial models were also fitted, and these also improve the fit, but these have less substantive meaning here (not presented in Table 4.2).

The next model of Table 4.2 is a latent growth model where the loadings $B_{[1]} = 0$ and $B_{[5]} = 1$ were fixed for the purposes of identification, but the other four $B_{[t]}$ coefficients were estimated from the data. This results in an large improvement over the baseline model [$LRT = 1120$ on $dDF = 7$] and over the linear growth model [$LRT = 796$ on $dDF = 4$]. The estimated basis coefficients, $B_{[1]} = [0, .93, 1.01, 1.06, 1.00, .97]$, define a shape that rises quickly between ages 4 and 14, peaks at age 42, and starts a small decline at age 65. The individual differences in this model are seen in the large variances of the level and the growth parameters. This latent growth model provides an omnibus test of nonlinearity, but it is somewhat exploratory.

A more rigorous hypothesis about nonlinear growth has been fitted in the Partial Adjustment model [M_3] with 4 free parameters. Because of the way we have written this model, individual differences are seen in the variances of the level (asymptote) and the growth (distance) parameters. This model requires all loadings to be an exponential function of a single rate parameter [estimated at $\pi = .103$]. In contrast to the previous latent model, this is an exponential shape that rises rapidly and then stays constant at the asymptote (or equilibrium point) at age 65. This model fit is not as good as the previous latent growth model, but the difference is relatively small compared to the difference in degrees of freedom [$dLRT = 59$ on $dDF = 3$].

The final model [M_4] is based on a Stochastic latent growth model and requires an additional latent component with nonlinear restrictions. As we have written it here, this is a Partial Adjustment model that allows individual differences (random coefficients) in the rate parameter [π_n]. The results show only a small change in the average rate [$\pi = .110$], and the random variance of these rates is very small [$< .01$]. This model fit [$-2LL = 4059$] is not much of an improvement on the simpler partial adjustment growth model [$dLRT = 14$ on $dDF = 4$].

The comparison of the latent [M_2] and the partial adjustment [M_3] model suggests that the decline in nonverbal intellectual abilities by age 65 is relatively small. Also, the further comparison of the stochastic [M_4] and the partial adjustment [M_3] model suggests that the same models of change in nonverbal intellectual abilities can be applied to all persons. Of course, these analyses illustrate only a limited set of substantive hypotheses about dynamic growth processes.

These models have been refit to separate subsets of these data. In one such analysis, the results for the complete data (Fig. 4.4a) and the incomplete data (Fig. 4.4b) have been examined separately, and the parameters are much the same. As a statistical test for parameter invariance over these two groups, we calculated the difference in the overall likelihood and the sum of the separate likelihoods, and these differences are trivial. This suggests that any selective dropout or subject attrition is random with respect to nonverbal abilities (Little & Rubin, 1987). This same MG-SEM framework has been used to examine the effects of other univariate and multivariate analyses of these data (McArdle & Hamagami, 1995).

MULTIVARIATE MULTILEVEL FACTOR MODELS

In a variety of previous studies we examined models of *factorial invariance over groups*. These models include the detailed statistical examination of the equality of the factor loadings over different groups and the examination of "measurement invariance" (see McArdle & Cattell, 1994; Meredith, 1964, 1993; Werts, Rock & Grandy, 1979). These models allow us to quantify fundamental measurement questions such as, "Are we measuring the same underlying constructs in each group?" (see Horn & McArdle, 1992; Humphreys & Taber, 1973). Second, we examine "dispersion invariance" or "Do these underlying constructs vary in the same way between groups?" (see McArdle & Prescott, 1992). Third, we examine "level invariance" or "Do these underlying constructs vary on average between groups?" This is similar but not identical to the standard MANOVA question about group differences (see McArdle & Cattell, 1994; Meredith, in press). We now examine some possible ML models for these MG-SEM models.

WAIS-R Data on Multiple Cognitive Measurements}

In one prior study (Horn & McArdle, 1992) we applied a variety of models of factorial invariance to measures from the *Wechsler Adult Intelligence Scale-Revised* (WAIS-R). These data come from the 1980 standardization sample of the WAIS, and include the measurement of 11 WAIS-R subscales on $N = 1,880$ adults over the age of 16. In Horn and McArdle (1992), we created 4 age groups to examine a variety of common factor models for these data. These models included: (a) single and multiple factor models, (b) factor models with configural and metric invariance, and (c) factor models based on correlations, covariances, and cross-products. These previous analyses suggest that the loadings associated with the so-called WAIS-Verbal subscales are invariant over age.

Fig. 4.5a is a plot of the factor loadings of each of four variables estimated separately in each of nine possible age groups. The variables plotted here are 4 measures from the Verbal subscales of the WAIS-R: Information, Comprehension, Similarities, and Vocabulary. The nine age groups represent the finest age groupings we could form from the existing data (i.e., chronological age was not available in years). The question we would now

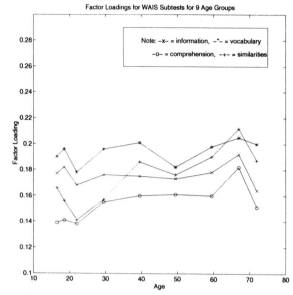

(a) WAIS–Verbal factor loadings over age groups

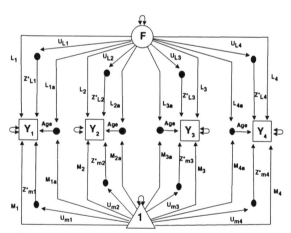

(b) A path diagram of a multilevel factor model

FIG. 4.5. A random coefficients common factor model from the WAIS-R study.

like to ask is, "Are there any changes over age in these factor loadings?" This kind of question was previously analyzed using the same data by McArdle and Rozeboom (1983) using a SEM with product variables, and we now develop an ML factor model for this problem.

A Multilevel Factor Model

In the MG-SEM studied, here we first write a common factor model for many groups as

$$Y_{[m],n}^{(g)} = I_{[m]}^{(g)} + L_{[m]}^{(g)} * F_n^{(g)} + U_{[m],n}^{(g)} \qquad (23)$$

where, for the mth variable, the $Y_{[m]}$ are observed measures, the $I_{[m]}$ are mean intercepts, the F are unobserved common factor scores, the $L_{[m]}$ are factor loadings, and the $U_{[m]}$ are unique factor scores. This is a well-known common factor model with multiple groups (Jöreskog & Sörbom, 1979; McArdle & Cattell, 1994).

The inclusion of common factors in ML models have been studied in some detail by Muthén and Satorra (1989), McDonald and Goldstein (1989), Muthén (1994), McDonald (1994), and Longford (1993). These authors have all suggested that the previous factor equation can be broken up into independent between (among) groups and within groups components. This kind of model extension may be written as

$$Y_{[m],n}^{(g)} = [I_{[m]}^{(g)} + L_{a,[m]}^{(g)} * F_a^{(g)} + U_{a,[m]}^{(g)}] + [L_{w,[m]} * F_{w,n} + U_{w[m],n}] \qquad (24)$$

where the L_a, F_a, and U_a represent a factor model for the differences among groups, and the L_w, F_w, and U_w represent a factor model for the differences within groups.

There has been some interesting work on this kind of two-level factor model. Goldstein and McDonald (1988) developed a general model for the analysis of multivariate multilevel data, McDonald and Goldstein (1989) provided a mathematical proof for the full-information MLE for the two-level structural equation model with latent variables, and McDonald (1994) discussed progress on a new computer program (BIRAM) for a general bilevel SEM. Muthén (1989) used a variation on the standard LISREL model to fit a multilevel covariance structural equation model using the conventional SEM computer programs (e,g. LISREL, LISCOMP). This modeling procedure uses a separate computation of within and between group cross-products matrices prior to the two-group SEM analysis, and the unequal sample sizes are taken into account by weighting. In practice, Muthén suggested that the quasi-MLE for unbalanced data approximates the full MLE of McDonald and Goldstein. This broad approach bears a strong similarity to analyses and models used in multivariate behavior genetic designs (see McArdle & Goldsmith, 1990).

The ML factor analysis problem we defined earlier is not stated in exactly the same way. Following the standard ML-VC model presented earlier, we can write

$$
\begin{aligned}
I_m^{(g)} &= I_{[m]} + S_i * i_{[m]}^{(g)} \text{ and} \\
L_m^{(g)} &= L_{[m]} + S_l * l_{[m]}^{(g)}
\end{aligned}
\tag{25}
$$

so the parameters are separated into the grand means $[I_{[m]}, L_{[m]}]$ and standard deviations $[S_i, S_l]$ over groups. To incorporate the ML-RC approach, we rewrite the model for the intercepts and loadings with regression parameters as

$$
\begin{aligned}
I_m^{(g)} &= I_{[m]} + A_{[m]} * Z^{(g)} + S_i * i_{[m]}^{(g)} \text{ and} \\
L_m^{(g)} &= L_{[m]} + B_{[m]} * Z^{(g)} + S_l * l_{[m]}^{(g)}
\end{aligned}
\tag{26}
$$

where the A_m and B_m terms represent linear coefficients relating the latent variable intercepts and loadings to a measured characteristic of the group (i.e., $Z^{(g)}$ = average age of group g). The standard deviations of the parameters $[S_i, S_l]$ now represent the residuals from this relationship.

A path diagram of this random coefficients factor model is given as Fig. 4.5b. The usually simple model of a single common factor for four variables is now complicated by (a) the age regression for each separate factor loading, (b) the mean intercepts, and (c) the age regressions for the means. This model differs from the previous factor analytic models because the intercepts and factor loadings are considered to be the random coefficients; but it also leads to a specific set of structural equations for each separate age group. All of these factor analytic models are latent variable generalizations of the ML-VC and ML-RC models discussed earlier.

Results of Multilevel Factor Analyses

The standard ML computer software do not have obvious provisions to fit this basic factor model with random loadings. However, the problem raised here requires structuring variation in the factor loadings across only nine age groups, and this turns out to be just manageable in SEM programs, which allow multiple groups with nonlinear constraints (e.g., LISREL-8, Mx). The MLE results from two ML factor models are presented in Table 4.3.

In all models for the four WAIS-Verbal variables over nine age groups we examined the fit of a model of a single common factor (i.e., Verbal Comprehension or Crystallized Intelligence). For the purposes of identi-

TABLE 4.3

Results from ML Factor Model Fitted to WAIS-R Age Data ($N = 1,880$)

4.3a: Selected Results from VC Factor Model ($\chi^2 = 150$ on $df = 32$)

Age Group	[Par.]	Information	Vocabulary	Comprehension	Similarities	Factor
Average Loadings	$[L_{[m]}]$	.883	.972	.771	.873	
		(.017)	(.018)	(.018)	(.021)	
S.D. Loadings	$[S_{L_{[m]}}]$	.001b	.002b	.004b	.011b	
		(.001)	(.002)	(.002)	(.004)	
Unique Variance	$[S^2_U]$	.010	.005	.012	.015	
		(.000)	(.000)	(.000)	(.001)	
Factor Variance	$[S^2_F]$	-	-	-	-	.040=
		-	-	-	-	(-)

Notes. Only parameters which are invariant over groups are listed here. Group deviation parameters for loadings and intercepts were also estimated. "b" refers to a constraint parameter.

Constraint: $\Sigma^G_g L^{(g)} = 0$, and $\Sigma^G_g L^{(g)^2} = S^2_L$.

Alternative: $\Sigma^G_g L^{(g)} = 0$, $\Sigma^G_g L^{(g)^2} = S^2_L$, and $L^{(G)} = -\Sigma^{G-1}_g L^{(g)} = 0$.

4.3b: Selected Results from RC Factor Model (χ^2 = 150 on df = 32)

Age Group	[Par.]	Information	Vocabulary	Comprehension	Similarities	Factor
Average Loadings	$[L_{[m]}]$	.904	1.012	.802	.865	
		(.037)	(.056)	(.054)	(.087)	
S.D. Loadings	$[S_{L_{[m]}}]$	.001b	.003b	.005b	.010b	
		(.001)	(.002)	(.003)	(.007)	
Unique Variance	$[S^2_U]$	.010	.005	.012	.015	
		(.000)	(.000)	(.000)	(.001)	
Age Regression	$[B_{age}]$	-.052	-.093	-.073	.019	
		(.093)	(.135)	(.130)	(.206)	
Factor Variance	$[S^2_F]$	-	-	-	-	.040=
		-	-	-	-	(-)

Notes. Only parameters which are invariant over groups are listed here. Group deviation parameters for loadings and intercepts were also estimated. "b" refers to a constraint parameter.

Constraint: $\Sigma_g^G L^{(g)} = 0$, and $\Sigma_g^G L^{(g)^2} = S^2_L$ and $\Sigma_g^G Age^{(g)} L^{(g)} = 0$.

Alternative: $\Sigma_g^G L^{(g)} = 0, \Sigma_g^G L^{(g)^2} = S^2_L, \Sigma_g^G Age^{(g)} L^{(g)} = 0$, and $L^{(1)}$ is fixed.

fication, we scaled the variance of the common factor to a length based on the variance of the scores [$V_f = .04$]. In a first model [M_0] we assumed all parameters of the factor models (including the means) were invariant over all 9 groups. This model of *total invariance* yielded a relatively poor fit [$LRT = 618$ on $df = 114$].

In a second model [M_1] we required *metric invariance*, or numerical equality of the factor loadings over groups, and we obtained a much improved fit [$LRT = 187$ on $df = 82$]. In a third model [M_2] we required *configural invariance*, or pattern equality of the factor loadings over groups, and again we obtained an improved fit [$LRT = 132$ on $df = 50$]. This is a very good fit with a large sample size, and the loadings obtained are those plotted in Fig. 4.5a.

On a statistical basis, the differences in fit between the last two models [$M_1 - M_2$] is not substantial [$dLRT = 55$ on $dDF = 32$], so metric invariance of the factor loadings is a reasonable interpretation. If the loadings are invariant over groups, it may not be worth pursuing the ML-VC and ML-RC factor models described earlier. For illustrative purposes, we continue to examine these new models anyway.

In a first ML factor model, we followed a ML-VC loadings model, and the results are listed in Table 4.3a. This parameterization required us to add nonlinear constraints on the mean deviations of the loadings—in this first case so they summed to zero. We explored several ways to do this, including adding more nodes to the model, but we eventually used the built-in nonlinear constraints defined earlier. As expected, the obtained fit remained at $LRT = 132$ on $df = 50$. In terms of fit, the VC factor model is simply a reparameterization of the standard model of configural invariance.

From this first VC factor model we obtained, for each variable m, one average loading $L_{[m]}$ and 9 group deviations $L_{[m]}^{(g)}$. The MLE standard errors of these deviations give a statistical indication about how far each group is away from the average loading (under the constraint that all deviations sum to zero with $G-1$ degrees of freedom). For example, the WAIS-Information scale has a loading of $L = .883$ (se $= .017$) with a standard deviation over age groups of only $S_L = .001$ (se $= .001$). This means that this loading does not vary much over age groups (as the previous LRT implied). Each WAIS-R variable shows only a small deviation from the average loading. These $L_{[m]}^{(g)}$ deviations are a part of the program output, and they do sum to zero, but we do not present them all here.

In other versions of this same VC factor model, we added a slightly different set of nonlinear constraints; we required the sum of the squares of these deviations to equal 1, and we tried to estimate the standard deviation S_l of all nine deviations as part of the model. This last model proved to be underidentified as expected. The calculation of this additional parameter required us to restrict at least one loading to obtain the needed *df* or constraint for each variable. In one sense this is similar to trying to find a reference group for L rather than create a numerical deviation $L_m^{(g)}$. These alternatives are directly related to the "centering problem" of ML analysis (see Kreft, deLeeuw, & Aiken, in press).

Next, we fitted an RC factor model based on the same kinds of programming constraints and model of Fig. 4.5b. Here we used the average Age (within group) as a linear predictor of the previous variation in the loadings, and we obtained the MLE results listed in Table 4.3b. These results yielded very small linear age effects; only a small change in the estimated loadings, and no change in goodness of fit. For example, the WAIS-R Information loading changed to $L = .904$ (se = .037) the regression $B_{[1]} = -.052$ (with se = .093), and the residual standard deviation in loadings of only $S_L = .001$ (se = .001). These results again suggest that these loadings are not changing linearly with age.

In broad terms, these results suggest that it is possible to run a ML-VC or ML-RC model for factor loadings within a common factor model. This is not particularly easy to program due to (a) the identification issues, (b) the nonlinear constraints required, and (c) the number of multiple groups that may be required. These problems need to be overcome before it will be practical for standard use of this ML factor model.

DISCUSSION

The purpose of this chapter was to examine some issues relating standard multiple group structural equation models (MG-SEM) and some of the new ideas from multilevel structural models (ML-SEM). In the first two sections, some of these relationships were formalized using the simplest possible models. The standard ML-VC and ML-RC models were seen to be MG-SEMs with specific nonlinear constraints over groups. We do not wish the reader to think these new ML techniques are simply subsets of the MG-SEM, because this is not completely true. The similarities of the basic conceptual models are striking, but we did not detail several important statistical and algorithmic contributions of ML research.

In the last three sections we used these MG-SEM concepts to describe three practical applications of ML modeling, and some differences became apparent. In a first analysis we used an ML-logit model, and here ML software was available to deal with the analysis (e.g., VARCL, ML3). The MG-SEM path diagram (Fig.4.3c) seemed to be a useful way of representing the modeling results. In a second analysis we used a ML-growth model, and here the ML software was used for models with fixed loadings. Latent variable ML-SEM models and programs (Mx) allow specific kinds of nonlinear growth representations that were hard to calculate otherwise. In a third analysis we used an ML-factor model, and here the standard ML software was not used at all. These ML-factor models were fitted with new SEM software (LISREL-8 and Mx) which allowed provisions for complex constraints over groups. Once again, we find similarities and differences between MG-SEM and ML-SEM models.

The knowledgeable user of MG-SEM software will certainly ask "So why can't we just fit these multiple group path models with programs like LISREL and LISCOMP?" We have shown how path diagrams can be written to give the exact model matrices needed to fit such a model, but this is a bit of a graphic illusion. Certainly for some models with small numbers of equal size groups (i.e., balanced) this is possible (following Muthén, 1994). But multilevel models are often fitted when the number of groups is relatively complex and large $(G > 50)$. Because a complete model for each group would require a very large diagram we do not even draw this kind of path model. More importantly, given large numbers of multiple groups, it turns out to be quite inefficient to fit this path model using a standard structural equation programs with multiple groups (e.g., LISREL-8).

The most serious practical problem we encountered was the necessity of adding constraints on the deviation scores across groups. That is, all ML calculations implicitly calculate the group level scores $[A^{(g)}$ and $B^{(g)}]$, and these constraints are added by the estimation equations used by the ML programs. Some of these constraints can be quite elaborate and far more complex than those described here (normality of $a^{(g)}$ and $b^{(g)}$; see the Appendix of Bryk & Raudenbush, 1993). In theory, however, these are all essentially nonlinear constraints and some new options are available to include such constraints. The kinds of practical issues raised here need to be explored further because, as such constraints become managable, ML models can benefit from other structural model developments. Until such time, the MG-SEM approach presented here may be most useful as a way to describe and present the ML models fitted with another approach.

Most importantly, the ML models have highlighted the benefits of separating different individuals into separate groups. The ML models described here provide one kind of model for group separation, and these ML results, here and elsewhere, suggest that disaggregation may affect both statistical efficiency and substantive interpretation. These groupings are defined based on observed variables only, and these models do not tell us which group variables should be used. But, unlike current MG-SEM, these ML models do provide opportunities for large numbers of groups. This leads us to a consideration of modeling raw data vectors on individuals rather than thinking about groups at all (McArdle, 1994; McArdle & Boker, 1992). These are ML lessons that are worthy of further consideration in MG-SEM research.

To reiterate, we think MG-SEM can lead to (a) the definition of the basic structural equation assumptions in ML models, (b) the drawing of *accurate path-graphic display* of ML models, and (c) opportunities to add *unobserved or latent variables* in ML models. Our current ML-SEM representation does not seem to lead to either improved statistical or algorithmic efficiency, but this may be improved by future work.

Over and over again we have seen that similar or even identical models have been studied in different substantive areas using different names. For example, the ML-longitudinal analysis has been termed "fragmentary data" in statistics (Wilks, 1932; Wishart, 1931), "pooled cross-sectional and time-series data" in economics (e.g., Dielman, 1989), and "incomplete pedigree analysis" in behavioral genetics (Lange et al, 1976). With this in mind, we hope our MG-SEM interpretation of ML-SEM models may help highlight the most useful concepts of both areas of research.

ACKNOWLEDGMENTS

We thank Bengt Muthén for suggesting we write this chapter, to the Editors for their patience, and to Steve Aggen and Tom Paskus for their editorial suggestions. The work described here has been supported since 1980 by the National Institute on Aging (Grants #AG-04704 and #AG-07137). All computer programs used here can all be obtained as ASCII files under the title of JJM MULTI95 from the Anonymous FTP server at the University of Virginia (VIRGINIA.EDU).

REFERENCES

Aitkin, M., & Longford, N. (1986). Statistical modelling issues in school effectiveness studies. *Journal of the Royal Statistical Society, Series A, 149*, 1–43.

Arminger, G. (1986). Linear stochastic differential equation models for panel data with unobserved variables. In N. Tuma (Ed.), *Sociological methodology 1986* (pp. 187–212). San Francisco: Jossey-Bass.

Bell, R. Q. (1954). An experimental test of the accelerated longitudinal approach. *Child Development, 25*, 281–286.

Bock, R. D. (Ed.) (1989). *Multilevel analysis of educational data*. New York: Academic Press.

Bradway, K. P., & Thompson, C. W. (1962). Intelligence at adulthood: A 25 year follow-up. *Journal of Educational Psychology, 53*(1), 1–14.

Browne, M., & DuToit, S. (1991). Analysis of learning curves. In L. Collins & J. L. Horn (Eds.), *Best methods for the analysis of change*. Washington, DC: APA Press.

Bryk, A. S., & Raudenbush, S. W. (1987). Application of hierarchical linear models to assessing change. *Psychological Bulletin, 101*, 147–158.

Bryk, A. S., & Raudenbush, S. W. (1993). *Hierarchical linear models: Applications and data analysis methods*. Newbury Park, CA: SAGE Press.

Cohen, J., & Cohen, P. (1985). *Multiple regression/correlation for the behavioral sciences*. Hillsdale, NJ: Lawrence Erlbaum Associates.

Coleman, J. S. (1964). The mathematical study of change. In H. M. Blalock & A. B. Blalock (Eds.), *Methodology in social research* (pp. 428–478). New York: McGraw-Hill.

Cronbach, L. J., Gleser, G. C., Nanda, H., & Rajaratnam, N. (1972). *The dependability of behavioral measurements: Theory of generalizability for scores and profiles.* New York: Wiley.

Dempster, A. P., Laird, N. M., & Rubin, D. B. (1977). Maximum likelihood from incomplete data via the EM algorithm. *Journal of the Royal Statistical Society, Series B, 39,* 1–38.

Dempster, A. P., Rubin, D. B., & Tsutakawa, R. D. (1981). Estimation in covariance components models. *Journal of the American Statistical Association, 76,* 341–353.

Dielman, T. E. (1989). *Pooled cross-sectional and times series data analysis.* New York: Marcel-Dekker.

Gibbons, R. D., & Hedeker, D. (1994). Application of random-effects probit regression models. *Journal of Consulting and Clinical Psychology, 62,* 285–96.

Goldstein, H. (1987). *Multilevel models in educational and social research.* New York: Oxford University Press.

Goldstein, H., & McDonald, R. P. (1988). A general model for the analysis of multilevel data. *Psychometrika, 53,* 455–467.

Hartley, H. O., & Rao, J. N. K. (1967). Maximum likelihood estimation for the mixed analysis of variance model. *Biometrika, 54,* 383–385.

Harville, D. A. (1977). Maximum likelihood approaches to variance component estimation and to related problems. *Journal of the American Statistical Association, 72,* 320–340.

Horn, J. L., & McArdle, J. J. (1980). Perspectives on mathematical and statistical model building (MASMOB) in research on aging. In L. Poon (Ed.), *Aging in the 1980's: Psychological issues* (pp. 503–541). Washington, DC: American Psychological Association.

Horn, J. L., & McArdle, J. J. (1992). A practical and theoretical guide to measurement invariance in aging research. *Experimental Aging Research, 18*(3), 117–144.

Hosmer, D. W., & Lemeshow, S. (1989). *Applied logistic regression.* New York: Wiley.

Hoc, J. J., & Kreft, I. G. G. (1994). Multilevel analysis methods. *Sociological Methods & Research, 22*(3), 288–299.

Humphreys, L. G., & Taber, T. (1973). Ability factors as a function of advantaged and disadvantaged groups. *Journal of Educational Measurement, 10*(2), 107–115.

Jennrich, R. I., & Sampson, P. F. (1976). Newton-Raphson and related algorithms for maximum likelihood variance component estimation. *Technometrics, 18,* 11–17.

Jennrich, R. I., & Schluchter, M. D. (1986). Unbalanced repeated-measures models with structured covariance matrices. *Biometrics, 42,* 805–820.

Jöreskog, K. G., & Sörbom, D. (1979). *Advances in factor analysis and structural equation models.* Cambridge, MA: Abt Books.

Jöreskog, K. G., & Sörbom, D. (1993). *LISREL 8.* Chicago: Scientific Software, Inc.

Kangas, J., & Bradway, K. P. (1971). Intelligence at middle age: A thirty-eight year follow-up. *Developmental Psychology, 5*(2), 333–337.

Kreft, I. G. G. (1993). Using multilevel analysis to assess school effectiveness: A study of Dutch secondary schools. *Sociology of Education, 66,* 104–129.

Kreft, I. G. G., DeLeeuw, J., & Kim, K. S. (1990). *Comparing four different statistical packages for hierarchical linear regression: GENMOD, HLM, ML2, and VARCL* (CSE Tech. Rep. 311). Los Angeles: UCLA Center for Research on Evaluation, Standards, and Student Testing.

Kreft, I. G. G., De Leeuw, J., & van de Leeden, R. V. D. (1994). Review of five multilevel analysis programs: BMDP-5V, GENMOD, HLM, ML3, VARCL. *The American Statistician, 48*(4), 324–335.

Kreft, I. G. G., DeLeeuw, J., & Aiken, L. S. (in press). The effect of different forms of centering in hierarchical linear models. *Multivariate Behavioral Research.*

Laird, N. M., & Ware, J. H. (1982). Random-effects models for longitudinal data. *Biometrics, 38,* 963–974.

Lange, K., Westlake, J., & Spence, M. A. (1976). Extensions to pedigree analysis: III. Variance components by the scoring method. *Annals of Human Genetics, 39,* 485–491.

Liang, K. Y., & Zeger, S. L. (1986). Longitudinal data analysis using generalized linear models. *Biometrika, 73,* 13–22.

Lindley, D. V., & Smith, A. F. M. (1972). Bayes estimates for the linear model. *Journal of the Royal Statistical Society, Series B, 34,* 1–41.

Little, R. J. A., & Rubin, D. B. (1987). *Statistical analysis with missing data.* New York: Wiley.

Longford, N. T. (1987). A fast scoring algorithm for maximum likelihood estimation in unbalanced mixed models with nested effects. *Biometrika, 74,* 812–827.

Longford, N. T. (1993). *Random coefficient models.* Oxford: Clarendon Press.

Marini, M. M., Olsen, A. R., & Rubin, D. R. (1979). Maximum likelihood estimation in panel studies with missing data. In K. F. Schuessler (Ed.), *Sociological methodology 1980* (pp. 314–357). San Francisco: Jossey-Bass.

Mason, W. M., Wong, G. Y., & Entwisle, B. (1984). Contextual analysis through the multilevel linear models. In S. Leighardt (Ed.), *Sociological methodology 1983–1984* (pp. 72–103). San Francisco: Jossey-Bass.

McArdle, J. J. (1994). Structural factor analysis experiments with incomplete data. *Multivariate Behavioral Research, 29*(4), 409–454.

McArdle, J. J., & Anderson, E. (1990). Latent variable growth models for research on aging. In J. E. Birren & K. W. Schaie (Eds.), *The Handbook of the Psychology of Aging* (pp. 21–43). New York: Plenum Press.

McArdle, J. J., & Boker, S. M. (1991). *RAMpath: Automatic path diagram software.* Hillsdale, NJ: Lawrence Erlbaum Associates.

McArdle, J. J., & Cattell, R. B. (1994). Structural equation models of factorial invariance in parallel proportional profiles and oblique confactor problems. *Multivariate Behavioral Research, 29*(1), 61–101.

McArdle, J. J., & Goldsmith, H. H. (1990). Some alternative structural equation models for multivariate biometric analyses. *Behavior Genetics, 20*(5), 569–608.

McArdle, J. J., & Hamagami, E. (1992). Modeling incomplete longitudinal and cross-sectional curves using latent growth structural models. *Experimental Aging Research, 18*(1), 145–166.

McArdle, J. J., & Hamagami, F. (1994). Logit and multilevel logit modeling studies of college graduation for 1984–85 freshman student athletes. *The Journal of the American Statistical Association, 89*(427), 1107–1123.

McArdle, J. J., & Hamagami, F. (1995, June). A Dynamic Structural Analysis of G_f and G_c. Paper presented at the *American Psychological Society Annual Meetings,* New York.

McArdle, J. J., & Rozeboom, W. W. (1983, October). A quadratic structural equation model used to estimate multiple group effects. *Society of Multivariate Experimental Psychologists Meeting,* Denver, CO.

McArdle, J. J., & Prescott, C. A. (1992). Age-based construct validation using structural equation models. *Experimental Aging Research, 18*(3), 87–115.

McCullagh, P., & Nelder, J. A. (1989). *Generalized linear models* (2nd ed.). London: Chapman Hall.

McDonald, R. P. (1994). The Bilevel Reticular Action Model for path analysis with latent variables. *Sociological Methods & Research, 22*(3), 399–413.

McDonald, R. P., & Goldstein, H. (1989). Balanced versus unbalanced designs for linear structural relations in two-level data. *British Journal of Mathematical and Statistical Psychology, 42,* 215–232.

Meredith, W. (1964). Notes on factorial invariance. *Psychometrika, 29*(2), 177–185.

Meredith, W. (in press). *Factorial Invariance from a Measurement Perspective.* Presidential address at the 1993 Annual Meetings of the Psychometric Society, Berkeley, CA. *Psychometrika.*

Meredith, W., & Tisak, J. (1990). Latent curve analysis. *Psychometrika, 55,* 107–122.

Muthén, B. O. (1988). *LISCOMP: Analysis of linear structural equations using a comprehensive measurement model: User's guide.* Chicago: Scientific Software, Inc.

Muthén, B. O. (1989). Latent variable modeling in heterogeneous populations. *Psychometrika, 54*(4), 557–585.

Muthén, B. O. (1994). Multilevel covariance structure analysis. *Sociological Methods & Research, 22*(3), 376–398.

Muthén, B. O., & Satorra, A. (1989). Multilevel aspects of varying parameters in structural models. In R. D. Bock (Ed.), *Multilevel analysis of educational data*. San Diego: Academic Press.

Neale, M. C. (1993). *Mx: Statistical modeling*. Richmond: Medical College of Virginia.

Novick, M. R., Jackson, P. H., Thayer, D. T., & Cole, N. S. (1972). Estimating multiple regressions in m groups—A cross validation study. *British Journal of Mathematical and Statistical Psychology, 25*, 33–50.

Prosser, R., Rabash, J., & Goldstein, H. (1991). *ML3: Software for three-level analysis user's guide for V.2*. London, England: Institute of Education, University of London.

Raudenbush, S. (1988). Educational applications of hierarchical linear models: A review. *Journal of Educational Statistics, 13*, 85–118.

Rindskopf, D. (1983). Parameterizing inequality constraints on unique variances in linear structural models. *Psychometrika, 48*(1), 73–83.

Rogosa, D. R., & Willett, J. B. (1985). Understanding correlates of change by modeling individual differences in growth, *Psychometrika, 50*, 203–228.

Singer, J. D. (1987). An intraclass correlation model for analyzing multilevel data. *The Journal of Experimental Education, 55*, 219–228.

Sörbom, D. (1974). A general method for studying differences in factor means and factor structures between groups. *British Journal of Mathematical and Statistical Psychology, 27*, 229–239.

Sörbom, D. (1978). An alternative to the methodology for analysis of covariance. *Psychometrika, 43*(3), 381–396.

Stiratelli, R., Laird, N. M., & Ware, J. H. (1984). Random effects models for serial observations with binary response. *Biometrics, 40*, 961–971.

Strenio, J. F. (1981). *Empirical Bayes estimation of linear model parameters*. Unpublished doctoral dissertation, Department of Statistics, Harvard University.

Vandenberg, S. G., & Falkner, F. (1965). Heredity factors in human growth. *Human Biology, 37*, 357–365.

Werts, C. E., Rock, D. A., & Grandy, J. (1979). Confirmatory factor analysis applications: Missing data problems and comparison of path models between populations. *Multivariate Behavioral Research, 14*, 199–213.

Williams, D. A. (1982). Extra-binomial variation in logistic linear models. *Applied Statistics, 31*, 144–148.

Wilks, S. S. (1932). Moments and distribution of estimates of population parameters from fragmentary samples. *Annals of Mathematical Statistics, 3*, 163–195.

Wishart, J. (1931). Growth-rate determination in nutrition studies with the bacon pig, and their analysis. *Biometrics*, 1–28.

Wong, G. Y., & Mason, W. M. (1985). The hierarchical logistic regression model for multilevel analysis. *Journal of the American Statistical Association, 80*(391), 513–524.

Wong, G. Y., & Mason, W. M. (1991). Conceptually specific effects and other generalizations of the hierarchical linear model for comparative analysis. *Journal of the American Statistical Association, 86*, 487–503.

CHAPTER FIVE

Cross-Domain Analyses of Change Over Time: Combining Growth Modeling and Covariance Structure Analysis

John B. Willett
Harvard University

Aline G. Sayer
Pennsylvania State University

Empirical researchers often inquire about systematic interindividual differences in change (i.e., whether individual change over time differs from person to person in systematic and interesting ways). Typically, such questions are concerned with the relationship between change in a single continuous outcome—mathematics achievement, say—and selected exogenous time-invariant predictors of that change, such as measures of a student's background, environment, and treatment. Examples include the following: Does the rate at which students learn mathematics differ by attributes of the academic programs in which they are enrolled? Are longitudinal changes in mathematics related to the student's health status, gender, and home background?

However, when individuals are growing, they may be changing simultaneously in several domains. It then becomes interesting to ask not only whether individual change in each domain is related to selected predictors but also whether the several changes themselves are related to each other. In the case of academic progress, for instance, we might ask whether concurrent individual changes in mathematics and reading achievement are mutually interrelated. Until recently, it has been difficult to answer such questions.

Questions about individual change require that longitudinal data be available in each domain on many individuals—that is, measurements on a representative sample of individuals are needed at a representative sample of time points. In the past, researchers have measured change by sampling individual status in each domain at only two points in time, thereby providing minimal information on individual change (Rogosa, Brandt, & Zimowski, 1982; Willett, 1989). When development follows an interesting trajectory, "snapshots" of status taken "before" and "after" cannot reveal the intricacies of individual change. In recent years, investigators have used individual growth modeling in order to capitalize on the richness of multiwave data and have provided better methods for investigating systematic interindividual difference in change (Bryk, 1977; Bryk & Raudenbush, 1987; Rogosa et al., 1982; Rogosa & Willett, 1985; Willett, 1988, 1994).

As a first step in the growth modeling approach, a suitable mathematical model must be chosen to represent individual change over time in each domain. These Level 1 models represent the outcomes of interest—mathematics and reading achievement, for instance—as a function of time and individual-specific "growth parameters." If the investigator decides, for instance, that individual change in mathematics achievement has a straight-line trajectory over time, then the Level 1 growth model for mathematics will contain two individual growth parameters: (a) an "intercept" parameter representing initial status, and (b) a "slope" parameter representing rate of change. If, on the other hand, individual change in reading achievement is thought to follow a curvilinear trajectory, that is quadratic with time, then the Level 1 model for change in reading will also contain a parameter representing curvature.

Within each domain, all population members are assumed to have growth trajectories of the same functional form, but different people may have different values of the Level 1 individual growth parameters. For instance, when individual change is linear with time, interindividual differences in progress may be due to heterogeneity in either intercept and slope (or both). Some individuals may start out at the same initial level, but make progress at vastly different rates, their trajectories diverging over time; others may be initially inept but progress so rapidly that they catch up and overtake their peers. If individual change is a quadratic function of time, then interindividual differences in curvature may also exist. When growth in one domain is related to growth in another, the individual growth parameters will covary across domains, perhaps with rate of change in one domain being related to curvature in the second, and so forth. Such hypothesized links between individual growth parameters in the two domains can be described in a between person or Level 2 statistical model.

Many methods have been proposed for estimating the parameters of the Level 1 and Level 2 models in the analysis of change, but most of the work has been restricted to growth in a single domain. For instance, Rogosa and his colleagues (Rogosa et al., 1982; Rogosa & Willett, 1985; Willett, 1985, 1994; Williamson, 1986; Williamson, Appelbaum, & Epanchin, 1991) described exploratory ordinary least-square (OLS) regression-based methods for estimating individual growth parameters and fitting Level 2 models of the relationship between growth in a single domain and time-invariant predictors of that change, with reliability-based adjustments to the latter based on the marginal maximum likelihood (ML) methods of Blomqvist (1977). In an extension of this approach, Willett (1988, based on Hanushek, 1974) provided weighted least squares (WLS) methods for obtaining asymptotically efficent estimates of the parameters of the Level 2 model. And, as part of their work on hierarchical linear modeling, Bryk and Raudenbush (1987, 1992) provided strategies for simultaneously estimating the parameters of the Level 1 and Level 2 models using empirical Bayes estimation, but again the methods were limited to individual growth in a single domain.

Recently, methodological pioneers have demonstrated how the analysis of change can be conducted conveniently by covariance structure analysis. Meredith and Tisak (1984, 1990; see also Tisak & Meredith, 1990) provided a technical framework for representing interindividual differences in individual development and gave examples of how model parameters can be estimated by covariance structure analysis. Their work extends earlier research on longitudinal factor analysis (Rao, 1958; Tucker, 1958) and subsumes more traditional approaches to the analysis of panel data, such as repeated-measures ANOVA and MANOVA (see also Jöreskog & Sörbom, 1989). The Meredith–Tisak approach is very general. It permits the evaluation of the general shape of the individual growth trajectories and provides not only estimates of the individual growth parameters (via the estimation of factor scores) but also estimates of the Level 2 means, variances, and covariances of the individual growth parameters across all members of the population. These latter statistics estimate the population average growth curve and provide evidence for the presence of interindividual differences in growth in the population.

In a linked body of applied work, McArdle and his colleagues extended the covariance structure approach of Meredith and Tisak, demonstrating its flexibility by application to a wide variety of developmental problems in psychology and the social sciences. For instance, they showed how covariance structure methods can be used to estimate average growth curves and to indicate the presence of interindividual differences in change, in a single domain and simultaneously in many domains (McArdle, 1986a, 1986b, 1989, 1991; McArdle & Epstein, 1987). They showed how average growth curves can be compared across groups (McArdle, 1989; McArdle & Epstein, 1987). They described how covariance structure methods can be used to conduct convergence analysis—in which segments of average growth curves that were estimated in overlapping cohorts are linked to provide a single trajectory (McArdle, Anderson, & Aber, 1987; McArdle & Hamagami, 1991).

Finally, in a separate but related stream of research, Muthén and his colleagues described the technical basis for, and provided data-analytic examples of, the modeling of multilevel data using covariance structure methods (Muthén, 1989; Muthén & Satorra, 1989). Of particular interest are a pair of recent papers (Muthén, 1991, 1992) in which the parameters of a linear individual growth model are allowed to vary across individuals in ways that are systematically related to selected time-invariant predictors of change. The latter paper also presents an application of a strategy based on multigroup analysis (see Bollen, 1989) for incorporating individuals with incomplete observed growth records into the analyses.

We are convinced that these new methods are another powerful weapon in the armory of the empirical researcher. Questions about change pervade psychology and the social sciences. In an earlier paper (Willett & Sayer, 1994), we reviewed the application of covariance structure methods to the investigation of systematic interindividual differences in change in a single domain. In the current chapter, we extend our presentation to include cross-domain analyses of change. Analytically, our work is closest to—and derivative of—the work of McArdle and Epstein (1987) and Muthén (1991, 1992). Our principal contribution is to provide a viewpoint that derives from our background in individual growth modeling. So, in this chapter, we link the pioneering contributions of McArdle, Muthén, Meredith, and Tisak to recent developments in the measurement of individual change (Bryk, 1977; Bryk & Raudenbush, 1987, 1992; Burchinall & Appelbaum, 1991; Rogosa et al., 1982; Rogosa & Willett, 1985; Willett, 1985, 1989, 1994; Williamson, 1986; Williamson et al., 1991).

This integration of the individual growth modeling and covariance structure approaches capitalizes on the fundamental mathematical equivalence of two alternative methods of representing the same data structure. The formulation of population Level 1 and Level 2 models for individual change in several domains, and for the interrelationships among those changes, is equivalent to postulating a specific structure for the matrix of population covariances among the multiple waves of observed data in the several domains. By using the LISREL model with mean structures to explicitly articulate this latter covariance structure and to fit it to the matrix of sample covariances, we can obtain ML estimates of the critical Level 2 parameters that answer our research questions about the interrelationship of changes in multiple domains.

The chapter has three sections and a concluding discussion. In the first section, we introduce the individual growth modeling perspective. We specify Level 1 growth models that represent individual change over time in multiple domains and we combine these into a composite "cross-domain" model for individual change. Then we formulate a Level 2 model for interindividual differences in change that describes heterogeneity in change across multiple domains. In this latter model, the individual growth parameters of the Level 1 individual growth models are permitted to covary across people. In the second section of the chapter, we illustrate how the Level 1 and Level 2 models of individual growth modeling perspective map smoothly onto the framework provided by the general LISREL model with mean structures. Then, in our third section, we demonstrate how the respective Level 2 means, variances, and covariances of the individual growth parameters that represent simultaneous change in several domains can be estimated straightforwardly by covariance structure analysis. To close out the chapter, we test and modify the critical assumptions made at Level 1 concerning the homoscedasticity and independence of the Level 1 measurement error covariance structure within each domain. We use a databased example to frame our presentation throughout the chapter and we provide, in an appendix, illustrative LISREL programs for conducting the proposed analyses.

THE INDIVIDUAL GROWTH MODELING PERSPECTIVE

To conduct analyses of individual change in several domains, a representative sample of individuals must be observed systematically over time and their status in each domain measured on several temporally spaced occasions. To use the methods described here, three or more, waves of data must be available on each individual in each domain. In addition, the data must be balanced in a particular way. In each domain, the occasions of measurement need not be equally spaced in time, but both the number and the spacing of assessments must be the same for all individuals—a pattern that is referred to as *time structuring*. The pattern of time structuring may differ from domain to domain.

Introducing the Data Example

Throughout this chapter, we illustrate the cross-domain analysis of change using panel data drawn from the National Child Development Study (NCDS), a longitudinal investigation of all children born in Britain between March 3 and 9, 1958.[1] In the NCDS, data on infant and maternal health were collected at birth for 17,614 babies (98% of the children born that week) and the survivors subsequently surveyed at ages 7, 11, 16, 23, and 33. Attrition was low—at age 16, for instance, 88% of the cohort remained. The subsample on which our analyses is based includes 437 children with

---

[1]The NCDS data set is available from the Murray Research Center for the Study of Women's Lives at Radcliffe College, Cambridge, Massachusetts.

chronic asthma, 72 with a seizure disorder, and 514 randomly selected healthy controls, for a sample size of 1,023.[2] Chronically ill children were identified by parent interview and medical examination. Some children suffered multiple disorders but, for our purposes, were defined as having the illness that was diagnosed as the most severe. To be included children had to fall within the normal range of intelligence and be free of severe emotional disturbance.

At ages 7, 11, and 16, children were administered a common set of achievement tests in two domains, reading and mathematics (Goldstein, 1979). Reading achievement was measured at age 7 by the Southgate Group Reading Test, a standardized measure designed for use during the first decade of life. The Watts–Vernon Reading Test was administered at ages 11 and 16. Mathematics achievement was measured at ages 7, 11, and 16 using tests that were designed and normed by the National Foundation of Educational Research (NFER). An important condition for the investigation of change is that outcome variables must be measured equatably over time. Unfortunately, in the NCDS, within each content domain, different tests were administered at different ages. However, because all tests were normed prior to data collection on independent nationally representative samples, we were able to convert all scores to a common metric suitable for growth analyses within each domain.[3] Although not ideal, this process permits the modeling of individual change over time and supports interpretations in terms of individual change in national rank order and is suitable for our purposes here.

In Table 5.1, for illustration, we provide three waves of observed reading and mathematics achievement scores (columns 2–4 and 5–7, respectively) for 16 children randomly selected from our data set. The table also contains a child identification code and a record of the child's health status. Inspection of the table—and the full data set—suggests that there is considerable heterogeneity in entry-level achievement and progress in both domains over the school career. In mathematics, for instance, Child 510121 begins at the 56th percentile and makes steady progress upward through the national rank order by the age of 16. Other children experience less success; in reading, for instance, Child 1010026 begins close to the 20th percentile but moves down the national rank order during the school career. Here, we use these data to illustrate the cross-domain analysis of change by addressing two research questions: Over the school career, are individual changes in reading and mathematics related? Is the pattern of

[2]The subsample of 514 healthy children was drawn at random from the sample of all healthy children with complete data ($N = 5,837$) to provide a control group.

[3]We thank Harvey Goldstein, statistician to the NCDS, for suggesting this approach.

TABLE 5.1

Longitudinal Panel Data on a Stratified Subsample of 16 Children
with 3 Waves of Reading and Mathematics Achievement Scores
at Ages 7, 11, and 16 Drawn at Random From the Larger NCDS Data Set

| | Reading | | | Mathematics | | | Health |
ID	Age 7	Age 11	Age 16	Age 7	Age 11	Age 16	Status
984011	37.5	84	78	80	44	80	H
400076	11.5	4.5	4	16	9.5	3.5	H
516031	1.5	1	7.5	28	6.5	19	H
289088	81	90.5	99	56	80.5	63.5	H
550343	18.5	35.5	34	42	40.5	55.5	H
223014	67.5	98.5	98	80	66	74	H
1082345	41.5	53	34	80	53	74	A
510121	99	65	92.5	56	78	92.5	A
620056	37.5	59	65	16	13	13.5	A
385077	11.5	29.5	19.5	6	6.5	59.5	A
287093	20.5	41	34	42	31	39	A
525088	81	80	78	89	76	85	A
740004	67.5	87.5	59	56	87.5	51	S
1010026	20.5	11.5	5	28	20	32.5	S
421062	99	59	85	80	76	82.5	S
1025119	99	11.5	26	16	34.5	32.5	S

Note. H = Healthy
       A = Chronic Asthma
       S = Chronic Seizures

interrelationship among these changes the same for populations of children with differing health status?

Modeling Individual Change Over Time

Classical test theory describes the properties of scores on a single occasion, distinguishing observed from true scores. We also make this distinction when change is investigated because it is change in underlying true score in which we are interested, not change in observed score. Measurement error randomly obscures the true growth trajectory from view. When individual growth is modeled, the model chosen must contain a component describing a person's true growth trajectory over time and a component representing the stochastic effect of measurement error.

Under the individual growth modeling framework, the "true" part of each person's growth trajectory is represented by an algebraic function of time. Choosing an appropriate mathematical function to represent true individual change is an important first step in any project.[4] One responsible preliminary strategy for choosing a valid model is to inspect each person's empirical growth record by plotting his or her observed status against time (see Willett, 1989). We believe that this type of individual-level data exploration is particularly important when covariance structure methods are being used to investigate change. Good data-analytic practice demands knowledge of the data at the lowest level of aggregation so that anomalous cases can be identified and assumptions checked. Once data have been summarized in a covariance matrix, all individual-level richness is lost. Nevertheless, it is possible, in subsequent covariance structure analyses, to confirm earlier "eyeball" suspicions in the aggregate by testing whether the addition of higher order nonlinear terms to the individual growth function improve model fit (see Willett & Sayer, 1994).

In our data example, initial exploratory, and later confirmatory, data analyses indicated that individual reading and mathematics trajectories were curvilinear. Specifically, we found that achievement in both domains could be represented well by a linear function of logarithmically transformed child age. Thus, the following Level 1 model was selected to represent the reading achievement $Y_{ip}^{(r)}$ of the pth child on the ith occasion of measurement ($i = 1, 2, 3$):

$$Y_{ip}^{(r)} = \pi_{0p}^{(r)} + \pi_{1p}^{(r)} t_i + \varepsilon_{ip}^{(r)} , \tag{1}$$

where the child's age has been transformed and recentered such that $t_i = \log_e(AGE_i - 6.5)$. The $\varepsilon_{ip}^{(r)}$ represent the Level 1 measurement errors that distinguish true and observed reading achievement. We adopted a similar growth model for individual change in mathematics achievement:

$$Y_{ip}^{(m)} = \pi_{0p}^{(m)} + \pi_{1p}^{(m)} t_i + \varepsilon_{ip}^{(m)} , \tag{2}$$

The shape of the hypothesized trajectory depends on the particular parameterization of time chosen and on the specific values of the individual growth parameters. The models in Equations 1 and 2 contain individual growth parameters representing the intercept and slope of each child's achievement trajectories in log-time. Thus, the slope parameter $\pi_{1p}^{(r)}$ represents change in true achievement per unit log-time for the pth child;

[4]If theory guides a rational choice of model, individual growth parameters will have powerful substantive interpretations. Often, however, the mechanisms governing change are poorly understood and a well-fitting polynomial is used to approximate the trajectory. In much research, only a restricted portion of the life span is observed and few waves of data collected, so the selected growth model must contain a small number of individual growth parameters if it is to be fitted successfully. Thus, a popular growth model is a linear or a quadratic function of time.

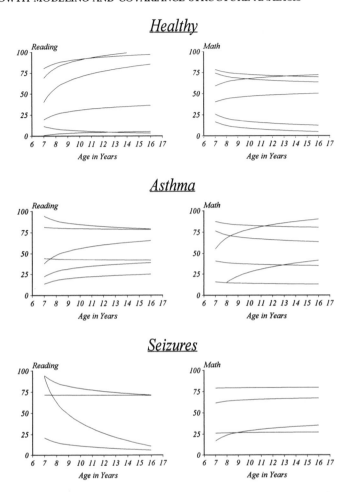

FIG. 5.1. OLS-fitted trajectories summarizing linear-logarithmic growth in reading and mathematics achievement between ages 7 and 16 (see Equations 1 and 2) for the subsample of 16 randomly selected children whose empirical growth records are displayed in Table 5.1.

children whose achievement increased the most rapidly over the school career will have the largest values of this parameter. The intercept parameter $\pi_{0p}^{(r)}$ represents the true achievement of Child p when t_i is equal to zero, that is at age 7.5 years; children whose achievement is higher early in their school careers will possess higher values of this parameter.

As an evocative summary of our data exploration, we fitted the models of Equations 1 and 2 to the empirical growth records of each of the children in Table 5.1 using "within-child" OLS regression analysis. Figure 5.1 presents these OLS-fitted trajectories. Notice that there is considerable evidence of heterogeneity in observed change across children, within each domain. In addition, a careful matching of reading and mathematics trajectories within child suggests that children who score highly early in their school careers tend to do so in both domains, and that children who grow rapidly in reading also grow rapidly in mathematics over the school career. It is these types of inference that the methods described in this chapter are intended to confirm.

A Matrix Representation for the Empirical Growth Records

In our example, three waves of longitudinal data were collected in each domain. Therefore, each child's empirical growth record contained three measurements of observed status, Y_{1p}, Y_{2p}, and Y_{3p}, in both reading and mathematics. Under the individual growth models in Equations 1 and 2, these records can be represented conveniently as:

$$\begin{bmatrix} Y_{1p}^{(r)} \\ Y_{2p}^{(r)} \\ Y_{3p}^{(r)} \end{bmatrix} = \begin{bmatrix} 1 & t_1 \\ 1 & t_2 \\ 1 & t_3 \end{bmatrix} \begin{bmatrix} \pi_{0p}^{(r)} \\ \pi_{1p}^{(r)} \end{bmatrix} + \begin{bmatrix} \varepsilon_{1p}^{(r)} \\ \varepsilon_{2p}^{(r)} \\ \varepsilon_{3p}^{(r)} \end{bmatrix} \tag{3}$$

and:

$$\begin{bmatrix} Y_{1p}^{(m)} \\ Y_{2p}^{(m)} \\ Y_{3p}^{(m)} \end{bmatrix} = \begin{bmatrix} 1 & t_1 \\ 1 & t_2 \\ 1 & t_3 \end{bmatrix} \begin{bmatrix} \pi_{0p}^{(m)} \\ \pi_{1p}^{(m)} \end{bmatrix} + \begin{bmatrix} \varepsilon_{1p}^{(m)} \\ \varepsilon_{2p}^{(m)} \\ \varepsilon_{3p}^{(m)} \end{bmatrix} \tag{4}$$

For reasons of pedagogy and parsimony, in Equations 3 and 4 and through-out the rest of the chapter, we have retained symbols t_1 through t_3 to represent the timing of the occasions of measurement. In any particular research project, of course, each of these symbols will have known constant value. In our data example, because of our recentering and logarithmic transformation of the time metric, t_1 through t_3 take on values -0.693, 1.504, and 2.251, respectively.

For the purposes of subsequent analysis, we must combine the separate Level 1 growth models of Equations 1 and 2 into a single composite "cross-domain" model that represents simultaneous individual change in both reading and mathematics achievement, as follows:

$$\begin{bmatrix} Y_{1p}^{(r)} \\ Y_{2p}^{(r)} \\ Y_{3p}^{(r)} \\ Y_{1p}^{(m)} \\ Y_{2p}^{(m)} \\ Y_{3p}^{(m)} \end{bmatrix} = \begin{bmatrix} 1 & t_1 & 0 & 0 \\ 1 & t_2 & 0 & 0 \\ 1 & t_3 & 0 & 0 \\ 0 & 0 & 1 & t_1 \\ 0 & 0 & 1 & t_2 \\ 0 & 0 & 1 & t_3 \end{bmatrix} \begin{bmatrix} \pi_{0p}^{(r)} \\ \pi_{1p}^{(r)} \\ \pi_{0p}^{(m)} \\ \pi_{1p}^{(m)} \end{bmatrix} + \begin{bmatrix} \varepsilon_{1p}^{(r)} \\ \varepsilon_{2p}^{(r)} \\ \varepsilon_{3p}^{(r)} \\ \varepsilon_{1p}^{(m)} \\ \varepsilon_{2p}^{(m)} \\ \varepsilon_{3p}^{(m)} \end{bmatrix} \tag{5}$$

Notice that for Person p, the joint observed growth record in both reading and mathematics (on the left-hand side of Equation 5) can be regarded as a combination of three distinct components: (a) a matrix of known times (and constants) that is identical across all individuals, multiplied by (b) an individual-specific vector of unknown individual growth parameters (which we refer to henceforth as the *latent growth vector*), added to (c) an individual-specific vector of unknown errors of measurement. The latent growth vector is the central focus of the subsequent cross-domain analysis of change. In our data example, the four elements of the latent growth vector represent the within-person "signal"—the individual growth parameters describing true change in both domains over time. The error vector, on the other hand, describes the within-person "noise" that disturbs measurement of true change over time. If the latter are large and erratic, we may never detect the former.

Distribution of the Level 1 Measurement Errors

In Equations 1 and 2, we stated that Level 1 measurement error ε_{1p} disturbs the true status of the pth person on the first occasion of measurement, ε_{2p} on the second occasion, ε_{3p} on the third, and so forth. However, we have made no claims about the shape of the distribution from which these errors are drawn—perhaps they are homoscedastic and independent over time within domain, perhaps they are heteroscedastic, or even autocorrelated. We usually begin by assuming that the measurement errors obey stringent "classical" assumptions within each domain (i.e., we assume initially that they are distributed independently and homoscedastically over time within domain). In other words, we assume that Child p draws his or her measurement error vector from the following distribution:

$$
\begin{bmatrix}
\varepsilon_{1p}^{(r)} \\
\varepsilon_{2p}^{(r)} \\
\varepsilon_{3p}^{(r)} \\
\varepsilon_{1p}^{(m)} \\
\varepsilon_{2p}^{(m)} \\
\varepsilon_{3p}^{(m)}
\end{bmatrix}
\sim N \left(
\begin{bmatrix}
0 \\
0 \\
0 \\
0 \\
0 \\
0
\end{bmatrix},
\begin{bmatrix}
\sigma_{\varepsilon^{(r)}}^{2} & 0 & 0 & 0 & 0 & 0 \\
0 & \sigma_{\varepsilon^{(r)}}^{2} & 0 & 0 & 0 & 0 \\
0 & 0 & \sigma_{\varepsilon^{(r)}}^{2} & 0 & 0 & 0 \\
0 & 0 & 0 & \sigma_{\varepsilon^{(m)}}^{2} & 0 & 0 \\
0 & 0 & 0 & 0 & \sigma_{\varepsilon^{(m)}}^{2} & 0 \\
0 & 0 & 0 & 0 & 0 & \sigma_{\varepsilon^{(m)}}^{2}
\end{bmatrix}
\right)
\tag{6}
$$

where the mean vector and covariance matrix on the right-hand side of Equation 6 are assumed identical across children. Notice that although we are assuming initially that the Level 1 measurement errors are homoscedastic within domain, we are not assuming that they are homoscedastic across domains, because there is no a priori reason to believe that measurement error variance will be identical in both reading and mathematics. If there were, then this constraint on the Level 1 measurement error variance could easily be tested and imposed.

The covariance structure approach that we describe permits great flexibility in the modeling of the Level 1 measurement error covariance structure and this flexibility is a major advantage for the method. We are not restricted only to "classical assumptions"—we can, in fact, permit each person to draw their measurement error vector at random from a distribution with mean vector zero and an unknown covariance matrix whose shape can be specified as necessary. This flexibility permits us to test the fit of the classical error structure here against other, more liberal, hypotheses and we can modify the Level 1 error covariance structure as necessary. And regardless of the final structure adopted, we can estimate all of the components of the hypothesized Level 1 error covariance matrix.[5] This facility is important in a study of individual change because knowledge of the magnitudes of the Level 1 error variances and covariances underpins the estimation of measurement reliability and measurement error autocorrelation.

Modeling Interindividual Differences in Change

Even though all population members are assumed to share a common functional form for their changes in each domain, the true growth trajectories may still differ across people within domain because of interindividual variation in the values of the individual growth parameters. Furthermore, the individual changes may be linked across domains because of covariation among the individual growth parameters from domain to domain. Thus, when we conduct cross-domain analyses of change, we necessarily express an interest in the population between-person distribution of the vector of individual growth parameters.

In our data example, for instance, we specify that everyone in the population draws their latent growth vector independently from a multivariate normal distribution of the following form:

$$\begin{bmatrix} \pi_{0p}^{(r)} \\ \pi_{1p}^{(r)} \\ \pi_{0p}^{(m)} \\ \pi_{1p}^{(m)} \end{bmatrix} \sim N\left(\begin{bmatrix} \mu_{\pi_0^{(r)}} \\ \mu_{\pi_1^{(r)}} \\ \mu_{\pi_0^{(m)}} \\ \mu_{\pi_1^{(m)}} \end{bmatrix}, \begin{bmatrix} \sigma^2_{\pi_0^{(r)}} & \sigma_{\pi_0^{(r)}\pi_1^{(r)}} & \sigma_{\pi_0^{(r)}\pi_0^{(m)}} & \sigma_{\pi_0^{(r)}\pi_1^{(m)}} \\ \sigma_{\pi_1^{(r)}\pi_0^{(r)}} & \sigma^2_{\pi_1^{(r)}} & \sigma_{\pi_1^{(r)}\pi_0^{(m)}} & \sigma_{\pi_1^{(r)}\pi_1^{(m)}} \\ \sigma_{\pi_0^{(m)}\pi_0^{(r)}} & \sigma_{\pi_0^{(m)}\pi_1^{(r)}} & \sigma^2_{\pi_0^{(m)}} & \sigma_{\pi_0^{(m)}\pi_1^{(m)}} \\ \sigma_{\pi_1^{(m)}\pi_0^{(r)}} & \sigma_{\pi_1^{(m)}\pi_1^{(r)}} & \sigma_{\pi_1^{(m)}\pi_0^{(m)}} & \sigma^2_{\pi_1^{(m)}} \end{bmatrix} \right) \tag{7}$$

This hypothesized distribution is a Level 2 between-person model for interindividual differences in true change. In the model, there are 14

---

[5]Provided the hypothesized covariance structure model is identified.

important between-person parameters: the 4 population means, 4 variances, and 6 covariances of the latent growth vector. These parameters provide information on the average trajectory of true change within domain, the variation and covariation of true intercept and slope within domain, and the covariation of true intercept and slope between domains, thereby answering the research questions cited earlier in this section. All of these Level 2 parameters can be estimated using the covariance structure approach that we describe next.

ADOPTING A COVARIANCE STRUCTURE PERSPECTIVE

In Table 5.2, we present the sample mean vectors and covariance matrices for the variables that were introduced in Table 5.1, estimated using data on all children in the illustrative data set. What kinds of statements do these statistics readily support? Focus, first, on the statistics that describe the three waves of observed reading achievement. Examining the wave-by-wave means (the first three entries in the left-hand part of the sample mean vector) we see that, on average, observed average national rank in reading tends to decline slightly for healthy children, increase slightly for asthamtic children, and plummet for children with seizures over the school career. The magnitudes of the variances in the leading diagonals of the covariance matrices for reading achievement (the [3 × 3] submatrices in the upper left-hand corner of the sample covariance matrices) suggest that, for all health status groups, observed reading achievement becomes generally less variable over time as adolescents' national rank converges with age. Inspection of the between-wave covariances among the reading scores (again in the [3 × 3] reading covariance submatrices) suggests a generally positive association among observed reading scores over the three occasions of measurement but contribute little to our understanding of change in reading achievement over time. Similar statements can be made about the sample means, variances, and covariances of the mathematics achievement scores. Finally, inspection of the submatrices of covariances among the three waves of reading scores and the three waves of mathematics score within each health status group (the [3 × 3] submatrices in the lower left corners of the sample covariance matrices), suggest that observed reading and mathematics scores are positively associated on each of the occasions of measurement but this does not allow us to craft statements about potential relationships between changes in the two domains.

So, even ignoring the distinction between observed and true scores, it is not easy to reach informed conclusions about interindividual differences in change by inspecting between-wave summary statistics (Rogosa et al., 1982; Rogosa & Willett, 1985; Willett, 1988). Between-wave statistics do not provide

TABLE 5.2

Estimated Means and Covariances for Three Waves of Reading and
Mathematics Achievement Scores at Ages 7, 11, and 16 for
(a) healthy children ($n = 514$), (b) children with chronic asthma
($n = 437$), and (c) children with chronic seizures ($n = 72$)

Health Status	Summary Statistic	Reading			Mathematics		
		Age 7	Age 11	Age 16	Age 7	Age 11	Age 16
Healthy	Means	56.97	54.28	53.78	56.72	54.87	55.01
	Covariances	972.18					
		583.33	823.82				
		519.94	683.15	824.68			
		431.75	369.76	371.11	773.68		
		542.41	564.72	574.97	430.86	775.30	
		448.83	504.99	549.05	380.74	563.86	764.40
Asthma	Means	55.12	56.47	57.15	58.58	54.08	53.63
	Covariances	986.71					
		548.25	802.96				
		520.82	657.57	849.52			
		481.10	372.74	381.45	800.32		
		566.74	567.08	531.00	442.87	788.15	
		463.27	494.04	546.13	349.44	589.60	819.31
Seizures	Means	53.05	43.81	44.06	49.89	45.38	46.72
	Covariances	1155.83					
		559.29	819.39				
		573.27	709.01	943.51			
		535.72	287.82	299.72	809.11		
		608.91	580.76	541.50	421.66	773.57	
		478.83	460.77	555.56	358.34	559.24	743.41

a "view" that supports easy inference about differences in individual change. To answer questions about change, one must adopt a perspective that emphasizes change. Rather than summarizing data as between-wave variances and covariances, one must use individual growth trajectories. For instance, in both domains, it is easier to see from Fig. 5.1 that observed change can be either positive or negative, that individuals are converging over time, and that there is heterogeneity in level and rate of change across people. The data are identical in both cases, but the view offered by the summary statistics differs—each view supporting a qualitatively different kind of interpretation.

Does this mean that we cannot recover information about change once data have been collapsed into between-wave means and covariances? No, it does not. We must simply "match up" the between-wave and change perspectives explicitly. If we could, for instance, figure out the between-wave implications of the individual growth modeling perspective adopted in

Equations 1 through 7, we could check whether they compared favorably with the data summaries in Table 5.2. For instance, in Equations 6 and 7, we have proposed what we believe are reasonable models for interindividual variation in the individual growth parameters and errors of measurement. If we are correct, then these models must underwrite the between-wave mean and covariance structure evident in Table 5.2. In other words, although we are dealing with two different perspectives on the problem—a "between-wave" perspective in Table 5.2 and a "growth" perspective in Equations 1 through 7—the between-wave covariance structure implied by the growth models must resemble the between-wave covariance structure observed in our data if our parameterization of change is correct.

Fortunately, well-developed methods are available for testing our suspicions—the methods of covariance structure analysis. Starting with the sample mean vector and covariance matrix in Table 5.2 as "input," we can claim that our hypothesized growth models fit when, having estimated the parameters of Equations 6 and 7, we can accurately predict the between-wave covariance structure of the observed data. As Meredith, Tisak, McArdle and Muthen pointed out, the growth formulation that we have posited—the Level 1 models of Equations 1 through 6 and the Level 2 model of Equation 7—falls naturally into the framework offered by the LISREL model with mean structures (Jöreskog & Sörbom, 1989). Thus, ML estimates of the important parameters in Equations 6 and 7 can be obtained by covariance structure analysis, as we now demonstrate.

Rewriting the Composite Cross-Domain Individual Growth Model as the LISREL Measurement Model for Y

When covariance structure analysis is used to conduct cross-domain analyses of change over time, the hypothesized composite cross-domain individual growth model in Equation 5 plays the role of the LISREL measurement model for the vector of endogenous variables Y. For instance, in our illustrative example, the combined empirical growth record of the pth child in both reading and mathematics achievement can be written as:

$$\begin{bmatrix} Y_{1p}^{(r)} \\ Y_{2p}^{(r)} \\ Y_{3p}^{(r)} \\ Y_{1p}^{(m)} \\ Y_{2p}^{(m)} \\ Y_{3p}^{(m)} \end{bmatrix} = \begin{bmatrix} 0 \\ 0 \\ 0 \\ 0 \\ 0 \\ 0 \end{bmatrix} + \begin{bmatrix} 1 & t_1 & 0 & 0 \\ 1 & t_2 & 0 & 0 \\ 1 & t_3 & 0 & 0 \\ 0 & 0 & 1 & t_1 \\ 0 & 0 & 1 & t_2 \\ 0 & 0 & 1 & t_3 \end{bmatrix} \begin{bmatrix} \pi_{0p}^{(r)} \\ \pi_{1p}^{(r)} \\ \pi_{0p}^{(m)} \\ \pi_{1p}^{(m)} \end{bmatrix} + \begin{bmatrix} \varepsilon_{1p}^{(r)} \\ \varepsilon_{2p}^{(r)} \\ \varepsilon_{3p}^{(r)} \\ \varepsilon_{1p}^{(m)} \\ \varepsilon_{2p}^{(m)} \\ \varepsilon_{3p}^{(m)} \end{bmatrix} \qquad (8)$$

which has the format of the LISREL measurement model for endogenous variables Y:

$$Y = \tau_y + \Lambda_y \eta + \varepsilon \tag{9}$$

with LISREL score vectors that contain the combined empirical growth record, the four individual growth parameters, and the six errors of measurement, respectively:

$$Y = \begin{bmatrix} Y_{1p}^{(r)} \\ Y_{2p}^{(r)} \\ Y_{3p}^{(r)} \\ Y_{1p}^{(m)} \\ Y_{2p}^{(m)} \\ Y_{3p}^{(m)} \end{bmatrix}, \eta = \begin{bmatrix} \pi_{0p}^{(r)} \\ \pi_{1p}^{(r)} \\ \pi_{0p}^{(m)} \\ \pi_{1p}^{(m)} \end{bmatrix}, \varepsilon = \begin{bmatrix} \varepsilon_{1p}^{(r)} \\ \varepsilon_{2p}^{(r)} \\ \varepsilon_{3p}^{(r)} \\ \varepsilon_{1p}^{(m)} \\ \varepsilon_{2p}^{(m)} \\ \varepsilon_{3p}^{(m)} \end{bmatrix} \tag{10}$$

and, unlike the usual practice of covariance structure analysis, the elements of the LISREL τ_y and Λ_y parameter matrices are entirely constrained to contain only known values and constants:

$$\tau_y = \begin{bmatrix} 0 \\ 0 \\ 0 \\ 0 \\ 0 \\ 0 \end{bmatrix}, \Lambda_y = \begin{bmatrix} 1 & t_1 & 0 & 0 \\ 1 & t_2 & 0 & 0 \\ 1 & t_3 & 0 & 0 \\ 0 & 0 & 1 & t_1 \\ 0 & 0 & 1 & t_2 \\ 0 & 0 & 1 & t_3 \end{bmatrix} \tag{11}$$

and the error vector ε is distributed with zero mean vector and covariance matrix Θ_ε which, under the classical assumptions of Equation 6, is given by:

$$\Theta_\varepsilon = Cov(\varepsilon) = \begin{bmatrix} \sigma_{\varepsilon^{(r)}}^2 & 0 & 0 & 0 & 0 & 0 \\ 0 & \sigma_{\varepsilon^{(r)}}^2 & 0 & 0 & 0 & 0 \\ 0 & 0 & \sigma_{\varepsilon^{(r)}}^2 & 0 & 0 & 0 \\ 0 & 0 & 0 & \sigma_{\varepsilon^{(m)}}^2 & 0 & 0 \\ 0 & 0 & 0 & 0 & \sigma_{\varepsilon^{(m)}}^2 & 0 \\ 0 & 0 & 0 & 0 & 0 & \sigma_{\varepsilon^{(m)}}^2 \end{bmatrix} \tag{12}$$

Rewriting the Model for Interindividual Differences in Change as the LISREL Structural Model

Notice that, unlike more familiar standard covariance structure analyses, we have chosen to specify the entire LISREL Λ_y parameter matrix in Equation 11 as a matrix of known times and constants rather than as a collection of unknown parameters to be estimated. This specification acts to "pass" the critical Level 1 individual growth parameters ($\pi_{0p}^{(r)}$, $\pi_{1p}^{(r)}$, $\pi_{0p}^{(m)}$, and $\pi_{1p}^{(m)}$) from the composite cross-domain Level 1 growth model into the LISREL endogenous construct vector $\mathbf{\eta}$, which we have then referred to as the latent growth vector. In other words, our fully constrained specification of Λ_y has forced the $\mathbf{\eta}$-vector to contain the very individual-level parameters whose Level 2 distribution must become the focus of our subsequent between-person analyses.

These required Level 2 analyses are conducted in the "structural" part of the general LISREL model—it is this part of the LISREL model that permits the distribution of the $\mathbf{\eta}$-vector to be modeled explicitly in terms of selected population means, variances, and covariances. And, of course, the particular population means, variances, and covariances that we select as parameters of the structural model are those that we have hypothesized are the important parameters in the joint distribution of the latent growth vector in Equation 7. All that is required is to rewrite the latent growth vector as follows:

$$\begin{bmatrix} \pi_{0p}^{(r)} \\ \pi_{1p}^{(r)} \\ \pi_{0p}^{(m)} \\ \pi_{1p}^{(m)} \end{bmatrix} = \begin{bmatrix} \mu_{\pi_0}^{(r)} \\ \mu_{\pi_1}^{(r)} \\ \mu_{\pi_0}^{(m)} \\ \mu_{\pi_1}^{(m)} \end{bmatrix} + \begin{bmatrix} 0 & 0 & 0 & 0 \\ 0 & 0 & 0 & 0 \\ 0 & 0 & 0 & 0 \\ 0 & 0 & 0 & 0 \end{bmatrix} \begin{bmatrix} \pi_{0p}^{(r)} \\ \pi_{1p}^{(r)} \\ \pi_{0p}^{(m)} \\ \pi_{1p}^{(m)} \end{bmatrix} + \begin{bmatrix} \pi_{0p}^{(r)} - \mu_{\pi_0}^{(r)} \\ \pi_{1p}^{(r)} - \mu_{\pi_1}^{(r)} \\ \pi_{0p}^{(m)} - \mu_{\pi_0}^{(m)} \\ \pi_{1p}^{(m)} - \mu_{\pi_1}^{(m)} \end{bmatrix} , \qquad (13)$$

which has the form of the reduced LISREL structural model:

$$\mathbf{\eta} = \mathbf{\alpha} + \mathbf{B\eta} + \mathbf{\zeta} \qquad (14)$$

with a latent residual vector $\mathbf{\zeta}$ that contains the deviations of the individual growth parameters from their respective population means:

$$\mathbf{\zeta} = \begin{bmatrix} \pi_{0p}^{(r)} - \mu_{\pi_0}^{(r)} \\ \pi_{1p}^{(r)} - \mu_{\pi_1}^{(r)} \\ \pi_{0p}^{(m)} - \mu_{\pi_0}^{(m)} \\ \pi_{1p}^{(m)} - \mu_{\pi_1}^{(m)} \end{bmatrix} , \qquad (15)$$

and parameter matrices:

$$\mathbf{\alpha} = \begin{bmatrix} \mu_{\pi_0}^{(r)} \\ \mu_{\pi_1}^{(r)} \\ \mu_{\pi_0}^{(m)} \\ \mu_{\pi_1}^{(m)} \end{bmatrix}, \mathbf{B} = \begin{bmatrix} 0 & 0 & 0 & 0 \\ 0 & 0 & 0 & 0 \\ 0 & 0 & 0 & 0 \\ 0 & 0 & 0 & 0 \end{bmatrix} \qquad (16)$$

Notice that we have removed the population averages of the individual growth parameters—a true intercept and slope, in both domains—into the LISREL α-vector. This permits these important mean parameters to be estimated explicitly. The elements of the LISREL latent residual vector, ζ, in Equations 14 and 15 contain deviations of $\pi_{0p}{}^{(r)}$, $\pi_{1p}{}^{(r)}$, $\pi_{0p}{}^{(m)}$, and $\pi_{1p}{}^{(m)}$ from their respective population means. The ζ vector of latent residuals is of special interest in the cross-domain analysis of change because it is distributed with zero mean vector and covariance matrix Ψ—the latter matrix containing the very variance and covariance parameters in which we are most interested in an investigation of interindividual differences in change:

$$\Psi = Cov(\zeta) = \begin{bmatrix} \sigma^2_{\pi_0^{(r)}} & \sigma_{\pi_0^{(r)}\pi_1^{(r)}} & \sigma_{\pi_0^{(r)}\pi_0^{(m)}} & \sigma_{\pi_0^{(r)}\pi_1^{(m)}} \\ \sigma_{\pi_1^{(r)}\pi_0^{(r)}} & \sigma^2_{\pi_1^{(r)}} & \sigma_{\pi_1^{(r)}\pi_0^{(m)}} & \sigma_{\pi_1^{(r)}\pi_0^{(m)}} \\ \sigma_{\pi_0^{(m)}\pi_0^{(r)}} & \sigma_{\pi_0^{(m)}\pi_1^{(r)}} & \sigma^2_{\pi_0^{(m)}} & \sigma_{\pi_0^{(m)}\pi_1^{(m)}} \\ \sigma_{\pi_1^{(m)}\pi_0^{(r)}} & \sigma_{\pi_1^{(m)}\pi_1^{(r)}} & \sigma_{\pi_1^{(m)}\pi_0^{(r)}} & \sigma^2_{\pi_1^{(m)}} \end{bmatrix} \tag{17}$$

To summarize, in Equations 1 through 7, the individual growth modeling framework provides baseline Level 1 (within-person) and Level 2 (between-person) models that represent our initial hypotheses about the growth structure underlying the three waves of panel data in reading and mathematics achievement in our data example. Then, in Equations 8 through 17 we have shown that these important models can be rewritten, without loss of generality, using the format and notation of the LISREL model with mean structures. By carefully choosing our specification of the various standard LISREL parameter matrices, we have forced the LISREL Y-measurement model to become our original Level 1 composite cross-domain individual growth model (including all existing assumptions on the distribution of the measurement errors), and we have forced a reduced form of the LISREL structural model to become our Level 2 model for interindividual differences in true change in both domains.

FITTING THE MODELS TO DATA: ARE CHANGES IN READING AND MATHEMATICS ACHIEVEMENT RELATED?

Because of the direct and explicit mapping of the individual growth modeling perspective onto that of covariance structure analysis, we can easily test whether our hypothesized growth formulation underpins the matrix of observed between-wave variances and covariances in Table 5.2 using the

LISREL program. If the implied covariance structure fits the data then we obtain, and can interpret, LISREL-provided ML estimates of the unknown parameters in our growth models that now reside in the α-vector, the Θ_ε-matrix and the Ψ-matrix.

Of course, in our data example, additional complications were present because there were three types of children included in the sample: (a) healthy children, (b) children with chronic asthma, (c) children suffering from chronic seizures. This complexity meant that we could not simply investigate the hypothesized interrelationships among simultaneous changes in reading and mathematics achievement as specified in the first research question. Instead, we had also to ascertain whether any pattern of interrelationship among the elements of the latent growth vector differed by the child's health status (the second research question). For this reason, we carried out all estimation and model fitting with LISREL multigroup analysis, the "groups" being defined by child health status. And, rather than simply fitting a single multigroup model, we fitted a taxonomy of such models so that comparisons among the goodness-of-fit statistics of nested models could be used to test hypotheses linked to the second research question.[6]

As is typical in multigroup analysis (Jörsekog & Sörbom, 1989), we began by fitting an "unconstrained" model in which the τ_y, Λ_y, Θ_ε, α, B, and Ψ parameter matrices for all children were patterned as described in Equations 11, 12, 16, and 17, but in which the unknown matrix elements to be estimated were permitted to take on different values for healthy, asthmatic, and seizure children.[7] In other words, although all children were assumed to be experiencing potentially interrelated linear-log growth in both reading and mathematics achievement, children with different health status could subscribe to their own average growth trajectories and interrelationships among the individual growth parameters in reading and mathematics. We summarize the goodness-of-fit of this model in Table 5.3 (as "Model I"). Model I fits moderately well—although the χ^2 statistic is a little large, given its degrees of freedom, the values of the LISREL goodness-of-fit index (GFI) are greater than .9 in each health status group (see Bollen, 1989, for a discussion of the use of summary statistics in model evaluation).

In the second model fitted in the taxonomy, we constrained the covariance structure of the latent growth vector and the Level 1 measurement errors—that is, the Θ_ε and Ψ matrices—to be identical across the three

---

[6]In the appendix, we provide annotated LISREL VII programs for our analyses.

[7]All hypothesized zero entries in the parameter matrices were fixed in the program and values of measurement times t_1 through t_3 were set to -0.693, 1.504, and 2.251 in accordance with the earlier recentering and transformation of the time metric.

TABLE 5.3
Comparing Covariance Structures Across Health Status Groups—
A Taxonomy of Multigroup Models

| | | Goodness-of-Fit Statistics | | | | |
| | | GFI | | | | |
Model Description		Healthy	Asthma	Seizure	χ^2	df
Model I	α unequal across groups	0.971	0.967	0.929	121.4	33
	Ψ unequal across groups					
	Θ_ε unequal across groups (errors independent and homoscedastic)					
Model II	α unequal across groups	0.966	0.963	0.903	141.5	57
	Ψ equal across groups					
	Θ_ε equal across groups (errors independent and homoscedastic)					
Model III	α unequal across groups	0.979	0.967	0.917	106.8	53
	Ψ equal across groups					
	Θ_ε equal across groups (errors autocorrelated and heteroscedastic)					

Note. Θ_ε represents the Level 1 population error covariance structure, α represents the Level 2 population mean vector of the individual growth parameters, and Ψ represents the Level 2 population covariance matrix of the individual growth parameters.

health status groups, but permitted the average growth trajectories (contained in the α vector) to differ from group to group (see Model II in Table 5.3). The imposition of these constraints led to an increase in the χ^2 goodness-of-fit statistic of 20.1 for an additional 24 degrees of freedom (but, again, GFI is greater than .9 in each group). Based on this nonsignificant change in the χ^2 goodness-of-fit statistic, we cannot reject the null hypothesis that the Θ_ε and Ψ matrices are identical across health status groups, implying that interrelationships among the individual growth parameters and the Level 1 error covariance structure are homogeneous across health status groups.

The imposition of the classical assumptions of independence and homoscedasticity on the Level 1 measurement errors in both domains is common but, with measurements being obtained repeatedly on the same child over time, these assumptions may not be tenable. The precision with which an attribute can be measured may not be identical at all ages, and so the measurement errors may be heteroscedastic. And, when measurements are closely spaced in time, there may be inadvertent autocorrelations among their errors. Therefore, in a final model in the sequence (Model III), we retained the equality constraints on the Θ_ε and Ψ matrices, continued to permit the α vector to differ by health status, but specified that the Level 1 measurement errors were autocorrelated and heteroscedastic. The Θ_ε matrix was hypothesized to be:

$$
\Theta_\varepsilon = \begin{bmatrix}
\sigma^2_{\varepsilon_1^{(r)}} & 0 & 0 & 0 & 0 & 0 \\
0 & \sigma^2_{\varepsilon_2^{(r)}} & \sigma_{\varepsilon_2^{(r)}\varepsilon_3^{(r)}} & 0 & 0 & 0 \\
0 & \sigma_{\varepsilon_3^{(r)}\varepsilon_2^{(r)}} & \sigma^2_{\varepsilon_3^{(r)}} & 0 & 0 & 0 \\
0 & 0 & 0 & \sigma^2_{\varepsilon_1^{(m)}} & 0 & 0 \\
0 & 0 & 0 & 0 & \sigma^2_{\varepsilon_2^{(m)}} & \sigma_{\varepsilon_2^{(m)}\varepsilon_3^{(m)}} \\
0 & 0 & 0 & 0 & \sigma_{\varepsilon_3^{(m)}\varepsilon_2^{(m)}} & \sigma^2_{\varepsilon_3^{(m)}}
\end{bmatrix}
\tag{18}
$$

with error variances on the second and third occasions being constrained equal, within each domain (for a discussion of the external empirical evidence on which these decisions were based, see Sayer & Willett, 1995). Model III fits considerably better than either of the two earlier models in the taxonomy and the change in the χ^2 goodness-of-fit statistic between Models II and III suggests that classical assumptions on the error structure are untenable ($\Delta\chi^2 = 34.7$ between Models II and III, for a loss of 4 df). We therefore report interpretations of Model III in the rest of the chapter.[8]

Average Trajectories of Change in Reading and Mathematics Achievement

In Table 5.4, we provide ML estimates of the population means of the true intercept and true slope in both reading and mathematics, along with approximate p values.[9] Notice that distinct values of each are provided within each health status group, as a consequence of the freeing of the α vector in Models II and III and the determination that average growth in both domains differed by health status. Of course, one must exercise caution in interpreting the findings of these analyses because of the nature of the achievement scores used in our analyses. As noted earlier, due to the failure of the NCDS designers to administer equatable tests over time within each domain, we had to convert achievement scores at each age to a common metric by the application of national percentiles provided by the NFER. Thus, when we begin to examine growth in these scores, we are implicitly examining an individual's change in national percentile—effectively their temporal trajectory through the national rank order. This accounts for the general horizontal nature of the fitted growth curves that we display.

---

[8]Interestingly, despite the change in the parameterization of the Level 1 error covariance structure between Models II and III, the parameter estimates describing the mean vector and covariance matrix of the latent growth vector—the central items in our interpretations of the cross-domain analysis of change—differed only negligibly between Models II and III. Output is available on request.

[9]The approximate p-value tests the null hypothesis that the value of a parameter is zero in the population, using a test statistic that is the ratio of the parameter estimate to its asymptotic standard error (see Bollen, 1989, p. 286).

TABLE 5.4
Estimated Average Growth Parameters in Reading and Mathematics
Achievement (Model III)

Health Status	Reading		Mathematics	
	True Status at 7.5 Years $\mu_{\pi_0}^{(r)}$	Rate of True Change $\mu_{\pi_1}^{(r)}$	True Status at 7.5 Years $\mu_{\pi_0}^{(m)}$	Rate of True Change $\mu_{\pi_1}^{(m)}$
Healthy	56.1***	−1.09**	56.1***	−0.62
Asthma	55.5***	0.69	57.1***	−1.74***
Seizures	50.2***	−3.10**	48.4***	−1.24

~ $p < .10$. * $p < .05$. ** $p < .01$. *** $p < .001$.

Inspection of the parameter estimates in Table 5.4 indicates that there are interesting differences among the health status groups, particularly between children with seizures and the other children. These differences are readily evident in Fig. 5.2, which presents plots of the average true growth trajectories in both domains for prototypical children with each health condition. Notice that children with seizures not only begin their school careers at a disadvantage in both domains but their relative standing, compared to other children regardless of health condition, declines as the years pass. Sayer and Willett (1995) suggested that this decline in relative standing may be due to the side effects of the lifelong medication that is required to control the seizure disorder. The average true growth trajectories of healthy and asthmatic children, on the other hand, are very similar to each other in the domain of mathematics but asthmatic children seem to enjoy a small advantage in the domain of reading, perhaps due to the fact that their illness prevents them from engaging in physical activity and consequently they tend to redirect their attention to more scholarly pursuits, both at school and in the home (see Sayer & Willett, 1995).

Heterogeneity in True Change in Reading and Mathematics

Based on ML estimates of the Ψ matrix, Table 5.5 summarizes interindividual differences in true change that were detected in both domains. As a consequence of the comparison described earlier between Models I and II of Table 5.3, we know that the magnitudes and directions of these interindividual differences are invariant across health status groups. In rows 1, 2, 4, and 5 of Table 5.5, there is evidence of considerable interindividual heterogeneity in true change in both domains; tests associated with the population variances of the four individual growth parameters (i.e., true intercept and true slope in each domain) indicate that children differ widely in their growth trajectories in both reading and mathemat-

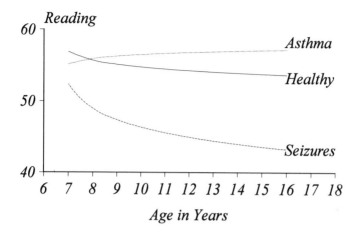

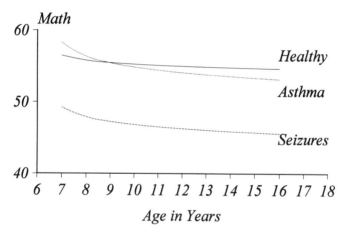

FIG. 5.2. Fitted average growth trajectories in true reading and mathematics achievement between the ages of 7 and 16 for prototypical children who are healthy and who are chronically ill.

ics.[10] In rows 3 and 6 we also present estimates of the correlation between true intercept and true rate of change for each domain. In mathematics, we are unable to reject the null hypothesis that the correlation is zero but, in reading, we find that true intercept and true rate of change are negatively

---

[10]The p values associated with these tests of variance components must be interpreted cautiously because they are sensitive to failures of the assumption of multivariate normality. As Miller (1986) commented on parametric tests of variance, "the effects of nonnormality on the distribution theories for the [variance component] test statistics . . . are catastrophic. For each test the actual significance level can be considerably different from the nominally stated level" (p. 264).

TABLE 5.5

Estimated Within-Domain Heterogeneity in the Individual Growth
Parameters in Reading and Mathematics Achievement (Model III)

Level 2 Parameter	Verbal Description	Estimate
$\sigma^2_{\pi_0^{(r)}}$	Variance of true status in reading at age 7.5	643.5***
$\sigma^2_{\pi_1^{(r)}}$	Variance of rate of true change in reading	30.6***
$\rho_{\pi_0^{(r)}\pi_1^{(r)}}$	Correlation of true status at age 7.5 and rate of true change in reading,	−.352**
$\sigma^2_{\pi_0^{(m)}}$	Variance of true status in mathematics at age 7.5	450.7***
$\sigma^2_{\pi_1^{(m)}}$	Variance of rate of true change in mathematics	39.7***
$\rho_{\pi_0^{(m)}\pi_1^{(m)}}$	Correlation of true status at age 7.5 and rate of true change in mathematics	0.111

~ $p < .10$. *$p < .05$. **$p < .01$. ***$p < .001$.

correlated, suggesting that children who begin their school careers with higher levels of reading skill tend to grow less rapidly in this domain over time. Of course, caution is required here because it is possible that this negative correlation is an artifact of the implicit score standardization that is involved in the use of national percentiles as a measure of achievement (see Rogosa et al., 1982; Rogosa & Willett, 1985; Willett, 1988).

In Table 5.6, we present the core findings of the cross-domain analysis of change in reading and mathematics. The table contains ML estimates of the pairwise correlations between individual growth parameters representing change in reading and those representing change in mathematics. Figure 5.3 presents these same estimates symbolically, with the width of each arrow proportional to the magnitude of the associated correlation coefficient. Notice that there are strong positive correlations between initial status in reading and initial status in mathematics and between rate of change in reading and rate of change in mathematics, suggesting that children who prosper in one domain will also prosper in the other. Interestingly, the estimated cor-

TABLE 5.6

Estimated Cross-Domain Relationships Among the Individual Growth
Parameters in Reading and Mathematics Achievement (Model III)

Level 2 Parameter	Verbal Description	Estimate
$\rho_{\pi_0^{(r)}\pi_0^{(m)}}$	Correlation of true status at age 7.5 in reading and mathematics	.880***
$\rho_{\pi_1^{(r)}\pi_1^{(m)}}$	Correlation of rate of true change in reading and mathematics	.564***
$\rho_{\pi_0^{(r)}\pi_1^{(m)}}$	Correlation of true status at age 7.5 in reading and rate of true change in mathematics	.130*
$\rho_{\pi_1^{(r)}\pi_0^{(m)}}$	Correlation of rate of true change in reading and true status at age 7.5 in mathematics	−.186*

~ $p < .10$. *$p < .05$. **$p < .01$. ***$p < .001$.

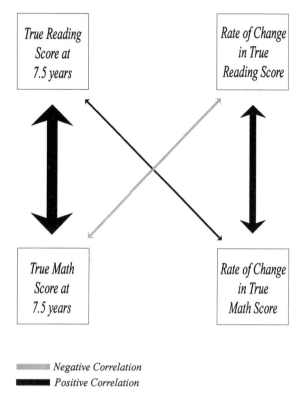

FIG. 5.3. Symbolic representation of the simultaneous bivariate relationships among the individual growth parameters represesenting change over time in true reading and true mathematics achievement. Arrow width is proportional to the magnitude of the estimated correlation coefficient and arrow shading represents the direction (black = positive correlation; grey = negative correlation)

relations between initial status in one domain and rate of change in the other differ in sign across domains. Children with higher reading scores early in the school career tend to progress more rapidly in mathematics, but children who were initially more adept in mathematics tend to progress less rapidly in reading.

DISCUSSION

In recent years, pioneering authors (McArdle & Epstein, 1987; Meredith & Tisak, 1990; Muthen, 1991) demonstrated how notions of individual growth modeling can be accommodated within the general framework offered by covariance structure analysis. In this chapter, we extended our

earlier work (Willett & Sayer, 1994) to explore and review the links between
these two formerly distinct conceptual arenas, carefully laying out in detail
the mapping of the one onto the other, and showing how the ensuing new
methods provide a convenient technique for addressing research questions
about the relationship between individual true growth in multiple domains.

Specifically, we reviewed and illustrated how the Level 1 (within-person)
and Level 2 (between-person) models of the individual growth modeling
framework can be reformatted to corrrespond, respectively, to the "measurement" and "structural" components of the general LISREL model with
mean structures. The direct correspondence between these two pairs of
models permits the population covariance matrix of the errors of measurement and the relationships among the individual growth parameters
in both domains to be modeled explicitly within a covariance structure
framework. Consequently, critical parameters in the investigation of interindividual differences in change can readily be estimated. This innovative
application of covariance structure analysis offers several important features
to the data analyst:

- *Cross-domain analyses of change can simultaneously examine individual
growth in many domains.* The cross-domain analysis of interindividual differences in change need not be limited to two domains, as in our example.
Within the normal constraints imposed by the requirements of statistical
power and the tenets of common sense, analyses can be conducted in many
domains; the model specifications that we have provided extend straightforwardly to these more complex situations.

- *The method can accommodate any number of waves of longitudinal data, with
differing numbers of waves in each domain.* Willett (1988, 1989) showed that
the collection of more waves of data leads to higher precision for the estimation of individual growth trajectories and greater reliability for the measurement of change. In the covariance structure analyses of change, extra
waves of data extend the length of the empirical growth record and expand
the sample between-wave covariance matrix (thereby increasing degrees of
freedom for model fitting), but do not change the fundamental parameterization of the Level 1 and Level 2 models.

- *Occasions of measurement need not be equally spaced, and can be spaced differently in each domain.* In our example, the first two measures of children's
achievement were separated by 4 years, the last two measurements by 5
years. Equal spacing of the occasions of measurement is not required.
Change data may be collected at irregular intervals either for convenience
(at the beginning and end of the school year, perhaps) or because the
investigator wishes to estimate certain features of the trajectory more precisely (by clustering data-collection points more closely at times of greater
research interest). Such irregularly spaced data is easily accommodated by

the method, provided everyone in the sample is measured on the same set of irregularly spaced occasions within each domain.

• *Individual change can be represented by either a straight line or a curvilinear trajectory, and different individual growth models can be adopted in each domain.* In the chapter, we have used linear-log growth models to represent individual change over time in both reading and mathematics. In fact, this approach can accommodate not only polynomial growth of any order but also any type of curvilinear growth model in which status is linear in the individual growth parameters. In addition, because the goodness-of-fits of nested models can be compared directly under the covariance structure approach, one can systematically evaluate the adequacy of contrasting individual growth models in any particular empirical setting (see Willett & Sayer, 1994).

• *The covariance structure of the occasion-by-occasion Level 1 measurement errors can be modeled explicitly, and different error covariance structures can be hypothesized in each domain.* Unlike other popular methods for longitudinal data analysis, the approach we have described does not restrict the population measurement error covariance matrix to a particular shape or pattern. The investigator need not accept unchecked the Level 1 independence and homoscedasticity assumptions of classical and HLM analyses, nor the band-diagonal configuration required by repeated-measures analysis of variance. Indeed, under the covariance structure approach, the researcher is completely in charge. The effectiveness of a variety of reasonable error structures can be systematically compared and the structure that is most appropriate for the particular problem adopted.

• *The method of ML is used to provide overall goodness-of-fit statistics, parameter estimates and asymptotic standard errors for each hypothesized model.* By using the covariance structure method, the investigator benefits from the flexibility and utility of a well-documented, popular, and widely disseminated statistical technique. Appropriate computer software is widely available. In this chapter, we relied on the LISREL computer package, but the techniques that we have reviewed can easily be implemented using other software such as EQS (Bentler, 1985), LISCOMP (Muthén, 1987), and PROC CALIS (SAS, 1991).

• *By comparing the goodness-of-fit of explicitly specified and nested models, the investigator can test complex hypotheses about the nature of interindividual differences in true change.* One benefit of fitting an explicitly parameterized covariance structure to data using a flexible software package like LISREL is that selected model parameters can be individually or jointly constrained during analysis to particular values. This allows the investigator to conduct a variety of nested tests on the variability of the individual growth parameters across people. Like other analytic approaches such as HLM (Bryk & Raudenbush, 1992), for instance, we can "fix" the value of one parameter in a given domain (the reading slope, say) to a value common across individuals but permit another parameter to be "random."

• *The flexibility of the LISREL model permits cross-domain analysis of change to be extended in substantively interesting ways.* There are several extensions of the covariance structure approach that are facilitated by the flexibility of the LISREL model. First, not only can we examine the interrelationships among several types of simultaneous change, we can also predict change in one or more domains by simultaneous changes in other domains. Second, we can introduce additional exogenous variables as predictors of any, or all, of these changes. Finally, the method enables the modeling of intervening effects, whereby a predictor may not act directly on change, but indirectly via the influence of intervening factors, each of which may be either time-invariant or a measure of change itself. We provide examples of these types of analyses in future efforts.

ACKNOWLEDGMENTS

This research was supported by the Henry A. Murray Center for the Study of Lives and the Harvard University Graduate School of Education Fund for Faculty Research and Development.

APPENDIX: SAMPLE LISREL VII PROGRAMS

Here, we present LISREL VII programs used in the multisample analyses for Models I through III, cited in the chapter. Programs for all models have a similar structure, thus we present the program for Model I in its entirety and, for remaining models, only the distinguishing lines.

Model I

In this model, the Level 1 errors of measurement are independent and homoscedastic within domain, and the Ψ, Θ_ε, and α matrices are invariant across health status groups.

Line 1 provides a title for the entire analysis. Lines 2 though 34 contain specifications for the first group (Healthy). After a subgroup title (Line 2), the data definition (DA) line specifies a three group multisample analysis (NG = 3), six input variables (NI = 6), and first group sample size (NO = 514). Lines 4 and 5 identify the source of the sample covariance matrix (CM) and mean vector (ME). We label the input variables (LA) in Lines 6 and 7.

The model definition (MO) line (8) describes the hypothesized LISREL variable and parameter matrices. Y and η score vectors are dimensioned (NY, NE) and the shape and initial contents of the τ_y, α, **B**, and Ψ parameter matrices are specified (TY, AL, BE, PS). In Lines 9 and 10, the elements of the latent growth record are labeled (LE). Then, we specify the fixed and free parameters of the measurement and structural models, as defined in the text. Lines 12 through 17 completely fix the contents of the Λ_y matrix (following the "MA LY" line). In Lines 18 through 21, we free appropriate elements of the Θ_ε vector (FR TE) and set them equal to each other (EQ TE) within domain, as per the hypothesized Level 1 error covariance structure.

Lines 22 through 33 provide starting values for the Θ_ε and Ψ matrices, following the "MA TE" and "MA PS" lines. In the "output" line (OU), we instruct LISREL to adopt the starting values we have provided (NS), and we limit the maximum number of iterations (IT = 10,000). We require the estimation and printing of standard errors (SE), t values (TV), and a residual analysis (RS), all to four decimal places (ND = 4).

The remaining lines of the program contain additional instructions required for the multisample analysis of the remaining groups. For the second group (Asthma), Lines 36 through 38 identify new data sources and Lines 39 and 49 repeat variable labeling information. Line 41 specifies the covariance structure model to be fitted. Notice that, consistent with the hypotheses underlying Model I, the α vector has the same pattern (SP), and the Ψ and Θ_ε matrices has the same pattern and starting values (PS), as those in the first group. Labeling and output details in Lines 42 through 44 are identical to the earlier group. Lines 45 through 54 contain similar required data, model and output specifications for the third group (Seizures).

The complete LISREL program follows, with line numbers inserted on the left to facilitate description.[11]

1. CROSS-DOMAIN ANALYSIS OF CHANGE

2. Healthy Sample

3. DA NG=3 NI=6 NO=514

4. CM FI=A:\HEALTHY.COV

5. ME FI=A:\HEALTHY.MEA

6. LA

---

[11]These line numbers should not be included in the LISREL program itself.

7.   'Read_7' 'Read_11' 'Read_16' 'Math_7' 'Math_11' 'Math_16'

8.   MO NY=6 TY=ZE NE=4 TE=SY,FI AL=FR BE=ZE PS=SY,FR

9.   LE

10.   'Pi0_R' 'Pi1_R' 'Pi0_M' 'Pi1_M'

11.   MA LY

12.   1 -.6931 0   0

13.   1 1.5041 0   0

14.   1 2.2513 0   0

15.   0   0   1 -.6931

16.   0   0   1 1.5041

17.   0   0   1 2.2513

18.   FR TE(1,1) TE(2,2) TE(3,3)

19.   EQ TE(1,1) TE(2,2) TE(3,3)

20.   FR TE(4,4) TE(5,5) TE(6,6)

21.   EQ TE(4,4) TE(5,5) TE(6,6)

22.   MA TE

23.   1

24.   0 1

25.   0 0 1

26.   0 0 0 1

27.   0 0 0 0 1

28.   0 0 0 0 0 1/

29.   MA PS

30.   1

31.   0 1

32.   0 0 1

33.   0 0 0 1/

34.   OU NS SE TV ND=4 IT=10000

35.   Asthma Sample

36.   DA NO=437

37.   CM FI=A:\ASTHMA.COV

38.   ME FI=A:\ASTHMA.MEA

39.   LA

40.   'Read_7' 'Read_11' 'Read_16' 'Math_7' 'Math_11' 'Math_16'

41.   MO NY=6 TY=ZE LY=IN NE=4 TE=PS AL=SP BE=ZE PS=PS

42.   LE

43.   'Pi0_R' 'Pi1_R' 'Pi0_M' 'Pi1_|M'

44.   OU NS SE TV ND=4 IT=10000

45.   Seizure Sample

46.   DA NO=72

47.   CM FI=A:\SEIZURE.COV

48.   ME FI=A:\SEIZURE.MEA

49.   LA

50.   'Read_7' 'Read_11' 'Read_16' 'Math_7' 'Math_11' 'Math_16'

51.   MO NY=6 TY=ZE LY=IN NE=4 TE=PS AL=SP BE=ZE PS=PS

52.   LE

53.   'Pi0_R' 'Pi1_R' 'Pi0_M' 'Pi1_M'

54.   OU NS SE TV ND=4 IT=10000

Model II

In this model, Level 1 errors of measurement remain independent and homoscedastic within domain. The Ψ and Θ_ε matrices are invariant (IN), and the α vector has the same pattern (SP), across the groups. These restrictions are imposed in Lines 41 and 51:

41.   MO NY=6 TY=ZE LY=IN NE=4 TE=IN AL=SP BE=ZE PS=IN

51.   MO NY=6 TY=ZE LY=IN NE=4 TE=IN AL=SP BE=ZE PS=IN

Model III

In this model, Level 1 errors of measurement are autocorrelated and heteroscedastic (Lines 18 through 21) within domain. As in Model II (Lines 41 and 51), the Ψ and Θ_ε matrices are invariant across health status groups (IN) and the α vector has the same pattern (SP).

18.   FR TE(1,1) TE(2,2) TE(3,3) TE(3,2)

19.   EQ TE(2,2) TE(3,3)

20.   FR TE(4,4) TE(5,5) TE(6,6) TE(6,5)

21.   EQ TE(5,5) TE(6,6)

41.   MO NY=6 TY=ZE LY=IN NE=4 TE=IN AL=SP BE=ZE PS=IN

51.   MO NY=6 TY=ZE LY=IN NE=4 TE=IN AL=SP BE=ZE PS=IN

REFERENCES

Bentler, P. M. (1985). *Theory and implementation of EQS: A structural equations program.* Los Angeles, CA: BMDP Statistical Software.

Blomqvist, N. (1977). On the relation between change and initial value. *Journal of the American Statistical Association, 72,* 746–749.

Bollen, K. A. (1989). *Structural equations with latent variables.* New York: Wiley.

Bryk, A. S. (1977). *An investigation of the effects of alternative statistical adjustment strategies in the analysis of quasi-experimental growth data.* Unpublished doctoral dissertation, Harvard University Graduate School of Education, Cambridge, MA.

Bryk, A. S., & Raudenbush, S. W. (1987). Application of hierarchical linear models to assessing change. *Psychological Bulletin, 101,* 147–158.

Bryk, A. S., & Raudenbush, S. W. (1992). *Hierarchical linear models: Applications and data analysis methods.* Beverly Hills, CA: Sage.

Burchinall, M., & Appelbaum, M. (1991). Estimating individual developmental functions: Methods and their assumptions. *Child Development, 62,* 23–43.

Goldstein, H. (1979). Some models for analysing longitudinal data on educational attainment. *Journal of the Royal Statistical Society, 142,* 407–442.

Hanushek, E. A. (1974). Efficient estimators for regressing regression coefficients. *The American Statistician, 28,* 66–67.

Jöreskog, K. G., & Sörbom, D. (1989). *LISREL 7 user's reference guide.* Mooresville, IN: Scientific Software.

McArdle, J. J. (1986a). Dynamic but structural equation modeling of repeated-measures data. In J. R. Nesselroade & R. B. Cattell (Eds.), *Handbook of multivariate experimental psychology* (Vol. 2, pp. 561–614). New York: Plenum.

McArdle, J. J. (1986b). Latent variable growth within behavior genetic models. *Behavior Genetics, 16*(1), 163–200.

McArdle, J. J. (1989). A structural modeling experiment with multiple growth functions. In P. Ackerman, R. Kanfer, & R. Cudek (Eds.), *Learning and individual differences: Abilities, motivation, and methodology* (pp. 71–117). Hillsdale, NJ: Lawrence Erlbaum Associates.

McArdle, J. J. (1991). Structural models of developmental theory in psychology. *Annals of Theoretical Psychology, 7,* 139–159.

McArdle, J. J., Anderson, E., & Aber, M. (1987). Convergence hypotheses modeled and tested with linear structural equations. *Proceedings of the 1987 Public Health Conference on Records and Statistics* (pp. 351–357). Hyattsville, MD: National Center for Health Statistics.

McArdle, J. J., & Epstein, D. (1987). Latent growth curves within developmental structural equation models. *Child Development, 58,* 110–133.

McArdle, J. J., & Hamagami, F. (1991). Modeling incomplete longitudinal and cross-sectional data using latent growth structural models. L. M. Collins & J. L. Horn (Eds.), *Best methods for the analysis of change: Recent advances, unanswered questions, future directions* (pp. 276–298). Washington, DC: American Psychological Association.

Meredith, W., & Tisak, J. (1984). *"Tuckerizing" curves.* Paper presented at the annual meeting of the Psychometric Society, Santa Barbara, California.

Meredith, W., & Tisak, J. (1990). Latent curve analysis. *Psychometrika, 55*(1), 107–122.

Miller, R. G., Jr. (1986). *Beyond ANOVA: Basics of applied statistics.* New York: Wiley.

Muthén, B. O. (1987). *LISCOMP: Analysis of linear structural equations with a comprehensive measurement model.* Mooresville, IN: Scientific Software, Inc.

Muthén, B. O. (1989). Latent variable modeling in heterogeneous populations. *Psychometrika, 54*(4), 557–585.

Muthén, B. O. (1991). Analysis of longitudinal data using latent variable models with varying parameters. In L. M. Collins & J. L. Horn (Eds.), *Best methods for the analysis of change: Recent advances, unanswered questions, future directions* (pp. 1–17). Washington, DC: American Psychological Association.

Muthén, B. O. (1992, September). *Latent variable modeling of growth with missing data and multilevel data.* Paper presented at the Seventh International Conference on Multivariate Analysis, Barcelona, Spain.

Muthén, B. O., & Satorra, A. (1989). Multilevel aspects of varying parameters in structural models. In D. Bock (Ed.), *Multilevel analysis of educational data* (pp. 87–99). San Diego, CA: Academic Press.

Rao, C. R. (1958). Some statistical methods for the comparison of growth curves. *Biometrics, 14,* 1–17.

Rogosa, D. R., Brandt, D., & Zimowski, M. (1982). A growth curve approach to the measurement of change. *Psychological Bulletin, 90,* 726–748.

Rogosa, D. R., & Willett, J. B. (1985). Understanding correlates of change by modeling individual differences in growth. *Psychometrika, 50,* 203–228.

SAS Institute. (1991). *User's guide: Statistics, Version 6.* Cary, NC: Author.

Sayer, A. G., & Willett, J. B. (1995). Does chronic illness affect academic progress?: An example of the integration of individual growth modeling and covariance structure analysis. Manuscript submitted for review.

Tisak, J., & Meredith, W. (1990). Descriptive and associative developmental models. In A. Von Eye (Ed.), *Statistical methods in longitudinal research* (Vol. 2, pp. 387–406). New York: Academic Press.

Tucker, L. R. (1958). Determination of parameters of a functional relation by factor analysis. *Psychometrika, 23,* 19–23.

Willett, J. B. (1985). *Investigating systematic individual differences in academic growth. Dissertation Abstracts International, 46,* 2863B (University Microfilms No. DA85-22251)

Willett, J. B. (1988). Questions and answers in the measurement of change. In E. Z. Rothkopf (Ed.), *Review of research in education* (Vol. 15, pp. 345–422). Washington, DC: American Educational Research Association.

Willett, J. B. (1989). Some results on reliability for the longitudinal measurement of change: Implications for the design of studies of individual growth. *Educational and Psychological Measurement, 49,* 587–602.

Willett, J. B. (1994). Measuring change more effectively by modeling individual change over time. In T. Husen & T. N. Postlethwaite (Eds.), *The international encyclopedia of education* (2nd ed.). Oxford, England: Pergamon Press.

Willett, J. B., & Sayer, A. G. (1994). Using covariance structure analysis to detect correlates and predictors of change. *Psychological Bulletin, 116,* 363–381.

Williamson, G. L. (1986). Assessing academic growth on multiple measures. *Dissertation Abstracts International, 47,* 4368A (University Microfilms No. DA87-07764)

Williamson, G. L., Appelbaum, M., & Epanchin, A. (1991). Longitudinal analyses of academic achievement. *Journal of Educational Measurement, 28*(1), 61–76.

CHAPTER SIX

A Hierarchy of Univariate and Multivariate Structural Times Series Models

Scott L. Hershberger
University of Kansas

Peter C. M. Molenaar
University of Amsterdam

Sherry E. Corneal
Pennsylvania State University

This chapter discusses a hierarchy of univariate and multivariate time series models. The term *hierarchy* was selected to suggest an ordering of complexity and generality among the models. Although the models differ on these two dimensions, they share two very important characteristics. As time series models, the models attempt to describe the behavior of a process across multiple occasions; in this chapter, the process is the emotional response patterns underlying daughter–father and stepdaughter–stepfather relationships. Yet, time series models of psychological processes are little employed despite their obvious appropriateness for describing developmental phenomena. Among the reasons given for this neglect include the perceived difficulty of the models, the necessity of collecting data across a large number of occasions, and a reflexive reliance on the repeated measures analysis of variance (MANOVA) paradigm (Glass, Willson, & Gottman, 1975). These conceptions concerning time series analyses underline the importance of the second characteristic the models share: All are relatively simple to analyze and do not require an extraordinary number of observations for their resolution, at least relative to the uniqueness of the information extractable from them. In this chapter, we are concerned with describing how some common, not-so-common, and original time series models may be resolved through a structural equation modeling (SEM) approach. We hope having another tractable analytic tool will encourage the broader use of time series methodology. For each model, we provide a basic description of the model, how the model may be analyzed through SEM, and the results of fitting the model to a specific data set. Throughout, the emphasis is on a confirmatory approach to modeling (i.e., specific factor structure is proposed), as well as a group comparison approach (i.e., stepdaughters are compared with daughters). LISREL-8 (Jöreskog & Sörbom, 1993) was selected as the SEM program, although any one of several others (e.g., EQS, Bentler, 1992) would have done equally as well. Of special note, all of the models discussed in this chapter describe phenomena in the time domain. Although frequency domain time series models have merit for behavioral and social science research, their implementation within current SEM programs is far more complex than in the time domain.

DATA

Seven daughters and seven stepdaughters were asked to keep a daily record of interactions that took place with their fathers or stepfathers. Examples of common interactions that took place are mealtimes, conversations, leisure activities, arguments, and routine activities (e.g., a trip to the store, a greeting, a request to or from family members). Data collection was terminated when 80 interactions were collected from each participant.

The measure used was the Positive and Negative Affect Schedule (PANAS; Watson, Clark, & Tellegen, 1988). This instrument is a 20-item inventory designed to measure emotions that characterize positive and negative affect simply and expediently; 8 emotions were added for this sample to measure a broader range of emotions. For each emotion, the possible responses are ordered along a 5-point Likert-type scale, and ranged from 1 (*very slightly or not at all*) to 5 (*extremely*). The 28 emotions were categorized into four factors: Anger, Involvement, Anxiety, and Affection. Table 6.1 indicates under which of the four factors each emotion is placed. All of the analyses reported in this chapter are conducted at the level of the four factors. In addition, it should be noted that only one of the seven

TABLE 6.1
Observed Variable Composition of the Four Factors

Anger	Involvement	Anxiety	Affection
Not wanted	Interested	Nervous	Liking
Distressed	Enthusiasm	Jittery	Accepted
Upset	Excited	Scared	Loved
Irritated	Inspired	Ashamed	Satisfied
Discouraged	Alert	Afraid	Proud
Hostile	Attentive		Content
Strong	Active		Close
Determined			
Humiliated			

28 × 80 data matrices of the daughters, as well as, only one of the seven 28 × 80 data matrices of the stepdaughters, were used in the analyses reported in this chapter. The selection of the two data matrices was based on which of the seven daughters and which of the seven stepdaughters had the most complete data across the 80 occasions, and which of the daughters' and stepdaughters' series had the greatest variability across time. Hershberger, Corneal, and Molenaar (1994) provided further details and preliminary analyses of this sample.

Definitions

Before describing the time series models, some basic terminology is needed.

Lagged Covariances. Lagged covariances provide information concerning how strongly measurements taken at earlier occasions are related to measurements taken at later occasions. The order of the lag signifies the distance between the occasions. A zero-order lagged covariance between two variables may be thought of as the covariance calculated between two columns of a data matrix, the rows representing different occasions. The first-order lagged covariance between the two variables is calculated by shifting one variable's column relative to the other variable's column down one row or occasion, the number of shifts down are equal to the order of the lag. A variable can also be lagged on itself by correlating its column with the same column shifted down the desired number of occasions; the covariance between a variable's column with its nonshifted counterpart is simply its variance.

One difficulty with the interpretation of lagged covariances is immediately apparent. The calculation of a lagged covariance results in the loss of two data points (occasions) for every unit increase in the order of the lag. This loss of data places a limit on the desirable interval size of the lag for most of the typically short time trajectories studied in the social and behavioral sciences. Further, it would seem reasonable to calculate each lagged covariance using a sample size that represents the actual number of data points contributing to the covariance because it yields an unbiased estimator. However, use of the full sample (occasions) N is preferable because it yields an estimate that often has a smaller mean square error (Jenkins & Watts, 1968). For users of SEM programs, the use of a common N is imperative because standard errors, significance tests, and other information provided are all given under the assumption that the same sample size pertains to each covariance. In practice, the order of the lag is so minor that it does not cause concern about the size of the N used.

Block Toeplitz Matrices. Time series analyses that model the lagged covariance structure among a set of variables frequently employ a toeplitz transform of the variances and covariances. A toeplitz transform replicates the symmetric blocks of 0-lagged covariances and higher order asymmetric blocks of lagged covariances so as to construct a variance–covariance matrix that is square and symmetric, overcoming the difficulties presented by the asymmetry of lagged covariances. Let $A(0)$ represent a symmetric variance–covariance matrix of 0-lagged covariances, $A(1)$ an asymmetric variance–covariance matrix of first-order lagged covariances, and $A(s)$ an asymmetric matrix of higher order $(s > 1)$ lagged covariances. The incorporation of $A(0)$, $A(1)$, and $A(s)$ into a single matrix using the toeplitz transform produces:

$$
A = \begin{bmatrix}
A(0) & & & \\
A(1) & A(0) & & \\
A(s) & A(1) & A(0) & \\
A(s+1) & A(s) & A(1) & A(0)
\end{bmatrix}
$$

By duplicating the blocks of variance–covariance matrices in a diagonal fashion, the square symmetry of a typical variance–covariance matrix is created.

An important point that should be emphasized is that covariance functions organized in a block toeplitz matrix imply the assumption of stationarity due to the invariance of the elements with respect to shifts in the direction of the main diagonal (Caines, 1988).

Autocorrelation Functions. In the special case where a variable is lagged on itself, the covariance is referred to as an *autocovariance.* A standardized autocovariance is referred to as an *autocorrelation.* Autocorrelation functions play an important role in time series model identification. An autocorrelation function is constructed between a variable and the same variable lagged successively, the magnitude of the autocorrelation being a function of the order of the lag. Closely related to the autocorrelation function is the *partial autocorrelation* function, representing a series of autocorrelations, where given the *s*th lagged autocorrelation, all *s*-1 prior autocorrelations are partialled from it. Less commonly used, but perhaps even more informative for the detection of deterministic trends, is the *inverse autocorrelation function* (Chatfield, 1980). This function may best be understood as the autocorrelation function of a series whose parameters are the complements or alternatives of the series (Schmitz, 1990).

Stationarity. An *m*-dimensional observed time series may be defined by the transposed vector:

$$y(t) = \{y_1(t), \cdots, y_m(t)\}'$$

where m refers to the number of variables measured on an individual at each of the k occasions. It is assumed that $y(t)$ is generated by the finite-dimensional probability distributions

$$P(y;t) = Prob[y(t) < y],$$

$$P(y_1, y_2; t_1, t_2) = Prob[y(t_1) < y_1; y(t_2) < y_2], \; etc.$$

As a random, time-dependent function, $y(t)$ has first-order mean and second-order covariance functions. If the mean function is a constant,

$$E[y(t)] = c_y,$$

then $y(t)$ is referred to as first-order stationary. When the covariance function only depends on the order of the lag between t_1 and t_2, $y(t)$ is referred to as second-order stationary:

$$E[y(t_1), y(t_2)'] = C_y(t_2 - t_1) = C_y(s), s = t_2 - t_1.$$

If $y(t)$ is both first- and second-order stationary, it is called weakly stationary. When all of $y(t)$s other, higher order moments are stationary as well, $y(t)$ is called strictly stationary. Identifying a time series as at least weakly stationary is critical for appropriately estimating its mean and covariance from any single realization of the series. This implies that the series has no deterministic trend (a rising or falling mean), and that its covariance function is invariant under a translation along the time axis.

Random Shocks (White Noise, Innovations). Nearly all time series models incorporate a stochastic component, referred to as either a random shock or white noise, or occasionally, as an *innovation*, to denote the novelty of this effect at a particular occasion. Random shocks (ε) are assumed to have the following properties:

$$E(\varepsilon_t) = 0,$$

$$var(\varepsilon_t) = \sigma_\varepsilon^2,$$

$$\gamma_k = E(\varepsilon_t \varepsilon_{t+k}) = \begin{cases} \sigma_\varepsilon^2, \; k = 0, \\ 0, \; k \neq 0, \end{cases}$$

$$\rho_k = \frac{\gamma_k}{\sigma_\varepsilon^2} = \begin{cases} 1, \; k = 0, \\ 0, \; k \neq 0, \end{cases}$$

where γ and ρ are general covariance and correlation functions, respectively.

Model-Fitting Criteria. Five incremental fit indices are reported in this chapter when various models are compared:

1. *Normed Fit Index (NFI*; Bentler & Bonett, 1980):

$$\frac{\chi^2_{null} - \chi^2_{target}}{\chi^2_{null}}.$$

2. *Non-normed Fit Index (NNFI*; Bentler & Bonett, 1980):

$$\frac{\dfrac{\chi^2_{null}}{df_{null}} - \dfrac{\chi^2_{target}}{df_{target}}}{\dfrac{\chi^2_{null}}{df_{null}} - 1}.$$

3. *Akaike's* (1987) *Information Criterion (AIC):*

$$\chi^2_{target} - 2df_{target},$$

expressed as an incremental fit index (Marsh, Balla, & McDonald, 1988; Wood & Brown, 1994):

$$\frac{AIC_{target} - AIC_{null}}{df_{null} - \chi^2_{null}}.$$

4. *Schwarz's* (1978) *Bayesian Information Criterion (SBIC):*

$$\chi^2_{target} - \ln(N)df_{target},$$

expressed as an incremental fit index (Marsh et al., 1988; Wood & Brown, 1994):

$$\frac{SBIC_{target} - SBIC_{null}}{df - \ln(N) - \chi^2_{null}}.$$

5. *Hannan–Quinn* (1979) *Criterion (HQ):*

$$\chi^2_{target} - c(\ln(\ln(N)))2df_{target}, \; c = 1,$$

expressed as an incremental fit index for this analysis:

$$\frac{HQ_{target} - HQ_{null}}{df - c(\ln(\ln(N))) - \chi^2_{null}}.$$

When comparing models, smaller values of the AIC, SBIC, and HQ indexes are considered desirable.

UNIVARIATE AUTOREGRESSIVE INTEGRATED MOVING AVERAGE (ARIMA) (p, d, q) AND MULTIVARIATE (P, D, Q) TIME SERIES MODELS

In this section, a general description of a time series model is given, followed by a discussion of its SEM form, and then the results of applying the model to the stepdaughter/daughter data are presented.

Model Description

Before combining the three autoregressive integrated moving-average parameters in *ARIMA* (*p,d,q*) models, where *p,d,* and *q* are univariate autoregression, differencing, and moving-average parameters, respectively, into one equation, each equation for each component is discussed separately.

The univariate equation for an *AR(p)* is:

$$y_t = \phi_1 y_{t-1} + \phi y_{t-2} + \ldots + \phi_p y_{t-p} + \varepsilon_t,$$

where ϕ and ε are scalars. This equation expresses the relation between one occasion and *p* preceding occasions, the number of preceding occasions corresponding to the order of the autoregressive process. The *AR(p)* described here is stationary; the stationarity arising from certain algebraic criteria imposed on the coefficients (Caines, 1988).

Figure 6.1 displays the autocorrelation, partial autocorrelation, and inverse autocorrelation functions expected when *AR(p)* = 2. For stationary models, the *AR* autocorrelation function should decrease exponentially or sinusoidally, the partial correlations corresponding to lag > *p* should equal zero, and the inverse autocorrelation function should decrease sinusoidally.

A multivariate autoregressive process of order *P* [*AR(P)*] may be expressed as:

$$y_t = \Phi_1 y_{t-1} + \Phi_p y_{t-p} + \varepsilon_t$$

where Φ_i, *i* = 1, . . . , *p* are $M \times M$ matrices of parameters and ε_t is a $M \times 1$ white noise vector. Both Φ_P and ε_t provide information concerning the univariate process of each variable, and the multivariate processes occurring among the variables. Significant diagonal elements in Φ indicate the order of the autoregressive process for each variable, and the off-diagonal elements indicate the order of the lagged relation between the variables.

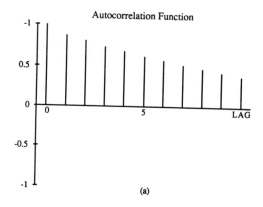

(a)

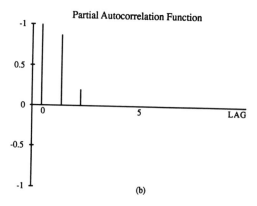

(b)

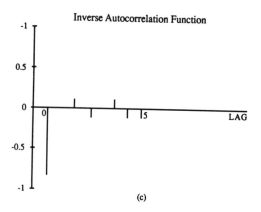

(c)

FIG. 6.1. Autocorrelation functions for *AR(2)* model.

166

As in the univariate case, the stationarity of the *AR(P)* process implies algebraic constraints placed on the coefficients.

In practice, autocorrelation, partial autocorrelation, and inverse autocorrelation functions for the *cross-correlations* among the variables would be inspected to determine *AR(P)*. This approach is preferable to the inspection of univariate autocorrelation functions when a set of variables is involved. In this chapter, prior to the time series analysis, we have combined the variables into orthogonal, common factors. When the goal is to determine the order of the autoregressive process of the common factor underlying the set of variables, the factor's univariate autocorrelation functions should be inspected. It is at the combined factorial level, and not at the level of the correlated observed variables, that our interest lies.

The univariate equation for a *MA(q)* process is:

$$y(t) = \varepsilon_t - \theta_1 \varepsilon_{t-1} - \theta_2 \varepsilon_{t-2} - \ldots - \theta_q \varepsilon_{t-q}.$$

This equation expresses the relation between one occasion and a weighted average of θ preceding random shocks, the number of preceding shocks corresponding to the order of the moving-average process. θ_q and ε_t are again scalars. Figure 6.2 displays the autocorrelation, partial autocorrelation, and inverse autocorrelation functions expected when *MA(q)* = 2. For stationary models, the MA autocorrelation function should equal zero for lags greater than *q*, the partial correlation should decrease exponentially or sinusoidally, and the inverse autocorrelation function should decrease sinusoidally.

A multivariate moving-average [*MA(Q)*] may be expressed as:

$$y_t = \varepsilon_t - \Theta_1 \varepsilon_{t-1} - \Theta_2 \varepsilon_{t-2} - \ldots - \Theta_Q \varepsilon_{t-Q}$$

where Θ is an $M \times M$ matrix of parameters and ε is defined as an $M \times 1$ vector of white noise. As in the case of the autoregressive parameter, we are concerned with the examination of the univariate moving-average process.

As previously noted, stationarity is desirable for time series analyses. Frequently, a nonstationary time series may be made so by differencing the time series, $y_t - y_{t-d}$, where *d* refers to the order of the difference. A nonstationary time series is most easily detected when the slope of the autocorrelation plot is fairly flat. Conversely, an over-differenced time series is most easily detected by an exponentially decreasing inverse autocorrelation plot (Cleveland, 1972). When both *AR* and *MA* processes co-occur in a differenced time series, the univariate *ARIMA (p,d,q)* equation is:

$$y_t = \phi_1 Y_{t-1} + \phi_2 y_{t-2} + \ldots + \phi_p y_{t-p} + \varepsilon_t - \theta_1 \varepsilon_{t-1} - \theta_2 \varepsilon_{t-2} - \ldots - \theta_q \varepsilon_{t-q}$$

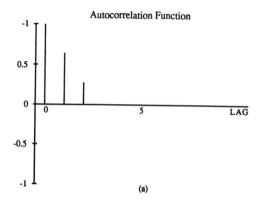

(a)

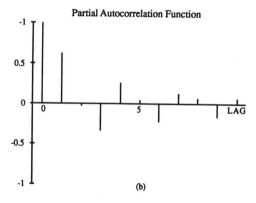

(b)

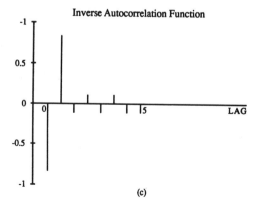

(c)

FIG. 6.2. Autocorrelation functions for *MA(2)* model.

168

where d may be of any feasible order. The comparable multivariate *ARIMA* *(P,D,Q)* equation is:

$$y_t = \Phi_1 y_{t-1} + \Phi_2 y_{t-2} + \ldots + \Phi_p y_{t-p} + \varepsilon_t - \Theta_1 \varepsilon_{t-1} - \Theta_2 \varepsilon_{t-2} - \ldots - \Theta_Q \varepsilon_{t-Q}.$$

Sufficient criteria for the stationarity of either an $ARMA(p,q)$ or $ARMA(P,Q)$ are: (a) the autoregressive and moving-average coefficients do not depend on time, (b) the autoregressive coefficients obey the necessary algebraic criteria, and (c) the variance of the innovations do not depend on time. Note that when the series is stationary, and therefore does not require differencing, it is referred to as either an *ARMA (p,q)* or *ARMA (P,Q)* process. In this chapter, a series is always referred to as $ARMA(p,q)$ due to the use of covariance functions organized in block toeplitz form, which are stationary by implication.

SEM Form

Figure 6.3 displays an *ARMA (2,2)* model spanning six measurement occasions. We are testing maximally for $p = 2$ and $q = 2$ because models with empirically higher terms are rare (Kendall & Ord, 1990). A series of six measurement occasions has been selected primarily for reasons of conciseness in the SEM setup.

It is also important to re-emphasize the character of the covariances tested in this analysis: The data are the five lagged covariances computable from a series of six measurement occasions, organized in block toeplitz form. For example, if $s =$ the order of the lag, then when $s(0) = .92$, $s(1)$

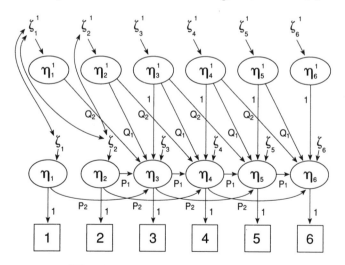

FIG. 6.3. Path diagram of *ARMA(2,2)* model.

$= .27$, $s(2) = .17$, $s(3) = .04$, $s(4) = .25$, and $s(5) = .13$, the block toeplitz matrix analyzed appears as:

$$\begin{bmatrix} 0.92 & & & & & \\ 0.27 & 0.92 & & & & \\ 0.17 & 0.27 & 0.92 & & & \\ 0.04 & 0.17 & 0.27 & 0.92 & & \\ 0.25 & 0.04 & 0.17 & 0.27 & 0.92 & \\ 0.13 & 0.25 & 0.04 & 0.17 & 0.27 & 0.92 \end{bmatrix}$$

The order of the *ARIMA* process will be identified through the examination of the relative significance of p_1, p_2, q_1, q_2. Appendix A contains the LISREL instructions for evaluating the model.

Results

Three steps were followed in the evaluation of the *ARIMA* model for the four factors: (a) the ARIMA procedure in the SAS/ETS statistical software program (SAS, 1993) was used to identify the order of p and q in each of the two groups (daughter and stepdaughters) as a way to validate the results from the SEM; (b) a two-group, SEM analysis was conducted testing for the equality of the *ARMA (2,2)* structures; and (c) given the equality of the *ARMA* structures, a series of hierarchically nested models were tested to assess the minimal order of p and q indicated by LISREL. The null or baseline model was an *ARMA(0,0)*, which essentially describes a white noise process.

Table 6.2 presents the results of the *ARMA* model fitting. When Model 1, the baseline model, is compared with Model 2, which equates the *ARMA(2,2)* structure between the two groups, an appreciable increase in fit appears for the factors, with the possible exception of Affection. For Affection, the fit indices χ^2_{diff}, *NFI*, *AIC*, and *HQ* suggest a nonsignificant improvement in fit, while *NNFI* and *SBIC* suggest the opposite. All fit indices indicate the superiority of Model 3, which allows the *ARMA(2,2)* structure to differ between daughters and stepdaughters, although the superiority of this fit compared with Model 2 is modest. Equating the structures of daughters and stepdaughters, and balancing the criteria of fit and parsimony, Anxiety is best described by an *AR(1)* model; Involvement, by an *AR(2)* model; Anger, by an *AR(1)* model, and Affection by the *ARMA(0,0)* model. Indeed, the problem of overparameterization is best illustrated by Involvement, where the *AIC* and *HQ* information indices penalize (in terms of relative fit) nearly all models with nonzero parameters.

Table 6.2 also indicates the individual parameters identified as significant by the separate evaluation of daughters and stepdaughters, in both LISREL and SAS. There is perfect agreement between the two programs for the nonexistence of any significant parameters for Affection and Anger, and near agreement for significant parameters with Involvement and Anxiety.

TABLE 6.2
ARIMA Modeling Results for Daughters and Stepdaughters

Model	$\chi^2_{diff}(df)$	NFI	NNFI	AIC	SBIC	HQ
			Anger			
1	-	-	-	−33.05	−130.71	−11.63
2	43.43(7)	.89	5.39	3.75	3.55	5.10
3	44.37(9)	.91	5.51	3.32	1.38	4.80
4	42.05(3)	.86	5.31	4.53	8.10	5.81
5	40.39(3)	.83	5.08	4.33	7.63	5.56
6	38.70(2)	.79	4.88	4.36	8.39	4.07
7	41.79(2)	.86	5.32	4.94	10.02	6.28
8	38.21(1)	.78	4.85	4.55	9.48	5.67
9	32.26(2)	.66	4.04	3.70	7.15	4.75
10	27.87(1)	.57	3.45	3.25	6.58	4.08
		p_1	q_1	p_2	q_2	
D-LIS		-	-	-	-	
S-LIS		-	-	-	-	
D-SAS		-	-	-	-	
S-SAS		-	-	-	-	
			Involvement			
1	-	-	-	−26.42	−124.08	−5.00
2	35.32(7)	.64	2.12	1.46	.46	1.91
3	42.26(11)	.83	2.91	1.66	.19	2.29
4	27.90(3)	.50	1.75	1.50	1.45	1.79
5	25.40(3)	.46	1.62	1.39	1.29	1.68
6	23.01(2)	.41	1.46	1.30	1.40	1.53
7	27.85(2)	.50	1.80	1.64	1.87	1.90
8	9.20(1)	.17	.56	.49	.47	.59
9	21.25(2)	.38	1.33	1.18	1.22	1.40
10	16.48(1)	.30	1.06	.99	1.19	1.15
D-LIS		-	-	-	1.95	
S-LIS		-	-	-	-	
D-SAS		-	−2.43	-	−2.98	
S-SAS		-	-	-	-	
			Anxiety			
1	-	-	-	−52.57	−147.85	−31.67
2	20.74(7)	.76	1.58	.70	.68	1.07
3	24.99(11)	.91	1.93	.08	3.90	.52
4	17.06(2)	.62	1.35	1.04	1.01	1.27
5	14.66(2)	.53	1.14	.85	.72	1.06
6	13.13(2)	.48	1.01	.80	.49	.77
7	16.68(2)	.61	1.21	1.08	.69	1.01
8	13.13(1)	.48	1.04	.89	1.07	1.05
9	11.36(2)	.42	.79	.70	.39	.67
10	10.44(1)	.38	.82	.67	1.27	.94
D-LIS		4.83	−4.80	-	-	
S-LIS		-	-	-	-	
D-SAS		-	-	-	-	
S-SAS		-	−2.90	-	-	

(Continued)

TABLE 6.2
(Continued)

Model	$\chi^2_{diff}(df)$	NFI	NNFI	AIC	SBIC	HQ
			Affection			
1	-	-	-	−51.63	−149.29	−30.21
2	13.39(7)	.44	.93	.06	2.76	.33
3	25.79(9)	.85	2.30	.73	2.18	1.36
4	3.06(3)	.10	.08	.28	1.61	.15
5	.35(3)	.01	.19	.53	2.05	.45
6	.35(2)	.01	.11	.34	1.35	.28
7	3.10(2)	.10	.15	.09	.38	.01
8	.34(1)	.01	.04	.16	.64	.12
9	1.72(2)	.06	.01	.19	.47	.11
10	.26(1)	.01	.05	.16	.66	.13
D-LIS		-	-	-	-	
S-LIS		-	-	-	-	
D-SAS		-	-	-	-	
S-SAS		-	-	-	-	

Note. NFI = Normed Fit Index, NNFI = Non-normed Fit Index, AIC = Akaike's Information Criterion, SBIC = Schwarz-Bayesian Information Criterion, HQ = Hannan-Quinn Criterion.

Model 1: ARMA(0,0) (Null Model);
Model 2: ARMA(2,2): Daughters = Stepdaughters;
Model 3: ARMA(2,2): Daughters ≠ Stepdaughters;
Model 4: ARMA(2,1);
Model 5: ARMA(1,2);
Model 6: ARMA(1,1);
Model 7: AR(2);
Model 8: AR(1);
Model 9: MA(2);
Model 10: MA(1).

D-LIS = Daughter's LISREL solution;
S-LIS = Stepdaughter's LISREL solution;
D-SAS = Daughter's SAS solution;
S-SAS = Stepdaughter's SAS solution.

RANDOM WALK MODELS

Model Description

One of the few inherently nonstationary time series models of interest is the *univariate random walk model*:

$$y_t = \mu_t + \varepsilon_t,$$

$$\mu_t = \mu_{t-1} + \alpha_t,$$

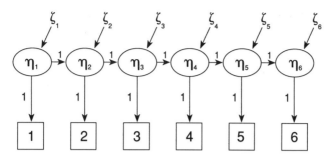

FIG. 6.4. Path diagram of random walk model.

where the prior t-1 occasion is contained within μ_t, with ε_t and α_t denoting measurement errors and random shocks, respectively. In addition to its own random shock, each occasion in a random walk model is influenced by the integration of all previous shocks. Because $\phi_1 = 1$, violating the stationarity assumption in an *AR(1)* model, the random walk model is nonstationary. However, by taking $d = 1$ (differencing once), the random walk model may be made stationary (Harvey, 1989).

SEM Form

A random walk model is simply an *AR(p)* model, with $p = 1$. This model is relatively straightforward to set up in LISREL, requiring only the fixing of each of the βs to unity, and freeing the diagonal of ψ. Figure 6.4 presents a path diagram of the random walk model.

Results

The random walk model was applied to each of the four factors. First, the model parameters were equated between daughters and stepdaughters, and then the parameters were free to differ between the two groups. The results of these analyses may be summarized succinctly: In no case was an adequately fitting model produced. This pertained to each of the four factors, regardless of whether the groups were equated or not. Given the apparent restrictedness of the random walk model, these results are not too surprising.

P-TECHNIQUE FACTOR ANALYSIS

Model Description

With the use of factor analytic techniques, we move from the analysis of the *ARMA* process of the four factors to the factor analysis of the 28 affective variables. *P*-technique factor analysis involves the factor analysis of covariances among variables, produced from occasion by variable data matrices for a single person. Cattell (1952) pointed out that the factor analysis of multiple measurements collected across multiple occasions on the same person might reveal the latent structure of the data responsible for the observed behavior across time. The P-technique factor analysis model may be expressed as:

$$y(t) = \Lambda \eta(t) + \varepsilon(t), \; t = 0, \pm 1, \ldots,$$

with Λ, $(N \times R)$, η, $(R \times 1)$, and ε, $(N \times 1)$. The covariance function of the model is:

$$C(0) = \Lambda \Xi(0) \Lambda^T + \Theta(0),$$

where $COV(0)$ signifies a matrix of nonlagged covariances. Although rarely noted explicitly, the P-technique factor analysis model requires at least weak stationarity.

SEM Form

As implemented in this study, the P-technique factor analysis model is merely a confirmatory measurement model. Due to its familiarity, further details concerning the organization of the model in LISREL are not given here.

Results

As a first step in the P-technique factor analysis, the 0-lagged covariance matrices of the daughters and stepdaughters were tested for equality, with equality rejected by a significant chi-square goodness-of-fit value: $\chi^2(406, N = 160) = 774.40, p < .001$. For daughters, an orthogonal four factor structure was rejected: $\chi^2(350, N = 80) = 617.99, p < .001$. Significant improvement in fit occurred with the addition of either an oblique factor structure ($\chi^2_{344} = 541.17, p < .001; \chi^2_{diff,6} = 76.82, p < .001$), or correlated measurement errors within each of the factors ($\chi^2_{345} = 603.45, p < .001; \chi^2_{diff,5} = 14.54, p < .05$). For stepdaughters, an orthogonal four-factor structure was also rejected: $\chi^2(350, N = 80) = 890.72, p < .001$. The incorporation of either an oblique factor structure ($\chi^2_{344} = 843.93, p < .001; \chi^2_{diff,6} = 46.79, p < .001$) or correlated errors within factors ($\chi^2_{336} = 736.17, p < .001; \chi^2_{diff,14} = 154.55, p < .001$) improved the fit significantly.

In the correlated measurement errors model, the errors of some of the observed indicators of a factor were allowed to correlate with each other within the factor; errors were not allowed to correlate across factors. Allowing measurement errors to correlate in this way would, if all possible measurement error correlations were evaluated, completely explain the within-time correlations among the observed variables. The detection of significant correlated measurement errors within factors suggests an un-modelled source of commonality among the observed variables. This commonality could in theory be attributable to the influence of higher order (lagged) processes in the data.

STATIONARY DYNAMIC FACTOR ANALYSIS (SDFA) MODEL

Model Description

The SDFA may be considered a generalization of the P-technique factor analysis model that includes the lagged-covariance structure among the variables (Molenaar, 1985). Under ordinary P-technique factor analysis, in which the covariances are of 0-lag (the covariances are among measurements taken within the same occasion), the obtained factor structure only represents the relations between variables within a single interval of time. The incorporation of lagged covariances in SDFA opens up the possibility of uncovering relations among variables across a specified interval of time, an interval defined by the order of the lag.

The SDFA model can be expressed as:

$$y(t) = \sum_{u=0}^{s} \Lambda(u)\eta(t-u) + \varepsilon(t),$$

where $y(t)$ is a weighted function of s matrices of lagged factor loadings, $\Lambda(u)\eta(t), \Lambda(u+1)\eta\ (t-1), \ldots, \Lambda(s)\eta(t-s)$ and a vector of random noise. The covariance function of the SDFA model is:

$$COV(u) = \sum_{v=0}^{s} \Lambda(v)\Xi\Lambda(u-v)' + \Theta(u),$$

where $\Lambda(u)$ is a series of $(M \times R)$ matrices of lagged loadings on the latent factors, $\Xi(u)$ is a series of $(R \times R)$ matrices of lagged covariances among the latent factors, and $\Theta(u)$ is a series of diagonal $(M \times M)$ white noise matrices.

Figure 6.5 displays a path diagram of the SDFA model. Note that within and between occasions, the covariances among the observed variables are a function (Λ) of the 0-lagged factors and a function (Λ^*) of the higher order lagged factors. Note also that a 0-lagged error of measurement is correlated with its higher order lagged counterpart.

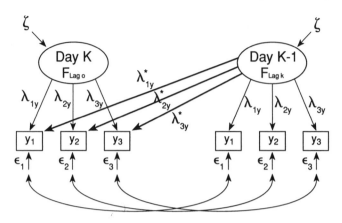

FIG. 6.5. Path diagram of dynamic factor analysis model.

SEM Form

Appendix B lists the LISREL program required to conduct the SDFA. For purposes of clarity, the organization of one model is described. Given a covariance structure among a set of y variables:

$$COV = \Lambda \Xi \Lambda^T + \Theta,$$

where COV and Θ are dimensional covariance matrices, $p(a+1) \times (a+1)p$, Ξ is an identity matrix, $q(a+s+1) \times (a+s+1)q$, and Λ is a dimensional matrix, $p(a+1) \times (a+s+1)q$, of factor loadings. Here, p refers to the number of observed variables, q to the number of factors, a to the *window* size, and s to the number of lags. The window size refers to the number of occasions used to construct each of the lags. Both COV and Θ are block toeplitz matrices.

Consider a four-factor, one-lag model, in which $a=1$, $s=1$, $p=28$, and $q=4$:

$$COV = \begin{bmatrix} COV(0) & \\ COV(1) & COV(0) \end{bmatrix}; \ (56 \times 56)$$

$$\Lambda = \begin{bmatrix} \Lambda(0) & \Lambda(1) & 0 \\ 0 & \Lambda(0) & \Lambda(1) \end{bmatrix}; \ (56 \times 12)$$

$$\Theta = \begin{bmatrix} \Theta(0) & \\ \Theta(1) & \Theta(0) \end{bmatrix}; \ (56 \times 56)$$

$$\Xi = I_q; \ (12 \times 12)$$

In this model, the covariance matrix is of order 56×56 because there are 56 observed variables (each of the 28 observed variables for both the 0-lag and first-lags), and therefore, the Λ matrix is of order 56×12 because each lag is represented by four factors, $(1(a) + 1(s) + 1) \times 4 = 12$.

Results

Due to the inequality of the 0-lagged covariance matrices of the daughters and stepdaughters, higher order lagged covariance matrices must necessarily be nonequivalent as well because whatever the equivalency status of higher order lagged covariances, the 0-lagged covariances form a part of the block toeplitz structure. For both daughters and stepdaughters, the SDFA model was rejected: for daughters, $\chi^2(1484, N = 80) = 2487.57$, $p < .001$; for stepdaughters, $\chi^2(1484, N = 80) = 2959.27$, $p < .001$. Because P-technique factor analysis (with uncorrelated factors and measurement errors) and SDFA use different covariance matrices, it is strictly inappropriate to conduct a chi-square difference test between the two models. We can compare their information indices: for daughters, $AIC_P = -82.01$, $AIC_{SDFA} = -480.43$; $SBIC_P = -915.72$, $SBIC_{SDFA} = -4015.36$; $HQ_P = 100.86$, $HQ_{SDFA} = 294.94$; for stepdaughters, $AIC_P = 190.72$, $AIC_{SDFA} = -8.73$; $SBIC_P = -642.99$, $SBIC_{SDFA} = -3543.66$; $HQ_P = 373.59$, $HQ_{SDFA} = 766.64$. Both the AIC and $SBIC$ indicate that the increase in chi-square for the SDFA model was more than compensated by the increase in degrees of freedom, relative to P-technique factor analysis.

NONSTATIONARY DYNAMIC FACTOR ANALYSIS MODEL (NDFA)

Molenaar, de Gooijer, and Schmitz (1992) proposed a nonstationary extension of the stationary dynamic factor analysis model. In the NDFA model, the temporal effects of trends are not removed prior to the analysis, but instead incorporated as an influence on the latent factor series. Repeating the equation for the SDFA model given above:

$$y(t) = \sum_{u=0}^{s} \Lambda(u)\eta(t - u) + \varepsilon(t) ,$$

we add the linear trend model:

$$\eta(t) = \gamma\tau(t) + w(t) ,$$

where γ is $(R \times 1)$, $\tau(t)$ denotes the linear trend, and $w(t)$ is a stochastic term. The covariance function of the NDFA model is then:

$$COV(u) = \sum_{v=0}^{s} \Lambda(v) \left\{ \varpi\varpi' + I_{(w+S+1)n} \right\} \Lambda' + \Theta$$

where ϖ is the $(w + s + 1)n$-dimensional vector $\{\gamma', \ldots, \gamma'\}'$, w = window size, and s = number of lags.

SEM Form

Implementation of the NDFA model requires a simple addition to the SDFA model: the construction of a time-ordered vector equal in length to that of the observed series, and the addition of this new variable to the existing set of variables. For example, because the number of observations on the daughters and stepdaughters was 80, we created a new variable with values from 1 to 80. The scaling of this time variable is completely arbitrary. During the construction of the block toeplitz matrix, both the original form and the lagged form of this time variable were added to the matrix, although it is only necessary to select the nonlagged form of the time variable for the analysis. With this new observed variable, one then creates a second-order factor model in which the observed variable is equated to a latent exogenous variable; the exogenous latent variable is allowed to influence all the lower order lagged and nonlagged factors. The values of the γ coefficients connecting the higher and lower order factors provide the values of the trend coefficients unique to each factor. Figure 6.6 presents a path diagram of the NDFA model (an extension of Fig. 6.5), and Appendix C the LISREL instructions. Note that Λ and Θ are dimensionalized in the SDFA model $\Gamma (w + s + 1)q \times (w + s + 1)q$ as:

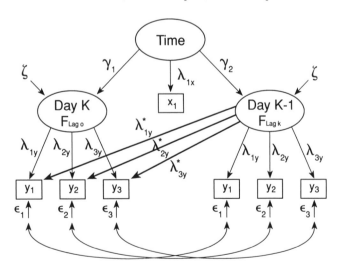

FIG. 6.6. Path diagram of nonstationary dynamic factor analysis model.

$$\Gamma = \begin{bmatrix} \gamma & 0 & \dots & 0 \\ 0 & \gamma & \dots & 0 \\ \vdots & \vdots & \vdots & \vdots \\ 0 & 0 & \dots & \gamma \end{bmatrix},$$

and ψ $(w + s + 1)q \times (w + s + 1)q$ is:

$$\Psi = \begin{bmatrix} I_q & \Psi(1) & \dots & \Psi(w+s) \\ \Psi(1) & I_q & \dots & \Psi(w+s-1) \\ \vdots & \vdots & \vdots & \vdots \\ \Psi(w+s) & \Psi(w+s-1) & \dots & I_q \end{bmatrix}.$$

However, the Γ matrix collapses to a vector in the LISREL instructions for the model given in Appendix C, as explained by Molenaar et al. (1992).

Results

The one-lagged, four-factor NDFA model for both the daughters and step-daughters was rejected: for daughters, $\chi^2(1528, N = 80) = 2658.71$, $p < .001$; for stepdaughters, $\chi^2(1528, N = 80) = 3192.73$, $p < .001$. The information indices for daughters are: $AIC_{NDFA} = -397.29$; $SBIC_{NDFA} = -4037.03$; $HQ_{NDFA} = 401.07$; for stepdaughters: $AIC_{NDFA} = 136.73$; $SBIC_{NDFA} = -3503.01$; $HQ_{NDFA} = 935.09$. When these information indices are compared with their counterparts for the SDFA model, it is not surprising that for the most part, they differ minimally: the data were stationary and did not require the incorporation of a linear trend term.

It is of some interest to perform a nonstationary P-technique factor analysis (NP) in order to assess how that model fares with the addition of a linear trend term. The nonstationary P-technique model was rejected for the daughters, $\chi^2(360, N = 80) = 638.36$, $p < .001$, and for the step-daughters, $\chi^2(360, N = 80) = 802.85$, $p < .001$. In this case, the information indices are, for daughters: $AIC_{NP} = -81.64$; $SBIC_{NP} = -939.17$; $HQ_{NP} = 106.46$; and for stepdaughters, $AIC_{NP} = 82.85$; $SBIC_{NP} = -774.68$; $HQ_{NP} = 442.85$. Similar to the SDFA versus NDFA results, little benefit is gained over the P-technique model by incorporating a linear trend term in the NP model.

STATE SPACE MODELS

Model Description

The *state space model* refers to a very general multivariate time series model defined by three simultaneous equations. The first is referred to as the *output measurement equation:*

$$y = H\alpha + Gc + \varepsilon,$$

where:

y = a $N \times 1$ vector of observed output variables;
α = an $q \times 1$ vector of latent state variables, H $(N \times q)$;
c = a $p \times 1$ vector of latent input variables, G $(N \times p)$;
ε = an $N \times 1$ white noise vector.

The second equation is referred to as the *transition equation*:

$$\alpha = T\alpha + Ac + R\eta,$$

where:

η = an $g \times 1$ white noise vector, R $(q \times g)$, A $(q \times p)$ and T $(q \times q)$.

The third equation is referred to as the *input measurement equation*:

$$x = Bc + \delta,$$

where:

x = an $M \times 1$ vector of observed input variables, B $(M \times p)$;
δ = an $M \times 1$ white noise vector.

The model underlying the state space system represents a process wherein a set of latent input variables (c) influences a set of observed output variables (y) directly, and through a system of latent state variables (α); the latent input variables are indicated by a set of observed input variables (x). The state space model is a time-dependent process describing the effect of observed input variables on observed output variables as mediated by their respective latent variables. This is the basis for the generality of the state space model: both the common factors (input and state) responsible for the behavior of an observed series *and* the relations among the factors are identified.

SEM Form

Figure 6.7 presents a path model of the state space model, and Appendix D provides the LISREL instructions for analyzing the model. We may use the model of Fig. 6.7 to illustrate the logic underlying the organization of the SEM.

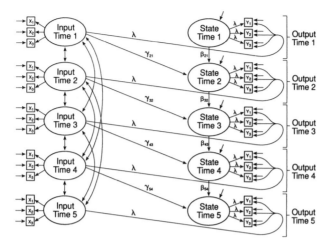

FIG. 6.7. Path diagram of state space model.

In this model, the observed x input measurement equations are defined as:

$$
\begin{bmatrix}
x_{1,1} \\
x_{1,2} \\
x_{1,3} \\
x_{2,1} \\
x_{2,2} \\
x_{2,3} \\
\vdots \\
x_{5,1} \\
x_{5,2} \\
x_{5,3}
\end{bmatrix}
=
\begin{bmatrix}
\lambda_{1,1} & 0 & 0 & 0 & 0 \\
\lambda_{2,1} & 0 & 0 & 0 & 0 \\
\lambda_{3,1} & 0 & 0 & 0 & 0 \\
0 & \lambda_{1,1} & 0 & 0 & 0 \\
0 & \lambda_{2,1} & 0 & 0 & 0 \\
0 & \lambda_{3,1} & 0 & 0 & 0 \\
\vdots & \vdots & \vdots & \vdots & \vdots \\
0 & 0 & 0 & 0 & \lambda_{1,1} \\
0 & 0 & 0 & 0 & \lambda_{2,1} \\
0 & 0 & 0 & 0 & \lambda_{3,1}
\end{bmatrix}
\begin{bmatrix}
\xi_1 \\
\xi_2 \\
\xi_3 \\
\xi_4 \\
\xi_5
\end{bmatrix}
+
\begin{bmatrix}
\delta_1 \\
\delta_2 \\
\delta_3 \\
\delta_1 \\
\delta_2 \\
\delta_3 \\
\vdots \\
\delta_1 \\
\delta_2 \\
\delta_3
\end{bmatrix}
$$

or

$$
x = \Lambda_x \xi + \delta ,
$$

where x is (15×1), representing three observed input variables measured over five occasions; Λ_x is (15×5), representing the loading of each of the three observed input variables on the latent input variable over five occasions; and δ is (15×1), representing the measurement errors of the three observed input variables measured over five occasions. Coefficients constrained to be equal have been given the same notation.

Further, the observed y output measurement equations are defined as:

$$
\begin{bmatrix} y_{1,1} \\ y_{1,2} \\ y_{1,3} \\ y_{2,1} \\ y_{2,2} \\ y_{2,3} \\ \vdots \\ y_{5,1} \\ y_{5,2} \\ y_{5,3} \end{bmatrix}
=
\begin{bmatrix}
\lambda_{1,1} & 0 & 0 & 0 & 0 \\
\lambda_{2,1} & 0 & 0 & 0 & 0 \\
\lambda_{3,1} & 0 & 0 & 0 & 0 \\
0 & \lambda_{1,1} & 0 & 0 & 0 \\
0 & \lambda_{2,1} & 0 & 0 & 0 \\
0 & \lambda_{3,1} & 0 & 0 & 0 \\
\vdots & \vdots & \vdots & \vdots & \vdots \\
0 & 0 & 0 & 0 & \lambda_{1,1} \\
0 & 0 & 0 & 0 & \lambda_{2,1} \\
0 & 0 & 0 & 0 & \lambda_{3,1}
\end{bmatrix}
\begin{bmatrix} \eta_1 \\ \eta_2 \\ \eta_3 \\ \eta_4 \\ \eta_5 \end{bmatrix}
+
\begin{bmatrix}
\lambda_{1,1} & 0 & 0 & 0 & 0 \\
\lambda_{2,1} & 0 & 0 & 0 & 0 \\
\lambda_{3,1} & 0 & 0 & 0 & 0 \\
0 & \lambda_{1,1} & 0 & 0 & 0 \\
0 & \lambda_{2,1} & 0 & 0 & 0 \\
0 & \lambda_{3,1} & 0 & 0 & 0 \\
\vdots & \vdots & \vdots & \vdots & \vdots \\
0 & 0 & 0 & 0 & \lambda_{1,1} \\
0 & 0 & 0 & 0 & \lambda_{2,1} \\
0 & 0 & 0 & 0 & \lambda_{3,1}
\end{bmatrix}
\begin{bmatrix} \xi_1 \\ \xi_2 \\ \xi_3 \\ \xi_4 \\ \xi_5 \end{bmatrix}
+
\begin{bmatrix} \varepsilon_1 \\ \varepsilon_2 \\ \varepsilon_3 \\ \varepsilon_1 \\ \varepsilon_2 \\ \varepsilon_3 \\ \vdots \\ \varepsilon_1 \\ \varepsilon_2 \\ \varepsilon_3 \end{bmatrix}
$$

or

$$ y = \Lambda_y \eta + \Lambda_x \xi + \varepsilon, $$

where y is (15×1), representing three observed output variables measured over five occasions; Λ_y is (15×5), representing the loading of each of the three observed output variables on the latent state variable over five occasions; ε is (15×1), representing the measurement errors of the three observed output variables measured over five occasions; and Λ_x now represents the loading of the three observed output variables on the latent input variable over five occasions.

The structural relations among the latent variables are defined as:

$$
\begin{bmatrix} \eta_1 \\ \eta_2 \\ \eta_3 \\ \eta_4 \\ \eta_5 \end{bmatrix}
=
\begin{bmatrix}
0 & 0 & 0 & 0 & 0 \\
\beta_{21} & 0 & 0 & 0 & 0 \\
0 & \beta_{32} & 0 & 0 & 0 \\
0 & 0 & \beta_{43} & 0 & 0 \\
0 & 0 & 0 & \beta_{54} & 0
\end{bmatrix}
\begin{bmatrix} \eta_1 \\ \eta_2 \\ \eta_3 \\ \eta_4 \\ \eta_5 \end{bmatrix}
+
\begin{bmatrix}
0 & 0 & 0 & 0 & 0 \\
\gamma_{21} & 0 & 0 & 0 & 0 \\
0 & \gamma_{32} & 0 & 0 & 0 \\
0 & 0 & \gamma_{43} & 0 & 0 \\
0 & 0 & 0 & \gamma_{54} & 0
\end{bmatrix}
\begin{bmatrix} \xi_1 \\ \xi_2 \\ \xi_3 \\ \xi_4 \\ \xi_5 \end{bmatrix}
+
\begin{bmatrix} \zeta_1 \\ \zeta_2 \\ \zeta_3 \\ \zeta_4 \\ \zeta_5 \end{bmatrix}
$$

or

$$ \eta_t = B\eta_{t-1} + \Gamma \xi_{t-1} + \zeta_t, $$

where ζ is (5×1), representing the unexplained variance (white noise) of the five latent state variable at each measurement occasion, and other terms are as defined earlier. Note that both latent input and latent state variables affect latent state variables on the subsequent occasion. The LISREL instructions in Appendix D follow the organization of the model as illustrated earlier, except that all observed variables have been defined in terms of y and all latent variables in terms of η.

A very clear illustration of the implementation of one version of the state space model in LISREL is provided by MacCallum and Ashby (1986), although the present analysis extends those authors' example by defining latent instead of observed variable inputs.

Results

As in the prior analyses, the covariances were organized in a block toeplitz matrix. Since the state space model involves the effect of one or more latent input (independent) variables on one or more output (dependent) variables, a recursive relation had to be defined among the four factors. As one example, it seemed most resemble to hypothesize that Involvement at one point in time (the input) would influence Affection at a later point in time (the output).

As in the prior analyses, daughters and stepdaughters were modeled separately. For daughters and stepdaughters, the model pictured in Fig. 6.7 was rejected: $\chi^2(2443, N = 80) = 4166.62$, $p < .001$; $\chi^2(2443, N = 80) = 6717.77$, $p < .001$. Nonetheless, for both daughters and stepdaughters, Involvement on one occasion significantly influenced Affection on the next occasion.

CONCLUDING REMARKS

This chapter presented a number of time series models appropriate for the type of data often of interest to behavioral and social scientists. Two issues not explicitly discussed before deserve at least some mention here due to their practical importance in structural time series modeling.

Difficulties With the Construction of Block Toeplitz Matrices

To our knowledge, no standard statistical software program exists that will directly compute the lagged covariances matrices and then perform a toeplitz transform. In this chapter, a FORTRAN program was used to conduct these tasks. One alternative has been provided by Wood and Brown (1994) who present a program written in the SAS Macro (SAS, 1990a) and SAS IML (SAS, 1990b) languages to construct the lagged covariances and block toeplitz matrices, among other important tasks required in time series modeling.

Model Identification Issues

Nowhere in this chapter have we commented on the restrictions required to achieve model identifiability. For two of the models in particular, SDFA and NDFA, the identification rules are complex, and are more involved than the identification restrictions required for the common factor model. Information concerning model identification may be found in Hershberger et al. (1994), Molenaar (1985, 1989), and Molenaar et al. (1992).

In closing, structural times series modeling is critical for the proper representation of developmental phenomena. Advances in SEM have now made the time series modeling more generally accessible. We hope this chapter has provided examples that will permit researchers to further investigate developmental phenomena.

ACKNOWLEDGMENTS

The authors would like to thank John Nesselroade and Philip Wood for their often insightful comments on the topic of this chapter.

APPENDIX A:
LISREL PROGRAM FOR ARMA(2,2) MODEL

```
ARMA(2,2) MODEL - INVARIANT ACROSS GROUPS
DAUGHTERS
DA NI = 6 MA = CM NO = 80 NG = 2
MO NY = 6 NE = 12 LY = FU,FI TE = ZE PS = SY,FI BE = FU,FI
VA 1.00 LY(1,1) LY(2,2) LY(3,3) LY(4,4) LY(5,5) LY(6,6)
FR PS(7,7)
EQ PS(7,7) PS(8,8) PS(9,9) PS(10,10) PS(11,11) PS(12,12)
FR BE(1,2)
EQ BE(1,2) BE(2,3) BE(3,4) BE(4,5)
FR BE(1,8) BE(1,9)
EQ BE(1,8) BE(2,9) BE(3,10) BE(4,11)
EQ BE(1,9) BE(2,10) BE(3,11) BE(4,12)
VA 1.0 BE(1,7) BE(2,8) BE(3,9) BE(4,10)
VA .99 PS(5,5) PS(6,6)
VA 0.10 PS(6,5)
ST .1 ALL
OU NS IT=250 AD=OFF
STEPDAUGHTERS
DA NI=6 NO=80 MA=CM
MO NY=6 NE=12 LY=FU,FI TE=ZE PS=SY,FI BE=IN
VA 1.00 LY(1,1) LY(2,2) LY(3,3) LY(4,4) LY(5,5) LY(6,6)
FR PS(7,7)
EQ PS(1,7,7) PS(7,7) PS(8,8) PS(9,9) PS(10,10) PS(11,11) C PS(12,12)
VA .99 PS(5,5) PS(6,6)
VA 0.19 PS(6,5)
```

```
ST .1 ALL
OU NS IT=250 AD=OFF
```

APPENDIX B: LISREL PROGRAM FOR FOUR-FACTOR, 0-, ONE-LAGGED DYNAMIC FACTOR ANALYSIS

```
DYNAMIC FACTOR ANALYSIS - FOUR FACTORS, 0, 1 LAGS
FACTOR PATTERN FOR INVOLVEMENT FACTOR
DA NI = 56 MA = CM NO = 80
MO NY = 56 NE = 12 LY = FU,FI PS=DI,FI TE = FU,FI
FR TE(1,1) TE(2,2) TE(3,3) TE(4,4) TE(5,5) TE(6,6) TE(7,7)
FR TE(8,8) TE(9,9) TE(10,10) TE(11,11) TE(12,12) TE(13,13)
FR TE(14,14) TE(15,15) TE(16,16) TE(17,17) TE(18,18) TE(19,19)
FR TE(20,20) TE(21,21) TE(22,22) TE(23,23) TE(24,24) TE(25,25)
FR TE(26,26) TE(27,27) TE(28,28)
FR TE(29,1) TE(30,2) TE(31,3) TE(32,4) TE(33,5) TE(34,6) TE(35,7)
FR TE(36,8) TE(37,9) TE(38,10) TE(39,11) TE(40,12) TE(41,13)
FR TE(42,14) TE(43,15) TE(44,16) TE(45,17) TE(46,18) TE(47,19)
FR TE(48,20) TE(49,21) TE(50,22) TE(51,23) TE(52,24) TE(53,25)
FR TE(54,26) TE(55,27) TE(56,28)
FR LY(1,2) LY(29,6)
FR LY(2,1) LY(30,5)
FR LY(3,4) LY(31,8)
FR LY(4,1) LY(32,5)
FR LY(5,1) LY(33,5)
FR LY(6,2) LY(34,6)
FR LY(7,1) LY(35,5)
FR LY(8,3) LY(36,7)
FR LY(9,1) LY(37,5)
FR LY(10,2) LY(38,6)
FR LY(11,1) LY(39,5)
FR LY(12,1) LY(40,5)
FR LY(13,4) LY(41,8)
FR LY(14,3) LY(42,7)
FR LY(15,2) LY(43,6)
FR LY(16,1) LY(44,5)
FR LY(17,4) LY(45,8)
FR LY(18,3) LY(46,7)
FR LY(19,1) LY(47,5)
FR LY(20,2) LY(48,6)
FR LY(21,2) LY(49,6)
FR LY(22,4) LY(50,8)
FR LY(23,4) LY(51,8)
FR LY(24,4) LY(52,8)
FR LY(25,3) LY(53,7)
```

```
FR LY(26,3) LY(54,6)
FR LY(27,3) LY(55,7)
FR LY(28,4) LY(56,8)
FR LY(1,6) LY(29,10)
FR LY(2,5) LY(30,9)
FR LY(3,8) LY(31,12)
FR LY(4,5) LY(32,9)
FR LY(5,5) LY(33,9)
FR LY(6,6) LY(34,10)
FR LY(7,5) LY(35,9)
FR LY(8,7) LY(36,11)
FR LY(9,5) LY(37,10)
FR LY(10,6) LY(38,10)
FR LY(11,5) LY(39,9)
FR LY(12,5) LY(40,9)
FR LY(13,8) LY(41,12)
FR LY(14,7) LY(42,11)
FR LY(15,6) LY(43,10)
FR LY(16,5) LY(44,9)
FR LY(17,8) LY(45,12)
FR LY(18,7) LY(46,11)
FR LY(19,5) LY(47,9)
FR LY(20,6) LY(48,10)
FR LY(21,6) LY(49,10)
FR LY(22,8) LY(50,12)
FR LY(23,8) LY(51,12)
FR LY(24,8) LY(52,12)
FR LY(25,7) LY(53,11)
FR LY(26,6) LY(54,10)
FR LY(27,7) LY(55,11)
FR LY(28,8) LY(56,12)
EQ LY(1,2) LY(29,6)
EQ LY(2,1) LY(30,5)
EQ LY(3,4) LY(31,8)
EQ LY(4,1) LY(32,5)
EQ LY(5,1) LY(33,5)
EQ LY(6,2) LY(34,6)
EQ LY(7,1) LY(35,5)
EQ LY(8,3) LY(36,7)
EQ LY(9,1) LY(37,5)
EQ LY(10,2) LY(38,6)
EQ LY(11,1) LY(39,5)
EQ LY(12,1) LY(40,5)
EQ LY(13,4) LY(41,8)
EQ LY(14,3) LY(42,7)
EQ LY(15,2) LY(43,6)
EQ LY(16,1) LY(44,5)
```

```
EQ LY(17,4) LY(45,8)
EQ LY(18,3) LY(46,7)
EQ LY(19,1) LY(47,5)
EQ LY(20,2) LY(48,6)
EQ LY(21,2) LY(49,6)
EQ LY(22,4) LY(50,8)
EQ LY(23,4) LY(51,8)
EQ LY(24,4) LY(52,8)
EQ LY(25,3) LY(53,7)
EQ LY(26,3) LY(54,6)
EQ LY(27,3) LY(55,7)
EQ LY(28,4) LY(56,8)
EQ LY(1,6) LY(29,10)
EQ LY(2,5) LY(30,9)
EQ LY(3,8) LY(31,12)
EQ LY(4,5) LY(32,9)
EQ LY(5,5) LY(33,9)
EQ LY(6,6) LY(34,10)
EQ LY(7,5) LY(35,9)
EQ LY(8,7) LY(36,11)
EQ LY(9,5) LY(37,10)
EQ LY(10,6) LY(38,10)
EQ LY(11,5) LY(39,9)
EQ LY(12,5) LY(40,9)
EQ LY(13,8) LY(41,12)
EQ LY(14,7) LY(42,11)
EQ LY(15,6) LY(43,10)
EQ LY(16,5) LY(44,9)
EQ LY(17,8) LY(45,12)
EQ LY(18,7) LY(46,11)
EQ LY(19,5) LY(47,9)
EQ LY(20,6) LY(48,10)
EQ LY(21,6) LY(49,10)
EQ LY(22,8) LY(50,12)
EQ LY(23,8) LY(51,12)
EQ LY(24,8) LY(52,12)
EQ LY(25,7) LY(53,11)
EQ LY(26,6) LY(54,10)
EQ LY(27,7) LY(55,11)
EQ LY(28,8) LY(56,12)
EQ TE(1,1) TE(29,29)
EQ TE(2,2) TE(30,30)
EQ TE(3,3) TE(31,31)
EQ TE(4,4) TE(32,32)
EQ TE(5,5) TE(33,33)
EQ TE(6,6) TE(34,34)
EQ TE(7,7) TE(35,35)
```

```
EQ TE(8,8) TE(36,36)
EQ TE(9,9) TE(37,37)
EQ TE(10,10) TE(38,38)
EQ TE(11,11) TE(39,39)
EQ TE(12,12) TE(40,40)
EQ TE(13,13) TE(41,41)
EQ TE(14,14) TE(42,42)
EQ TE(15,15) TE(43,43)
EQ TE(16,16) TE(44,44)
EQ TE(17,17) TE(45,45)
EQ TE(18,18) TE(46,46)
EQ TE(19,19) TE(47,47)
EQ TE(20,20) TE(48,48)
EQ TE(21,21) TE(49,49)
EQ TE(22,22) TE(50,50)
EQ TE(23,23) TE(51,51)
EQ TE(24,24) TE(52,52)
EQ TE(25,25) TE(53,53)
EQ TE(26,26) TE(54,54)
EQ TE(27,27) TE(55,55)
EQ TE(28,28) TE(56,56)
ST 1 ALL
ST 1 PS(1,1) PS(2,2) PS(3,3) PS(4,4) PS(5,5) PS(6,6)
ST 1 PS(7,7) PS(8,8) PS(9,9) PS(10,10)
ST 1 PS(11,11) PS(12,12)
OU NS
```

APPENDIX C: LISREL PROGRAM FOR FOUR-FACTOR, 0-, ONE-LAGGED NONSTATIONARY DYNAMIC FACTOR ANALYSIS

```
DYNAMIC FACTOR ANALYSIS - FOUR FACTORS, 0, 1 LAGS - NONSTATIONARY
FACTOR PATTERN FOR INVOLVEMENT FACTOR
DA NI = 57 MA = CM NO = 80
MO NY = 56 NE = 12 NX = 1 NK = 1 LY = FU,FI PS=DI,FI TE = FU,FI C
   GA = FU,FI PH=SY,FI LX = FU,FR TD = ZE
VA 1.00 PH(1,1)
FR GA(1,1) GA(2,1) GA(3,1) GA(4,1) GA(5,1) GA(6,1) GA(7,1)
FR GA(8,1) GA(9,1) GA(10,1) GA(11,1) GA(12,1)
EQ GA(1,1) GA(5,1) GA(9,1)
EQ GA(2,1) GA(6,1) GA(10,1)
EQ GA(3,1) GA(7,1) GA(11,1)
EQ GA(4,1) GA(8,1) GA(12,1)
FR TE(1,1) TE(2,2) TE(3,3) TE(4,4) TE(5,5) TE(6,6) TE(7,7)
FR TE(8,8) TE(9,9) TE(10,10) TE(11,11) TE(12,12) TE(13,13)
```

```
FR TE(14,14) TE(15,15) TE(16,16) TE(17,17) TE(18,18) TE(19,19)
FR TE(20,20) TE(21,21) TE(22,22) TE(23,23) TE(24,24) TE(25,25)
FR TE(26,26) TE(27,27) TE(28,28)
FR TE(29,1) TE(30,2) TE(31,3) TE(32,4) TE(33,5) TE(34,6) TE(35,7)
FR TE(36,8) TE(37,9) TE(38,10) TE(39,11) TE(40,12) TE(41,13)
FR TE(42,14) TE(43,15) TE(44,16) TE(45,17) TE(46,18) TE(47,19)
FR TE(48,20) TE(49,21) TE(50,22) TE(51,23) TE(52,24) TE(53,25)
FR TE(54,26) TE(55,27) TE(56,28)
VA 1.00 LY(1,2) LY(29,6)
VA 1.00 LY(2,1) LY(30,5)
VA 1.00 LY(3,4) LY(31,8)
FR LY(4,1) LY(32,5)
FR LY(5,1) LY(33,5)
FR LY(6,2) LY(34,6)
FR LY(7,1) LY(35,5)
VA 1.00 LY(8,3) LY(36,7)
FR LY(9,1) LY(37,5)
FR LY(10,2) LY(38,6)
FR LY(11,1) LY(39,5)
FR LY(12,1) LY(40,5)
FR LY(13,4) LY(41,8)
FR LY(14,3) LY(42,7)
FR LY(15,2) LY(43,6)
FR LY(16,1) LY(44,5)
FR LY(17,4) LY(45,8)
FR LY(18,3) LY(46,7)
FR LY(19,1) LY(47,5)
FR LY(20,2) LY(48,6)
FR LY(21,2) LY(49,6)
FR LY(22,4) LY(50,8)
FR LY(23,4) LY(51,8)
FR LY(24,4) LY(52,8)
FR LY(25,3) LY(53,7)
FR LY(26,3) LY(54,6)
FR LY(27,3) LY(55,7)
FR LY(28,4) LY(56,8)
FR LY(1,6) LY(29,10)
FR LY(2,5) LY(30,9)
FR LY(3,8) LY(31,12)
FR LY(4,5) LY(32,9)
FR LY(5,5) LY(33,9)
FR LY(6,6) LY(34,10)
FR LY(7,5) LY(35,9)
FR LY(8,7) LY(36,11)
FR LY(9,5) LY(37,10)
FR LY(10,6) LY(38,10)
FR LY(11,5) LY(39,9)
```

```
FR LY(12,5) LY(40,9)
FR LY(13,8) LY(41,12)
FR LY(14,7) LY(42,11)
FR LY(15,6) LY(43,10)
FR LY(16,5) LY(44,9)
FR LY(17,8) LY(45,12)
FR LY(18,7) LY(46,11)
FR LY(19,5) LY(47,9)
FR LY(20,6) LY(48,10)
FR LY(21,6) LY(49,10)
FR LY(22,8) LY(50,12)
FR LY(23,8) LY(51,12)
FR LY(24,8) LY(52,12)
FR LY(25,7) LY(53,11)
FR LY(26,6) LY(54,10)
FR LY(27,7) LY(55,11)
FR LY(28,8) LY(56,12)
EQ LY(4,1) LY(32,5)
EQ LY(5,1) LY(33,5)
EQ LY(6,2) LY(34,6)
EQ LY(7,1) LY(35,5)
EQ LY(9,1) LY(37,5)
EQ LY(10,2) LY(38,6)
EQ LY(11,1) LY(39,5)
EQ LY(12,1) LY(40,5)
EQ LY(13,4) LY(41,8)
EQ LY(14,3) LY(42,7)
EQ LY(15,2) LY(43,6)
EQ LY(16,1) LY(44,5)
EQ LY(17,4) LY(45,8)
EQ LY(18,3) LY(46,7)
EQ LY(19,1) LY(47,5)
EQ LY(20,2) LY(48,6)
EQ LY(21,2) LY(49,6)
EQ LY(22,4) LY(50,8)
EQ LY(23,4) LY(51,8)
EQ LY(24,4) LY(52,8)
EQ LY(25,3) LY(53,7)
EQ LY(26,3) LY(54,6)
EQ LY(27,3) LY(55,7)
EQ LY(28,4) LY(56,8)
EQ LY(1,6) LY(29,10)
EQ LY(2,5) LY(30,9)
EQ LY(3,8) LY(31,12)
EQ LY(4,5) LY(32,9)
EQ LY(5,5) LY(33,9)
EQ LY(6,6) LY(34,10)
```

```
EQ LY(7,5) LY(35,9)
EQ LY(8,7) LY(36,11)
EQ LY(9,5) LY(37,10)
EQ LY(10,6) LY(38,10)
EQ LY(11,5) LY(39,9)
EQ LY(12,5) LY(40,9)
EQ LY(13,8) LY(41,12)
EQ LY(14,7) LY(42,11)
EQ LY(15,6) LY(43,10)
EQ LY(16,5) LY(44,9)
EQ LY(17,8) LY(45,12)
EQ LY(18,7) LY(46,11)
EQ LY(19,5) LY(47,9)
EQ LY(20,6) LY(48,10)
EQ LY(21,6) LY(49,10)
EQ LY(22,8) LY(50,12)
EQ LY(23,8) LY(51,12)
EQ LY(24,8) LY(52,12)
EQ LY(25,7) LY(53,11)
EQ LY(26,6) LY(54,10)
EQ LY(27,7) LY(55,11)
EQ LY(28,8) LY(56,12)
EQ TE(1,1) TE(29,29)
EQ TE(2,2) TE(30,30)
EQ TE(3,3) TE(31,31)
EQ TE(4,4) TE(32,32)
EQ TE(5,5) TE(33,33)
EQ TE(6,6) TE(34,34)
EQ TE(7,7) TE(35,35)
EQ TE(8,8) TE(36,36)
EQ TE(9,9) TE(37,37)
EQ TE(10,10) TE(38,38)
EQ TE(11,11) TE(39,39)
EQ TE(12,12) TE(40,40)
EQ TE(13,13) TE(41,41)
EQ TE(14,14) TE(42,42)
EQ TE(15,15) TE(43,43)
EQ TE(16,16) TE(44,44)
EQ TE(17,17) TE(45,45)
EQ TE(18,18) TE(46,46)
EQ TE(19,19) TE(47,47)
EQ TE(20,20) TE(48,48)
EQ TE(21,21) TE(49,49)
EQ TE(22,22) TE(50,50)
EQ TE(23,23) TE(51,51)
EQ TE(24,24) TE(52,52)
EQ TE(25,25) TE(53,53)
```

```
EQ TE(26,26) TE(54,54)
EQ TE(27,27) TE(55,55)
EQ TE(28,28) TE(56,56)
ST 1 ALL
OU NS
```

APPENDIX D: LISREL PROGRAM FOR STATE SPACE MODEL: INVOLVEMENT AND AFFECTION

```
STATE SPACE MODEL: INPUT INVOLVEMENT FACTOR; OUTPUT AFFECTION FACTOR
DA NI = 70 NO = 108 MA = CM
MO NY = 70 NE = 10 LY = FU,FI TE = DI BE = FU,FI PS = SY,FR
VA 1.0 LY(1,1) LY(8,2) LY(15,3) LY(22,4) LY(29,5)
VA 1.0 LY(36,6) LY(43,7) LY(50,8) LY(57,9) LY(64,10)
FR LY(2,1) LY(3,1) LY(4,1) LY(5,1) LY(6,1) LY(7,1)
FR LY(36,1) LY(37,1) LY(38,1) LY(39,1) LY(40,1) LY(41,1) LY(42,1)
FR LY(9,2) LY(10,2) LY(11,2) LY(12,2) LY(13,2) LY(14,2)
FR LY(43,2) LY(44,2) LY(45,2) LY(46,2) LY(47,2) LY(48,2) LY(49,2)
FR LY(16,3) LY(17,3) LY(18,3) LY(19,3) LY(20,3) LY(21,3)
FR LY(50,3) LY(51,3) LY(52,3) LY(53,3) LY(54,3) LY(55,3) LY(56,3)
FR LY(23,4) LY(24,4) LY(25,4) LY(26,4) LY(27,4) LY(28,4)
FR LY(57,4) LY(58,4) LY(59,4) LY(60,4) LY(61,4) LY(62,4) LY(63,4)
FR LY(30,5) LY(31,5) LY(32,5) LY(33,5) LY(34,5) LY(35,5)
FR LY(64,5) LY(65,5) LY(66,5) LY(67,5) LY(68,5) LY(69,5) LY(70,5)
EQ LY(2,1) LY(9,2) LY(16,3) LY(23,4) LY(30,5)
EQ LY(3,1) LY(10,2) LY(17,3) LY(24,4) LY(31,5)
EQ LY(4,1) LY(11,2) LY(18,3) LY(25,4) LY(32,5)
EQ LY(5,1) LY(12,2) LY(19,3) LY(26,4) LY(33,5)
EQ LY(6,1) LY(13,2) LY(20,3) LY(27,4) LY(34,5)
EQ LY(7,1) LY(14,2) LY(21,3) LY(28,4) LY(35,5)
EQ LY(36,1) LY(43,2) LY(50,3) LY(57,4) LY(64,5)
EQ LY(37,1) LY(44,2) LY(51,3) LY(58,4) LY(65,5)
EQ LY(38,1) LY(45,2) LY(52,3) LY(59,4) LY(66,5)
EQ LY(39,1) LY(46,2) LY(53,3) LY(60,4) LY(67,5)
EQ LY(40,1) LY(47,2) LY(54,3) LY(61,4) LY(68,5)
EQ LY(41,1) LY(48,2) LY(55,3) LY(62,4) LY(69,5)
EQ LY(42,1) LY(49,2) LY(56,3) LY(63,4) LY(70,5)
VA 1.00 LY(36,6) LY(43,7) LY(50,8) LY(57,9) LY(64,10)
FR LY(37,6) LY(38,6) LY(39,6) LY(40,6) LY(41,6) LY(42,6)
FR LY(44,7) LY(45,7) LY(46,7) LY(47,7) LY(48,7) LY(49,7)
FR LY(51,8) LY(52,8) LY(53,8) LY(54,8) LY(55,8) LY(56,8)
FR LY(58,9) LY(59,9) LY(60,9) LY(61,9) LY(62,9) LY(63,9)
FR LY(65,10) LY(66,10) LY(67,10) LY(68,10) LY(69,10) LY(70,10)
EQ LY(37,6) LY(44,7) LY(51,8) LY(58,9) LY(65,10)
EQ LY(38,6) LY(45,7) LY(52,8) LY(59,9) LY(66,10)
```

```
EQ LY(39,6) LY(46,7) LY(53,8) LY(60,9) LY(67,10)
EQ LY(40,6) LY(47,7) LY(54,8) LY(61,9) LY(68,10)
EQ LY(41,6) LY(48,7) LY(55,8) LY(62,9) LY(69,10)
EQ LY(42,6) LY(49,7) LY(56,8) LY(63,9) LY(70,10)
EQ TE(1,1) TE(8,8) TE(15,15) TE(22,22) TE(29,29)
EQ TE(2,2) TE(9,9) TE(16,16) TE(23,23) TE(30,30)
EQ TE(3,3) TE(10,10) TE(17,17) TE(24,24) TE(31,31)
EQ TE(4,4) TE(11,11) TE(18,18) TE(25,25) TE(32,32)
EQ TE(5,5) TE(12,12) TE(19,19) TE(26,26) TE(33,33)
EQ TE(6,6) TE(13,13) TE(20,20) TE(27,27) TE(34,34)
EQ TE(7,7) TE(14,14) TE(21,21) TE(28,28) TE(35,35)
EQ TE(36,36) TE(43,43) TE(50,50) TE(57,57) TE(64,64)
EQ TE(37,37) TE(44,44) TE(51,51) TE(58,58) TE(65,65)
EQ TE(38,38) TE(45,45) TE(52,52) TE(59,59) TE(66,66)
EQ TE(39,39) TE(46,46) TE(53,53) TE(60,60) TE(67,67)
EQ TE(40,40) TE(47,47) TE(54,54) TE(61,61) TE(68,68)
EQ TE(41,41) TE(48,48) TE(55,55) TE(62,62) TE(69,69)
EQ TE(42,42) TE(49,49) TE(56,56) TE(63,63) TE(70,70)
PA PS
2
4 2
5 4 2
6 5 4 2
7 6 5 4 2
0 0 0 0 0 10
0 0 0 0 0 0 3
0 0 0 0 0 0 0 3
0 0 0 0 0 0 0 0 3
0 0 0 0 0 0 0 0 0 3
PA BE
0 0 0 0 0 0 0 0 0 0
0 0 0 0 0 0 0 0 0 0
0 0 0 0 0 0 0 0 0 0
0 0 0 0 0 0 0 0 0 0
0 0 0 0 0 0 0 0 0 0
0 0 0 0 0 0 0 0 0 0
8 0 0 0 0 9 0 0 0 0
0 8 0 0 0 0 9 0 0 0
0 0 8 0 0 0 0 9 0 0
0 0 0 8 0 0 0 0 9 0
OU
```

REFERENCES

Akaike, H. (1987). Factor analysis and AIC. *Psychometrika, 52,* 333–342.

Bentler, P. M. (1992). *EQS: Structural equations program manual.* Los Angeles: BMDP Statistical Software.

Bentler, P. M., & Bonett, D. G. (1980). Significance tests and goodness of fit in the analysis of covariance structures. *Psychological Bulletin, 88*, 588–606.

Caines, P. E. (1988). *Linear stochastic systems.* New York: Wiley.

Cattell, R. B. (1952). *Factor analysis.* New York: Harper.

Chatfield, C. (1980). Inverse autocorrelations. *Journal of the Royal Statistical Society, A142,* 363–377.

Cleveland, W. W. (1972). The inverse autocorrelation of a time series and their applications. *Technometrics, 14*, 277–293.

Glass, G. V., Willson, V. L., & Gottman, J. M. (1975). *Design and analysis of time-series experiments.* Boulder, CO: Associated University Press.

Hannan, E. J., & Quinn, B. G. (1979). The determination of the order of an autoregression. *Journal of the Royal Statistical Society, 41*, 190–195.

Harvey, A. C. (1989). *Forecasting, structural time series models and the Kalman filter.* Cambridge, MA: Cambridge University Press.

Hershberger, S. L., Corneal, S. E., & Molenaar, P. C. M. (1994). Dynamic factor analysis: An application to emotional response patterns underlying daughter/father and stepdaughter/stepfather relationships. *Structural Equation Modeling, 2*, 31–52.

Jenkins, G. M., & Watts, D. G. (1968). *Spectrum analysis and its applications.* San Francisco: Holden-Day.

Jöreskog, K. G., & Sörbom, D. (1993). *LISREL VIII user's reference guide.* Chicago: Scientific Software International.

Kendall, M., & Ord, J. K. (1990). *Time series* (3rd ed.). England: Edward Arnold.

MacCallum, R., & Ashby, F. G. (1986). Relationships between linear systems theory and covariance structure modeling. *Journal of Mathematical Psychology, 30*, 1–27.

Marsh, H. W., Balla, J. R., & McDonald, R. P. (1988). Goodness-of-fit indexes in confirmatory factor analysis: The effect of sample size. *Psychological Bulletin, 103*, 391–410.

Molenaar, P. C. M. (1985). A dynamic factor model for the analysis of multivariate time series. *Psychometrika, 50*, 181–202.

Molenaar, P. C. M. (1989). Aspects of dynamic factor analysis. In *Annals of statistical information* (pp. 183–199). Tokyo: The Institute of Statistical Mathematics.

Molenaar, P. C. M., de Gooijer, J. G., & Schmitz, B. (1992). Dynamic factor analysis of nonstationary multivariate time series. *Psychometrika, 57*, 333–349.

SAS Institute. (1990a). *SAS guide to macro processing. 2nd edition.* Cary, NC: Author.

SAS Institute. (1990b). *SAS/IML software.* Cary, NC: Author.

SAS Institute. (1993). *SAS/ETS user's guide.* Cary, NC: Author.

Schmitz, B. (1990). Univariate and multivariate time-series models: The analysis of intraindividual variability and interindividual relationships. In A. von Eye (Ed.), *Statistical methods in longitudinal research. Vol. II: Time series and categorical longitudinal data* (pp. 351–386). San Diego, CA: Academic Press.

Schwarz, G. (1978). Estimating the dimension of a model. *Annals of Statistics, 6*, 461–464.

Watson, D., Clark, L. A., & Tellegen, A. (1988). Development and validation of brief measures of positive and negative affect: The PANAS scales. *Journal of Personality and Social Psychology, 54*, 1063–1070.

Wood, P., & Brown, D. (1994). The study of intraindividual differences by means of dynamic factor models: Rationale, implementation, and interpretation. *Psychological Bulletin, 116*, 166–186.

CHAPTER SEVEN

Bootstrapping Techniques in Analysis of Mean and Covariance Structures

Yiu-Fai Yung
University of North Carolina, Chapel Hill

Peter M. Bentler
University of California, Los Angeles

It has been more than 15 years since Efron's (1979) monumental paper on bootstrap methods. This paper has had a major impact on the field of statistics. In Kotz and Johnson's (1992) book *Breakthroughs in Statistics*, which selected, highlighted, and reprinted the most significant works in statistics since the 1980s, Efron's (1979) paper is the latest one selected. Therefore, although Efron's paper is quite "young" relative to the history of statistics, its significance has already been well recognized. The beauty of the bootstrap, of course, lies in its relaxation of severe distributional assumptions of parametric models (e.g., multivariate normality of the population distribution). Statistical inferences using the bootstrap are usually made by computations, thus providing solutions to statistical problems that would otherwise be intractable. The bootstrap has been applied to many areas in statistics, and a vast amount of research on it has been published since Efron's introduction. The bootstrap also has diffused into the field of behavioral sciences, though at a much slower pace. In the psychological literature, there has been a heated debate about the usefulness of the bootstrap applied to the correlation coefficient (cf. Efron, 1988; Lunneborg, 1985; Rasmussen, 1987, 1988; Strube, 1988). A recent application has been tied to coefficients in discriminant analysis (Dalgleish, 1994). In the sociological literature, to the best of our knowledge, the earliest introduction of the bootstrap methodology into the field can be traced back to the work by Bollen and Stine (1988), Dietz, Frey, and Kalof (1987), and Stine (1989). Although not primarily written for social scientists, articles and books also exist that introduce the basic bootstrap ideas in a way comprehensible to social scientists with minimal formal statistical training (e.g., Efron & Gong, 1983; Efron & Tibshirani, 1986, 1993; for a recent critical review of the bootstrap research, see Young, 1994).

The present chapter focuses on bootstrap applications to covariance structure analysis, of which exploratory and confirmatory factor analysis are considered leading cases. Because general introductions to bootstrap methods already are available to behavioral scientists (e.g., Lambert, Wildt, & Durand, 1991; Mooney & Duval, 1993; Stine, 1989), our introduction to the bootstrap is minimal. Of course, we present all necessary definitions and basic ideas so that this chapter will be self-explanatory. Our main emphasis is on abstracting relevant bootstrap methods into a framework suitable to covariance structures, and on judging whether the bootstrap "works" for the given situations. Thus, the present exposition is more evaluative than introductory. Following a critical review of the literature, an analysis using a real data set illustrates the validity of the bootstrap method for estimating standard errors when the normality assumption may not be true. Some related issues in the application of the bootstrap to covariance structure analysis are also discussed here. Next, by extending Beran and Srivastava's (1985; see also Bollen & Stine, 1993) method of bootstrap testing, we suggest two additional applications of the bootstrap to mean and covariance structures. Finally, some concluding comments are given.

APPLICATION OF THE BOOTSTRAP
TO COVARIANCE STRUCTURE ANALYSIS

Covariance Structure Analysis

Suppose the target population P has a (cumulative) distribution function $\mathcal{F}$ for a $p \times 1$ vector of variables. A sample of size n is drawn from P according to the distribution $\mathcal{F}$. Denote the $p \times 1$ vector of observed variables (random) for the i-th individual as x_i (i = 1, 2, . . . , n). Then a covariance structure model, here called the null model M_0 (not to be confused with the model of uncorrelated variables used in Bentler-Bonett fit indices), is fitted to the sample data, of which $\mathcal{F}_n$ is the empirical distribution function. The model fitting procedure is characterized by the solution $\theta = \hat{\theta}$ satisfying the equation

$$F(S_n, \Sigma(\hat{\theta})) = \min_{\theta \in \Theta} \{ F(S_n, \Sigma(\theta)) \} , \tag{1}$$

where $F(\cdot , \cdot)$ is a discrepancy function which measures the discrepancy between its two ordered arguments; S_n is a $p \times p$ symmetric matrix of the observed variances and covariances; $\Sigma(\theta)$ is a $p \times p$ matrix of theoretical covariances "structured" in terms of θ, θ is considered to be a vector of model parameters, and Θ is an admissible set of values for θ. Usually, $\hat{\theta}$, the solution of θ in Equation 1 must be obtained by iterative procedures. If the value of $F(S_n, \Sigma(\hat{\theta}))$ in Equation 1 is denoted by $\hat{F}$, then the corresponding model test statistic is defined as $T \equiv (n-1)\,\hat{F}$. For many functions F, in regular situations and under the null hypothesis, T is distributed in large samples as a χ^2 variate. Without further specification, we assume that the discrepancy function defined in Equation 1 is the normal theory maximum likelihood (ML) discrepancy function [i.e., $F(S_n, \Sigma(\theta)) = \log|\Sigma(\theta)| - \log |S_n| + \mathrm{trace}(S_n\Sigma(\theta)^{-1}) - p$].

The Bootstrap Applied to Covariance Structure Analysis

The bootstrap method can be summarized in the following three steps:

Step 1. Define a resampling space R, which usually contains n data points denoted by $y_1, y_2, \ldots, y_n$. Each y_i is a p $\times$ 1 vector and is associated with the original observed data point x_i through the same indices for individuals.

Step 2. Fix a point mass $\frac{1}{n}$ for each point in R, draw a sample of n observations randomly from R with replacement. The vector of the variances and covariances of such *bootstrap* sample is denoted by $S_{n,j}^*$, where j is an index for bootstrap samples drawn from R and the starred symbol signifies its pertinence to the bootstrap sample, to be distinguished from the symbol for the original sample. Such starred notation for bootstrap samples will be used througout this chapter. Fit the covariance structure model M_0 to this bootstrap sample by feeding $S_{n,j}^*$ into Equation 1 using some computer program (e.g., Bentler & Wu, 1995) and obtain θ_j^* as the solution for θ. Accordingly, we have $F_j^* \equiv F(S_{n,j}^*, \Sigma(\theta_j^*))$ and hence $T_j^* \equiv (n-1)F_j^*$.

Step 3. Repeat Step 2, B times, and obtain a set of bootstrapped values of parameter estimates and test statistic: $\{(\theta_j^*, T_j^*), j = 1, 2, \ldots, B\}$.

In the most natural situation, y_i is just set to be x_i for all i in the resampling space R in Step 1. In this case, the distribution on R is just $\hat{\mathcal{F}}_n$, the empirical distribution function. To distinguish this "natural" method from others, we call it the *completely nonparametric bootstrap*, or simply *the bootstrap* when there is no further specification. It is completely nonparametric because the resampling from R does not depend on any assumption about the distributional family or on any covariance structure model for the data. In contrast, we also define some "model-based" bootstrap methods that are *semi-nonparametric* in nature, in the sense that R depends on certain covariance structural information, but *without* any assumption about the distributional family for the data. Theoretically, an ideal (nonparametric, semi-nonparametric) bootstrapping method would be one that generates all possible samples of size n from R. In this case, B would equal n^n, the total number of possible samples from R of size n each. However, B is then too large to be practical for implementation. Moreover, a large number of samples would be ill-defined in the sense that these samples will have singular covariance matrices and thus will not be suitable for the fitting of a covariance structure model. Therefore, in practice bootstrap sampling is carried out with B being chosen to be some hundreds, say 500 or more, and ill-defined bootstrap samples from R must be dropped without being further analyzed. In Step 2 and Step 3, although only θ_j^*s and T_j^*s are listed, it is also possible to include any function of the bootstrap sample data into the list. For example, suppose β is an element of θ and the standard error of $\hat{\beta}$ can be estimated by $\hat{\sigma}_{\hat{\beta}}$ in the parental sample, then it is also possible to estimate the standard error of $\hat{\beta}_j^*$ by $\hat{\sigma}_{\hat{\beta}_j}^*$ in the j-th bootstrap sample. In this case, the set of bootstrapped values would also contain all the $\hat{\sigma}_{\hat{\beta}_j}^*$s. For brevity in presentation, such a possibility had been made implicit in Steps 2 and 3. A final remark about the bootstrap procedures already described is about the sample size for resampling. Typically, the size of resampling is set to be the same as the actual sample size, as treated in Step 2. But there are some theoretical reasons that bootstrap resampling based on a fewer sample size, say m_n ($m_n < n$), would be preferred for some cases. In fact, using m_n for boot-strapping would revive some well-known failure of the bootstrapping using a resampling of size n (e.g., for estimating the sampling distribution of the smallest or the largest order statistics, see a recent technical paper by Bickel, Götze, & van Zwet, 1994, and references therein). However, we only consider the case of bootstrapping with size n here.

The basic bootstrap principle can be simply stated as:

The relation between a population P and its samples *can be modeled by* the relation between the resampling space R and its bootstrap samples.

A direct consequence of this principle is that the distribution of the set of bootstrapped values $\{(\theta_j^*, T_j^*), j = 1, 2, \ldots, B\}$ from R in Step 3 can be used as an estimator of the sampling distribution of $(\hat{\theta}, T)$ from P. Notice that up to this point, we have not assumed any knowledge about the population distribution $\mathcal{F}$ (not to be confused with the discrepancy function F). In fact, this is exactly why the bootstrap is so attractive as an alternative to fitting covariance structure models without the multivariate normality as-sumption. By doing the bootstrapping procedures described previously, the non-normality problem can be taken into account implicitly in the boot-strapping. Because most of the statistical problems in covariance structure analysis are about the sampling properties of parameter estimators and the test statistic, and it is always possible to do bootstrapping based on the parental sample, it seems that the bootstrap principle is general enough to address a wide variety of statistical problems in covariance structure analysis without making any distributional assumption.

However, these assertions are based on *faith* in the bootstrap principle. We purposely italicized the phrase *can be modeled* in the bootstrap principle to signify that the bootstrap is merely a plausible method, whether it is good or bad in a given situation. The real applicability of the bootstrap to covariance structure analysis, as well as to all other innovative statistical techniques, is subject to examination. In contrast, blind faith can be characterized by replacing the phrase with *is* in the bootstrap principle. Blind faith in the bootstrap principle unfortunately may lead to over-optimism regarding the bootstrap results. Therefore, rather than simply advocate the bootstrap without any critical evaluation, we take a more critical stance in the hope that the usefulness of the bootstrap to the analysis of covariance structures can be grounded appropriately.

A Critical Review of Bootstrap Applications

We now look at four main applications of the bootstrap to covariance structure analysis in the literature. They are: (a) bias estimation, (b) estimation of standard errors, (c) construction of confidence intervals, and (d) model testing.

Bias Estimation

Usually, the bias of an estimator $\hat{\theta}$ for θ is defined as

$$\mathbf{B}(\hat{\theta}) = \mathcal{E}(\hat{\theta}) - \theta, \tag{2}$$

where $\mathcal{E}(\cdot)$ is the expectation operator taken with respect to the true distribution function $\mathcal{F}$. The bootstrap principle implies the following estimator for $\mathbf{B}(\hat{\theta})$:

$$\mathbf{B}^*(\hat{\theta}) = \mathcal{E}^*(\theta^*) - \hat{\theta}, \tag{3}$$

where $\mathcal{E}(\cdot)$ is an expectation operator taken with respect to the distribution function on R, the resampling space. Notice how the analogous features in Equations 2 and 3 realize the bootstrap principle. As discussed before, the ideal evaluation of $\mathcal{E}^*(\theta^*)$ should be based on all possible samples of size n drawn from R. In practice, however, the expectation is replaced by the simple average of the B sample values of θ^*. As a result, Equation 3 becomes

$$\mathbf{B}^*(\hat{\theta}) = \bar{\theta}^* - \theta, \tag{4}$$

where $\bar{\theta}^* = \frac{1}{B}\sum_{j=1}^{B}\theta_j^*$ is the mean value of the B bootstrapped values θ_j^*'s. It is tempting to use (4) to define a bias-corrected estimator of θ as

$$\hat{\theta}_{BC} = \hat{\theta} - (\bar{\theta}^* - \hat{\theta}) = 2\hat{\theta} - \bar{\theta}^*. \tag{5}$$

In the literature of structural equation modeling, the use of $\mathbf{B}^*(\hat{\theta})$ as an estimator of $\mathbf{B}(\hat{\theta})$ has not been studied extensively. Chatterjee (1984) examined specific data ($n = 50$) and found that the biases estimated using the bootstrap were "very small" for the loadings of the first factor when an exploratory factor model was applied. He then concluded, "Since both biases and standard errors are very small [estimated by the bootstrap method], it is possible to accept Factor 1 as a legitimate factor with its high loadings" (p. 256). However, it is possible that Chatterjee's conclusion was too optimistic, if not mistaken. The reason is that $\mathbf{B}^*(\hat{\theta})$ in Equation 4 is intended to estimate $\mathbf{B}(\hat{\theta})$ in Equation 2, and it is good if $\mathbf{B}^*(\hat{\theta})$ can provide reliable estimates that are stochastically close to $\mathbf{B}(\hat{\theta})$. To our knowledge, no research before Chatterjee (1984) studied the statistical properties (e.g., unbiasedness and variability) of $\mathbf{B}^*(\hat{\theta})$ as an estimator of the true bias in the context of exploratory factor analysis. If $\mathbf{B}^*(\hat{\theta})$ itself is a biased estimator of the true bias, then observing a "very small" value of $\mathbf{B}^*(\hat{\theta})$ need not be good news. It follows that the empirical bias correction, as in Equation 5, may not be appropriate either. Therefore, Chatterjee's (1984) argument was not based on the established trustworthiness of the bootstrap bias estimator for factor loadings, but only on faith in the bootstrap. Such faith may be dangerous in real applications.

Perhaps it can be argued that since bootstrap bias estimation has been proven successful in other statistical contexts, Chatterjee's argument should be justifiable, in the sense that there should be some cross-validity of such bootstrap results to the analysis of covariance structures. This may or may not be true. Consider the simplest example in which bootstrap bias estimation "works," namely the case of the sample mean $\bar{X}$, an estimator of population mean μ. In this case, it can be proven that $\mathbf{B}^*(\bar{X})$ is always zero without regard to any real data set. Of course, this matches exactly the real bias of $\bar{X}$, which is well-known to be zero. A less optimistic case is the following. Consider the sample biased variance estimator $\hat{\sigma}^2$ for estimating the population variance σ^2. According to the definition in Equation 2, the real bias is $-\frac{1}{n}\sigma^2$, the well-known under-estimation using $\hat{\sigma}^2$. Doing some algebra shows that the bootstrap estimator of the real bias, that is, $\mathbf{B}^*(\hat{\sigma}^2)$, is $-\frac{1}{n}\hat{\sigma}^2$. Two things can be noticed here. First, unlike the case in which

$\mathbf{B}^*(\overline{X})$ is a constant, the realization of $\mathbf{B}^*(\hat{\sigma}^2)$ is a random quantity which depends on the observed value of $\hat{\sigma}^2$. Second, unlike the case in which $\mathbf{B}^*(\overline{X})$ is an unbiased estimator for $\mathbf{B}(\overline{X})$, $\mathbf{B}^*(\hat{\sigma}^2)$ is a biased estimator for $\mathbf{B}(\hat{\sigma}^2)$. The bias of $\mathbf{B}^*(\hat{\sigma}^2)$ is exactly $\frac{1}{n^2}\sigma^2$, an under-estimation (in absolute magnitude) of the real bias. On the other hand, it remains true that applying the bias correction in Equation 5 yields an estimator $\hat{\sigma}^2_{BC}$ which is less biased than the original estimator $\hat{\sigma}^2$ (the bias for the bias-corrected estimator is now just $-\frac{1}{n^2}\sigma^2$).

Although one might think that the bootstrap actually is not so bad in the case of $\hat{\sigma}^2$, the two examples together illustrate that the bootstrap estimator for biases may not work equally well in all cases (ideal for sample means but worse for the biased sample variance estimator). It would seem risky indeed to have blind faith in the bootstrap principle in the hope that bootstrap estimation of biases in the context of structural equation modeling will work out correctly. In our opinion, there should be established evidence for supporting the bootstrap estimation of bias within covariance structure analysis before a lot of faith is placed in interpretations of bootstrapping results. To overcome this shortcoming, Ichikawa and Konishi (1995) carried out an extensive simulation study on the use of the bootstrap in exploratory factor analysis. They found that if analytic rotation is employed, the bootstrap bias estimator $\mathbf{B}^*(\hat{\theta})$, on average, provided estimates that were quite close to the "true" bias $\mathbf{B}^*(\hat{\theta})$ (obtained empirically by the Monte Carlo method), where the elements in θ are factor loadings and error variances. Therefore, their results should provide some support for using the bootstrap bias estimator $\mathbf{B}^*(\hat{\theta})$ in covariance structure analysis. Unfortunately, bias estimation for the unrotated solution did not work as well. In fact, the sampling variability of the estimates using $\mathbf{B}^*(\hat{\theta})$ were very large in some cases, especially for unrotated factor loadings. These results led to the impression that even though bias estimation using the bootstrap may be close to the true bias on average, the precision (or reliability) of the estimates are still in doubt.

A related issue here is the mean square error (MSE, which can be defined as the sum of variance and bias squared) of $\hat{\theta}_{BC}$. It may be the case that $\hat{\theta}_{BC}$ is less biased than $\hat{\theta}$ as an estimator for θ, but in the meantime it has a much larger variability. As a result, a decrease in bias obtained by using the bias correction in Equation 5 may not compensate for the increase in variability, and the MSE of $\hat{\theta}_{BC}$ could thus be much larger than that of $\hat{\theta}$. Efron and Tibshirani (1993) also warned against the indiscriminate use of the bias correction. It seems that in the present stage of development, the use of the bootstrap estimator of bias $\mathbf{B}^*(\hat{\theta})$ in covariance structure analysis is still limited. It is not clear whether one can trust the bias estimates given by the bootstrap or whether the empirical bootstrap correction is always a good thing to do.

Estimation of Standard Errors

Estimation of variances and standard errors using the bootstrap is a relatively well-studied topic in structural equation modeling. First, let us define the covariance matrix of $\hat{\theta}$ as:

$$\mathbf{V}(\hat{\theta}) = \mathcal{E} \, [\hat{\theta} - \mathcal{E}\hat{\theta}] \, [\hat{\theta} - \mathcal{E}\hat{\theta}]^{\mathrm{T}}, \tag{6}$$

where, again, the expectation is taken with respect to the true distribution $\mathcal{F}$. The bootstrap estimator for $\mathbf{V}(\hat{\theta})$ is the (estimated) covariance matrix of the bootstrap values θ_j^*s. That is,

$$\mathbf{V}^*(\hat{\theta}) = \frac{1}{B-1} \sum_{j=1}^{B} [\theta_j^* - \bar{\theta}^*] \, [\theta_j^* - \bar{\theta}^*]^{\mathrm{T}}. \tag{7}$$

The corresponding bootstrap estimators of standard errors for the elements in $\hat{\theta}$ are simply the square roots of the diagonal elements in $\mathbf{V}^*(\hat{\theta})$. Chatterjee (1984) was probably the first one to propose using Equation 7 in the context of exploratory factor analysis. He argued that the factor loadings should be interpreted relative to their standard errors so as to determine their significance on a particular factor. Common rules of thumb, such as requiring standardized loadings to be greater than 0.4, do not take the sampling variability into account, and thus might not be appropriate. Lambert et al. (1991) also endorsed this point and proposed the use of the bootstrap method for setting up confidence intervals. Moreover, it was recognized that because of the use of rotation in getting a factor solution and a possibly non-normal distribution of the population, the standard errors of estimates were difficult to derive by using standard parametric methods. In such a situation, the bootstrap provides a very useful alternative. Similarly, Boomsma (1986) suggested the use of the bootstrap for estimating standard errors in analysis of covariance structures when the correlation matrix instead of the covariance matrix was the focus of interest, or when the population distribution was skewed. Stine (1989) and Bollen and Stine (1990), went a step further and proposed the use of the bootstrap method to estimate the standard errors of the estimates of standardized regression coefficients, and direct, indirect, and total effects. Basically, for any parametric function, $h(\theta)$ (including various effects, standardized regression coefficients), the estimator is just $h(\hat{\theta})$, where $h(\,\cdot\,)$ is a vector-valued function with any desirable dimensions. Then, the bootstrap estimator of the covariance matrix of $h(\hat{\theta})$ is:

$$\mathbf{V}^*(h(\hat{\theta})) = \frac{1}{B-1} \sum_{j=1}^{B} [h(\theta_j^*) - \bar{h}^*] \, [h(\theta_j^*) - \bar{h}^*]^{\mathrm{T}}, \tag{8}$$

where $\bar{h}^* = \frac{1}{B}\sum_{j=1}^{B} h(\theta_j^*)$. Certainly, Equation 8 is just a generalization of Equation 7, where $h(\hat{\theta}) \equiv \hat{\theta}$.

How does the bootstrap work in estimating standard errors? As previously mentioned, Chatterjee's (1984) study was limited to an example and virtually did not show much evidence for supporting the use of the bootstrap. And, although Bollen and Stine's (1990) study was full of real examples, it did not give much information for evaluating the performance of the bootstrap under finite samples. A more relevant result concerning the justification of the bootstrap was given by Boomsma (1986). He found, by simulation (Boomsma, 1983), that the ML method for estimating standard errors was inadequate in two cases: (a) They were too large when the correlation instead of the covariance matrix was analyzed; and (b) they were too small when the population distribution was skewed. Thus, a potential justification of the bootstrap was that it would provide smaller estimates of standard errors in the first case and larger estimates of standard errors in the second case. In fact, Boomsma (1986) did demonstrate such behavior of the bootstrap. Another piece of evidence about the validity of using the bootstrap came from the study by Ichikawa and Konishi (1995). By comparing the empirical standard errors obtained in simulation, they showed that the bootstrap did provide better (less biased) estimates of standard errors than the standard ML method when the distribution was nonnormal. When the underlying distribution was actually multivariate normal, the bootstrap, however, was not as good as the ML estimator. This is certainly natural because the bootstrap has to pay a price for not having any distributional assumption. Additional qualifications concerning the performance of the bootstrap in Ichikawa and Konishi (1995) must be made here. First, the bootstrap seems not to have worked well for a small sample size such as 150 in their study. Evidently, the bootstrap consistently overestimated the empirical standard errors when $n = 150$. But this was not a problem when $n = 300$. Therefore, it should be noticed that the empirical performance of the bootstrap must depend somewhat on sample sizes. Second, there was evidence that the bootstrap worked better for rotated loadings than for unrotated loadings. This is conceivably the case because, as the authors noted, "The unrotated solutions were not so well defined" (p. 89). The more important implication here is that the bootstrap may perform quite differently for different estimators within the same setting, let alone across different statistical settings. Therefore, it is risky to assume that the bootstrap can work well in the context of covariance structure analysis on the basis of faith, or on the basis of evidence outside the field. Nonetheless, Boomsma (1986) and Ichikawa and Konishi (1995) have provided supporting evidence for using the bootstrap to estimate standard errors in some nonstandard situations in the analysis of covariance structures.

Constructing Confidence Intervals

Constructing confidence intervals for parameters or parametric functions using the bootstrap is a more controversial topic (Efron, 1988). Unfortunately, this is also not a very well-studied topic in covariance structure analysis. Let us first define a $(1 - 2\alpha)100\%$ confidence interval (L, U) for a parameter β (an element of θ) by

$$\text{Prob}\{L < \beta < U\} = 1 - 2\alpha. \tag{9}$$

Notice in (9) that L and U, but not β, are considered to be random. This is the typical, classical (versus Bayesian) set-up. Now, by assuming the (asymptotic) sampling distribution of $\hat{\beta}$ to be normal with mean β and standard deviation $\sigma_{\hat{\beta}}$, we can have the following probability statement:

$$\text{Prob}\{z(\alpha) < \frac{(\hat{\beta} - \beta)}{\sigma_{\hat{\beta}}} < z(1 - \alpha)\} = 1 - 2\alpha \text{ (as } n \text{ goes to infinity)}, \tag{10}$$

where $z(\alpha)$ is the $\alpha \cdot 100$th percentile of the standard normal distribution. By changing the terms in (10), we can obtain the form similar to (9) as

$$\text{Prob}\{\hat{\beta} - z(1 - \alpha) \cdot \sigma_{\hat{\beta}} < \beta < \hat{\beta} - z(\alpha) \cdot \sigma_{\hat{\beta}}\} = 1 - 2\alpha \text{ (as } n \text{ goes to infinity)}, \tag{11}$$

so that $(L, U) \equiv (\hat{\beta} - z(1 - \alpha) \cdot \sigma_{\hat{\beta}}, \hat{\beta} - z(\alpha) \cdot \sigma_{\hat{\beta}})$ is the $(1 - 2\alpha)100\%$ confidence interval. When $\sigma_{\hat{\beta}}$ is not known and estimated by $\hat{\sigma}_{\hat{\beta}}$, the usual treatment is to replace the percentiles of the standard normal distribution in Equation 11 by the percentiles of the t-distribution, with appropriate degrees of freedom. That is, the $(1 - 2\alpha)100\%$ confidence interval of β is

$$(\hat{\beta} - t(1 - \alpha) \cdot \hat{\sigma}_{\hat{\beta}}, \hat{\beta} - t(\alpha) \cdot \hat{\sigma}_{\hat{\beta}}) \tag{12}$$

Three commonly used bootstrap methods are described as follows:

The Bootstrap-t. This method is intuitively valid because it was motivated by the form in Equation 12. Instead of relying on the tabled values of the t-distribution, which assumes a normal distribution in the population, the bootstrap-t method will empirically construct a "table," which is considered to be more appropriate under any distributional assumption. However, for this method to work, an estimator for $\sigma_{\hat{\beta}}$ must exist. Otherwise, a nested bootstrap (bootstrapping within bootstrap samples) may be used. Suppose such an estimator does exist and is denoted by $\hat{\sigma}_{\hat{\beta}}$, then it is certainly possible to get $\hat{\sigma}_{\hat{\beta}j}^*$ for the j-th bootstrap sample (by using the estimator $\hat{\sigma}_{\hat{\beta}}$ on the j-th bootstrap sample). Now define

$$t_j^* = \frac{\beta_j^* - \hat{\beta}}{\hat{\sigma}_{\beta_j^*}}. \tag{13}$$

After B times of bootstrapping, the bootstrap-t table is formed by the B t_j^* values. Then the bootstrapped $(1 - 2\alpha)100\%$ confidence interval for β is

$$(\hat{\beta} - t^*(1 - \alpha) \cdot \hat{\sigma}_{\hat{\beta}}, \hat{\beta} - t^*(\alpha) \cdot \hat{\sigma}_{\hat{\beta}}), \tag{14}$$

where $t^*(\alpha)$ is the $\alpha \cdot 100$-th percentile of the bootstrap distribution of t^*. Essentially, $t^*(\alpha)$ can be defined by the values which satisfy:

$$\frac{1}{B}\sum_{j=1}^{B} I\{t_j^* \le t^*(\alpha)\} = \alpha, \tag{15}$$

where $I\{\cdot\}$ is an indicator function. Usual interpolation methods can be used for finding a unique value of $t^*(\alpha)$. (See chapter 12 of Efron & Tibshirani, 1993, for determining a unique value of $t^*(\alpha)$ when such a value is restricted to be in the set of the bootstrapped t^* values.)

Percentile Method. Instead of bootstrapping those t^* values as in the bootstrap-t method, one can focus on the bootstrapped values of β_j^*s when using the percentile method. The $(1 - 2\alpha)100\%$ confidence interval for β is

$$(\beta^*(\alpha), \beta^*(1 - \alpha)), \tag{16}$$

where $\beta^*(\alpha)$ is the $\alpha \cdot 100$th percentile of the bootstrap distribution for β^*.

Bias-Corrected and Bias-Corrected-and-Accelerated Methods. To adjust the median biasedness of $\hat{\beta}$, the bias-corrected percentile method can be used (Efron, 1982, 1985, 1987). Define the estimated bias of $\hat{\beta}$ in standardized units by

$$\hat{z}_0 = \Phi^{-1}(\frac{1}{B}\sum_{j=1}^{B} I\{\beta_j^* \le \hat{\beta}\}), \tag{17}$$

where $\Phi(\cdot)$ is the distribution function of the standard normal variable. Notice that if $\hat{\beta}$ is unbiased, $\hat{z}_0$ should be zero on average. The $(1 - 2\alpha)100\%$ bias-corrected confidence interval for β is then

$$(\beta^*(\alpha_1), \beta^*(\alpha_2)), \tag{18}$$

where $\alpha_1 = \Phi(2\hat{z}_0 + z(\alpha))$ and $\alpha_2 = \Phi(2\hat{z}_0 + z(1-\alpha))$. Certainly, Expression 18 reduces to Expression 16 when $\hat{z}_0 = 0$, where no bias is detected by using Equation 17. An improvement over (18) proposed by Efron (1987) is called the bias-corrected and accelerated method (BC_a). The BC_a method differs from the bias-corrected method by incorporating an acceleration $\hat{a}$, which is computable from a given set of data (see chapter 14 of Efron & Tibshirani, 1993, or Lambert et al., 1991, for the exact formula), in setting up the confidence intervals. That is, the $(1 - 2\alpha)100\%$ BC_a confidence interval for β is

$$(\beta^*(\alpha_{a1}), \beta^*(\alpha_{a2})), \tag{19}$$

where $\alpha_{a1} = \Phi(\hat{z}_0 + \frac{\hat{z}_0 + z(\alpha)}{1 - \hat{a}(\hat{z}_0 + z(\alpha))})$ and $\alpha_{a2} = \Phi(\hat{z}_0 + \frac{\hat{z}_0 + z(1-\alpha)}{1 - \hat{a}(\hat{z}_0 + z(1-\alpha))})$. Again, if both $\hat{a}$ and $\hat{z}_0$ are zero, this reduces to the percentile method in Equation 16.

Which bootstrap method is the best? Efron and Tibshirani (1993) recommend the BC_a method because its good mathematical properties are not completely shared by other bootstrap methods (i.e., transformation respecting and second-order correctness). Bollen and Stine (1990) introduced use of the percentile method in covariance structure analysis. Lambert et al. (1991) investigated the applications of the percentile, bias-corrected, and BC_a methods for constructing confidence intervals for factor loadings by using hypothetical data sets. From our point of view, neither Bollen and Stine (1990) nor Lambert et al. (1991) provided supporting evidence on the applicability of the bootstrap construction of confidence intervals to covariance structure analysis. Ichikawa and Konishi (1995) investigated the performance of the bootstrap-t method for constructing confidence intervals in the context of exploratory factor analysis. They showed by simulation ($n = 150$ and $n = 300$) that *on average* the 0.01 and 0.99 percentage points of the bootstrap-t table (regarding factor loadings as well as error variances) are close to the actual percentage points (obtained empirically), even under some contaminated normal distributions (non-normal distributions). They thus advocated the use of Expression 14 for constructing confidence intervals. However, it can be argued that Ichikawa and Konishi's basis of judgment is not without problem. The reason is that the bootstrap-t method assumes that $t = \frac{\hat{\beta} - \beta}{\hat{\sigma}_\beta}$ is an (asymptotic) pivot (i.e., a statistic whose distribution does not depend on the actual population value of β) so that the probability statement in Equation 12 could be (asymptotically) correct. It may be the case that when sample size is not so large, such as $n = 150$, t is not quite pivotal. As a result, merely showing the closeness of the (averaged) bootstrap-t table to the "actual" t-table (obtained from a simulation method), but without the pivotal property, may not necessarily lead to a correct coverage probability as claimed in Expression 14 (see Schenker, 1985, for an expository note for the need of the pivotal quantity for bootstrapping and the coverage problems of bootstrap confidence intervals for small and moderate samples). A more direct method to judge the performance of the bootstrap-t confidence intervals is by observing their empirical coverage probability. That is, we can just verify whether the proportion of samples of which the $(1-2\alpha)\,100\%$ confidence intervals covers the true β is $(1-2\alpha)$. A close match to theoretical coverage probability should indicate a good performance of the bootstrap-t method. Lambert et al. (1991) attempted to use such a criterion for judging the bootstrap methods for constructing confidence intervals, but unfortunately, as they noted, they did not have independent samples for arriving at concrete conclusions about the coverage performance of the bootstrap.

Model Testing

Model testing using the bootstrap is an area that has not received as much attention as the other bootstrap applications in the analysis of covariance structures, possibly because the model test statistic T has long been deemphasized as a suitable measure of model fit in the field. Beran and Srivastava (1985) were probably the first to propose a bootstrap method for testing patterns of covariance structures (see also Zhang, Pantula, & Boos, 1991). Their set up is somewhat different from the present framework, however. In their notation, the null hypothesis on a covariance structure model is H_0: $\Sigma = \pi(\Sigma)$, where $\pi(\cdot)$ is a continuous function which is not an identity mapping and Σ is p × p square symmetric. An example for the null hypothesis of this kind is the equicorrelation model of the form:

$$\Sigma = \begin{pmatrix} \sigma^2 & \rho\sigma^2 & \rho\sigma^2 & \dots & \rho\sigma^2 \\ \rho\sigma^2 & \sigma^2 & \rho\sigma^2 & \dots & \rho\sigma^2 \\ \rho\sigma^2 & & \ddots & & \rho\sigma^2 \\ \vdots & & & \ddots & \rho\sigma^2 \\ \rho\sigma^2 & \rho\sigma^2 & \dots & \rho\sigma^2 & \sigma^2 \end{pmatrix}. \tag{20}$$

For the null hypothesis, the structure of Σ in (20) can be defined by the following function $\pi(\cdot)$ (see Zhang et al., 1991):

$$\pi(A) = b\{(1-a)\,\mathrm{I}_p + a\,1_p 1'_p\}, \tag{21}$$

with

$$a = \left\{\frac{(\mathrm{sum}(A))}{\mathrm{trace}(A)} - 1\right\}/(p-1), \tag{22}$$

and

$$b = \frac{\mathrm{trace}(A)}{p}, \tag{23}$$

where A is a p × p square symmetric matrix, I_p is a p × p identity matrix, 1_p is a p × 1 vector with all 1s as its elements, trace($\cdot$) is the scalar function of a matrix that sums up the diagonal elements of the matrix, and sum($\cdot$) is a scalar function of a matrix that sums up all elements of the matrix. As noted already, under the null hypothesis, the normal theory likelihood ratio test statistic, say T, is distributed as a central χ^2 variate with df degrees of freedom, where $df = \frac{p(p+1)}{2} - $ #(parameters). For the equicorrelation model in Equation 20, $df = \frac{p(p+1)}{2} - 2$, the two parameters being ρ and σ^2, respectively. Suppose the model under the null hypothesis is fitted to the observed covariance matrix S_n, and the fitted covariance matrix is denoted by $\hat{\Sigma}$ so that $\hat{\Sigma} = \pi(\hat{\Sigma})$ is satisfied. Again, for the equicorrelation model, $\hat{\rho}$ and $\hat{\sigma}^2$ are simply estimated respectively by the solutions of a and b in Equations 22 and 23 into which $A = S_n$ is substituted. Then $\hat{\Sigma}$ is obtained by Equation 20, with the sample estimates replacing the unknown parameters. In general, to obtain an estimate of the sampling distribution of T, instead of resampling from the original data, Beran and Srivastava (1985) essentially suggested the following resampling space for bootstrapping:

$$R = \left\{ y_i = \hat{\Sigma}^{\frac{1}{2}} S_n^{-\frac{1}{2}} x_i, i = 1, 2, \ldots, n \right\}. \tag{24}$$

By doing the bootstrapping procedures as described before, Beran and Srivastava (1985) claimed that the bootstrap distribution of T^* can be used as an estimator for the sampling distribution of T, virtually under any distribution (provided the existence of the first four mixed moments). They proved analytically that the bootstrap distribution of T^* converges to the limiting sampling distribution of T asymptotically.

Bollen and Stine (1993), in the same context as our present framework for covariance structure analysis, proposed a similar strategy for estimating the sampling distribution of the test statistic under the null model M_0. Their proposed resampling space was essentially of the form:

$$R = \left\{ y_i = \Sigma(\hat{\theta})^{\frac{1}{2}} S_n^{-\frac{1}{2}} x_i, i = 1, 2, \ldots, n \right\}. \tag{25}$$

which is very similar to Beran and Srivastava (1985, although Bollen & Stine used $x_i - \bar{x}$ in place of x_i in Equation 25; however, this does not affect the covariance structure of R in Equation 25). To distinguish this procedure from completely nonparametric bootstrapping, we call the resampling from R in Equation 25 the bootstrap-M_0 method, for the reason that the covariance structure assumed in the null model M_0 has been utilized in the transformation (i.e., $\Sigma(\cdot)$) in Equation 25. Then, the significance of the original test statistic (under any distribution) is referred to the bootstrapped distribution of T^*. Basically, the p value of the original test statistic is estimated by

$$p^* = \frac{1}{B} \sum_{j=1}^{B} I\left\{ T_j^* > T \right\}. \tag{26}$$

It is, of course, very interesting to know why Equation 24 or Equation 25 is needed. What would happen if we had not transformed the original data according to Equation 24 and used the completely nonparametric method of bootstrapping? Under multivariate normality and the null model M_0, Bollen and Stine (1993) showed that if the completely nonparametric bootstrap is employed, the distribution of T^* would be more like a noncentral χ^2, instead of a central χ^2. They argued that the key for bootstrap-M_0 is to "force" the resampling space to satisfy the null hypothesis so that the null distribution of T can be estimated. That is, for the transformed data y_is, the covariance matrix would be $\Sigma(\hat{\theta})$, which by definition satisfies the null hypothesis. Details about the argument can be found in Bollen and Stine (1993). In addition, they proposed procedures for estimating the sampling distribution of the χ^2 difference test statistic for two nested models, with the model in the null hypothesis being more restrictive. This requires the same transformation as in Equation 25 and the two nested models are fitted to the bootstrap samples, respectively. Then the bootstrap distribution of the pairwise difference in χ^2 for the two nested models is used as an estimate of the sampling distribution of the χ^2-difference test statistic.

Although Bollen and Stine (1993) did not prove analytically the validity of the bootstrap-M_0 for estimating the null distribution of T under arbitrary distributions, as was done by Beran and Srivastava (1985), they did give evidence that the completely nonparametric bootstrap (i.e., in their terms, the naive bootstrap) would not work. The examples and a single simulation given by Bollen and Stine (1993) are illustrative, but do not provide strong evidence regarding the validity of their bootstrapping procedures. We believe, however, that Bollen and Stine's (1993) bootstrapping methods can be justified asymptotically, using a proof similar to that of Beran and Srivastava (1985). Recently, simulation results by Ichikawa and Konishi (1995) showed that the bootstrap-M_0 method does lead to an appropriate estimation of the null distribution of T, even under some contaminated normal distributions with sample size less than 300. Their conclusion is based on the fact that there is a close matching of the "averaged" bootstrap estimation of the null distribution of T to the "actual" (obtained by an extensive Monte Carlo method) distribution of T.

Another line of "bootstrap" research on model testing in covariance structures analysis was done by Yung and Bentler (1994). Their main contribution was to propose the use of empirical corrections to the ADF (asymptotically distribution-free; see Browne, 1984) test statistic using the bootstrap. They showed by simulation that the bootstrap-corrected ADF test statistic behaved much more closely to what is expected than the uncorrected statistic. Also, it was shown that the corrections worked better for $n = 500$ than $n = 250$. Unfortunately, their bootstrapping procedures do not fit our present bootstrapping framework very well. To reduce com-

putations, their procedures just produce one bootstrapped value of the
test statistic, say T^*. Basically, the single T^* value is obtained by fitting the
model to a "typical bootstrap sample" with its covariance matrix equal to
the mean of the bootstrapped values of covariance matrices and its "weight"
matrix (required for the ADF test statistic) proportional to the covariance
matrix of the elements of the bootstrapped covariance matrices. Then the
two types of corrections they proposed are of the following forms:

$$T_{BC,I} = 2T - T^*, \tag{27}$$

and

$$T_{BC,II} = T^2 / T^*, \tag{28}$$

where $T_{BC,I}$ is called the ADF test statistic with an additive bias correction and
$T_{BC,II}$ is the ADF test statistic with a proportional bias correction. Although
the "bootstrap" method proposed by Yung and Bentler (1994) was substantiated by simulation results, their procedures are not quite the same as the
usual bootstrap. Therefore, because of the lack of more detailed theoretical
justification, one must question whether their simulation results could be
generalizable to other setups. To evaluate this requires further research.

Does the Bootstrap "Work"?

To answer the question whether the bootstrap "works," we have to define
what we mean by this phrase. Let us list three criteria in order of strictness:

1. Analytic results show that the bootstrap method is correct.
2. Simulation results show that the bootstrap method is adequate.
3. Examples show that the bootstrap method is adequate.

In principle, there are statistical standards for judging a method as
"correct" or "adequate" in these criteria, for example, consistency, convergence to the true limiting distribution, match to the empirical "true" values,
and so on. Of course it may be difficult to apply these criteria. In addition,
because the bootstrap is designed primarily for situations where severe
statistical assumptions such as large sample size and multivariate normality
may not hold, it would be reasonable to require the bootstrap to have
adequate performance even under situations which violate these assumptions, and where existing or standard methods may not work satisfactorily.
  To classify the supporting evidence according to the listed criteria for the
validity of the bootstrap applied to covariance structure analysis, we see that
only the Beran and Srivastava (1985) or Bollen-Stine (1993) type of bootstrap
tests have strong analytical results. For simulation results, Boomsma (1986)

provided evidence that supports the use of bootstrap estimation of standard errors. In addition, simulation results from Ichikawa and Konishi (1995) give support to the use of the bootstrap for bias estimation and confidence interval construction (only for the bootstrap-t method), as well as the bootstrap testing using T. If their method can be counted as a standard bootstrap, Yung and Bentler (1994) also provide supporting evidence for the bootstrap correction to the ADF χ^2 test statistic. Much weaker supporting evidence for the validity of the bootstrap is given by Chatterjee (1984), Bollen and Stine (1990), and Lambert et al. (1991), who gave examples to demonstrate the plausibility and reasonableness of the bootstrap method. Therefore, in the present stage of development, the strongest evidence is for the validity of bootstrap tests. Supporting evidence for bias estimation, estimation of standard errors, and confidence intervals (only for bootstrap-t) by the bootstrap are mainly on exploratory factor-analytic models (except for Boomsma, 1986). More evidence is needed for confirmatory models, especially for bias estimation and variants of confidence interval construction by the bootstrap.

It must be stressed here that we do not mean that examples (e.g., Chatterjee, 1984; Bollen & Stine, 1990; and Lambert et al., 1991) are not helpful to judging the usefulness of the bootstrap. In fact, it is usually interesting and motivating to justify the bootstrap by an example, especially if this is then followed up with simulation or analytical results. However, examples usually do not permit the use of strict criteria that could be used to judge the reasonableness of the bootstrap. As stated earlier, any bootstrap application on a particular sample is still an estimation; hence it is subject to error and cannot be an infallible standard. Then, how should one evaluate the performance of the bootstrap if there is only a single application on a particular sample? Here we suggest a plausible strategy. That is, we can compare the bootstrap with another well-justified method that has been shown to work well even under situations where severe statistical assumptions may not be true. If the bootstrap really "works," then its performance under such situations should resemble the performance of such a well-justified method. Next, we illustrate this strategy with an example. In addition, we hope to get some further insights about the bootstrap from this example.

JUSTIFYING BOOTSTRAP ESTIMATION
OF STANDARD ERRORS WITH AN EXAMPLE

The Data and Some Preliminary Considerations

The example considered here is Holzinger and Swineford's (1939) data for cognitive ability of the seventh and eighth grade students in a suburb of Chicago. Only part of the data is used here ($n = 145$). A confirmatory factor-analytic model with three factors is hypothesized for nine observed variables. The three factors are labeled *Space, Verbal,* and *Memory.* The original scores for all nine variables are divided by their ranges so that they are approximately at the same scale. Then the factor-analytic model is fitted by the ML method. Sörbom (1974), in the context of multiple-group factor analysis, formulated a confirmatory factor-analytic model by assuming the existence of high and low ability groups. Yung (1994) gave evidence for the heterogeneity of the samples. According to Yung, the data may be considered to be a mixture of two multivariate normals. That is, the data is not quite multivariate normal, but has about 10% contaminated cases with high performance scores. Therefore, the ML method is not completely appropriate because the estimates of standard errors would be (approximately) correct only if the data were drawn from a multivariate normal population. However, there is a method (called the ML-Robust method in EQS; Bentler, 1989, Equation 10.13), which provides asymptotically correct estimates of standard errors even if the distribution is not multivariate normal. These robust standard errors were developed for covariance structure analysis by Dijkstra (1981), Browne (1984), and more generally by Bentler and Dijkstra (1985).

On the other hand, because the bootstrap method does not assume multivariate normality, it can be claimed also to provide adequate estimates of standard errors in such a situation. Because we just have one data set and do not know the actual population, a possible justification regarding the appropriateness of the bootstrap estimates of standard errors could be their "closeness" to the robust standard errors, as compared to the usual information matrix ML standard errors. In other words, if the bootstrap method really "works," it should improve over the ordinary ML method by providing more adequate estimates of standard errors which are closer to the robust ones. Thus we have established a criterion for judging the validity of the bootstrap estimation of standard errors.

There remains a question of which bootstrap method to use here, the completely nonparametric bootstrap or the bootstrap-M_0. According to Bollen and Stine (1993), the completely nonparametric bootstrap should be used for estimating the standard errors, whereas the bootstrap distribution of the test statistic should be estimated by the bootstrap-M_0 (see note 11 of Bollen and Stine). We postpone a discussion on this while we just apply the two types of bootstrapping on the data and see what happens to the results.

In addition, in line with the ideas appeared in Jorgensen (1987), Stine (1989), and Bollen and Stine (1990, 1993) proposed a so-called 1-iteration method for model fitting (characterized by Equation 1) within the bootstrapping loop. The argument for using one iteration instead of full iterations for the bootstrap samples is that, because the estimates obtained in the parental sample are consistent, one iteration would be enough to attain (asymptotic) efficiency of estimates for the bootstrap samples in which consistent estimates are provided as the initial values. Bentler and Dijkstra (1985) provide the theory for such linearized estimation in standard situations. Of course, the 1-iteration method would be a very economic alternative to the full iteration model fitting procedure if it actually provides results which are not very discrepant from those of the full iteration procedure. Therefore, it is also interesting to see whether this is the case for the present example, so that hopefully, we can gain some insights about the plausibility of the 1-iteration fitting procedure.

Bootstrapping Results and Interpretations

Estimation of Bias. Estimates of biases using the bootstrap (1-iteration or full-iteration) are very small in absolute values. This means that the two variants of the bootstrap actually provide estimates that are close to those provided by the model fitting of the parental sample. Notice that we do not mean that the bootstrap shows that the estimates are "unbiased." Results for estimation of biases are not shown because this is not the main concern here.

Estimation of Standard Errors. The estimates of standard errors are shown in Table 7.1. The entries for the bootstrap methods ("B-F" for the completely non-parametric bootstrap with full-iterations and "B-M_0-F" for the bootstrap-M_0 with full-iterations) in Table 7.1 were intended to be based on B = 500 bootstrap samples. However, because of the occurrence of improper solutions and non-convergence problems, estimation of the standard errors using the bootstrap was based on the non-problematic cases alone. The number of bootstrap samples deleted were 20 and 10 respectively for B-F and B-M_0-F. For the 1-iteration versions, the number of bootstrap samples deleted (for samples with improper solutions) were 5 and 7 respectively for the completely non-parametric bootstrap and the bootstrap-M_0. The corresponding results for the 1-iteration bootstrap methods are not shown in Table 7.1, but are compared to their full-iteration versions in Table 7.2.

Table 7.2 indicates (Comparison 1) that, on average, the estimates of standard errors using B-1 are different from the full iteration version by .41%. Therefore, it seems that the B-1 method can be used without the risk of being far off from the solution obtained by B-F. The same conclusion can be drawn for the difference between B-M_0-1 and B-M_0-F (Comparison 2 in Table 7.2), because the average percentage difference is 2.66%. Without much loss of generality, we only consider the full-iteration versions of the bootstrap for comparison to the ML and ML-Robust methods. First of all, estimates of standard errors by the ML-Robust (ML-R in Table 7.1) method are usually larger than that of the ML method (11 out of 16 cases). Table 7.2

TABLE 7.1
Estimation of Standard Errors Using the Maximum Likelihood
and the Bootstrap Methods

	ML	ML-R	B-F	B-M_0-F
Φ_{12}	9169	11747	12947	12192
Φ_{13}	9841	10695	11822	10816
Φ_{23}	9668	11936	12506	12092
Ψ_{11}	307	335	368	360
Ψ_{22}	266	311	309	303
Ψ_{33}	276	292	312	310
Ψ_{44}	197	202	207	208
Ψ_{55}	247	254	251	251
Ψ_{66}	180	175	184	183
Ψ_{77}	445	431	505	461
Ψ_{88}	309	387	365	364
Ψ_{99}	558	584	678	607
Λ_{11}	1622	1720	1790	1727
Λ_{21}	1495	1378	1471	1400
Λ_{31}	1536	1740	1831	1728
Λ_{42}	1306	1466	1370	1405
Λ_{52}	1457	1451	1541	1556
Λ_{62}	1246	1662	1706	1642
Λ_{73}	1958	1817	2210	1889
Λ_{83}	1630	1812	2171	1939
Λ_{93}	2185	2138	2495	2156

Note. Entries should be multiplied by 10^{-5}. ML: Maximum Likelihood; ML-R: Maximum Likelihood-Robust method; B-F: Completely nonparametric bootstrap with full iterations; B-M_0-F: Bootstrap-M_0 with full iterations. Entries under column B-F are based on 480 bootstrap replications with proper and converged solutions. Entries under column B-M_0-F are based on 490 bootstrap replications with proper solutions.

(Comparison 3) indicates that on average the estimate of standard errors of the ML-Robust method is 8.54% larger than those of the ML method. Theoretically, the estimates provided by ML-R should be more adequate here. How do the bootstrap methods compare to these methods? From Table 7.2 (Comparisons 4 and 5), it is obvious that B-F behaves more closely to the ML-R than to the ML method. On average, the standard errors provided by the B-F are 16.01% larger than those from the ML method, whereas they are just 7.20% larger than those of the ML-R method. The same pattern of results as for B-F is observed for the B-M_0-F methods (Comparisons 6 and 7). That is, B-M_0-F standard error estimates are closer to ML-R (2.06% difference on average) than to ML (10.60% difference on average). Moreover, Comparisons 5 and 7 show that B-M_0-F is closer to ML-R than is B-F.

The possible implications of these results are as follows. (a) The bootstrap did some automatic adjustment to the ML standard errors, taking

TABLE 7.2
Comparisons Between Methods for Estimating Standard Errors

Method A	Method B	Average Percentage Difference (Standard Deviation)	
1 B-F	B-1	.41%	(6.29%)
2 B-M_0-F	B-M_0-1	2.66%	(2.93%)
3 ML	ML-R	8.54%	(11.58%)
4 ML	B-F	16.01%	(11.75%)
5 ML-R	B-F	7.20%	(7.81%)
6 ML	B-M_0-F	10.60%	(10.60%)
7 ML-R	B-M_0-F	2.06%	(3.84%)

Note. In all comparisons, Method A is treated as a baseline for assessing the percentage differences in estimating the standard errors by Method B. That is, the percentage difference is defined as $(s(B)/s(A) - 1) \times 100\%$, where $s(A)$ and $s(B)$ are the estimates of standard errors for the same estimate using methods A and B, respectively.

into account distributional violations in a way that is comparable to the adjustment done by the ML-Robust method. So, there is weak evidence that bootstrap estimation of standard errors would work adequately even for non-normal data using ML estimation. (b) The fact that the standard errors obtained by B-M_0-F are closer than B-F to those obtained by ML-R is compatible with the notion that the usual estimates of standard errors in covariance structure analysis are, in fact, *model-based*. That is, the estimates of standard errors provided by ML or ML-R methods are based on the assumption that the null model M_0 is true. Judged from this perspective, it seems that B-M_0-F, which incorporates information regarding the covariance structure model, is the legitimate bootstrap method that is compatible with traditional estimation procedures. This also explains why one should observe the results of Comparisons 5 and 7 in Table 7.2. On the other hand, because the completely nonparametric bootstrap does not utilize any model information, the estimates of standard errors by it are not necessarily comparable to those obtained from ordinary model-based estimation methods such as ML-R. Does it follow that one should use the bootstrap-M_0 indiscriminately? Not quite. The argument is as follows.

Completely Nonparametric Bootstrap Versus Bootstrap-M_0. Certainly, if the estimation of the null sampling distribution of the test statistic is required, then only the bootstrap-M_0 is appropriate. This was argued forcefully by Bollen and Stine (1993). They also proposed that one can use a completely nonparametric bootstrap for estimating standard errors. Is such an eclectic approach inconsistent? It may not be. If one believes the philosophy that structural models are never exactly true (even at the population level), then the completely nonparametric bootstrap is the right approach. Cudeck and Henly (1991; see also Cudeck & Browne, 1983; Browne & Cudeck, 1989), based on the general framework of Linhart and Zucchini (1986), suggested an approach to covariance structure modeling that puts an emphasis on this philosophy. Their framework should naturally lead to a completely nonparametric bootstrap. Although this is still an open issue and one should not rush to a definite conclusion at this time, the distinction between the completely nonparametric bootstrap and the bootstrap-M_0 methods should be clear: The former is designed for distribution- and model-free situations, whereas the latter is designed for distribution-free situations only. Such a distinction is important to the future development of bootstrap procedures in covariance structure modeling.

1-Iteration or Full-Iteration for the Test Statistic. The aforementioned results regarding the estimation of standard errors indicate that the B-1 method can replace the more computational demanding B-F method without much risk. How about the difference in performance between B-M_0-1 and B-M_0-F regarding the estimation of p-value of the test statistic? Using Equation 26, one can estimate the p-value using p* when bootstrap-M_0 is used. In Table 7.3, bootstrapping results using B-M_0-1 and B-M_0-F are compared to the theoretical $\chi^2(24)$ distribution (the distribution for the test statistic under multivariate normality and the null model M_0). In order to be more careful about the results of the bootstrap, we repeated the bootstrapping procedure to assess if there was uncertainty about the bootstrap results due to simulation using finitely many samples (B = 500 was intended). Again, those bootstrap samples with nonconverged (not applied to B-M_0-1) and improper solutions were deleted from the analysis. The two blocks of results for B-M_0-1 and B-M_0-F respectively show that there is little to worry about regarding the stability of the bootstrapping. The p value of the test statistic is .0229 when compared to the theoretical χ^2 distribution. All bootstrapping results give more conservative estimates of the p values. However, it is obvious that the B-M_0-1 method does not resemble B-M_0-F in the present situation. Whereas the $p*$ value is around .108 using B-M_0-1, it is just around .057 by B-M_0-F (averaging the two blocks of results in each case). Therefore, the present results indicate that even though the 1-iteration procedure claims to have the same asymptotic efficiency as the full-iteration version (in our example, it even needs the normality assumption to be qualified), it may act quite differently in finite samples in certain aspects (e.g., the significance of the test statistics). This result demonstrates a danger to using the 1-iteration model fitting procedures for bootstrap samples. In addition, in the present example, if the estimates from the parental sample are set to be the initial values for the bootstrap samples, it was observed that only 3 to 4 iterations were needed to get converged solutions for most of the bootstrap samples. Thus, using

TABLE 7.3
The Significance Level of the χ^2 Test Statistic

	$\chi^2(24)$	B-M_0-1, I	B-M_0-1, II	B-M_0-F, I	B-M_0-F, II
Replications	0	493	494	490	493
Mean	24	28.260	28.355	25.066	24.934
SD	6.928	9.629	9.810	8.522	8.225
p value	0.0229	0.1034	0.1134	0.0592	0.0548

Note. The number of bootstrap replications attempted was 500 for each bootstrapping. The number of replications shown in Table 7.3 are those results with converged and proper solutions. The obtained p values using the bootstrap are based on those converged and proper solutions only. B-M_0-1, I: Bootstrap-M_0 with a single iteration, the first block. B-M_0-1, II: Bootstrap-M_0 with a single iteration, the second block. B-M_0-F, I: Bootstrap-M_0 with full iterations, the first block. B-M_0-F, II: Bootstrap-M_0 with full iterations, the second block.

full iterations actually did not seem to create much of a computational burden. In fact, in the present example, B-M_0-1 on average consumed 1.282 cpu for a bootstrap sample, whereas B-M_0-F consumed 1.944 cpu on average (based on computations by EQS using a 486 IBM/PC computer). Therefore, it seems that in practice there is no need to minimize the computations by using the 1-iteration alternative, as the computation-accuracy trade-off does not favor the 1-iteration procedure, at least for the estimation of the significance levels of the test statistics.

TWO MORE APPLICATIONS OF BOOTSTRAP TESTS IN STRUCTURAL EQUATION MODELING

The idea of the bootstrap (as expressed in the bootstrap principle) is simple but useful, and different types of applications to analysis of covariance structures based on this principle have been explored as noted before. These seem to cover most problems in this field. Nonetheless, let us try to extend the logic of bootstrap tests to two more areas in structural equation modeling.

Testing Structural Equation Models with Mean and Covariance Structures: Bootstrap-M_0 Method

Beran and Srivastava's (1985), or Bollen and Stine's (1993) idea of bootstrapping can be extended easily to structural equation models with mean and covariance structures. This is achieved by transforming the observed sample such that its first and second moments satisfy the hypothesized mean and covariance structure completely. In this case, we can define the following resampling space according to the null model, M_0, as:

$$R(M_0) \equiv \left\{ y_i = \hat{\Sigma}_0^{\frac{1}{2}} S_n^{-\frac{1}{2}} (x_i - \bar{x}_n) + \hat{\mu}_0, \ i = 1, 2, \ldots, n \right\}, \qquad (29)$$

where $\hat{\Sigma}_0 = \Sigma(\hat{\theta})$ and $\hat{\mu}_0 = \mu(\hat{\theta})$ are estimated under the null hypothesis. The bootstrap distribution of T^* will be used as an estimate for the sampling distribution of the original test statistic T. The bootstrap estimate of the p value of T would be p^*, which is defined in Equation 26. The above real-data example shows that p^* may be quite different from the original p value using the standard ML method. This is natural because the bootstrap does not require any distributional assumption and captures the nonnormality as indicated in samples for bootstrapping. Although the justification of Equation 29 for bootstrapping awaits further evidence, it would seem that the work by Beran and Srivastava (1985) and Bollen and Stine (1993) would back up the current approach to bootstrapping. Loosely speaking, the transformation in Equation 29 is intended to achieve the goal that the mean and covariance matrix of the resampling space $R(M_0)$ satisfy exactly the mean and covariance structures hypothesized by the null model M_0.

We stress that p^* is an estimator because it is estimated from samples, whereas the original p value obtained from the ML method is not an estimate but is an exact value provided that the population distribution is exactly multivariate normal. Here, the distinction is important because it implies that the bootstrapped p^* value is a random variable and thus it may or may not be reliable. This is due, of course, to abandoning the assumption of a normal distribution. Therefore, as we judge any estimation method, the bootstrap method can rarely be justified by just one simulation or one example alone. In the present context, this means that without knowing the sampling variability of p^*, we cannot trust the bootstrap blindly (especially when the sample size is extremely small). We will elaborate on this point in the next section.

Power Calculations with Specified Alternative Models: Bootstrap-M_A Method

The transformation in Equation 29 according to M_0 motivates another type of transformation. That is, we can transform the observed data in a way that the resampling space R will have certain specified covariance and mean structures, but not necessarily according to the null model M_0. How about a bootstrap-M_A method which has a resampling space $R(M_A)$ according to the alternative model M_A? What can one achieve by using this bootstrap-M_A method? The answer is: estimation of power.

Satorra and Saris (1985) discussed the importance of using power calculations as a tool for evaluating models. By assuming the multivariate normal distribution, they proposed a practical method for approximating the power calculation of the likelihood ratio test (essentially based on the

TABLE 7.4
Distinctions Between Several Methods for Calculating/Estimating the
Power of the Likelihood Ratio Test of Structural Equation Models

	Empirical	*Approximate*	*Bootstrap-M$_A$*	*Bootstrap-$\hat{M}_A$*
Structural Equations	✓	✓	✓	✓
Parameter Values	✓	✓	✓	
Distribution	✓	✓		
Simulation	✓		✓	✓

Note. "✓": need to be specified/conducted.

ML test statistic T) for a specified alternative structural equation model, say M_A. They showed that the approximation is good when compared to the empirical (the "true") power, which was obtained by simulations. Columns 2 and 3 in Table 7.5 show the power calculations under different α-levels in the Satorra and Saris (1985) study. Basically, there are close agreements between the empirical and approximate calculations of the power for the likelihood ratio tests at different α levels. As shown in Table 7.4, where distinctions between several methods for calculating power are made, an advantage of using approximate power calculation is that no simulation is needed. However, it also can be observed that both the empirical and approximate methods would require the specification of the distribution under the alternative model. The distributional assumption made by Satorra and Saris (1985) was multivariate normality. This is an assumption that one may not be willing to make in many practical situations.

To relax the assumption of multivariate normality, two variants of the bootstrap are now introduced. They are also included in Table 7.4 for comparison. The first one is called the "bootstrap-M_A" method. Basically, for this method to work, one has to specify the alternative structural model (M_A) completely, just as for the two methods proposed by Satorra and Saris (1985). That is, the structural equations and the parameter values (θ_A) should all be hypothesized. Consequently, Σ_A and μ_A are just vectors with known values. Now, define the following resampling space for the bootstrap-M_A method as:

$$R(M_A) \equiv \left\{ y_i = \Sigma_A^{\frac{1}{2}} S_n^{-\frac{1}{2}} (x_i - \bar{x}_n) + \mu_A, i = 1, 2, \dots, n \right\}. \tag{30}$$

Once the resampling space has been specified, the usual bootstrapping procedures (still fitting the null model M_0 for the bootstrap samples), as described previously, can be carried out. By focusing on the set of boot-strapped T_j^* values, the power of the test at a specific α-level is estimated by:

$$W^*(M_A, \alpha) = \frac{1}{B} \sum_{j=1}^{B} I\left\{ T_j^* > K_{df}^{-1}(1 - \alpha) \right\}, \tag{31}$$

TABLE 7.5
Power Calculations/Estimation Using Satorra and Saris (1985) Example
($n = 100$)

	Emp.	Appr.	"Best" B-M_A	"Best" B-$\hat{M}_A$	"Ave." B-M_A	"Ave." B-$\hat{M}_A$
$\alpha = .001$	.033	.061	.027	.060	.065 (.018)	.075 (.083)
$\alpha = .005$	.103	.141	.102	.122	.143 (.022)	.148 (.142)
$\alpha = .010$	.177	.198	.159	.182	.203 (.025)	.198 (.165)
$\alpha = .025$	.297	.302	.284	.288	.307 (.022)	.282 (.201)
$\alpha = .050$	.390	.407	.412	.404	.415 (.022)	.369 (.222)
$\alpha = .100$	.520	.535	.558	.528	.540 (.023)	.472 (.231)

Note. Emp.: Empirical power obtained from simulations by Satorra and Saris (1985); Appr.: Approximate power calculations proposed by Satorra and Saris (1985); B-M_A: The bootstrap-M_A result with assumed parameter values under H_A; B-$\hat{M}_A$: The bootstrap-$\hat{M}_A$ result without assuming parameter values under H_A. "Best": The bootstrapping results of the sample among the total of ten samples which shows the closest agreement with the empirical power calculation. "Ave.": The averaged results based on ten random samples. Parenthesized values are standard deviations.

where df is the degrees of freedom of the test statistic, $K_{df}(\cdot)$ is the distribution function of the central χ^2 variable with df degrees of freedom. Here, df should be the same as the degrees of freedom in the null model. Up to now, we have not made any distributional assumption about the data with the bootstrap-M_A method, as is clearly shown in Table 7.4. Instead, the distribution under the alternative model M_A is estimated by the distribution of y_i, say $\hat{\mathcal{F}}_{n,A}$, and has been taken into account implicitly in the bootstrapping procedures.

Furthermore, we can actually relax one more specification of the alternative model. That is, only the structural equation model is hypothesized but without any specified parameter values for θ_A. This will be our "bootstrap-$\hat{M}_A$" method introduced here. If the parameter values, say θ_A, are not specified, we can get some estimates, say $\hat{\theta}_A$, by using the minimization using Equation 1 for fitting the alternative model M_A. However, $\hat{\theta}_A$ must be consistent for the method to work appropriately. Denote the estimated theoretical moments as $\hat{\Sigma}_A = \Sigma(\hat{\theta}_A)$ and $\hat{\mu}_A = \mu(\hat{\theta}_A)$, then the resampling space for bootstrap-$\hat{M}_A$ method is defined as:

$$R(\hat{M}_A) \equiv \left\{ y_i = \hat{\Sigma}_A^{\frac{1}{2}} S_n^{-\frac{1}{2}} (x_i - \bar{x}_n) + \hat{\mu}_A, i = 1, 2, \ldots, n \right\}. \quad (32)$$

As in the bootstrap-M_A method, the power of the test at a specific α level can be estimated using Equation 31 after bootstrapping on $R(\hat{M}_A)$. The estimator is denoted here by $W^*(\hat{M}_A, \alpha)$.

We stress that the two bootstrap methods proposed here are intended to provide "estimates" of power because the population distribution has been estimated implicitly from the data instead of being assumed. This approach should be clearly distinguished from the empirical and approximate *calculations* suggested by Satorra and Saris (1985) in Table 7.4. If the multivariate normality assumption can be assumed, then the power calculation given by the empirical method used by Satorra and Saris (1985) is exact (subject to numerical accuracy due to simulation). The approximation method, on the other hand, only gives values of power that are exact for extremely large samples. In order to obtain some *initial* evidence about the proposed bootstrap-M_A and bootstrap-$\hat{M}_A$ methods, a small simulation was conducted (for $n = 100$). We did not simulate the case for $n = 600$, as was done by Satorra and Saris (1985), because the power at all α levels are essentially too high (all of them are greater than .94) to make a useful comparison between methods. The setup of the simulation is the same as specified in Satorra and Saris (1985), and the corresponding results here would be comparable to theirs. For the two proposed bootstrap methods, the number of bootstrap replications B was set to be 1000.

In Column 4 of Table 7.5, the result of a *single* simulation using the bootstrap-M_A is shown. Ignoring the label of Column 4 at this moment, it seems that the power estimates using the bootstrap-M_A are quite close to those of the empirical method, which are supposed to be exact. However, the bootstrap-M_A did this without assuming normality (although the data are actually drawn from a multivariate normal distribution). In Column 5, where the result of a *single* simulation using the bootstrap-$\hat{M}_A$ is shown, the estimates of power at all α levels still are close to the empirical power, except perhaps for $\alpha = .001$ (but it is no worse than the approximation method). However, the bootstrap-$\hat{M}_A$ method did this without any knowledge about the distribution and parameter values under the alternative model M_A!

We have purposely misled our readers by showing the most optimistic results in Columns 4 and 5 out of ten repeated sampling from a multivariate normal distribution. That is why we label *Best* in Columns 4 and 5. In fact, not all ten random samples yielded good estimates of power using the bootstrap methods. Some of them are really bad, as compared to the empirical method. As a usual strategy for studying any innovative estimation method, we usually assess the quality of estimators by looking at their expected values and standard errors. The last two columns in Table 7.5 for the two bootstrap methods serve such a purpose. In Column 6, where the results based on ten repeated samplings for the bootstrap-M_A are shown, it is observed that the mean values of the power estimates are still close to the empirical method, but it seems that they are much closer to those of the approximation method. The standard errors are quite small, as compared to the estimates of power. Therefore, we may conclude that the bootstrap-M_A method works fine for power estimation even without the normality information. In contrast, Column 7 shows that although the average values of the power estimates using the bootstrap-$\hat{M}_A$ method seem to be close enough to either of the empirical and approximation methods, their standard errors of estimates are quite large (i.e., they are really not reliable). Apparently, this is due to the price one pays for not assuming parameter values, as compared to the bootstrap-M_A method.

Certainly, our simulation results are quite limited because we just have 10 repeated samples drawn from a multivariate normal distribution. In addition, we did not examine these bootstrap methods under nonnormal distributions, which is usually more interesting for judging the validity of bootstrap methods. Nonetheless, our results suffice to show that a *single* simulation result about any innovative bootstrap method can be misleading. Our crude sampling experiment clearly shows that the reliability of the estimates using the bootstrap must also be taken into account. In this respect, we show initial evidence that the bootstrap-M_A method may work well, whereas the bootstrap-$\hat{M}_A$ method may not be reliable enough. Further research should extend the present methodology to nonnormal conditions and increase the number of repeated (independent) samples to have a clearer picture about the proposed bootstrap-M_A and bootstrap-$\hat{M}_A$ methods.

A final comment about the present methodology is best illustrated in Table 7.4. That is, the proposed bootstrap methods are very much like the empirical method, in which simulation is used for getting solutions, but notably without a distributional assumption (and parameter values for bootstrap-$\hat{M}_A$). Such resemblance to the empirical method suggests the following conceptual formula for the bootstrap-M_A:

"Bootstrap-M_A" = "Empirical Method Without Distributional Assumption."

CAUTIONARY NOTES AND CONCLUSIONS

There are some cautionary notes that we have not mentioned explicitly but that are quite important for a better understanding of the bootstrap. Let us now have a brief look at these, and then make our final conclusions.

1. *Assumption of iid (Independent and Identical Distributed) Property of Observations.* This is a central assumption for the bootstrap to work in the present framework. Such an assumption is essential for justifying the replacement sampling from R of the bootstrap. Bollen and Stine (1988) illustrated the problem of lacking such iid property for bootstrapping. Had this iid property not been true, the bootstrap resampling would have to be modified. An obvious example that lacks the iid property is multilevel covariance structure analysis.

2. *Adequacy of Estimation of Standard Errors by the Bootstrap Does Not Mean That It Is the "Best" Method.* Although the bootstrap may give accurate esti-

mates of standard errors, this does not mean that estimation using the bootstrap (coupled with certain estimation methods) must yield (asymptotically) efficient estimates. For example, when applying the bootstrap to the Ordinary Least Squares (OLS) method for model estimation, one may get unbiased estimates of standard errors, but this by no means implies that the bootstrap with OLS estimation is the "best" method available. A method such as ADF (Browne, 1984) may be more efficient asymptotically for parameter estimates under arbitrary distributions. The point here is that even if the bootstrap may help a particular estimation method to work more accurately under a set of less severe assumptions, one may still prefer to use some other estimation method due to the desire to achieve certain statistical properties like efficiency, robustness and so on.

   3. *Sample Size Requirement.* It must be emphasized that the bootstrap method is not a panacea for small sample sizes. The reason is obvious because the success of the bootstrap depends on the accuracy of the estimation of the parent distribution (and/or under a particular model) by the observed sample distribution. For an acceptable degree of accuracy, one cannot expect a very small sample for the bootstrap to work satisfactorily. Such argument is supported by the simulation results obtained by Ichikawa and Konishi (1995) and Yung and Bentler (1994). In structural equation modeling, perhaps the real advantage of using the bootstrap may be its "automatic" refinement on standard asymptotic theories (e.g., higher order accuracy) so that the bootstrap can be applied even for samples with moderate (but not extremely small) sizes.

   Now, let us conclude the present chapter with the following points:

   1. *Applicability of the Bootstrap to Covariance Structure Analysis.* Certainly, the bootstrap may yield results that will be useful for covariance structure analysis and structural equation modeling. However, this conclusion is based on differential evidence supporting the use of bootstrapping, as discussed previously. The bootstrap principle cannot be blindly trusted because there are cases in which it will not work (see, e.g., Bollen & Stine, 1988, 1993; Bickel et al., 1994, for some interesting examples of bootstrap failures). But the worst thing is that it is usually difficult to give a general rule to predict when the bootstrap principle will fail. More evidence for the validity of the bootstrap should be gathered for different areas of applications in structural equation modeling. In addition, there are some issues regarding evaluation of bootstrap methods. Since the bootstrap is designed to address situations without strong distributional assumptions, the trade-off is that one can only get "estimates," instead of exact values in some occasions, as opposed to traditional estimation methods with distributional assumptions. The p level of test statistics and the power of the test

are two examples of this. In these cases, we must assess the precision (or the variability) of the bootstrap estimates. The bootstrap estimates must also be precise to be useful. Certainly, the evaluation of the precision of the bootstrap estimation cannot be done simply by using a single example or a single simulation. More extensive simulation studies are needed. Practically, it would be nice to have a method for assessing (or estimating) the precision of the bootstrap estimates in each single application. The jack-knife-after-bootstrap method introduced in Efron and Tibshirani (1993, pp. 275–280) may provide a useful empirical technique for estimating the standard errors of the bootstrap estimates (see also Efron, 1992). This would be an important aspect of the bootstrap that needs to be investigated more in structural equation modeling.

2. *Completely Nonparametric Bootstrap Versus Bootstrap-M_0 and Bootstrap-M_1.* Modifications in the resampling space for bootstrapping are needed in some applications such as estimating the sampling distribution of a test statistic and the power of the test against an alternative model. In other situations, it seems that the completely non-parametric approach is more reasonable and realistic.

3. *1-Iteration Versus Full-Iteration.* It is safe to use full-iteration model fitting procedures within a bootstrapping loop because this does not require much additional computer time and appears to give more accurate results (e.g., estimation of significance levels) in practical applications, as compared to the 1-iteration method.

ACKNOWLEDGMENTS

This research was supported in part by a University Research Council grant of the University of North Carolina at Chapel Hill to the first author, and grants DA01070 and DA00017 from the National Institute on Drug Abuse to the second author. We thank Dr. Kenneth A. Bollen for his useful comments that helped to correct some mistakes in an earlier version of the chapter.

REFERENCES

Bentler, P. M. (1989). *EQS structural equations program manual.* Los Angeles, CA: BMDP Statistical Software, Inc.

Bentler, P. M., & Dijkstra, T. (1985). Efficient estimation via linearization in structural models. In P. R. Krishnaiah (Ed.), *Multivariate analysis VI* (pp. 9–42). Amsterdam: North-Holland.

Bentler, P. M., & Wu, E. J. C. (1995). *EQS for windows user's guide.* Encino, CA: Multivariate Software.

Beran, R., & Srivastava, M. S. (1985). Bootstrap tests and confidence regions for functions of a covariance matrix. *Annals of Statistics, 13*, 95–115.

Bickel, P. J., Götze, F., & van Zwet, W. R. (1994). Resampling fewer than *n* observations: Gains, losses, and remedies for losses. *Diskrete Strukturen in der Mathematik* (Preprint 94-084). Bielefeld, Germany: Universität Bielefeld.

Bollen, K. A., & Stine, R. (1988). *Bootstrapping structural equation models: Variability of indirect effects and goodness of fit measures.* Paper presented at the Annual Meetings of the American Sociological Association, Atlanta, GA.

Bollen, K. A., & Stine, R. (1990). Direct and indirect effects: Classical and bootstrap estimates of variability. In C. C. Clogg (Ed.), *Sociological methodology* (pp. 115–140). Oxford: Basil Blackwell.

Bollen, K. A., & Stine, R. A. (1993). Bootstrapping goodness-of-fit measures in structural equation models. In K. A. Bollen & J. S. Long (Eds.), *Testing structural equation models* (pp. 111–135). Newbury Park, CA: Sage.

Boomsma, A. (1983). *On the robustness of LISREL (maximum likelihood estimation) against small sample size and non-normality.* Amsterdam: Sociometric Research Foundation.

Boomsma, A. (1986). On the use of bootstrap and jackknife in covariance structure analysis. *Compstat 1986,* 205–210.

Browne, M. W. (1984). Asymptotically distribution-free methods for analysis of covariance structures. *British Journal of Mathematical and Statistical Psychology, 37*, 62–83.

Browne, M. W., & Cudeck, R. (1989). Single sample cross-validation indices for covariance structures. *Multivariate Behavioral Research, 24*, 445–455.

Chatterjee, S. (1984). Variance estimation in factor analysis: An application of the bootstrap. *British Journal of Mathematical and Statistical Psychology, 37*, 252–262.

Cudeck, R., & Browne, M. W. (1983). Cross-validation of covariance structures. *Multivariate Behavioral Research, 18*, 147–167.

Cudeck, R., & Henly, S. J. (1991). Model selection in covariance structures analysis and the "problem" of sample size: A clarification. *Psychological Bulletin, 109*, 512–519.

Dalgleish, L. I. (1994). Discriminant analysis: Statistical inference using the jackknife and bootstrap procedures. *Psychological Bulletin, 116*, 498–508.

Dietz, T., Frey, R. S., & Kalof, L. (1987). Estimation with cross-national data: Robust and nonparametric methods. *American Sociological Review, 52*, 380–390.

Dijkstra, T. K. (1981). *Latent variables in linear stochastic models.* Groningen: Rijksuniversiteit.

Efron, B. (1979). Bootstrap methods: Another look at the jackknife. *Annals of Statistics, 7*, 1–26.

Efron, B. (1982). *The jackknife, the bootstrap and other resampling plans.* Philadelphia: SIAM.

Efron, B. (1985). Bootstrap confidence intervals for a class of parametric problems. *Biometrika, 72*, 45–58.

Efron, B. (1987). Better bootstrap confidence intervals (with discussion). *Journal of the American Statistical Association, 82*, 171–200.

Efron, B. (1988). Bootstrap confidence intervals: Good or bad? *Psychological Bulletin, 104*, 293–296.

Efron, B. (1992). Jackknife-after-bootstrap standard errors and influence functions. *Journal of the Royal Statistical Society: Series B, 54*, 83–127.

Efron, B., & Gong, G. (1983). A leisurely look at the bootstrap, the jackknife and cross-validation. *American Statistician, 37*, 36–48.

Efron, B., & Tibshirani, R. (1986). Bootstrap measures for standard errors, confidence intervals, and other measures of statistical accuracy. *Statistical Science, 1*, 54–77.

Efron, B., & Tibshirani, R. J. (1993). *An introduction to the bootstrap.* New York: Chapman & Hall.

Holzinger, K. J., & Swineford, F. (1939). A study in factor analysis: The stability of a bi-factor solution. *Supplementary Educational Monographs, 48*, 1–91.

Ichikawa, M., & Konishi, S. (1995). Application of the bootstrap methods in factor analysis. *Psychometrika, 60,* 77–93.

Jorgensen, M. A. (1987). Jackknifing fixed points of iterations. *Biometrika, 74,* 207–211.

Kotz, S., & Johnson, N. L. (1992). *Breakthroughs in statistics: Volumes 1 and 2.* New York: Springer-Verlag.

Lambert, Z. V., Wildt, A. R., & Durand, R. M. (1991). Approximating confidence intervals for factor loadings. *Multivariate Behavioral Research, 26,* 421–434.

Linhart, H., & Zucchini, W. (1986). *Model selection.* New York: Wiley.

Lunneborg, C. E. (1985). Estimating the correlation coefficient: The bootstrap approach. *Psychological Bulletin, 98,* 209–215.

Mooney, C. Z., & Duval, R. D. (1993). *Bootstrapping: A nonparametric approach to statistical inference.* Newbury Park, CA: Sage.

Rasmussen, J. L. (1987). Estimating the correlation coefficient: Bootstrap and parametric approaches. *Psychological Bulletin, 101,* 136–139.

Rasmussen, J. L. (1988). "Bootstrap confidence intervals: Good or bad": Comments on Efron (1988) and Strube (1988) and further evaluation. *Psychological Bulletin, 104,* 297–299.

Satorra, A., & Saris, W. E. (1985). Power of the likelihood ratio test in covariance structure analysis. *Psychometrika, 50,* 83–90.

Schenker, N. (1985). Qualms about bootstrap confidence intervals. *Journal of the American Statistical Association, 80,* 360–361.

Sörbom, D. (1974). A general method for studying differences in factor means and factor structures between groups. *British Journal of Mathematical and Statistical Psychology, 27,* 229–239.

Stine, R. A. (1989). An introduction to bootstrap methods: Examples and ideas. *Sociological Methods and Research, 8,* 243–291.

Strube, M. J. (1988). Bootstrap type I error rates for the correlation coefficient: An examination of alternate procedures. *Psychological Bulletin, 104,* 290–292.

Young, G. A. (1994). Bootstrap: More than a stab in the dark? (with comments). *Statistical Science, 9,* 382–415.

Yung, Y.-F., & Bentler, P. M. (1994). Bootstrap-corrected ADF test statistics in covariance structure analysis. *British Journal of Mathematical and Statistical Psychology, 47,* 63–84.

Yung, Y.-F. (1994). *Finite mixtures in confirmatory factor-analytic models.* Unpublished doctoral dissertation, UCLA.

Zhang, J., Pantula, S. G., & Boos, D. D. (1991). Robust methods for testing the pattern of a single covariance matrix. *Biometrika, 78,* 787–795.

CHAPTER EIGHT

A Limited-Information Estimator for LISREL Models With or Without Heteroscedastic Errors

Kenneth A. Bollen
University of North Carolina, Chapel Hill

The estimation of structural equation models (SEMs) is marked by two traits. One is the use of full-information estimators such as maximum likelihood (ML) or generalized least squares (GLS). The other is that the derivations of these estimators assumes that the variances of the disturbances or errors in each equation are constant across observations, that is, they are homoscedastic. This chapter has two primary purposes. First, I present an alternative two-stage least squares (2SLS) estimator and its asymptotic standard errors for the coefficients of LISREL[1] models developed in Bollen (1995, in press) under the assumption of homoscedastic errors. Second, I apply results from econometrics and sociometrics to expand the model to allow for heteroscedasticity of the disturbance term. This is done by providing heteroscedastic-consistent standard errors and developing alternative estimators that allow known or unknown forms of heteroscedasticity.

The 2SLS estimator recommended is a limited-information estimator in that researchers estimate coefficients one equation at a time. The full-information estimators (e.g., ML) that dominate the SEM field estimate all parameters in all equations simultaneously. This is both an asset and a liability. It is an asset in that information from the whole system can improve the efficiency of the estimator. However, a key drawback is that

---

[1]The term *LISREL* is used in the generic sense of SEMs with latent variables that include confirmatory factor analysis, recursive and nonrecursive equations, and simultaneous equation models as special cases.

specification error in one part of the system can bias coefficient estimates throughout the system. Limited-information estimators sometimes better isolate the biases due to specification error. Given that virtually all SEMs are misspecified, limited-information estimators are a viable option to pursue.

Heteroscedasticity of errors or disturbances is scarcely discussed in the SEM literature outside of the special case of econometric and regression models. This refers to the problem of errors or disturbances in either the latent variable or measurement models having variances that differ across observations. That is, the same disturbance might have a variance of 10 for the first case, a variance of 5 for the second case, and so on. The problem is not unusual in regression applications and there is no reason to think that it is less common in the more general SEM models.

Homoscedasticity, or equal variances of errors and disturbances across observations, is implicit in the LISREL model.[2] Heteroscedastic disturbances raise doubts about the appropriateness of the significance tests derived from the ML estimator. It is possible to find heteroscedastic-consistent asymptotic standard errors for the 2SLS estimator of LISREL models. Furthermore, the 2SLS estimator can take into account heteroscedasticity so as to increase its efficiency, an option that is not yet developed for the full-information estimators of LISREL models.

The first section briefly reviews the literature on limited-information estimators. The next section presents the notation, model, and the 2SLS estimator developed in Bollen (in press). The third section generalizes the estimator to allow heteroscedasticity of errors in the measurement or latent variable model. I then present a simulation example, and the last section in the chapter contains the conclusions.

LIMITED-INFORMATION ESTIMATORS IN LISREL MODELS

The literature on limited-information estimators in simultaneous equation models and econometric applications is vast and I do not review it here (see, e.g., Bowden & Turkington, 1984). The research on limited-information estimators of factor analysis or LISREL models is less extensive. Madansky (1964) suggested an instrumental variable (IV) estimator for the factor loadings in factor analysis models. Hägglund (1982) and Jöreskog (1983) proposed IV and 2SLS estimators for factor analysis models with uncorrelated errors of measurement. Other studies have examined issues such as scaling and computational algorithms (Cudeck, 1991; Jennrich, 1987), al-

---

[2]An explicit statement of the assumptions of homoscedasticity is in Bollen (1989, pp. 14–15, 18).

lowing correlated errors of measurement (Bollen, 1989, p. 415), and providing an overall test statistic for a factor analysis estimated by IV (Satorra & Bentler, 1991). Gerbing and Hamilton (1994) provided an iterative limited-information estimator for factor analysis models where all variables have a factor complexity of one. The Monte-Carlo evidence to date shows that the IV and 2SLS estimators perform well in factor analysis models (Brown, 1990; Hägglund, 1983; Lukashov, 1994).

Less frequent is work on limited-information estimators for the latent variable model (or "structural model"). Jöreskog and Sörbom (1986) and Lance, Cornwell, and Mulaik (1988) proposed estimators for the latent variable model. They first estimated the covariance (correlation) matrix of the latent variables by estimating the measurement model and then they used the formulas for 2SLS applied to the covariance matrix of the latent variables. A drawback of these estimators is that little is known about the distribution of the coefficient estimators. The analytical results for the distribution are complicated by the use of an estimate of the covariance (correlation) matrix of the latent variables for the estimates of the coefficients of the latent variable equation. In addition, in the case of Jöreskog and Sörbom's (1986) estimator, it depends on having uncorrelated errors of measurement in the measurement model. The next section describes an alternative 2SLS estimator that does not have these restrictions.

MODEL AND ESTIMATOR

This section presents the model and 2SLS estimator for the LISREL model under the assumption of homoscedastic errors. It draws heavily from Bollen (1995, in press). The model is presented in LISREL matrix notation (Jöreskog & Sörbom, 1986), although the same estimator applies when using other notational systems. The latent variable model is:

$$\eta = \alpha + \mathbf{B}\eta + \mathbf{\Gamma}\xi + \zeta \tag{1}$$

where η is an m x 1 vector of latent endogenous random variables, $\mathbf{B}$ is a m x m matrix of coefficients that give the impact of the ηs on each other, ξ is an n x 1 vector of latent exogenous variables, $\mathbf{\Gamma}$ is the m x n coefficient matrix giving ξ's impact on η, α is an m x 1 vector of intercept terms, and ζ is an m x 1 vector of random disturbances with the $E(\zeta) = 0$ and $COV(\xi, \zeta') = 0$. Assume for now that the disturbance for each equation is homoscedastic and nonautocorrelated across observations.

Two equations summarize the measurement model of the SEM:

$$\mathbf{x} = \tau_x + \mathbf{\Lambda}_x \xi + \delta \tag{2}$$

$$\mathbf{y} = \boldsymbol{\tau}_y + \boldsymbol{\Lambda}_y \boldsymbol{\eta} + \boldsymbol{\varepsilon} \tag{3}$$

where $\mathbf{x}$ is a q x 1 vector of observed indicators of ξ, $\boldsymbol{\Lambda}_x$ is a q x n matrix of "factor loadings" (regression coefficients) giving the impact of ξ on $\mathbf{x}$, $\boldsymbol{\tau}_x$ is q x 1 vector of intercept terms, and $\boldsymbol{\delta}$ is a q x 1 vector of measurement errors with $E(\boldsymbol{\delta}) = \mathbf{0}$ and $COV(\xi, \boldsymbol{\delta}') = \mathbf{0}$. The δ_i for the *i*th equation is homoscedastic and nonautocorrelated across cases. Similarly in Equation 3 $\mathbf{y}$ is a p x 1 vector of indicators of $\boldsymbol{\eta}$, $\boldsymbol{\Lambda}_y$ is the p x m matrix of factor loadings, $\boldsymbol{\tau}_y$ is a p x 1 vector of intercept terms, and $\boldsymbol{\varepsilon}$ is a p x 1 vector of errors with $E(\boldsymbol{\varepsilon}) = \mathbf{0}$ and $COV(\boldsymbol{\eta}, \boldsymbol{\varepsilon}') = \mathbf{0}$. And ε_i is homoscedastic and nonautocorrelated across observations. Another assumption is that $\boldsymbol{\varepsilon}$, $\boldsymbol{\delta}$, and ζ are mutually uncorrelated.

Suppose that for scaling purposes the model has one indicator per latent variable for which its factor loading is set to one and its intercept is set to zero (see Bollen, 1989, pp. 350–352). Assume that the scaling variable is only influenced by a single latent variable and an error term. Although most models will satisfy this condition, there are some, such as multitrait–multimethod models, that will not. I do not consider such cases here.

We begin by sorting the $\mathbf{y}$ and $\mathbf{x}$ vectors so that the indicators that scale the latent variables come first. Then we can create partitioned vectors for $\mathbf{y}$ and $\mathbf{x}$:

$$\mathbf{y} = \begin{bmatrix} \mathbf{y}_1 \\ \mathbf{y}_2 \end{bmatrix} \text{ and } \mathbf{x} = \begin{bmatrix} \mathbf{x}_1 \\ \mathbf{x}_2 \end{bmatrix}$$

where $\mathbf{y}_1$ is the m x 1 vector of y's that scale $\boldsymbol{\eta}$, $\mathbf{y}_2$ consists of the (p-m) x 1 vector of remaining y variables, $\mathbf{x}_1$ is the n x 1 vector of x's that scale ξ, and $\mathbf{x}_2$ is the (q-n) x 1 vector of remaining x variables.

This means that

$$\mathbf{y}_1 = \boldsymbol{\eta} + \boldsymbol{\varepsilon}_1 \tag{4}$$

or

$$\boldsymbol{\eta} = \mathbf{y}_1 - \boldsymbol{\varepsilon}_1 \tag{5}$$

and

$$\mathbf{x}_1 = \xi + \boldsymbol{\delta}_1 \tag{6}$$

or

$$\xi = \mathbf{x}_1 - \boldsymbol{\delta}_1 \tag{7}$$

where ε_1 and δ_1 contain the errors that correspond to y_1 and x_1. Substituting Equations 5 and 7 into Equation 1 leads to:

$$y_1 = \alpha + By_1 + \Gamma x_1 + u \qquad (8)$$

where $u = \varepsilon_1 - B\varepsilon_1 - \Gamma\delta_1 + \zeta$. Note that these manipulations recast the latent variable model into a simultaneous equation model where all variables are observed except for the composite disturbance term. The main difference is that in general u and x_1 are correlated rather than uncorrelated as is assumed in econometric simultaneous equation models. In some models, all or a subset of the variables in x_1 could be exogenous and hence uncorrelated with u.

Consider a single equation from Equation 8. Represent the ith equation from y_1 as:

$$y_i = \alpha_i + B_i y_1 + \Gamma_i x_1 + u_i \qquad (9)$$

where y_i is the ith y from y_1, α_i is the corresponding intercept, B_i is the ith row from B, Γ_i is the ith row from Γ, and u_i is the ith element from u.

Define A_i to be a column vector that contains α_i and all of the nonzero elements of B_i and Γ_i strung together in a column. Let N equal the number of cases and Z_i be an N row matrix that contains 1s in the first column and the N rows of elements from y_1 and x_1 that have nonzero coefficients associated with them in the remaining columns. The N x 1 vector y_i contains the N values of y_i in the sample and u_i is an N x 1 vector of the values of u_i. Then we can rewrite Equation 9 as:

$$y_i = Z_i A_i + u_i \qquad (10)$$

In all but exceptional situations, at least some of the variables in Z_i will be correlated with u_i and ordinary least squares (OLS) is inappropriate to estimate the coefficients in Equation 10. However, the 2SLS estimator provides an alternative consistent estimator of A_i.

To apply 2SLS we must find IVs for Z_i. The IVs must be: (a) correlated with Z_i, (b) uncorrelated with u_i, and (c) at least as many IVs as there are variables in Z_i. The pool of potential IVs comes from those ys and xs *not* included in Z_i (excluding, of course, y_i) and any variables in Z_i that are uncorrelated with u_i. We can check condition (a) by looking at the sample correlations between the potential IVs and Z_i. Identification requires that the third condition be satisfied and it is a simple counting rule that is easy to check. The second condition is more difficult to establish and the full model structure is essential in evaluating it. Recall that u_i equals $(\varepsilon_i - B_i\varepsilon_1 - \Gamma_i \delta_1 + \zeta_i)$. The IVs must be uncorrelated with each component in the composite. The $\mathbf{B_i\epsilon_1}$ term rules out using ys that both scale the latent variables and that have a nonzero impact on y_i. In addition, because of $\mathbf{B_i\epsilon_1}$ we cannot use ys as IVs that have correlated errors of measurement with those ys in $\mathbf{y_1}$ that appear in the y_i equation.

The $\mathbf{\Gamma_i\delta_1}$ term rules out xs as IVs that scale the latent ξs and that have a nonzero direct impact on y_i. In addition, any xs with correlated errors of measurement with such xs that appear in the y_i equation cannot be IVs. Finally, the ζ_i in the $\mathbf{u_i}$ eliminates any ys as IV that correlate with ζ_i. This means, for example, that ys that are indicators of ηs that are influenced by η_i would be ineligible as IVs. If any doubt on the suitability of an IV, say v_i, remains, then the researcher can check its correlation by determining the $COV(v_i, u_i)$. The equation for u_i should be substituted in and the reduced form for v_i should replace v_i. The reduced form is the equation for v_i with only exogenous and error variables on the right-hand side. Then the researcher can find whether the $COV(v_i, u_i)$ is zero. See Bollen (1995, in press) for further discussion of the selection of IVs in these models.

For now assume that we collect all eligible IVs for $\mathbf{Z_i}$ in an N row matrix $\mathbf{V_i}$. Then the first stage of 2SLS is to regress $\mathbf{Z_i}$ on $\mathbf{V_i}$ where Equation 11 provides the coefficient estimator:

$$(\mathbf{V_i'V_i})^{-1}\mathbf{V_i'Z_i} \tag{11}$$

Form $\overset{\wedge}{\mathbf{Z}}_i$ as:

$$\overset{\wedge}{\mathbf{Z}}_i = \mathbf{V_i}(\mathbf{V_i'V_i})^{-1}\mathbf{V_i'Z_i} \tag{12}$$

The second stage is the OLS regression of y_i on $\overset{\wedge}{\mathbf{Z}}_i$ so that

$$\overset{\wedge}{\mathbf{A}}_i = (\overset{\wedge}{\mathbf{Z}}_i'\overset{\wedge}{\mathbf{Z}}_i)^{-1}\overset{\wedge}{\mathbf{Z}}_i'\mathbf{y_i} \tag{13}$$

The 2SLS estimator assumes that:

$$plim\,(\tfrac{1}{N}V_i'Z_i) = \Sigma_{VZ_i} \tag{14}$$

$$plim\,(\tfrac{1}{N}V_i'V_i) = \Sigma_{V_iV_i} \quad\text{and} \tag{15}$$

$$plim\,(\tfrac{1}{N}V_i'\mathbf{u_i}) = \mathbf{0} \tag{16}$$

where plim refers to the probability limits as N goes to infinity of the term in parentheses. The right-hand side matrices of Equations 14 through 16 are finite, $\Sigma_{V_iV_i}$ is nonsingular, and Σ_{VZ_i} is nonzero. We assume that $E[\mathbf{u_iu_i'}] = \sigma_{u_i}^2\mathbf{I}$ and $E(\mathbf{u_i}) = \mathbf{0}$.

Under these assumptions, the 2SLS estimator, $\hat{A}_i$, is a consistent estimator of A_i. Assume that:

$$\frac{1}{\sqrt{N}} \hat{Z}_i' u_i \sim AN(O, \sigma_{u_i}^2 \Sigma_{\hat{Z}_i \hat{Z}_i}) \tag{17}$$

$$plim(\frac{1}{N} \hat{Z}_i' \hat{Z}_i)^{-1} = \Sigma_{\hat{Z}_i \hat{Z}_i}^{-1} \tag{18}$$

where $AN(O, \sigma_{u_i}^2 \Sigma_{\hat{Z}_i \hat{Z}_i})$ refers to an asymptotic normal distribution. With these assumptions, the asymptotic distribution of $\hat{A}_i$ is normal with a covariance matrix of $\sigma_{u_i}^2 \Sigma_{\hat{Z}_i \hat{Z}_i}^{-1}$.

The estimate of the asymptotic covariance matrix is:

$$acov(\hat{A}_i) = \hat{\sigma}_{u_i}^2 (\hat{Z}_i' \hat{Z}_i)^{-1} \tag{19}$$

where

$$\hat{\sigma}_{u_i}^2 = (y_i - Z_i \hat{A}_i)' (y_i - Z_i \hat{A}_i)/N \tag{20}$$

and acov signifies the sample estimate of the asymptotic covariance. The square root of the main diagonal of Equation 19 gives an estimate of the asymptotic standard errors of the coefficient estimates.

It should be noted that we have not assumed that the observed variables (xs, ys, or zs) are normally distributed. So the 2SLS estimator is applicable even for some observed variables that come from nonnormal distributions.

Estimates of the intercepts and factor loadings of the measurement model follow an analogous procedure to that of the latent variable model. More specifically, consider the measurement model for **x** in Equation 2. Substitute Equation 7 for ξ into Equation 2, which leads to:

$$x = \tau_x + \Lambda_x x_1 - \Lambda_x \delta_1 + \delta \tag{21}$$

Since x_1, the scaling variables, come first in **x**, the first n rows of τ_x are zero and the first n rows and n columns of Λ_x form an identity matrix.

Choosing one of the xs from the x_2 vector of nonscaling xs leads to:

$$x_i = \tau_{x_i} + \Lambda_{x_i} x_1 + d_i \tag{22}$$

where d_i equals $(- \Lambda_{x_i} \delta_1 + \delta_i)$, τ_{x_i} is the intercept for the x_i equation, Λ_{x_i} is the ith row of Λ_x, δ_i is the error of measurement for x_i. Define C_i to be a column vector that contains τ_{x_i} and all of the nonzero factor loadings in Λ_{x_i} put together in a column. N is the number of observations and let W_i be an N row matrix that contains 1s in the first column and the N rows of elements from x_1 that have nonzero factor loadings associated with them in the remaining columns. The $\mathbf{x}_i$ vector is N x 1 and contains the N values of x_i in the sample and $\mathbf{d}_i$ is an N x 1 vector of the values of d_i.

These definitions are similar to those for the latent variable model. In the measurement model for $\mathbf{x}$, they lead to

$$\mathbf{x}_i = \mathbf{W}_i\mathbf{C}_i + \mathbf{d}_i \tag{23}$$

Equation 23 is analogous to Equation 10. In fact, the 2SLS estimator applies to this equation as it did to Equation 10. The major difference is that a researcher must select IVs that are correlated with $\mathbf{W}_i$ and uncorrelated with $\mathbf{d}_i$. The 2SLS estimator for the $\mathbf{x}$ measurement model is:

$$\hat{\mathbf{C}}_i = (\hat{\mathbf{W}}_i'\hat{\mathbf{W}}_i)^{-1}\hat{\mathbf{W}}_i'\mathbf{x}_i \tag{24}$$

where

$$\hat{\mathbf{W}}_i = V_i(V_i'V_i)^{-1}V_i'\mathbf{W}_i$$

The $\mathbf{V}_i$ is the matrix of IVs that are suitable for the ith equation of the measurement model for $\mathbf{x}$. The procedure is so similar to that described for the latent variable model that it need not be described any further here. In addition, the same steps apply to estimating the equations for the measurement model for $\mathbf{y}$ (see Equation 3).

The results up to this point provide the means to estimate magnitudes and asymptotic standard errors for intercepts and coefficients for all the equations in the latent variable and in the measurement model. See Bollen (in press) for a discussion of a method to estimate the variances and covariances of the latent exogenous variables (ξ), of the equation disturbances (ζ), or of the errors of measurement (ε, δ).

HETEROSCEDASTIC DISTURBANCES

So far we have assumed that the disturbances of each equation are homoscedastic—have the same variances across observations. For some cross-sectional or longitudinal data, this may be too restrictive an assumption. In this section, heteroscedasticity, its consequences, methods to estimate heteroscedastic consistent standard errors, and estimators that take account of heteroscedasticity are discussed. A latent variable model is developed, but it is easy to see that an analogous method applies to the measurement model.

A useful starting point is to return to the previous model components of the disturbance u_i from the y_i Equation 9:

$$u_i = \varepsilon_i - \beta_i \varepsilon_1 - \Gamma_i \delta_1 + \zeta_i \qquad (25)$$

Heteroscedasticity can enter u_i in several ways. If the y_i variable that scales η_i has a heteroscedastic measurement error, ε_i, then this leads u_i to be heteroscedastic even if all the other components in Equation 25 are homoscedastic. An interesting implication of this is that the choice of scaling variable can determine whether heteroscedasticity is present. Thus, a consideration in choosing a scaling variable is whether its measurement error is homoscedastic. The $\beta_i \varepsilon_1$ and $\Gamma_i \delta_1$ terms mean that heteroscedasticity in the measurement errors for the other scaling variables that enter the y_i equation also can create heteroscedasticity of u_i. Finally, heteroscedasticity of the original error in the latent variable equation, ζ_i, means heteroscedasticity. This latter heteroscedasticity is not influenced by the choice of scaling indicators.

Two consequences follow the presence of heteroscedasticity in u_i. One is that it is possible to develop a 2SLS estimator with a "smaller" asymptotic covariance matrix. The other is that the usual uncorrected asymptotic covariance matrix for 2SLS is incorrect and this could lead to inaccurate statistical tests.

I discuss the second point first. Define the N x N nonsingular covariance matrix of u_i (from Equation 10) to be $\Omega_i (E(u_i u_i') = \Omega_i)$. In the case of homoscedasticity $\Omega_i = \sigma_{u_i} I$ where I is an N x N identity matrix. In Equation 17 the asymptotic covariance matrix of A_i under homoscedasticity is:

$$N^{-1} \sigma_{u_i}^2 \ \text{plim} \left(\frac{1}{N} \hat{Z}_i' \hat{Z}_i \right) \qquad (26)$$

Following Bollen (1984, p. 4) the asymptotic covariance matrix of $\hat{A}_i$ with heteroscedasticity is:

$$\text{ACOV}(\hat{A}_i) = N^{-1} \ \text{plim} \left(\frac{\hat{Z}_i' \hat{Z}_i}{N} \right)^{-1} \text{plim} \left(\frac{\hat{Z}_i' \Omega_i \hat{Z}_i}{N} \right) \text{plim} \left(\frac{\hat{Z}_i' \hat{Z}_i}{N} \right)^{-1} \qquad (27)$$

where ACOV is the population asymptotic covariance matrix. Equation 27 simplifies to Equation 26 when $\Omega_i = \sigma_{u_i}^2 I$. More generally, it shows that the homoscedasticity derived asymptotic covariance matrix departs from the one appropriate for heteroscedastic disturbances.

Eicker (1963), Horn, Horn, and Duncan (1975), and White (1980), among others, suggested a heteroscedastic consistent asymptotic covariance matrix for OLS regression models. Here, I use White's (1982) extension of these results to the 2SLS estimator that allows a heteroscedastic-consistent estimator of the asymptotic covariance matrix with unknown forms of heteroscedasticity. White (1982) began with a set of less restrictive assumptions than those I used earlier in this chapter. Assume that $\mathbf{Z}_i$ and $\mathbf{u}_i$ consist of independent but not (necessarily) identically distributed random variables. This assumption allows heteroscedasticity of $\mathbf{u}_i$. Earlier I assumed that

$$plim\left(\frac{V_i'Z_i}{N}\right) = \Sigma_{V_iZ_i}, \; plim\left(\frac{V_i'V_i}{N}\right) = \Sigma_{V_iV_i}, \text{ and } plim\left(\frac{V_i'\mathbf{u}_i}{N}\right) = \mathbf{0}$$

(see Equations 14 through 16). That is, I assumed that the moment matrices of the instrumental variables $\mathbf{V}_i$ and $\mathbf{Z}_i$, of $\mathbf{V}_i$ and $\mathbf{V}_i$, and of $\mathbf{V}_i$ and $\mathbf{u}_i$ stochastically converged to fixed matrices. White replaced these assumptions with the less restrictive ones of uniform boundedness of the error variances, the cross-moments of the elements of $\mathbf{V}_i$ and $\mathbf{Z}_i$, and the moments of the elements of $\mathbf{V}_i$ with itself. Also assumed is that the mean across observations of the cross-moment matrix of $\mathbf{V}_i$ and $\mathbf{Z}_i$ has uniformly full column rank, that the mean moment matrix of $\mathbf{V}_i$ with itself is uniformly positive definite, and that $E(\mathbf{V}_i'\mathbf{u}_i) = \mathbf{0}$ for all observations. These assumptions are less demanding than the previous ones in that the cross-moment and moment matrices need not converge to fixed matrices and the IVs, $\mathbf{V}_i$, and the disturbances $\mathbf{u}_i$ can have different distributions across observations.

Under general conditions (see White, 1982, pp. 487–490) the 2SLS estimator, $\hat{\mathbf{A}}_i$, has a heteroscedastic consistent asymptotic covariance matrix that is estimated by:

$$\text{acov}(\hat{\mathbf{A}}_i) = \left(\frac{\hat{\mathbf{Z}}_i'\hat{\mathbf{Z}}_i}{N}\right)^{-1} \left(\frac{\sum_{j=1}^{N} \hat{u}_{ij}^2 \hat{\mathbf{Z}}_{ij}' \hat{\mathbf{Z}}_{ij}}{N}\right) \left(\frac{\hat{\mathbf{Z}}_i'\hat{\mathbf{Z}}_i}{N}\right)^{-1} \tag{28}$$

where $\hat{\mathbf{Z}}_{ij} = \mathbf{V}_{ij}(\mathbf{V}_i'\mathbf{V}_i)^{-1}\mathbf{V}_i'\mathbf{Z}_i$, $\hat{u}_{ij} = Y_{ij} - \mathbf{Z}_{ij}\hat{\mathbf{A}}_i$, $j = 1, 2, \ldots, N$ indexes the observations in a sample, and the lower case "acov" stands for the sample estimate of the asymptotic covariance matrix.

Although Equation 28 is a consistent estimator of the asymptotic covariance matrix, there may be other consistent ones with better finite sample properties. One issue is that $\hat{u}_{ij}^2$ may not be the best estimator to use given the relation between $\hat{\mathbf{u}}_i$ and $\mathbf{u}_i$:

$$\begin{aligned}
\hat{\mathbf{u}}_i &= Y_i - \mathbf{Z}_i\hat{\mathbf{A}}_i \\
&= \mathbf{Z}_i\mathbf{A}_i + \mathbf{u}_i - \mathbf{Z}_i\hat{\mathbf{A}}_i \\
&= \mathbf{Z}_i(\mathbf{A}_i - \hat{\mathbf{A}}_i) + \mathbf{u}_i \\
&= \mathbf{u}_i - \mathbf{Z}_i(\hat{\mathbf{Z}}_i'\hat{\mathbf{Z}}_i)^{-1}\hat{\mathbf{Z}}_i'\mathbf{u}_i \\
&= (\mathbf{I} - \mathbf{Z}_i(\hat{\mathbf{Z}}_i'\hat{\mathbf{Z}}_i)^{-1}\hat{\mathbf{Z}}_i')\mathbf{u}_i \\
&= \hat{\mathbf{H}}\mathbf{u}_i
\end{aligned} \tag{29}$$

where $\hat{\mathbf{H}} = (\mathbf{I} - \mathbf{Z}_i(\hat{\mathbf{Z}}_i'\hat{\mathbf{Z}}_i)^{-1}\hat{\mathbf{Z}}_i')$. An estimator that takes account of the relation between $\hat{\mathbf{u}}_i$ and $\mathbf{u}_i$ might better estimate the variance of u_{ij} than $\hat{u}_{ij}^2$. Analogous concerns in the context of developing heteroscedastic-consistent standard error for OLS regression has led Horn et al. (1975) and MacKinnon and White (1985) to propose other estimators of the disturbance variances for each observation that have better finite sample performance than using $\hat{u}_{ij}^2$. The same might be true in this context.

Rather than estimating a heteroscedastic-consistent asymptotic covariance matrix of the 2SLS estimator, it is possible to develop an alternative estimator that incorporates unknown heteroscedasticity. White (1982, p. 491) called this the two-stage instrumental variable (2SIV) estimator and it is:

$$\hat{\mathbf{A}}_{i2SIV} = (\mathbf{Z}_i'\mathbf{V}_i\hat{\mathbf{\Omega}}_i^{-1}\mathbf{V}_i'\mathbf{Z}_i)^{-1}\mathbf{Z}_i'\mathbf{V}_i\hat{\mathbf{\Omega}}_i^{-1}\mathbf{V}_i'\mathbf{Y}_i \tag{30}$$

where $\mathbf{\Omega}_i$ is a diagonal matrix containing $\hat{u}_{ij}^2$ in the main diagonals. It has an estimated asymptotic covariance matrix of:

$$\mathrm{acov}(\hat{\mathbf{A}}_{i2SIV}) = (\mathbf{Z}_i'\mathbf{V}_i(\mathbf{V}_i'\hat{\mathbf{\Omega}}_i\mathbf{V}_i)^{-1}\mathbf{V}_i'\mathbf{Z}_i)^{-1} \tag{31}$$

The 2SIV estimator is generally asymptotically efficient relative to 2SLS under heteroscedastic disturbances (White, 1982, p. 492). Analysts can estimate $\hat{u}_{ij}^2$ by applying the usual 2SLS to the model and using these residuals to form $\hat{u}_{ij}^2$.

Another alternative available when a researcher knows $\mathbf{\Omega}_i$ or can consistently estimate it is GLS approach to 2SLS (Bollen, 1984; Bollen & Kmenta, 1986; Bowden & Turkington, 1984). The procedure is to: (a) estimate the reduced form of $\mathbf{Z}_i$ on $\mathbf{V}_i$ using $\mathbf{\Omega}_i^{-1}$ (or $\hat{\mathbf{\Omega}}_i^{-1}$) as a weight in a weighted least squares procedure, (b) estimate the second-stage structural equation with $\mathbf{\Omega}_i^{-1}$ (or $\hat{\mathbf{\Omega}}_i^{-1}$) as a weight substituting $\tilde{\mathbf{Z}}_i$ for $\mathbf{Z}_i$ where $\tilde{\mathbf{Z}}_i = \mathbf{V}_i\tilde{\mathbf{\Pi}}$ and $\tilde{\mathbf{\Pi}}$ is the matrix of reduced form coefficients from (a). More formally,

$$\hat{\mathbf{A}}_{iG2SLS} = (\tilde{\mathbf{Z}}_i'\mathbf{\Omega}_i^{-1}\tilde{\mathbf{Z}}_i)^{-1}\tilde{\mathbf{Z}}_i'\mathbf{\Omega}_i^{-1}\mathbf{Y}_i \tag{32}$$

where

$$\tilde{Z}_i = V_i(V_i'\mathbf{\Omega}_i^{-1}V_i)^{-1}V_i'\mathbf{\Omega}_i^{-1}Z_i$$

The estimate $\hat{\mathbf{\Omega}}_i^{-1}$ replaces $\mathbf{\Omega}_i^{-1}$ in the common case that the latter is not available. The estimated asymptotic variance of this coefficient estimator is $s^2 (\tilde{Z}'\mathbf{\Omega}_i^{-1}\tilde{Z})^{-1}$ where s^2 estimates the residual variance. The estimate $\hat{\mathbf{\Omega}}_i^{-1}$ replaces $\mathbf{\Omega}_i^{-1}$ when $\mathbf{\Omega}_i$ is not available. A valuable feature of the $\hat{A}_{iG2SLS}$ is that this estimator also applies to autocorrelated disturbances. Because the focus of the chapter is heteroscedasticity, I do not pursue the issue of auto-correlation here.

In summary, this section proposes several approaches to the problem of heteroscedasticity in latent variable models estimated with 2SLS. One is to estimate a heteroscedastic-consistent covariance matrix for the coefficients. Another is the 2SIV estimator of White (1982) that corrects for heteroscedasticity of an unknown form. The last is a GLS analog for 2SLS, G2SLS. These alternatives are illustrated in the next section.

EXAMPLE

To illustrate the estimators of the last section, I simulated a data set with the following structure:

$$
\begin{aligned}
\eta &= 5 + 2\xi + \zeta \\
x_1 &= \xi + \delta_1 \\
x_2 &= 5 + \xi + \delta_2 \\
x_3 &= \xi + \delta_3 \\
y_1 &= \eta + \varepsilon_1 \\
y_2 &= 5 + \eta + \varepsilon_2 \\
y_3 &= 5 + \eta + \varepsilon_3
\end{aligned}
\tag{33}
$$

where $\zeta = \zeta^* \xi$, $\delta_2 = \delta_2^* \xi$, $\delta_3 = \delta_3^* \xi$, $\varepsilon_3 = \varepsilon_3^* \xi$, and ζ^*, δ_1, δ_2^*, δ_3^*, ε_1, ε_2, ε_3^* are generated as independent, standardized normal variables using the "rndn" function in GAUSS (Aptech Systems, 1993). The ξ is a nonstochastic variable whose initial values are generated with a normal variable generator. This simulation leads to heteroscedasticity in the disturbances for the first, third, fourth, and seventh equations in Equation 33.

Consider the latent variable equation that is the first equation in Equation 33. Substituting $(x_1 - \delta_1)$ for ξ and $(y_1 - \varepsilon_1)$ for η leads to:

$$
y_1 = 5 + 2x_1 - 2\delta_1 + \varepsilon_1 + \zeta
\tag{34}
$$

The IVs for x_1 in this equation are x_2 and x_3. Table 8.1 provides the 2SLS, 2SIV, and G2SLS estimates for the latent variable model at the top of Equation 33 using Equation 34 as the observed variable form of the equation. The intercept and coefficient estimates are fairly close across estimators and are close to the population parameters for the equation. Because all estimators are consistent estimators under heteroscedasticity, this is not surprising. The estimates of the asymptotic standard errors are in parentheses (). Those for the 2SLS estimator would generally be inaccurate due

TABLE 8.1
2SLS, 2SIV, and G2SLS, Coefficient Estimates and Estimated Asymptotic
Standard Errors for Latent Variable Equation Using Simulated Data
($N = 200$)

| | η | | |
	2SLS	2SIV	G2SLS
Intercept	5.041	5.038	5.146
	$(0.212)^a$	(0.210)	(0.192)
	$[0.212]^b$		
ξ	2.273	2.275	2.187
	(0.245)	(0.301)	(0.295)
	[0.302]		

[a] estimated asymptotic standard error
[b] estimated heteroscedastic-consistent standard error

to the heteroscedasticity of the disturbance. The heteroscedastic-consistent
estimates of the asymptotic standard errors for the 2SLS estimates in the
first column are in brackets []. In this case the uncorrected standard errors
are smaller than the corrected standard errors for the regression coefficient, but not for the intercept. In other examples I found that the uncorrected standard errors are generally smaller than the corrected ones for
2SLS. The heteroscedastic-consistent asymptotic standard errors for 2SLS
are close to the standard errors for 2SIV and G2SLS estimates. I observed
a similar pattern in other examples with the G2SLS standard errors usually
the smallest. A far more extensive Monte-Carlo simulation study would be
required to determine whether general relations hold between these estimates and their asymptotic standard errors.

CONCLUSIONS

No SEM package fails to include full information estimators such as ML
or GLS. But most omit an option for limited-information estimators. A
major exception is the Jöreskog and Sörbom (1986) LISREL software. Even
LISREL, however, does not provide asymptotic standard errors for the limited-information estimators and the LISREL limited-information estimator
differs from that described here. Given the computational advantages, the
elimination of convergence problems, the decreased sensitivity to specification errors, and the possibility of significance testing under nonnormality, the 2SLS estimator presented here has great potential.

Furthermore, I explained how this estimator could be adapted to handle
heteroscedastic disturbances or errors. One modification I presented was

heteroscedastic-consistent asymptotic standard errors. Another is to apply estimators that correct for unknown or known forms of heteroscedasticity using 2SIV or G2SLS. The latter ability, to have an estimator that takes account of heteroscedasticity, is one that is not yet available for full-information estimators of LISREL models.

In other work, I show that equation-by-equation tests of overidentification apply to the 2SLS estimator (Bollen, in press). These should prove helpful in better isolating problems in the specification of a model. A different paper shows that the 2SLS estimator easily applies to models with interactions or other nonlinear functions of latent variables (Bollen, 1995).

Although the features of the 2SLS estimator sound extremely promising, I caution the reader that these properties are asymptotic. Analytical and simulation results should illuminate the finite sample behavior of the estimator and asymptotic standard errors. Then we will have a better sense of the practical advantages of the 2SLS, 2SIV, and G2SLS estimators.

ACKNOWLEDGMENTS

I gratefully acknowledge support for this research from the Sociology Program of the National Science Foundation (SES-9121564) and the Center for Advanced Study in the Behavioral Sciences, Stanford, California.

REFERENCES

Aptech Systems. (1993). *GAUSS: The GAUSS System Version 3.1*. Maple Valley, WA: Author.

Bollen, K. A. (1984). *A note on 2SLS under heteroscedastic and/or autoregressive disturbances*. Paper presented at the annual American Sociological Association Convention, San Antonio, TX.

Bollen, K. A. (1989). *Structural equations with latent variables*. New York: Wiley.

Bollen, K. A. (1995). Structural equation models that are nonlinear in latent variables: A least squares estimator. In P. M. Marsden (Ed.), *Sociological methodology* (pp. 223–251). Cambridge, MA: Blackwell.

Bollen, K. A. (in press). An alternative 2SLS estimator for latent variable equations. *Psychometrika*.

Bollen, K. A., & Kmenta, J. (1986). Estimation of simultaneous equation models with autoregressive or heteroscedastic disturbances. In J. Kmenta (Ed.), *Elements of econometrics* (pp. 704–711). New York: Macmillan.

Bowden, R. J., & Turkington, D. A. (1984). *Instrumental variables*. Cambridge: Cambridge University Press.

Brown, R. L. (1990). The robustness of 2SLS estimation of a non-normally distributed confirmatory factor analysis model. *Multivariate Behavioral Research, 25*, 455–466.

Cudeck, R. (1991). Noniterative factor analysis estimators, with algorithms for subset and instrumental variable selection. *Journal of Educational Statistics, 16*, 35–52.

Eicker, F. (1963). Asymptotic normality and consistency of the least squares estimators for families of linear regression. *Annals of Mathematical Statistics, 34*, 447–456.

Gerbing, D. M., & Hamilton, J. G. (1994). The surprising viability of a simple alternate estimation procedure for construction of large-scale structural equation measurement models. *Structural Equation Modeling, 1*, 103–115.

Hägglund, G. (1982). Factor analysis by instrumental variables. *Psychometrika, 47*, 209–222.

Hägglund, G. (1983). *Factor analysis by instrumental methods: A Monte Carlo study of some estimation procedures.* (Rep. No. 80-2). Sweden: University of Uppsala, Department of Statistics.

Horn, S. D., Horn, R. A., & Duncan, D. B. (1975). Estimating heteroscedastic variances in linear models. *Journal of the American Statistical Association, 70*, 380–385.

Jennrich, R. I. (1987). Tableau algorithms for factor analysis by instrumental variable method. *Psychometrika, 52*, 469–476.

Jöreskog, K. G. (1983). Factor analysis as an error-in-variables model. In H. Wainer & S. Messick (Eds.), *Principles of modern psychological measurement* (pp. 185–196). Hillsdale, NJ: Lawrence Erlbaum Associates.

Jöreskog, K. G., & Sörbom, D. (1986). *LISREL VI: Analysis of linear structural relationship by maximum likelihood, instrumental variables, and least squares methods* [computer program]. Mooresville, IN: Scientific Software.

Lance, C. E., Cornwell, J. M., & Mulaik, S. A. (1988). Limited information parameter estimates for latent or mixed manifest and latent variable models. *Multivariate Behavioral Research, 23*, 155–167.

Lukashov, A. (1994). *A Monte Carlo study of the IV estimator in factor analysis.* Unpublished master's thesis, Department of Sociology, University of North Carolina, Chapel Hill.

MacKinnon, J. G., & White, H. (1985). Some heteroskedasticity-consistent covariance matrix estimators with improved finite sample properties. *Journal of Econometrics, 29*, 305–325.

Madansky, A. (1964). Instrumental variables in factor analysis. *Psychometrika, 29*, 105–113.

Satorra, A., & Bentler, P. M. (1991). Goodness-of-fit test under IV estimation: Asymptotic robustness of a NT test statistic. In R. Gutiérrez & M. J. Valderrana (Eds.), *Applied stochastic models and data analysis* (pp. 555–566). Singapore: World Scientific.

White, H. (1980). A heteroskedasticity-consistent covariance matrix and a direct test for heteroskedasticity. *Econometrica, 48*, 721–746.

White, H. (1982). Instrumental variables regression with independent observations. *Econometrica, 50*, 483–499.

CHAPTER NINE

Full Information Estimation in the Presence of Incomplete Data

James L. Arbuckle
Temple University

Most multivariate methods require complete data, but most multivariate data contain missing values. This problem is usually dealt with by fixing the data in some way so that the data can be analyzed by methods that were designed for complete data. The most commonly used techniques for treating missing data are ad hoc procedures that attempt to make the best of a bad situation in ways that are seemingly plausible but have no theoretical rationale. A theory-based approach to the treatment of missing data under the assumption of multivariate normality, based on the direct maximization of the likelihood of the observed data, has long been known. The theoretical advantages of this method are widely recognized, and its applicability in principle to structural modeling has been noted. Unfortunately, theory has not had much influence on practice in the treatment of missing data. In part, the underutilization of maximum likelihood (ML) estimation in the presence of missing data may be due to the unavailability of the method as a standard option in packaged data analysis programs. There may also exist a (mistaken) belief that the benefits of using ML rather than conventional missing data techniques will, in practice, be small.

Recently, ML estimation for incomplete data has begun to appear as an option in structural modeling programs, giving new relevance to the theoretical work that demonstrates the advantages of this approach. This chapter has two purposes: (a) to demonstrate that ML estimation is a practical method that can be used on a routine basis, and (b) to give a rough indication of how much one can expect to benefit from its use. The chapter is organized as follows:

1. Current practice in the treatment of missing data is summarized.
2. ML estimation is described and its advantages stated.
3. Computational details are given for ML estimation and for some competing methods.
4. Two simulations are reported, comparing the performance of ML to the performance of competing missing data techniques. The first simulation demonstrates the efficiency of ML estimates. The second demonstrates the reduced bias of ML estimates when values that are missing fail to be missing "completely at random."
5. A simple "how to" example is presented to show how a ML analysis with incomplete data differs in practice from an analysis with complete data.
6. A second example shows how it can pay to design a study so that some data values are intentionally missing.
7. An approach to the imputation of missing values is described.
8. The computational cost of ML is addressed.

CURRENT PRACTICE IN THE TREATMENT
OF MISSING DATA

This chapter does not attempt to review extant approaches to the treatment of missing data. Summaries are provided, for example, by Kim and Curry (1977), Little and Rubin (1989), and Brown (1994). The purpose of this chapter is to focus on current practice in the handling of missing data, which appears to be dominated by the methods sometimes known as pairwise deletion (PD) and listwise deletion (LD). Kim and Curry remarked on the widespread reliance on these two methods. Roth (1994) made the same observation after examining 132 analyses in 75 studies taken from two psychology journals, *Journal of Applied Psychology* and *Personnel Psychology*. Roth noted that it was often hard to tell whether the data in an analysis contained any missing values. When it appeared that data values were missing, it was often unclear what technique was used to handle them. Guessing where necessary, Roth concluded that 86 of the 132 analyses were based on data that contained missing values. LD was used in 29 of those analyses. PD was used 24 times. Mean substitution and regression imputation (see, e.g., Kim & Curry, 1977) were each used once. In the remaining 31 cases, Roth could not tell which missing data technique was used. Because of the popularity of LD and PD, this paper was prepared with users of those two methods in mind.

ML ESTIMATION

The principles of ML estimation with incomplete data are well known (Anderson, 1957; Beale & Little, 1975; Hartley, 1958; Hartley & Hocking, 1971; Little, 1976; Rubin, 1974, 1976; Wilks, 1932). Finkbeiner (1979) used ML for common factor analysis with missing data. Allison (1987) and Muthén, Kaplan, and Hollis (1987) showed how the method applies to structural modeling.

Missing Data Mechanisms

In order to state the advantages of ML estimation over PD and LD, it is necessary to discuss mechanisms by which missing data can arise. In particular, it is necessary to make use of Rubin's (1976; Little & Rubin, 1989) distinction between data that are missing completely at random (MCAR) and data that are missing at random (MAR). Rubin's formal conditions for these two types of randomness are not easy to paraphrase. The distinction can be illustrated with the following simple example, which draws upon examples employed by Allison (1987) and by Little and Rubin. Suppose a questionnaire contains two items: One item asks about years of schooling, and the other asks about income. Suppose that everyone answers the schooling question, but that not everyone answers the income question.

Under these conditions, what is the mechanism that decides who answers the income question? Rubin considered several possibilities. First, suppose that whether a respondent answers the income question is independent of both income and education. Then the data are MCAR. Respondents who answer the income question are a random sample of all respondents. Suppose, on the other hand, that highly educated people are less likely (or more likely) than others to reveal their income, but that among those with the same level of education, the probability of reporting income is unrelated to income. Then the data no longer qualify as MCAR, but they are still MAR. A third possibility to consider is that, even among people with the same level of education, high income people may be less likely (or more likely) to report their income. Then the data are not even MAR.

The MAR condition is weaker than the MCAR condition. That is, data that are MCAR are also MAR. Some confusion over the use of the terms can result from the fact that, as Muthén et al. (1987) observed, MCAR is what people usually mean by the term *missing at random*. Many people would say that data that are MAR (but not MCAR) are not missing at random in the everyday sense.

The advantages of ML relative to PD and LD can now be stated. PD and LD estimates are consistent, although not efficient, provided that the data are MCAR. With data that are not MCAR but only MAR, PD and LD estimates can be biased. ML estimates, on the other hand, are consistent and efficient under the weaker condition that the data be MAR. Furthermore, Muthén et al. (1987) and Little and Rubin (1989) suggest that the use of ML will reduce bias even when the MAR assumption is not strictly satisfied. Finally, to add to the list of PD's shortcomings, PD does not provide a means to obtain estimated standard errors or a method for testing hypotheses.

Implementations of ML in Structural Modeling

Allison (1987) and Muthén et al. (1987) proposed a method by which the LISREL program can be used to obtain maximum likelihood estimates with missing data. Bentler (1990) showed how to use the same technique with EQS (Bentler, 1989). Werts, Rock, and Grandy (1979) described a similar method for use in confirmatory factor analysis.

The application of the method of Allison (1987) and Muthén et al. (1987) is impeded by the fact that in practice it can only be used when there are not many distinct patterns of missing data. The method is impractical in the more frequent situation where each pattern of missing values occurs only once or a handful of times. Situations can indeed arise in which only a few distinct patterns of missing data occur. Both Allison and Muthén et al. described situations where only a few missing data patterns would be expected. On the other hand, this is not the most prevalent type of missing data problem. It is also fair to say that using the Allison and Muthén et al. method requires an exceptionally high level of expertise, and this has no doubt been a limiting factor in its use.

At present, ML estimation with missing data is available in at least two structural modeling programs, Amos (Arbuckle, 1995) and Mx (Neale, 1994). These programs do not place a limit on the number of missing data patterns, and do not require the user of the programs to take elaborate steps to accommodate missing data.

COMPUTATIONAL DETAILS

ML estimation for structural modeling under the assumption of multivariate normality is described here. Computational details for LD and PD, as implemented in the simulations to be reported later, are also given. A

TABLE 9.1
Data for Seven Cases Including Three Variables

Case	X	Y	Z
1	13	23	21
2	14	22	17
3	15	—	11
4	16	18	—
5	17	17	12
6	—	20	8
7	—	20	15

small, artificial data set with missing data is used to explain all three methods. In this data set there are three variables, X, Y, and Z. There are seven cases. The data are shown in Table 9.1.

Maximum Likelihood Estimation

Finkbeiner (1979) gave computational details for maximum likelihood estimation in confirmatory factor analysis with incomplete data. The generalization to structural modeling is straightforward. Let n be the number of variables and N the number of cases. In the numerical example given, $n = 3$ and $N = 7$. Let n_i be the number of observed data values for case i, and let $\mathbf{x}_i$ be the vector of length n_i that contains those observed values. In the numerical example, $n_1 = n_2 = n_5 = 3$, $n_3 = n_4 = n_6 = n_7 = 2$, and

$$\mathbf{x}'_1 = [13\ 23\ 21]$$
$$\mathbf{x}'_2 = [14\ 22\ 17]$$
$$\mathbf{x}'_3 = [15\ 11]$$
$$\mathbf{x}'_4 = [16\ 18]$$
$$\mathbf{x}'_5 = [17\ 17\ 12]$$
$$\mathbf{x}'_6 = [20\ 8]$$
$$\mathbf{x}'_7 = [20\ 15]$$

Let the n observed variables have the population mean vector $\boldsymbol{\mu}$ and covariance matrix $\boldsymbol{\Sigma}$. In the numerical example,

$$\boldsymbol{\mu}' = [\mu_1\,\mu_2\,\mu_3] \text{ and } \boldsymbol{\Sigma} = \begin{bmatrix} \sigma_{11} & \sigma_{12} & \sigma_{13} \\ \sigma_{21} & \sigma_{22} & \sigma_{23} \\ \sigma_{31} & \sigma_{32} & \sigma_{33} \end{bmatrix}.$$

Let $\boldsymbol{\mu}_i$ and $\boldsymbol{\Sigma}_i$ be the population mean vector and covariance matrix for the variables that are observed for case i. Each $\boldsymbol{\mu}_i$ can be obtained by deleting elements of $\boldsymbol{\mu}$, and each $\boldsymbol{\Sigma}_i$ can be obtained by deleting rows and columns of $\boldsymbol{\Sigma}$. In the numerical example,

$$\boldsymbol{\mu}_1 = \boldsymbol{\mu}_2 = \boldsymbol{\mu}_5 = \boldsymbol{\mu},$$
$$\boldsymbol{\mu}_3' = [\mu_1\,\mu_3], \boldsymbol{\mu}_4' = [\mu_1\,\mu_2], \text{ and } \boldsymbol{\mu}_6' = \boldsymbol{\mu}_7' = [\mu_2\,\mu_3],$$
$$\boldsymbol{\Sigma}_1 = \boldsymbol{\Sigma}_2 = \boldsymbol{\Sigma}_5 = \boldsymbol{\Sigma}, \text{ and}$$
$$\boldsymbol{\Sigma}_3 = \begin{bmatrix} \sigma_{11} & \sigma_{13} \\ \sigma_{31} & \sigma_{33} \end{bmatrix}, \boldsymbol{\Sigma}_4 = \begin{bmatrix} \sigma_{11} & \sigma_{12} \\ \sigma_{21} & \sigma_{22} \end{bmatrix}, \text{ and } \boldsymbol{\Sigma}_6 = \boldsymbol{\Sigma}_7 = \begin{bmatrix} \sigma_{22} & \sigma_{23} \\ \sigma_{32} & \sigma_{33} \end{bmatrix}.$$

Assuming multivariate normality the log likelihood of the ith case is

$$\log L_i = K_i - \tfrac{1}{2}\log|\boldsymbol{\Sigma}_i| - \tfrac{1}{2}(\mathbf{x}_i - \boldsymbol{\mu}_i)'\boldsymbol{\Sigma}_i^{-1}(\mathbf{x}_i - \boldsymbol{\mu}_i)$$

where K_i is a constant that depends only on n_i. The log likelihood of the entire sample is then

$$\log L(\boldsymbol{\mu}, \boldsymbol{\Sigma}) = \sum_{i=1}^{N} \log L_i.$$

Given a model that specifies $\boldsymbol{\mu} = \boldsymbol{\mu}(\boldsymbol{\gamma})$ and $\boldsymbol{\Sigma} = \boldsymbol{\Sigma}(\boldsymbol{\gamma})$ as a function of some parameter vector, $\boldsymbol{\gamma}$, maximum likelihood estimates of $\boldsymbol{\gamma}$ are obtained by maximizing

$$\log L(\boldsymbol{\mu}(\boldsymbol{\gamma}), \boldsymbol{\Sigma}(\boldsymbol{\gamma})),$$

or, equivalently, by minimizing

$$C(\boldsymbol{\gamma}) = -2\log L(\boldsymbol{\mu}(\boldsymbol{\gamma}), \boldsymbol{\Sigma}(\boldsymbol{\gamma})) + 2\sum_{i=1}^{N} K_i = \sum_{i=1}^{N} \log|\boldsymbol{\Sigma}_i| + \sum_{i=1}^{N} (\mathbf{x}_i - \boldsymbol{\mu}_i)'\boldsymbol{\Sigma}_i^{-1}(\mathbf{x}_i - \boldsymbol{\mu}_i). \quad (1)$$

Listwise Deletion

LD is a two-step procedure. In the first step, every case that contains any missing values is discarded. Sample moments are then calculated from the cases that are left. With the artificial data set given earlier, sample moments would be calculated from the three cases in Table 9.2.

TABLE 9.2
Cases with Complete Data on All Variables

Case	X	Y	Z
1	13	23	21
2	14	22	17
5	17	17	12

TABLE 9.3
Sample Covariance Matrix After LD

	X	Y	Z
X	4.333		
Y	−6.667	10.333	
Z	−9.167	13.833	20.333

The sample covariance matrix is presented in Table 9.3. The sample means of X, Y, and Z are 14.67, 20.67, and 16.67.

The second step of the two-step procedure is to carry out ML estimation in the same way as if the sample moments had been calculated from complete data.

Pairwise Deletion

Like LD, PD is a two-step procedure in which the calculation of sample moments is followed by ML estimation, treating the sample moments as though they had been calculated from complete data. A case is excluded from the calculation of an individual moment only when the case lacks a value that is needed for the computation of that particular moment. The method of pairwise deletion uses all available data in the sense that every observed value enters into the calculation of the sample moments. To this extent it appeals to common sense. Nevertheless, the method lacks a theoretical basis, and in fact has known weaknesses as a method of estimation.

Because there is more than one way to implement PD, the implementation that was used for this chapter is described in some detail. Pairwise deletion was carried out using the following formula (Jöreskog & Sörbom, 1993) for the covariance between variables i and j:

$$s_{ij} = \frac{1}{N_{ij} - 1} \sum_k (x_{ki} - \bar{x}_{ij})(x_{kj} - \bar{x}_{ji})$$

The summation is over those cases where both variable i and variable j are observed, N_{ij} is the number of such cases, x_{ki} is the value of variable i for case k, and $\bar{x}_{ij}$ is the mean of variable i for those cases that have observations on variables i and j. In other words, the covariance between X and Y in the earlier data set is calculated entirely from the data in Table 9.4. Note in particular that the means used in the calculation of the covariance are calculated from these four cases only.

The mean and variance of Y in the example are calculated from the six cases in Table 9.5.

The sample covariance matrix after pairwise deletion is given in Table 9.6. The sample means of X, Y, and Z are 15, 20, and 14, based on sample sizes of 5, 6, and 6. This example shows that a covariance matrix calculated using

TABLE 9.4
Cases with Complete Data on Variables X and Y

Case	X	Y
1	13	23
2	14	22
4	16	18
5	17	17

TABLE 9.5
Cases with Complete Data on Variable Y

Case	Y
1	23
2	22
4	18
5	17
6	20
7	20

TABLE 9.6
Sample Covariance Matrix After PD

	X	Y	Z
X	2.500		
Y	−5.333	5.200	
Z	−6.583	7.950	21.600

pairwise deletion can fail to be nonnegative definite. The fact that this covariance matrix fails to be nonnegative definite can be seen from the fact that the covariance of X and Y is larger (in magnitude) than the variances of both X and Y. Calculating the correlation between X and Y from the covariance and the variances gives

$$r = \frac{-5.333}{\sqrt{2.5 \times 5.2}} = -1.48,$$ an impossible value for a correlation.

SIMULATION 1: MCAR DATA

A simulation was carried out to demonstrate the efficiency of ML estimates relative to PD and LD for a single, more or less typical estimation problem in which the data are MCAR. Numerous data sets were constructed randomly with varying amounts of missing data. A single model was fitted to each random sample, first using ML, once again using PD, and a third time

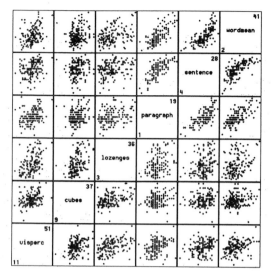

FIG. 9.1. Simulation 1: Matrix scatterplot of the six measures in the original
Holzinger-Swineford sample.

using LD. Estimates produced by each method were then evaluated by
comparing them to their known population values.

The simulation was based on a subset of data collected by Holzinger
and Swineford (1939). Six tests were administered to 145 seventh and
eighth graders. A matrix scatterplot of the six tests is shown in Fig. 9.1.
The sample of 145 cases served as the simulated population from which
repeated samples were drawn.

Figure 9.2 depicts the technique for generating 200 random samples
from the original sample of 145 examinees. In order to obtain 200 samples,
the following two-stage procedure was carried out 200 times:

1. Select a random sample with replacement from the original Holzinger-Swineford sample (i.e., the simulated "population").
2. Using the sample generated at the previous stage, randomly delete
   a prespecified number of data values. Give every observation on every
   variable an equal chance of being deleted. Delete one value at a
   time, always giving the survivors an equal chance of being deleted,
   until the missing data target has been reached.

The simulation was performed under 10 conditions, with a new set of 200
samples for each condition. The 10 conditions were obtained by pairing a
sample size (either 145 or 500), with a missing data rate (either 0%, 5%, 10%,
20%, or 30%). Altogether, $200 \times 2 \times 5 = 2,000$ samples were generated. Some
samples of size 1,500 were generated in the early stages of the simulation.
However, it became apparent that samples of 1,500 cases were yielding about

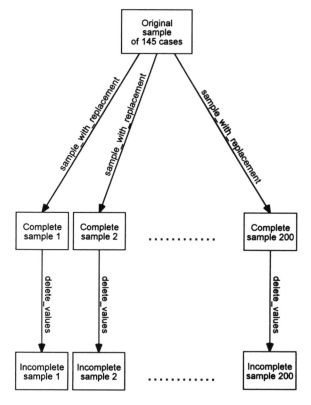

FIG. 9.2. Simulation 1: Simulation procedure.

the same results as samples of 500 cases. Consequently, the practice of generating samples of 1,500 was discontinued. Results from samples of 1,500 are not reported.

Figure 9.3 shows the model that was fitted to each simulated sample. Figure 9.3 also shows standardized parameter values obtained by fitting the model to the original Holzinger-Swineford sample. The performance of a single estimation method (say ML) in fitting this model under a particular condition (say a sample size of 145 with 20% missing data) is assessed in the following way. First, the method is used to fit the model of Fig. 9.3 to each of the 200 samples in the bottom row of Fig. 9.2. The accuracy of the estimates is then judged by comparing them to the values obtained from fitting the model to the original sample at the top of Fig. 9.2. The estimates obtained from the original sample, and shown in Fig. 9.3, are the "correct" values in the sense that ML, PD, and LD will all yield estimates that converge to these values with increasing sample size. The question to be answered is which of the three methods will produce estimates that come closest to the "correct" values in finite samples of sizes 145 or 500.

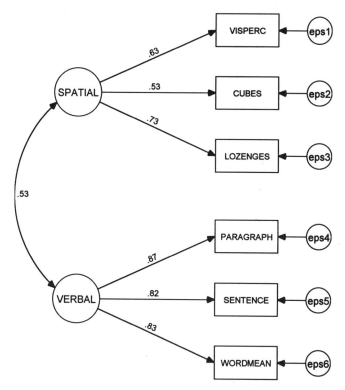

FIG. 9.3. Simulation 1: Standardized parameter values for original sample.

Comparing the Performance of ML and PD

To illustrate this type of comparison, focus on a single estimate, say the standardized regression weight for predicting PARAGRAPH from VERBAL. Also, focus on a single condition, say a sample size of 145 with 20% missing data. We know that in the "population" (i.e., the original Holzinger-Swineford sample) the standardized regression weight is .87. How far do the 200 PD estimates depart from .87? This question is answered by the histogram at the top of Fig. 9.4. The histogram shows the distribution of estimation errors across the 200 samples represented by the boxes along the bottom of Fig. 9.2. The bottom histogram in Fig. 9.4 shows the distribution of errors across the same 200 samples, but for ML estimation. Both histograms are nearly centered around zero. The mean error for PD is −.0028. For ML it is .0015. Thus both PD and ML estimates appear to have little or no bias. The ML histogram looks normal in shape. This is in accord with maximum likelihood theory. The ML histogram is also less spread out than the PD histogram. This is what you would expect in comparing an efficient estimator to an inefficient one. The mean square errors for PD and ML are .005121 and .001859,

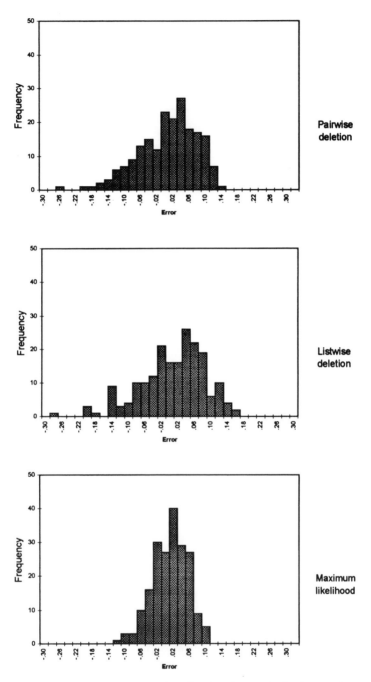

FIG. 9.4. Simulation 1: Errors in estimating the standardized regression weight for PARAGRAPH.

respectively. Because of the small mean errors, the mean square error (mse) for each method is, for practical purposes, the same as its variance, so the two standard deviations are about $\sqrt{.005121} = .0716$ and $\sqrt{.001859} = .0431$. The ratio of the two standard deviations, $\sqrt{.005121/.001859} = \sqrt{2.75} = 1.66$, conforms relatively closely to the visual impression that the PD histogram is a little more than half again as spread out as the ML histogram. The ratio 1.66 can be taken as a quantitative indicator of the superiority of ML over PD, at least with regard to this particular parameter in this particular situation. However, the square of this figure, in other words the ratio of the mean square errors, is arguably a more meaningful figure of comparison under the assumption that the variance (and hence the mse for practical purposes) for each method is an approximate multiple of the inverse of sample size. In the present case the ratio of the mse's, or the *relative mean square error*, is 2.75, implying that switching from PD to ML provides the same improvement in accuracy of estimation that would be obtained by increasing the sample size by a factor of 2.75.

Of course the relative mse of 2.75 just referred to is specific to a single parameter, a single sample size, and a single missing data rate. Figure 9.5 shows relative mse's for all six standardized regression weights under a variety of conditions. One of the points (indicated by an arrow) in Fig. 9.5 represents the relative mse of 2.75 that was just discussed.

The points in Fig. 9.5 are affected by an undetermined amount of sampling error. Nevertheless, some broad trends seem clear. Figure 9.5 shows that the relative mse increases as the missing data rate increases. It also seems clear that the relative mse is different for some estimates than for others. In particular, the relative mse's for the verbal tests are larger than for the spatial tests. One possible explanation for the superior relative performance of ML in the case of the verbal tests lies in the fact that the verbal tests, taken individually, are more predictable from the remaining five tests than the spatial tests are. Using the original "population" (i.e., the original Holzinger-Swineford sample of 145 cases), a squared multiple correlation was computed, giving the proportion of variance in each test that is accounted for by the other five tests. The verbal tests, PARAGRAPH, SENTENCE and WORDMEAN, had squared multiple correlations of .62, .58, and .58, respectively, whereas the spatial tests, VISPERC, CUBES, and LOZENGES, had squared multiple correlations of .27, .20, and .32, respectively.

Figure 9.6 compares ML and PD in their ability to estimate the correlation between SPATIAL and VERBAL.

Comparing the Performance of ML and LD

Figures 9.7 and 9.8 show relative mse's for LD compared to ML. The number of cases retained for analysis by LD falls rapidly as the proportion of missing data increases. The number of cases with complete data was,

N=145

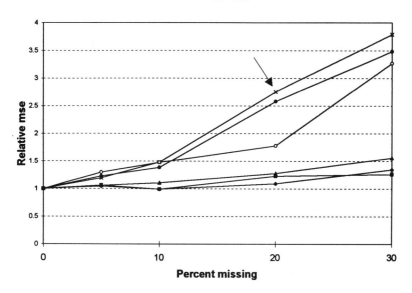

N=500

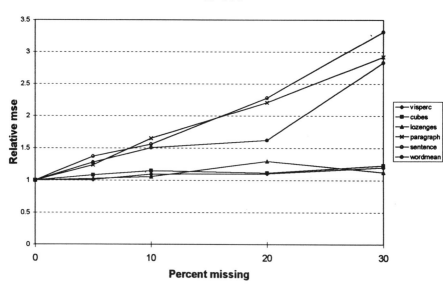

FIG. 9.5. Simulation 1: Relative mean square errors (PD vs. ML) for standardized regression weights.

N=145

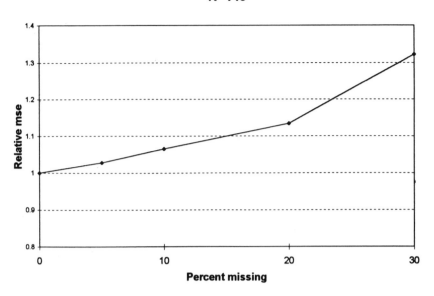

N=500

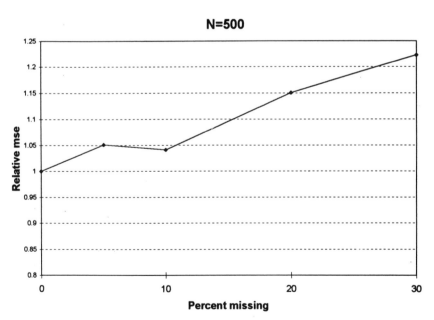

FIG. 9.6. Simulation 1: Relative mean square error (PD vs. ML) for the correlation between SPATIAL and VERBAL.

N=145

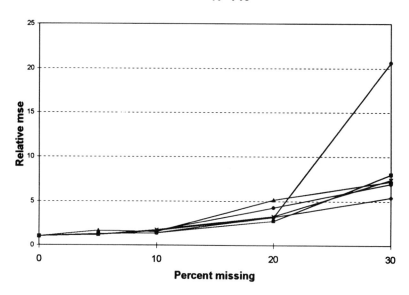

N=500

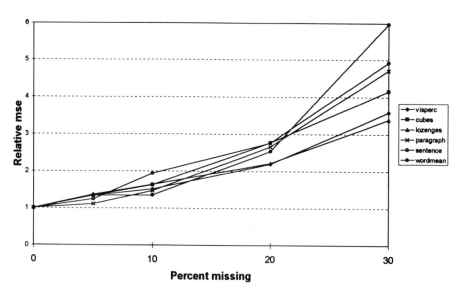

FIG. 9.7. Simulation 1: Relative mean square errors (LD vs. ML) for standardized regression weights.

N=145

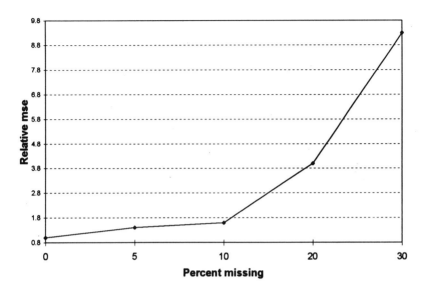

N=500

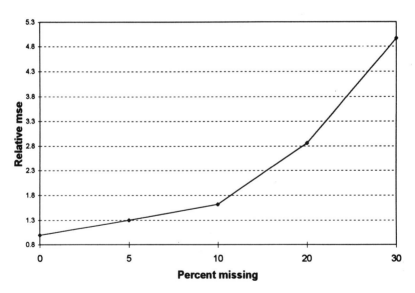

FIG. 9.8. Simulation 1: Relative mean square error (LD vs. ML) for the correlation between SPATIAL and VERBAL.

on average, extremely close to its expected value, $n(1 - p)^6$, where p is the proportion of data that is missing. For example, with 30% missing data and a sample size of 145, you would expect about $145(1 - .3)^6 = 17.06$ cases with complete data. In fact the average number of complete cases was 17.22. In one sample, the number of complete cases was 8. With such small effective sample sizes it is not surprising that, for some samples, it was not possible to find a numerical solution to the estimation problem using LD. With 30% missing data and a sample size of 145, a solution was obtained for only 165 of 200 samples. With 20% missing data and a sample size of 145 (with an average of 37.8 cases with complete data), a solution was obtained for 195 out of 200 samples. Figures 9.7 and 9.8 are based on only those samples where an LD solution was obtained. An ML solution was successfully obtained for every sample.

Figure 9.7 shows that the relative mse for the SENTENCE regression weight is unusually high for the condition of 30% missing data and a sample size of 145. An examination of the 165 cases where an LD solution was obtained showed that the deviant relative mse is due to the influence of four samples for which the estimate of the SENTENCE regression weight was exceptionally far from its population value.

Discussion

It is impossible to put a single figure on the gain in accuracy of estimation to be had by abandoning PD or LD in favor of ML. The advantage of ML depends on the amount of missing data, and it differs from one parameter to another. The simulation reported here was based on resampling from one particular sample, fitting one particular model, and using a single, oversimplified mechanism for generating missing values. Moreover, although the results reported here were not materially affected by the choice of sample size, one suspects that in other circumstances, possibly with a different range of sample sizes, the sample size would matter. It can only be presumed that systematically manipulating these features of the simulation would produce varying results and additional insight. Nevertheless, it is clear that ML can under realistic conditions be superior to PD and LD by a wide margin. Additional, informal simulations not reported here suggest that the results that were reported do not exaggerate the advantages of ML relative to PD and LD.

SIMULATION 2: MAR DATA

A second simulation was performed to illustrate the benefits of ML with data that are MAR (but not MCAR). The second simulation was identical to the first except for the missing data mechanism. In the second simulation, SENTENCE and PARAGRAPH scores were deleted (i.e., caused to be missing) for every examinee whose WORDMEAN score was 12 or less, and retained for examinees with WORDMEAN scores greater than 12. No scores were deleted on the VISPERC, CUBES, LOZENGES, or WORDMEAN tests. The threshold of 12 was chosen so as to delete approximately 30% of the SENTENCE and PARAGRAPH scores. The 30% figure was picked arbitrarily. This missing data mechanism is intended to emulate the situation in which an examiner administers the WORDMEAN test first, and then administers the other verbal tests only to the examinees who "passed" the WORDMEAN test. The same sort of selection would occur, in less extreme form, if examinees had a tendency to drop out or to refuse to take the remaining verbal tests after obtaining low scores on WORDMEAN.

It is particularly easy to see how LD would lead to biased estimates in this simulation. LD would exclude examinees with low WORDMEAN scores so that it would lead to estimates based on a sample of examinees that tended to be high in verbal ability. The effect of the missing data pattern on PD is not so clear-cut. Some of the sample moments using PD would be based on the full sample, whereas others would be based on a subsample with high verbal ability. Some sample moments would be biased and some would not.

Results of the Simulation

We have already observed the efficiency of ML estimates in Simulation 1, where, because the data were MCAR, the bias in the estimates was small relative to their variance. By contrast, estimation bias is of central concern in the present simulation. Table 9.7 shows the average error (an estimate of bias) for several estimates when averaged across 200 samples of size 145. For almost every estimate (i.e., for almost every row of the table) ML has the lowest mean error. In the rare cases where ML has a higher mean error than PD or LD, the standard errors (in parentheses) suggest that the difference may be due to sampling error. For several estimates, the mean error for ML is dramatically smaller than for PD or LD.

When the simulation was carried out with 200 samples of size 500, the results in Table 9.8 were obtained. Broadly speaking, the mean errors did not change very much when the sample size was increased from 145 to 500 (although the standard errors of the means became smaller). In contrast to the loss of efficiency that is incurred by the use of PD or LD, the bias that can result from using PD or LD with data that are MAR (but not MCAR) cannot be compensated for by increasing the sample size.

Although this simulation succeeded in illustrating that ML estimates have smaller bias than PD or LD estimates, it is also a fact that a few of the mean errors in Tables 9.7 and 9.8 are large relative to their standard errors. That is, ML, while doing a better job than PD or LD, does not appear to have entirely compensated for the bias introduced by the missing data process.

TABLE 9.7
Simulation 2: Mean Error (Approximate Bias) When Drawing a Sample of 145 From the Holzinger-Swineford Population With Missingness Dependent on WORDMEAN

Parameter	Mean error		
	ML	LD	PD
Regr. Weights			
visperc	.000 (.000)	.000 (.000)	.000 (.000)
cubes	.033 (.010)	.049 (.018)	.028 (.011)
lozenges	.078 (.027)	.235 (.053)	.114 (.031)
paragraph	.000 (.000)	.000 (.000)	.000 (.000)
sentence	-.189 (.010)	-.188 (.010)	-.180 (.010)
wordmean	.081 (.020)	-.157 (.021)	-.077 (.022)
Intercepts			
visperc	-.014 (.040)	.909 (.050)	-.014 (.040)
cubes	.009 (.025)	.539 (.034)	.009 (.025)
lozenges	-.016 (.048)	1.097 (.056)	-.016 (.048)
paragraph	-.023 (.024)	1.043 (.022)	1.043 (.022)
sentence	.398 (.030)	1.579 (.025)	1.579 (.025)
wordmean	-.017 (.048)	3.449 (.046)	-.017 (.048)
Covariance	-.089 (.158)	-1.372 (.171)	-.913 (.157)
Variances			
spatial	-.694 (.435)	-1.445 (.583)	-.564 (.483)
verbal	-.225 (.132)	-1.795 (.111)	-1.964 (.109)
eps1	-.703 (.425)	3.682 (.626)	-.513 (.465)
eps2	-.258 (.154)	2.405 (.204)	.017 (.160)
eps3	-.724 (.640)	2.407 (.987)	-1.467 (.729)
eps4	.392 (.059)	.418 (.060)	.587 (.059)
eps5	-1.870 (.077)	-1.836 (.078)	-1.760 (.079)
eps6	-1.854 (.369)	-3.417 (.319)	12.267 (.398)
Stand. Regr. Wts.			
visperc	-.011 (.007)	-.054 (.009)	-.012 (.007)
cubes	.000 (.005)	-.056 (.007)	-.010 (.005)
lozenges	-.004 (.006)	-.021 (.009)	.004 (.007)
paragraph	-.023 (.004)	-.051 (.004)	-.061 (.004)
sentence	-.009 (.003)	-.039 (.003)	-.043 (.003)
wordmean	.013 (.003)	-.032 (.004)	-.135 (.004)
Correlation	.013 (.008)	-.031 (.010)	.002 (.008)
SMCs			
visperc	-.004 (.008)	-.048 (.011)	-.005 (.009)
cubes	.005 (.005)	-.047 (.007)	-.005 (.006)
lozenges	.002 (.009)	-.012 (.013)	.017 (.010)
paragraph	-.037 (.006)	-.082 (.007)	-.099 (.007)
sentence	-.013 (.005)	-.061 (.005)	-.067 (.005)
wordmean	.024 (.006)	-.049 (.006)	-.202 (.005)

TABLE 9.8
Simulation 2: Mean Error (Approximate Bias) When Drawing a Sample of 500 From the Holzinger-Swineford Population With Missingness Dependent on WORDMEAN

Parameter	Mean error		
	ML	LD	PD
Regr. Weights			
visperc	.000 (.000)	.000 (.000)	.000 (.000)
cubes	.024 (.005)	.026 (.008)	.019 (.005)
lozenges	.039 (.015)	.105 (.023)	.057 (.017)
paragraph	.000 (.000)	.000 (.000)	.000 (.000)
sentence	-.207 (.005)	-.207 (.005)	-.199 (.004)
wordmean	.045 (.012)	-.193 (.012)	-.116 (.013)
Intercepts			
visperc	.021 (.022)	.923 (.029)	.021 (.022)
cubes	.013 (.014)	.541 (.017)	.013 (.014)
lozenges	.044 (.028)	1.108 (.035)	.044 (.028)
paragraph	-.047 (.012)	1.011 (.013)	1.011 (.013)
sentence	.395 (.015)	1.557 (.015)	1.557 (.015)
wordmean	-.038 (.025)	3.420 (.026)	-.038 (.025)
Covariance	-.206 (.081)	-1.503 (.090)	-1.098 (.081)
Variances			
spatial	-.520 (.252)	-1.689 (.341)	-.524 (.273)
verbal	-.167 (.071)	-1.729 (.061)	-1.890 (.060)
eps1	.422 (.250)	4.956 (.360)	.521 (.269)
eps2	-.245 (.087)	2.472 (.124)	-.078 (.092)
eps3	-.173 (.349)	3.694 (.537)	-.782 (.406)
eps4	.458 (.032)	.456 (.032)	.617 (.031)
eps5	-1.595 (.040)	-1.591 (.040)	-1.519 (.040)
eps6	-1.103 (.190)	-2.802 (.160)	12.656 (.203)
Stand. Regr. Wts.			
visperc	-.011 (.004)	-.054 (.005)	-.012 (.004)
cubes	.009 (.003)	-.043 (.004)	.002 (.003)
lozenges	-.001 (.004)	-.025 (.005)	.005 (.004)
paragraph	-.021 (.002)	-.047 (.002)	-.057 (.002)
sentence	-.015 (.001)	-.045 (.002)	-.049 (.002)
wordmean	.008 (.002)	-.038 (.002)	-.137 (.002)
Correlation	-.002 (.004)	-.043 (.005)	-.018 (.004)
SMCs			
visperc	-.011 (.005)	-.059 (.006)	-.011 (.005)
cubes	.011 (.003)	-.041 (.004)	.004 (.003)
lozenges	.001 (.005)	-.030 (.008)	.010 (.006)
paragraph	-.035 (.003)	-.078 (.004)	-.094 (.004)
sentence	-.024 (.002)	-.072 (.002)	-.078 (.002)
wordmean	.014 (.003)	-.060 (.004)	-.207 (.003)

Tables 9.7 and 9.8 show that parameters associated with the SENTENCE test have particularly large mean errors. A possible explanation for this pattern can be found in Fig. 9.1, which shows a pronounced nonlinearity in the scatterplot of SENTENCE and WORDMEAN. Several attempts were made to eliminate the nonlinearity by transformations of SENTENCE and WORD-MEAN, but none were successful in reducing the mean errors to the point where they could plausibly be attributed to sampling error. Ultimately, it was suspected that the significant mean errors for ML in Tables 9.7 and 9.8 are due to the failure of the model of Fig. 9.3 to fit the population (i.e., the original Holzinger-Swineford sample) perfectly, as well as to departures from multivariate normality. To confirm this explanation, the simulation was repeated using a new, artificial population in which the six test scores were multivariate normally distributed, and in which the model of Fig. 9.3 held exactly, with parameter values identical to the estimates obtained by fitting the model to the Holzinger-Swineford sample. The threshold for WORDMEAN, used for determining whether SENTENCE and PARAGRAPH would be observed, was adjusted so that SENTENCE and PARAGRAPH were unobserved with probability .3. When drawing samples of 145 from this population, the simulation yielded the mean errors shown in Table 9.9. In Table 9.9 it can be seen that the ML estimates not only have less bias than the PD and LD estimates, but now appear to be essentially free of bias.

EXAMPLE 1: FACTOR ANALYSIS

This section provides a "how to" on structural modeling with incomplete data, showing how an analysis with incomplete data differs in practice from an analysis with complete data. The data for the example consist of scores obtained by 39 students on four quizzes in an undergraduate statistics course. Missing values are fairly common in this set of data. Here is a listing of the frequencies with which each missing data pattern occurred. The first row shows, for instance, that 2 students took the first quiz and missed the remaining three quizzes.

Pattern	Frequency
x???	2
xx??	2
xxx?	6
?xx?	2
xx?x	3
?x??	1
?xxx	1

It may be instructive in this example to speculate on why students miss quizzes. When students miss quizzes as a result of illness or accident it is

TABLE 9.9

Simulation 2: Mean Error (Approximate Bias) When
Drawing a Sample of 145 With a Correct Model and
With Missingness Dependent on WORDMEAN

Parameter	Mean error		
	ML	LD	PD
Regr. Weights			
visperc	.000 (.000)	.000 (.000)	.000 (.000)
cubes	.005 (.009)	.021 (.012)	.003 (.009)
lozenges	.032 (.020)	.097 (.034)	.038 (.024)
paragraph	.000 (.000)	.000 (.000)	.000 (.000)
sentence	.021 (.014)	.022 (.014)	.033 (.013)
wordmean	.030 (.020)	-.508 (.020)	-.372 (.022)
Intercepts			
visperc	-.063 (.043)	.889 (.047)	-.063 (.043)
cubes	-.017 (.025)	.518 (.032)	-.017 (.025)
lozenges	-.062 (.043)	1.305 (.053)	-.062 (.043)
paragraph	-.010 (.023)	1.202 (.019)	1.202 (.019)
sentence	-.022 (.035)	1.571 (.028)	1.571 (.028)
wordmean	-.050 (.048)	3.883 (.042)	-.050 (.048)
Covariance	.038 (.126)	-2.327 (.121)	-1.805 (.113)
Variances			
spatial	.070 (.359)	-1.518 (.467)	.321 (.385)
verbal	.130 (.150)	-2.872 (.094)	-3.079 (.090)
eps1	.055 (.347)	-.055 (.446)	.135 (.377)
eps2	-.280 (.154)	-.239 (.194)	-.149 (.157)
eps3	-1.052 (.544)	-1.630 (.769)	-.917 (.652)
eps4	-.030 (.052)	-.003 (.053)	.204 (.051)
eps5	-.114 (.114)	-.051 (.115)	.094 (.115)
eps6	-.608 (.335)	-5.184 (.215)	24.588 (.469)
Stand. Regr. Wts.			
visperc	-.005 (.005)	-.027 (.007)	-.004 (.006)
cubes	-.004 (.007)	-.023 (.008)	-.007 (.007)
lozenges	.001 (.005)	-.010 (.007)	.001 (.006)
paragraph	-.003 (.003)	-.055 (.004)	-.070 (.004)
sentence	.000 (.004)	-.061 (.004)	-.067 (.004)
wordmean	.003 (.003)	-.102 (.005)	-.287 (.005)
Correlation	.007 (.007)	-.079 (.009)	-.042 (.009)
SMCs			
visperc	-.001 (.006)	-.023 (.009)	.001 (.007)
cubes	.004 (.007)	-.010 (.008)	.002 (.007)
lozenges	.008 (.008)	-.003 (.011)	.010 (.009)
paragraph	-.003 (.006)	-.088 (.007)	-.113 (.006)
sentence	.002 (.006)	-.094 (.006)	-.102 (.006)
wordmean	.007 (.005)	-.155 (.007)	-.388 (.005)

probably reasonable to regard the missing scores as MCAR. When students get low scores on early quizzes, and then drop the course because of the low scores, their missed scores are MAR. However, if students tend not to take quizzes when they are poorly prepared, and if their lack of preparation cannot be inferred from previous test scores, their missing scores will not be MAR. It seems likely that students miss quizzes for all of these reasons, so that ML could be expected to be useful in reducing estimation bias that results from the missing data mechanism, but not to eliminate it.

Figure 9.9 shows a factor analysis model for these data with one common factor called ACHIEVE (for achievement). Fitting a model to an incomplete data set differs in three ways from an analysis with complete data. First, the analysis requires raw data, and not just sample moments. Second, your model must include a mean for each exogenous variable and an intercept in each equation that predicts an endogenous variable. Some models include explicit means and intercepts anyway. However, if an existing model does not include explicit means and intercepts, you need to add these parameters to the model. You can accomplish this without affecting the fit of the model or altering the estimates of other model parameters by taking the following steps: Allow the mean of each observed, exogenous variable, and the intercept for each observed, endogenous variable to be an unconstrained parameter. Fix all other means and intercepts at zero. Amos can make these changes to an existing model automatically. It is also quite easy to add mean and intercept parameters to an existing model using Mx. The model in Fig. 9.9 can be suitably modified by adding four additional parameters (one intercept for each of the observed test scores) and fixing the means of the exogenous variables at zero. ML estimates for the model parameters, including intercepts, are shown in Table 9.10. Estimates obtained by PD and LD are also shown for comparison.

The third, and final, way in which an incomplete-data analysis differs from a complete-data analysis is in the way one tests the hypothesis that a model is correct. The usual likelihood-ratio chi-square statistic is computed as the difference, $C_{model} - C_{saturated}$, where C_{model} is the minimum of (1) for the model being tested and $C_{saturated}$ is the minimum of (1) for the saturated model. If the model being tested is correct, $C_{model} - C_{saturated}$ has, approximately, a chi square distribution with degrees of freedom equal to the difference between the number of parameters in the model being tested and the number of parameters in the saturated model. In a complete-data analysis $C_{saturated}$ can be computed rapidly, so that $C_{model} - C_{saturated}$ is always reported as a matter of course. In an incomplete-data analysis, $C_{saturated}$ is as hard to obtain as C_{model} is. Consequently, both C_{model} and $C_{saturated}$ must be obtained in separate analyses, and then subtracted by hand. In the present example, fitting the model in Fig. 9.9 yielded $C_{model} = 450.366$. The model in Fig. 9.9 has 12 parameters (five variances, three regression

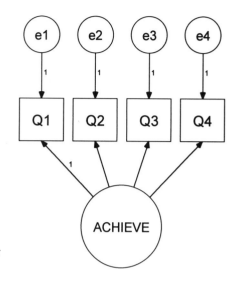

FIG. 9.9. Example 1: One factor model for four quizzes.

TABLE 9.10
Example 1: Parameter Estimates for the One Factor Model

	LD	PD	ML
Regression weights			
Q1	1.00 (*)	1.00 (*)	1.00 (*)
Q2	.97 (.47)	.95 (.56)	.97 (.22)
Q3	.84 (.44)	1.72 (1.01)	.99 (.24)
Q4	.12 (.17)	.37 (.23)	.13 (.10)
Intercepts			
Q1	15.77 (.61)	15.09 (.63)	14.92 (.63)
Q2	16.18 (.76)	15.89 (.64)	15.42 (.71)
Q3	15.55 (.83)	15.06 (.67)	14.30 (.80)
Q4	16.18 (.38)	16.19 (.27)	16.07 (.32)
Variances			
ACHIEVE	5.89 (3.40)	3.26 (2.83)	12.00 (3.96)
e1	1.83 (2.55)	11.64 (3.25)	2.53 (2.16)
e2	6.48 (3.09)	12.74 (3.41)	7.92 (2.72)
e3	10.38 (3.66)	7.31 (5.28)	10.10 (3.29)
e4	2.88 (.90)	2.27 (.59)	2.51 (.70)

Note. Standard errors in parentheses. Parameters marked with an asterisk were fixed in order to identify the model.

weights, and four intercepts). In order to obtain $C_{saturated}$, it is necessary to fit the model in Fig. 9.10, which yields $C_{saturated} = 446.772$. The saturated model has 14 parameters (10 variances and covariances, and 4 means). If the one-factor model is correct, the difference, $C_{model} - C_{saturated} = 450.366 - 446.772 = 3.594$, is from a chi square distribution with $14 - 12 = 2$ degrees of freedom.

In general, if two models are "nested" the more restricted model can be tested against the more general one (the one with more parameters) in the following way. Fit each model separately. Let C_r be the minimum of (1) for the more restricted model, and let C_g be the minimum of (1) for the more general model. Let q_r be the number of parameters in the more restricted model, and let q_g be the number of parameters in the more general model. Then if the more restricted model is correct, $C_r - C_g$ will have an approximate chi-square distribution with $q_g - q_r$ degrees of freedom. To illustrate the making of model comparisons, the model in Fig. 9.9 was fitted a second time under the assumption that the four quizzes are tau-equivalent (i.e., that they have equal regression weights), and then a third time under the assumption that the four quizzes are parallel tests (i.e., that they have equal regression weights and equal error variances). In all analyses the intercepts in the model remained unconstrained. The results of fitting Fig. 9.10 and three variations of Fig. 9.9 are summarized in Table 9.11.

Testing the parallel tests model against the tau-equivalent model gives $\chi^2 = 476.651 - 467.026 = 9.625$ with df $= 9 - 6 = 3$. Testing the parallel tests model against the congeneric model gives $\chi^2 = 476.651 - 450.366 =$

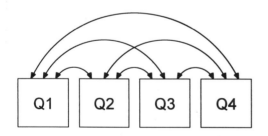

FIG. 9.10. Example 1: Saturated model for four quizzes.

TABLE 9.11
Results of Fitting Models and Variations

Model	C	Number of Parameters
Saturated	446.772	14
1-factor (congeneric)	450.366	12
Tau-equivalent	467.026	9
Parallel	476.651	6

26.285 with df = 12 − 6 = 6. In a similar way, each model can be tested against the models that precede it on the previous list.

EXAMPLE 2: DATA THAT ARE INCOMPLETE
BY DESIGN

Numerous writers have suggested the possibility of designing studies in which some measurements are intentionally not made (Lord, 1955a, 1955b; Matthai, 1951; Rubin & Thayer, 1978; Thayer, 1983; Trawinski & Bargmann, 1964). In the context of structural modeling, Allison (1987) described designs for data collection in which some (inexpensive) measurements are made on an entire sample, whereas other (expensive) measurements are made on a random subsample of cases.

In order to illustrate this type of analysis, it was necessary to contrive a suitable data set by discarding values from a set of complete data. Judd and McClelland (1989) provided self-reported SAT scores for 170 students who gave permission for their university records to be used in follow-up studies and for whom the university had SAT scores on record. The data set that was presented by Judd and McClelland contained complete data on the following variables: SATM (self-reported SAT quantitative score), SATV (self-reported SAT verbal score), RSATM (recorded SAT quantitative score from university records), and RSATV (recorded SAT verbal score from university records).

For purposes of the present example, a new data set was created from the Judd and McClelland (1989) data by discarding the recorded scores for 130 randomly selected students. The resulting data set contained complete data (four measurements) for 40 students, and self-reported scores alone (two measurements) for 130 students. The data that were missing were MCAR. The purpose of this example is to show how data obtained from students who provided only SATM and SATV scores can be used to improve inferences about the distribution of RSATM and RSATV scores. In order to get into the spirit of this example, it will help to pretend that the entire purpose of collecting the data was to obtain information about RSATM and RSATV, but that scores on those variables are costly, whereas self-reported SATM and SATV scores are plentiful and cheap.

Consider first the problem of estimating the means and the variance–covariance matrix of RSATM and RSATV. These parameters can be estimated by fitting either of the models in Fig. 9.11 and Fig. 9.12. If the data set were complete, the two models would yield the same estimates for the moments or RSATM and RSATV (and the same standard errors). The model in Fig. 9.12 would merely yield estimates of additional parameters. With the current data, however, fitting the model of Fig. 9.12 allows the use of the entire set of data from all 170 subjects (including the 130 subjects for whom only self-reported scores are available). Table 9.12 shows

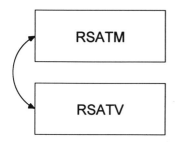

FIG. 9.11. Example 2: Path diagram to estimate moments of RSATM and RSATV.

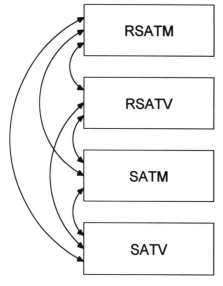

FIG. 9.12. Example 2: Using SATM and SATV to help estimate the moments of RSATM and RSATV.

estimates of the moments of RSATM and RSATV obtained by fitting Fig. 9.11 (or Fig. 9.12) to the 40 complete cases, and also the estimates obtained by fitting Fig. 9.12 to all 170 cases. The standard errors shown in parentheses are the usual approximate standard errors obtained from the information matrix. Treating these standard errors as roughly correct indicates that it would take somewhere between $40(10.56/7.29)^2 = 84$ and $40(1.04/.60)^2 = 120$ complete cases to match the accuracy of estimation that was achieved with 40 complete cases and 130 incomplete cases.

Using the same data again, suppose one wished to fit the regression model in Fig. 9.13, involving only RSATM and RSATV. The path diagram in Fig. 9.14 introduces new variables (SATV and SATM) into the model, as well as new parameters. The advantage of the model in Fig. 9.14 is that it allows the "extra" data from the students who supplied only self-reported scores to be used in estimating the parameters of interest. Table 9.13 shows estimates obtained by fitting Fig. 9.13 (or Fig. 9.14) to the 40 complete cases, and also the estimates obtained by fitting Fig. 9.14 to all 170 cases. Once again, the benefit of including the 130 pairs of self-reported scores

TABLE 9.12
Example 2: Estimates of Population Moments

Parameter	40 complete cases	40 complete cases + 130 incomplete cases
Means		
RSATM	58.85 (1.04)	58.23 (.60)
RSATV	52.08 (1.09)	50.94 (.64)
Variances		
RSATM	42.43 (9.61)	47.77 (6.36)
RSATV	46.62 (10.56)	55.51 (7.29)
Covariance	20.51 (7.84)	15.57 (4.92)
Correlation	.46	.30

Note. Standard errors are in parentheses.

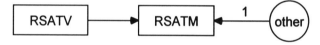

FIG. 9.13. Example 2: Regression of RSATM on RSATV.

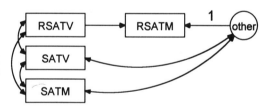

FIG. 9.14. Example 2: Using SATM and SATV to help estimate the regression of RSATM on RSATV.

can be seen in the reduced standard errors of the estimates in the incomplete-data solution.

It should be acknowledged that the correlations between self-reported scores and recorded scores were atypically high. The correlation between SATM and RSATM was .94. The correlation between SATV and RSATV was .91. These high correlations made SATM and SATV exceptionally useful in drawing inferences about RSATM and RSATV.

IMPUTATION OF MISSING VALUES

It is not necessary either to impute values for missing data or to estimate the population moments as a prerequisite to model fitting by ML. These

TABLE 9.13
Example 2: Estimates for Regression Model

Parameter	40 complete cases	40 complete cases + 130 incomplete cases
Mean of RSATV	52.08 (1.09)	50.94 (.64)
Intercept	35.94 (7.12)	43.94 (4.35)
Regression Weight	.44 (.14)	.28 (.08)
Variances		
RSATV	46.62 (10.56)	55.51 (7.29)
other	33.40 (7.56)	43.40 (6.05)
Standardized regression weight	.46	.30
Squared Multiple correlation	.21	.09

Note. Standard errors are in parentheses.

are optional steps which, if they are performed at all, are best performed after the model is fitted, not before.

Estimates of population means, variances, and covariances, calculated from parameter estimates under the assumption of a correct model, are reported by most structural modeling programs. Let μ^* and Σ^* be the population means and covariances of all the variables in the model, including measured and unmeasured variables, and let $\hat{\mu}^*$ and $\hat{\Sigma}^*$ be their estimates assuming a correct model. $\hat{\mu}^*$ and $\hat{\Sigma}^*$ are referred to by various names. LISREL (Jöreskog & Sörbom, 1989, p. 28) reports them as "fitted" moments. EQS (Bentler, 1989, p. 91) reports them in the "model covariance matrix for V and F variables." Amos follows Bollen (1989, p. 95) and calls them "implied" moments. The implied moments from Example 1 are

$$\hat{\mu}^* = \begin{bmatrix} 0.0000 \\ 14.9209 \\ 15.4166 \\ 14.2980 \\ 16.0734 \end{bmatrix}, \hat{\Sigma}^* = \begin{bmatrix} 11.9976 & 11.9976 & 11.6951 & 11.8451 & 1.5520 \\ 11.9976 & 14.5266 & 11.6951 & 11.8451 & 1.5520 \\ 11.6951 & 11.6951 & 19.3212 & 11.5465 & 1.5129 \\ 11.8451 & 11.8451 & 11.5465 & 21.7900 & 1.5323 \\ 1.5520 & 1.5520 & 1.5129 & 1.5323 & 2.7079 \end{bmatrix} \begin{matrix} Achieve \\ Q1 \\ Q2 \\ Q3 \\ Q4 \end{matrix}$$

In Amos, these two matrices are obtained by using the command "$all implied moments."

TABLE 9.14
Scores of Two Examinees

Case #	ACHIEVE	Q1	Q2	Q3	Q4
24	—	12	19	20	16
25	—	12	6	—	—

Once μ^* and Σ^* have been estimated by $\hat{\mu}^*$ and $\hat{\Sigma}^*$, the imputation of missing values is no different from the well-known problem of estimating scores on latent variables (i.e., *factor scores* in the case of factor analysis). In fact, latent variables can be thought of as differing from other variables only in the fact that all of their values are missing. This point of view is central to the use of the EM algorithm with latent variable models (Dempster, Laird, & Rubin, 1977; Orchard & Woodbury, 1972; Rubin & Thayer, 1982). To make the following discussion concrete it will be useful to have a specific example in mind. The scores of Examinees 24 and 25 from the factor analysis of Example 1 are presented in Table 9.14. Examinee 24 of course has no score on the latent variable ACHIEVE, but has complete data otherwise. Examinee 25 has no score on ACHIEVE, and also no scores on Q3 or Q4. So Examinee 24 has one score that needs to be filled in, and Examinee 25 has three.

For an individual case (i.e., an individual member of the sample) let $\mathbf{x}_m$ contain the measurements that are observed for that case, and let $\mathbf{x}_u$ be the vector of (unknown) values of the measurements that are unobserved or missing. Obviously, $\mathbf{x}_m$ and $\mathbf{x}_u$ will be of different sizes for different cases. Let μ_m and μ_u contain the elements of μ^* corresponding to measured and unmeasured values, respectively. Let Σ_{mm} and Σ_{uu} contain the rows and columns of Σ^* corresponding to measured and unmeasured values, respectively. Let Σ_{mu} be the submatrix obtained from Σ^* by deleting the rows corresponding to unmeasured variables and deleting the columns corresponding to measured variables. Finally, let the estimates $\hat{\mu}_m$, $\hat{\mu}_u$, $\hat{\Sigma}_{mm}$, $\hat{\Sigma}_{uu}$, and $\hat{\Sigma}_{mu}$ be similarly defined as submatrices of $\hat{\mu}^*$ and $\hat{\Sigma}^*$.

For Examinee 24 in Example 1, $\mathbf{x}'_m = [12, 19, 20, 16]$, $\mathbf{x}_u$ contains one (unknown) element,

$$\hat{\mu}_m = \begin{bmatrix} 14.9209 \\ 15.4166 \\ 14.2980 \\ 16.0734 \end{bmatrix}, \hat{\Sigma}_{mm} = \begin{bmatrix} 14.5266 & 11.6951 & 11.8451 & 1.5520 \\ 11.6951 & 19.3212 & 11.5465 & 1.5129 \\ 11.8451 & 11.5465 & 21.7900 & 1.5323 \\ 1.5520 & 1.5129 & 1.5323 & 2.7079 \end{bmatrix},$$

$$\hat{\mu}_u = [0.0000], \hat{\Sigma}_{uu} = [11.9976] \text{ and } \hat{\Sigma}_{mu} = \begin{bmatrix} 11.9976 \\ 11.6951 \\ 11.8451 \\ 1.5520 \end{bmatrix}.$$

For Examinee 25 in Example 1, $\mathbf{x'_m} = [12, 6]$, $\mathbf{x_u}$ contains three (unknown) elements,

$$\boldsymbol{\mu}_m = \begin{bmatrix} 14.9209 \\ 15.4166 \end{bmatrix}, \boldsymbol{\mu}_u = \begin{bmatrix} 0.0000 \\ 14.2980 \\ 16.0734 \end{bmatrix}, \boldsymbol{\Sigma}_{mm} = \begin{bmatrix} 14.5266 & 11.6951 \\ 11.6951 & 19.3212 \end{bmatrix}$$

$$\boldsymbol{\Sigma}_{uu} = \begin{bmatrix} 11.9976 & 11.8451 & 1.5520 \\ 11.8451 & 21.7900 & 1.5323 \\ 1.5520 & 1.5323 & 2.7079 \end{bmatrix} \text{ and } \boldsymbol{\Sigma}_{mu} = \begin{bmatrix} 11.9976 & 11.8451 & 1.5520 \\ 11.6951 & 11.5465 & 1.5129 \end{bmatrix}.$$

Under the assumption of multivariate normality, the distribution of $\mathbf{x_u}$ given $\mathbf{x_m}$ is multivariate normal with mean

$$E(\mathbf{x_u}|\,\mathbf{x_m}) = \boldsymbol{\mu}_u + \boldsymbol{\Sigma}_{um}\boldsymbol{\Sigma}_{mm}^{-1}(\mathbf{x_m} - \boldsymbol{\mu}_m), \tag{2}$$

and covariance matrix

$$\text{Cov}(\mathbf{x_u}|\,\mathbf{x_m}) = \boldsymbol{\Sigma}_{uu} - \boldsymbol{\Sigma}_{um}\boldsymbol{\Sigma}_{mm}^{-1}\boldsymbol{\Sigma}_{mu}. \tag{3}$$

Substituting estimates for the moments on the right hand sides of Equations 2 and 3 shows that examinees who have Examinee 24's measured scores have scores on ACHIEVE that are normally distributed with a mean of approximately

$$\overline{E(\mathbf{x_u}|\,\mathbf{x_m})} = \hat{\boldsymbol{\mu}}_u + \hat{\boldsymbol{\Sigma}}_{um}\hat{\boldsymbol{\Sigma}}_{mm}^{-1}(\mathbf{x_m} - \hat{\boldsymbol{\mu}}_m) = [-.228],$$

and a variance of approximately

$$\overline{\text{Cov}(\mathbf{x_u}|\,\mathbf{x_m})} = \hat{\boldsymbol{\Sigma}}_{uu} - \hat{\boldsymbol{\Sigma}}_{um}\hat{\boldsymbol{\Sigma}}_{mm}^{-1}\hat{\boldsymbol{\Sigma}}_{mu} = [1.425].$$

Similarly, examinees who have Examinee 25's measured scores have scores on ACHIEVE, Q3, and Q4 are normally distributed with means of approximately

$$\overline{E(\mathbf{x_u}|\,\mathbf{x_m})} = \hat{\boldsymbol{\mu}}_u + \hat{\boldsymbol{\Sigma}}_{um}\hat{\boldsymbol{\Sigma}}_{mm}^{-1}(\mathbf{x_m} - \hat{\boldsymbol{\mu}}_m) = \begin{bmatrix} -3.865 \\ 10.483 \\ 15.574 \end{bmatrix},$$

and covariance matrix of approximately

$$\overline{\text{Cov}(\mathbf{x_u}|\,\mathbf{x_m})} = \hat{\boldsymbol{\Sigma}}_{uu} - \hat{\boldsymbol{\Sigma}}_{um}\hat{\boldsymbol{\Sigma}}_{mm}^{-1}\hat{\boldsymbol{\Sigma}}_{mu} = \begin{bmatrix} 1.670 & 1.649 & .216 \\ 1.649 & 11.723 & .213 \\ .216 & .213 & 2.535 \end{bmatrix}.$$

TABLE 9.15
Scores of Examinees 24 and 25

Case #	ACHIEVE	Q1	Q2	Q3	Q4
24	−.228	12	19	20	16
25	−3.865	12	6	10.483	15.574

If it is necessary to impute a single number for each missing value, the estimated conditional means may be used for Examinees 24 and 25, as shown in Table 9.15. With complete data, this approach gives the usual regression estimates of factor scores provided by many structural modeling programs. An alternative is to employ $\overline{E(x_u|x_m)}$ and $\overline{Cov(x_u|x_m)}$ in *stochastic regression imputation* (Little & Rubin, 1989), where x_u is replaced by a random sample from a multivariate normal distribution with mean $\overline{E(x_u|x_m)}$ and covariance $\overline{Cov(x_u|x_m)}$. Repeated samples can be drawn in order to carry out *multiple imputation* (Rubin, 1987). Little and Rubin point out that this approach to multiple imputation can be improved by taking into account the uncertainty in the estimation of $E(x_u|x_m)$ and $Cov(x_u|x_m)$, but they add, "This is an important adjustment when the fraction of missing data is large, but subtle relative to the improvements afforded by multiple rather than single imputation" (p. 304).

The foregoing discussion used the factor analysis model from Example 1 to illustrate the estimation of population moments and the imputation of missing values. If model-free (although not distribution-free) estimates and imputed values are desired, they can be obtained by using a saturated model.

COMPUTATIONAL COST

The presence of missing data adds to the computational effort needed to get maximum likelihood estimates. The amount of additional effort needed depends on the number of cases and the number of distinct missing value patterns. Table 9.16 gives representative computing times from Simulation 1. The table does not give raw computing times inasmuch as such figures would vary from one computer to another. Instead, each table entry gives the time required to perform an incomplete-data analysis as a multiple of the time required to perform a complete-data analysis with the same number of observations. The table includes timing information from samples of size 1,500 that were discarded from Simulation 1.

CONCLUSION

ML estimation with incomplete data is feasible and should be the preferred method of treating missing data when the alternative is PD or LD. ML's lack of reliance on the MCAR requirement is a characteristic that remains

TABLE 9.16
Representative Computing Times for Missing Data Analysis,
as a Multiple of Computing Times for Complete Data Analysis

Percent	Sample size		
missing	145	500	1500
0%	1.0	1.0	1.1
5%	2.6	3.8	4.1
10%	3.8	5.4	4.3
20%	6.6	7.8	6.3
30%	9.7	9.4	7.3

to be fully exploited. It should not be overlooked that structural modeling can be used to solve missing data problems that arise in conventional analyses, such as regression with observed variables or the simple estimation of means and variances.

REFERENCES

Allison, P. D. (1987). Estimation of linear models with incomplete data. In C. C. Clogg (Ed.), *Sociological methodology 1987* (pp. 71–103). San Francisco: Jossey-Bass.

Anderson, T. W. (1957). Maximum likelihood estimates for a multivariate normal distribution when some observations are missing. *Journal of the American Statistical Association, 52,* 200–203.

Arbuckle, J. L. (1995). *Amos user's guide.* Chicago: SmallWaters.

Beale, E. M. L., & Little, R. J. A. (1975). Missing values in multivariate analysis. *Journal of the Royal Statistical Society, Series B, 37,* 129–145.

Bentler, P. M. (1989). *EQS structural equations program manual.* Los Angeles, CA: BMDP Statistical Software.

Bentler, P. M. (1990). EQS structural models with missing data. *BMDP Communications, 22,* 9–10.

Bollen, K. A. (1989). *Structural equations with latent variables.* New York: Wiley.

Brown, R. L. (1994). Efficacy of the indirect approach for estimating structural equation models with missing data: A comparison of five methods. *Structural Equation Modeling, 1,* 287–316.

Dempster, A. P., Laird, N. M., & Rubin, D. B. (1977). Maximum likelihood from incomplete data via the EM algorithm. *Journal of the Royal Statistical Society Series B, 39,* 1–22.

Finkbeiner, C. (1979). Estimation for the multiple factor model when data are missing. *Psychometrika, 44,* 409–420.

Hartley, H. O. (1958). Maximum likelihood estimation from incomplete data. *Biometrics, 14,* 174–194.

Hartley, H. O., & Hocking, R. R. (1971). The analysis of incomplete data. *Biometrics, 27,* 783–823.

Holzinger, K. J., & Swineford, F. A. (1939). A study in factor analysis: The stability of a bi-factor solution. *Supplementary Educational Monographs, No. 48.* Chicago: University of Chicago, Department of Education.

Jöreskog, K. G., & Sörbom, D. (1989). *LISREL-7 user's reference guide.* Mooresville, IN: Scientific Software.

Jöreskog, K. G., & Sörbom, D. (1993). *Prelis 2 user's reference guide.* Chicago: Scientific Software.

Judd, C. M., & McClelland, G. H. (1989). *Data analysis: A model-comparison approach.* New York: Harcourt Brace Jovanovich.

Kim, J.-O., & Curry, J. (1977). The treatment of missing data in multivariate analysis. *Sociological Methods and Research, 6,* 215–240.

Little, R. J. A. (1976). Inference about means from incomplete multivariate data. *Biometrika, 63,* 593–604.

Little, R. J. A., & Rubin, D. B. (1989). The analysis of social science data with missing values. *Sociological Methods and Research, 18,* 292–326.

Lord, F. M. (1955a). Equating test scores—a maximum likelihood solution. *Psychometrika, 20,* 193–200.

Lord, F. M. (1955b). Estimation of parameters from incomplete data. *Journal of the American Statistical Association, 50,* 870–876.

Matthai, A. (1951). Estimation of parameters from incomplete data with application to design of sample surveys. *Sankhya, 11,* 145–152.

Muthén, B., Kaplan, D., & Hollis, M. (1987). On structural equation modeling with data that are not missing completely at random. *Psychometrika, 52,* 431–462.

Neale, M. C. (1994). *Mx: Statistical modeling* (2nd ed.). Richmond, VA: Department of Psychiatry, Medical College of Virginia.

Orchard, T., & Woodbury, M. A. (1972). A missing information principle: Theory and applications. *Proceedings of the 6th Berkeley Symposium on Mathematical Statistics and Applied Probability* (Vol. 1). Berkeley, CA: University of California Press.

Roth, P. L. (1994). Missing data: A conceptual review for applied psychologists. *Personnel Psychology, 47,* 537–560.

Rubin, D. B. (1974). Characterizing the estimation of parameters in incomplete-data problems. *Journal of the American Statistical Association, 69,* 467–474.

Rubin, D. B. (1976). Inference and missing data. *Biometrika, 63,* 581–592.

Rubin, D. B. (1987). *Multiple imputation for nonresponse in surveys.* New York: Wiley.

Rubin, D. B., & Thayer, D. (1978). Relating tests given to different samples. *Psychometrika, 43,* 3–10.

Rubin, D. B., & Thayer, D. T. (1982). EM algorithms for ML factor analysis. *Psychometrika, 47,* 69–76.

Thayer, D. T. (1983). Maximum likelihood estimation of the joint covariance matrix for sections of tests given to distinct samples with application to test equating. *Psychometrika, 48,* 293–297.

Trawinski, I. M., & Bargmann, R. E. (1964). Maximum likelihood estimation with incomplete multivariate data. *Annals of Mathematical Statistics, 35,* 647–657.

Werts, C. E., Rock, D. A., & Grandy, J. (1979). Confirmatory factor analysis applications: Missing data problems and comparison of path models between populations. *Multivariate Behavioral Research, 14,* 199–213.

Wilks, S. S. (1932). Moments and distributions of estimates of population parameters from fragmentary samples. *Annals of Mathematical Statistics, 3,* 163–195.

CHAPTER TEN

Inference Problems With Equivalent Models

Larry J. Williams
Purdue University

Hamparsum Bozdogan
University of Tennessee

Lynda Aiman-Smith
Purdue University

Researchers in the social and behavioral science areas have become increasingly interested in using structural equation models (SEM) to address substantive questions. The steps a researcher typically takes in conducting SEM applications are: (a) the researcher translates the proposed theoretical processes into a path diagram; (b) the structural equations represented by the diagram are developed; (c) data are collected and the resulting covariance matrix prepared; (d) the parameters in the structural equations are estimated using one of the available software packages; and (e) the researcher judges the adequacy of the model, via the use of goodness-of-fit indices, by comparing the difference between the sample covariance matrix and a corresponding reproduced covariance matrix based on the parameter estimates.

The SEM approach to data analysis was described more than 10 years ago as "perhaps the most important and influential statistical revolution to have occurred in the social sciences" (Cliff, 1983, p. 115). One reason for the popularity is that SEM techniques permit researchers to effectively study substantive problems that could not easily be investigated using experimental approaches (Bentler, 1986). Additionally, SEMs provide many statistical advantages that are important to substantive researchers, including the capability to account for random and nonrandom measurement error, the ability to easily accommodate models with correlated dependent variables via the use of full-information estimators, and the effective manner in which even quite complex models can be efficiently compared.

In the time during which applications of SEMs have increased, there has been a corresponding explosion of research on different technical aspects of SEM techniques. For example, one stream of investigations has examined and compared the performance of alternative parameter estimation techniques (e.g., Muthén & Kaplan, 1992). Alternatively, the impact of the distributions of variables on estimation and fit has been studied (e.g., Mislevy, 1986). There has also been considerable attention given to the development of goodness-of-fit indices for use in the model assessment process (e.g., Bollen & Long, 1993). Finally, there has been an attempt to identify optimal strategies for the comparison of competing theoretical models (e.g., Anderson & Gerbing, 1988).

In spite of the proliferation of substantive applications of SEM techniques and the technical developments noted above, there is still a fundamental difficulty which users of this approach confront every time they fit and evaluate a model. This difficulty has been known since the earliest stages of SEM development, and it occurs in the last step of the modeling process (Step (e) previously mentioned), as the adequacy of the model examined is being judged. Simply, regardless of the strength of the substantive theory underlying the model and the adequacy of the values for the fit indices used, it is always the case that alternative models might exist which fit the data equally well. As a result, researchers are unable to "confirm" the model being evaluated; instead, they may only fail to "disconfirm" the model (e.g., Cliff, 1983; Duncan, 1975; James, Mulaik, & Brett, 1982).

This chapter focuses on a special case of the problem of alternative models, in which the competing models have the special property of being "equivalent" (i.e., they result in identical implied or predicted covariance matrices and have identical chi-square, degrees of freedom, and traditional goodness of fit values). First we provide some background on equivalent models and a summary of the literature on this problem. Next, we discuss an important question that results from this problem: Are researchers' substantive conclusions about relationships in their models impacted when they pick one from among a set of equivalent models? Having raised this question, we then present results of analyses from both simulated and real sample data that indicate conclusions are impacted by this choice. Finally, we discuss statistical and nonstatistical approaches to dealing with this problem, including the role of complexity based fit measures.

BACKGROUND ON EQUIVALENT MODELS

Even though researchers have been aware of the problem of equivalent models, the understanding of associated issues was slowed by a basic difficulty: How can one identify the possible equivalent models for a given model being considered? Fortunately, Stelzl (1986) stimulated subsequent work on the topic by presenting four rules for generating equivalent path models. These rules focused on cases in which the direction of a causal path was reversed, or the causal path was replaced with a correlation among disturbance terms for the equations associated with the two variables. Stelzl used these rules to develop equivalent models for two empirical examples, the results of which were also reported. Stelzl closed by discussing how equivalent models can be avoided by careful selection of additional variables for the model.

In an important follow-up article, Lee and Hershberger (1990) introduced the replacing rule as a simplification of Stelzl's (1986) four rules. To explain the replacing rule, we make reference to an hypothetical model that has (a) one or more predictors influencing Y1 (labeled our "source" variable), and (b) Y1 influencing Y2 (labeled our "effect" variable). With such a model, as long as the predictors of Y1 are the same as or include those of Y2, equivalent models will result if (a) the path from Y1 to Y2 is reversed such that Y2 becomes a cause of Y1, or (b) if the path from Y1 to Y2 is replaced by a correlation between the disturbance terms for the Y1 and Y2 equations. Lee and Hershberger demonstrated the replacement rule with several examples, and concluded with some guidance concerning how the indeterminancy associated with equivalent models could be resolved.

Finally, in a more recent review, MacCallum, Wegener, Uchino, and Fabrigar (1993) applied the replacement rule to 53 studies from the areas of educational psychology, industrial–organizational psychology, and social-personality psychology. MacCallum et al. determined that the number of studies in each of the three areas for which the existence of equivalent models could be identified were 86%, 74%, and 100%, respectively. Moreover, for the three areas of research, the median number of equivalent models was 16.5, 12, and 21. MacCallum et al. also selected one application from each of the three areas for reanalysis and presented the results for the equivalent models obtained from this reanalysis. Finally, these authors discussed the implications of their findings, and provided some strategies for managing problems associated with equivalent models.

ARE CONCLUSIONS COMPROMISED BY IGNORING EQUIVALENT MODELS?

For substantive researchers, the lesson from the aforementioned studies is that when they pick a model to examine, they should be aware that other models exist that fit the data equally well. Although this has been known for some time, tools such as those developed by Stelzl (1986) and Lee and Hershberger (1990) make it easier for researchers to identify the specific form of the equivalent models. Unfortunately, it is not clear whether researchers are motivated to undertake the process of examining these models or take the design steps necessary to preclude these models, because the impact of this problem on substantive conclusions has not been well documented. It is obvious that conclusions associated with the path(s) being manipulated to obtain the equivalent models will be impacted. Thus, in the previous example for the three equivalent models, which propose that either Y1 > Y2, Y2 > Y1, or Y1 and Y2 are linked via a correlated disturbance term, inferences about the relationship between Y1 and Y2 will be different. There are other paths, however, that are constant across the equivalent models, namely the paths linking the predictors to Y1 and Y2. An important question arises as to whether the conclusions associated with these paths will be impacted by a failure to consider equivalent models. If so, equivalent models might pose an even bigger threat to inferences made during the modeling process, because the magnitude and significance of every relationship in the model might be dependent on the researcher's choice among the three possible relationships between Y1 and Y2.

In the literature on equivalent models, little attention has been paid to the parameter estimates resulting from a set of equivalent models. Stelzl (1986) did present the path coefficients for some of the equivalent models examined. In Stelzl's Example II, the coefficients for 5 of 7 paths that were constant across the models changed noticeably, although information on their statistical significance was not provided. In Example III, which contained three paths among three latent variables, significance levels for path coefficients were presented. Stelzl noted that one important parameter estimate was significant in one model but nonsignificant in a different equivalent model, which reversed the direction of one of the other paths. Alternatively, MacCallum et al. (1993) presented parameter estimates and significance levels for the models examined, and some variability in these estimates and their significance was obtained. Jöreskog and Sörbom (1989) also presented an empirical examination of a set of equivalent models, and reported differences in estimates and statistical significance in their example.

TWO EXAMPLES BASED ON POPULATION MODELS

It is apparent that more information is needed about how the parameter estimates from a set of equivalent models differ. This information should address the question of how the inference process is impacted by the selection of a given model from among a set of equivalent models. We examine two sets of examples in pursuit of this issue. These examples are referred to as population models because a population covariance matrix was used to examine parameter values for three equivalent models. This approach has the advantage that the actual parameter values from the model are known, which facilitates the comparison of the results of the equivalent models.

Example 1. In this example, the population covariance matrix from Model A by MacCallum (1986) was used and three equivalent models were evaluated. The first model for this example is shown in Fig. 10.1. It should be noted that this model includes a path that actually has a value of zero (ga 2,3). This path was included to meet the conditions necessary for equivalent models (the predictors of Y1 must be the same as or include those of Y2), and to provide an example of how alternative specifications can incorrectly yield nonzero path values. Because this model is based on Y1 being a determinant of Y2, it will be referred to as Model Y1Y2. The first alternative model examined is Model Y2Y1; it is based on changing the direction of the path between Y1 and Y2 so that Y2 is a determinant of Y1. The second equivalent model examined is Model CD; the path from Y1 to Y2 was replaced with a correlation between the disturbance terms for the Y1 and Y2 equations.

The parameter values resulting from the three equivalent models are presented in Table 10.1. The first column presents the values for Model Y1Y2, and because these values are the standardized estimates used by MacCallum to generate the original covariance matrix, the results of the other two models will be compared to them. In the second column, reversing the direction of the path such that Y2 is a determinant of Y1, changes the values for the paths from the exogenous variables to both Y1 and Y2. Specifically, two of the paths are much smaller in the second model than in the first model, including GA (1,1) and GA (1,2), whereas the GA (1,3) path dropped by a smaller amount. Alternatively, two other paths [GA (2,1) and GA (2,2)] increased considerably in the second model, as did the GA (2,3) path that originally had a value of zero. In one sense, these changes are not very surprising, because the paths leading to Y1 in

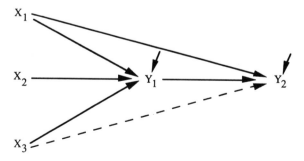

FIG. 10.1. Model for Example 1. Correlations among predictor variables omitted for clarity. Dotted line represents path with a value of zero.

TABLE 10.1
Standardized Parameter Values for Example 1 Equivalent Models

Path	Model Y1Y2	Model Y2Y1	ModelCD
GA 1,1	.32	.11	.32
GA 1,2	.48	.30	.48
GA 1,3	.32	.28	.32
GA 2,1	.42	.53	.53
GA 2,2	.28	.45	.45
GA 2,3**	.00	.11	.11
BE 2,1	.35	—	—
BE 1,2	—	.39	—
PS 1,2	—	—	.11
R2X	.68	.72	.68
R2Y	.75	.71	.71

*True parameter values from chosen starting model. **Specified to be zero in true model.

the second model control for the impact of Y2, and thus would be expected to drop. Similarly, the paths leading to Y2 do not control for the impact of Y1 in the second model, since Y1 is no longer a determinant of Y2. Thus, they would be expected to increase in value with the second model. Finally, the values in Column 3 for Model CD with the correlated disturbance terms are a combination of those presented for the other models. Specifically, the paths leading to Y1 [GA (1,1), GA (1,2), GA (1,3)] have the same values as in Model Y1Y2, whereas the paths leading to Y2 [GA (2,1), GA (2,2), GA (2,3)] have the same values as in Model Y2Y1.

Example 2. The second example to be studied is based on the model presented by Mulaik et al. (1989). As shown in Fig. 10.2, this model contains four exogenous constructs and three endogenous constructs, and a total of eight nonzero paths are included. Three paths with values of zero are

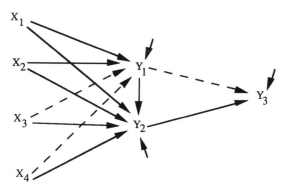

FIG. 10.2. Model for Example 2. Correlations among predictor variables omitted for clarity. Dotted line represents path with a value of zero.

included in this analysis to yield a model that would allow equivalent models to be generated using the replacement rule. In this example, the population covariance matrix is not available (as it was with Example 1), so one had to be generated by assuming values for the various paths in the model. Specifically, the correlations among the exogenous constructs were set at .3, the structural paths were set at either .2, .3, or .4 (unstandardized values), and the error variances of the structural equations were assumed to be .5. The factor loadings in the measurement model were set at .8, whereas the indicator error variances were assumed to be .6. The obtained population covariance matrix based on these fixed values was then used as input for the examination of the three equivalent models.

The standardized parameter values for the three equivalent models in this example are provided in Table 10.2. Model Y1Y2 refers to the model used to generate the covariance matrix and contains the path from Y1 to Y2. This path is reversed in the second equivalent model, Model Y2Y1. In the other equivalent model (Model CD), the path from Y1 to Y2 is replaced with a correlated disturbance term. As noted earlier, three paths with values of zero were included in Model Y1Y2 [GA (1,3), GA (1,4), and BE (3,1)]. The results for Model Y2Y1 shown in the second column indicate a pattern similar to that obtained in Example 1. Specifically, two of the paths from the exogenous constructs to Y1 were attenuated, in that GA (1,1) dropped from .46 in Model Y1Y2 to .24 in Model Y2Y1. Similarly, the value for GA (1,2) changed from .23 to −.03 in the second equivalent model. Perhaps even more interesting, the values changed for the two paths that were actually zero, GA (1,3) became

TABLE 10.2
Standardized Parameter Values for Example 2 Equivalent Models

Path	Model Y1Y2	Model Y2Y1	Model CD
GA 1,1	.46	.24	.46
GA 1,2	.23	−.03	.23
GA 1,3**	.00	−.20	.00
GA 1,4**	.00	−.10	.00
GA 2,1	.15	.32	.32
GA 2,2	.29	.38	.38
GA 2,3	.29	.29	.29
GA 2,4	.15	.15	.15
BE 3,1**	.00	.00	.00
BE 3,2	.61	.61	.61
BE 2,1	.38	—	—
BE 1,2	—	.70	—
PS 1,2	—	—	.25
R2X	.33	.51	.33
R2Y	.73	.64	.64

*True parameter values from chosen starting model. **Specified to be zero in true model.

–.20 and GA (1,4) became –.10. Also, there was an increase in two of the paths leading to Y2, in that GA (2,1) increased from .15 in Model Y1Y2 to .32 in Model Y2Y1, and GA (2,2) increased from .29 to .38. Finally, as in Example 1, the results for Model CD were a mixture of those obtained in the first two models, with the values for the paths leading to Y1 being the same as with Model Y1Y2, and the values for the paths leading to Y2 being the same as with Model Y2Y1.

SIX EXAMPLES BASED ON SAMPLE DATA

The two previous examples provided information about how the values of paths in a structural equation model vary as equivalent models are examined. It is clear from these results that the common paths (paths that do not change) in a set of equivalent models can be impacted by the specification of a path that does change. However, an important follow-up question needs attention. Specifically, in addition to differences in value, can the statistical significance of these paths be impacted by the specification of a path that changes in a set of equivalent models? To address this question, we examined a set of three equivalent models in six samples (referred to as Examples 3–8). We selected the six samples from a single content area, involving the study of predictors of employee attitudes of job satisfaction and organizational commitment. Also, we selected the samples so that they would share the same dependent variables, as well as have several predictors in common. Selecting the samples in this fashion permits a pattern to emerge so as to indicate how the development of a specific theoretical model can be affected by problems associated with equivalent models.

There were other reasons for selecting these specific examples for comparative analysis. First, the models were not unusually complex and they used constructs very common in organizational studies. Second, the models fit criteria outlined in Lee and Hershberger (1990) for application of the replacement rule. Also, all of the studies included job satisfaction and organizational commitment as endogenous variables, and these variables served as the source and effect variables (e.g., MacCallum et al., 1993). Previous research has shown that these two variables have a number of common predictors. Equally as important, empirical literature on the relationship between job satisfaction and organizational commitment has provided support for three models: Satisfaction causes commitment, commitment causes satisfaction, and the two variables are not related but share some common causes. As such, the structure of the models are consistent with the requirements for using the replacement rule proposed by Lee and Hershberger.

Thus, in each study, there are three equivalent models. The first is a model in which a path is specified to go from satisfaction to commitment;

it will be identified as Model SC. The second model reverses that path, so that it goes from commitment to satisfaction; it will be identified as Model CS. The third model allows the disturbance terms of commitment and satisfaction to correlate freely, and it will be identified as Model CD.

We used data from six separate published papers in Examples 3–8. Each article included a correlation matrix, and four of the studies also included the standard deviations that allowed for a covariance matrix to be generated. Thus, four of the examples are based on the analysis of a covariance matrix, and two others are based on an analysis of a correlation matrix. Although the analysis of correlation matrices is not without its problems (e.g., Cudeck, 1989), the latter two examples are included to supplement the first four examples based on a covariance matrix, recognizing that their results should be interpreted cautiously. As previously noted, each study had organizational commitment and job satisfaction as dependent variables. The predictor variables differed in each study. The sources for all of the variables in each study are included in their respective tables presenting the results for each study.

The results from Examples 3–8 focus on how the conclusions that substantive researchers would reach from a set of analyses are different across three equivalent models. We will focus on changes in a set of parameter estimates, where the term set refers to the three estimates from a predictor to a dependent variable for the three equivalent models. For example, the three estimates for the path linking a predictor to job satisfaction from the three equivalent models will be referred to as a set. Three types of changes within sets of estimates are identified. First, we note instances where a parameter is statistically significant (T value > 1.96) in one model, but not significant in one of the other two models. This type of change is referred to as Category 1. Next, we note instances where a parameter estimate increases or decreases by more than 20% across the three models, and this type of change is referred to as Category 2. Finally, we note a change of a more dramatic nature; the case where a parameter is significant in one model, and significant but with the opposite sign in the other models. This type of change will be labeled Category 3. The use of these categories will facilitate the discussion and summary of results from the analyses of the equivalent models.

Example 3. For this example, we drew on a previous analysis done by Williams and Hazer (1986), who used data from Bluedorn (1982) consisting of 154 employees from a corporate division. Although the research by Williams and Hazer was concerned with developing a unified model of turnover, only a subset of the data will be presented here. Specifically, organizational commitment and job satisfaction were dependent variables, and equity, routinization, instrumental information, and age were used as the predictor variables.

The results of the three equivalent models for Example 3 are in Table 10.3. In Table 10.3, it can be seen that across the equivalent models the

TABLE 10.3
Standardized Parameter Estimates for Example 3 Equivalent Models

Exogenous Variables	Estimates of Paths to Satisfaction			Type of Change	Estimates of Paths to Commitment			Type of Change
	Model SC	Model CS	Model CD	Change	Model SC	Model CS	Model CD	Change
Equity	.48*	.28	.48*	2	-.11	.28*	.28*	1
Routine	-.04	.11	-.04		-.18*	-.21*	-.21*	
InstrInfo	.39*	.15*	.39*	2	.01	.34*	.34*	1
Age	.19*	.01	.19*	1	.09	.25*	.25*	1

Note. Variables: Equity = equity (adapted by Bluedorn, 1982, from Adams, 1963); Routine = routinization (Price & Bluedorn, 1980); InstrInfo = instrumental information (Price & Bluedorn, 1980); Age = person's chronological age.

Change categories: 1 = change in statistical significance; 2 = change in value of estimate ≥ 20%; 3 = change in direction of significant estimate.

*indicates significance at p < .05.

parameter estimates shift in size and in significance. For example, in Model SC, the value of the parameter between equity and satisfaction is significant with a value of .48; in Model CS, that same parameter remains significant, but decreases in value to .28. Alternatively, in Model SC, the parameter linking equity and commitment is nonsignificant (−.11); however, in Model CS this parameter becomes significant with a value of .28. The parameters associated with the variables *instrumental information* and *age* also show changes in significance and/or magnitude. For example, the path between instrumental information and satisfaction in Model SC has a parameter value of .39 (significant at $p < .05$); however, in Model CS that parameter value shrinks by over 50% to .15. Alternatively, in Model SC, the path between instrumental information and commitment is nonsignificant (.01), yet, in Model CS, that path is not only significant, but it has a moderate value of .34. With respect to the variable age, its impact on satisfaction changes in significance in moving from Model SC to Model CS, and the same is true of its effects on commitment. The parameters from age to both commitment and satisfaction are significant in Model CD where the disturbance terms are allowed to correlate freely. Finally, the variable routinization remains stable when the equivalent models are examined, in that its effects on satisfaction are nonsignificant across the three models, and its effects on commitment are significant across the three models. In summary, four out of the eight sets of parameter estimates had a change in the significance of a parameter (Category 1 change), whereas in two cases there was a change in the magnitude of the parameter (Category 2 change).

Example 4. Data used in this example was published by Podsakoff, Niehoff, MacKenzie, and Williams (1993). Three diverse samples were pooled to form an overall sample of 612 employees, representing custodial, clerical, supervisory, technical, and managerial positions. The original research addressed the topic of substitutes for leadership. As noted earlier, a subset of variables were used with organizational commitment and job satisfaction as the dependent variables, and predictor variables including role conflict, role ambiguity, group cohesion, routinization, task feedback, professional orientation, and leader supportive behavior.

Table 10.4 presents the results for these equivalent models, and once again changes in magnitude and significance of the parameter estimates are observed across the equivalent models. For example, the parameter estimate for the path from role conflict to satisfaction is −.21 in Model SC; it drops by nearly 50% to −.11 in Model CS. At the same time, the parameter from role conflict to commitment in Model SC has a value of −.10, and it more than doubles in value to −.24 in Model CS. As another example, in Model SC, the path between group cohesiveness and commitment is nonsignificant (value of −.01), whereas the same path in Model

TABLE 10.4
Standardized Parameter Estimates for Example 4 Equivalent Models

Exogenous Variables	Estimates of Paths to Satisfaction			Type of Change	Estimates of Paths to Commitment			Type of Change
	Model SC	Model CS	Model CD	Change	Model SC	Model CS	Model CD	Change
RoleConflict	-.21*	-.11*	-.21*	2	-.10*	-.24*	-.24*	2
RoleAmbiguity	-.06	-.04	-.06		-.01	-.05	-.05	
GroupCohesion	.19*	.13*	.19*	2	.01	.13*	.13*	1
Routine	-.27*	-.14*	-.27*	2	-.14*	-.32*	-.32*	2
Feedbck	.27*	.20*	.27*	2	.00	.18*	.18*	1
Professional	.18*	.07*	.18*	2	.13*	.25*	.25*	2
LeaderSupport	.16*	.14*	.16*	2	-.06	.05	.05	2

Note. Variables: RoleConflict = role conflict (8 items taken from Rizzo, House, & Lirtzman, 1970); RoleAmbiguity = role ambiguity (6 items from Rizzo et al., 1970); GroupCohesion = cohesive interdependent work groups (from Podsakoff, Niehoff, MacKenzie, & Williams, 1993); Routine = routine tasks (Podsakoff et al., 1993); Feedbck = task provided feedback (Podsakoff et al., 1993); Professional = professional orientation (Podsakoff et al., 1993); LeaderSupport = supportive leader behavior (Schriesheim, 1978).

Change categories: 1 = change in statistical significance; 2 = change in value of estimate ≥ 20%; 3 = change in direction of significant estimate.
*indicates significance at $p < .05$.

CS is significant (value of .13). Similar changes are observable in the routinization, task feedback, and professionalism parameter estimates. In sum, for two of the 14 sets of parameter estimates, there were Category 1 changes, and in eight cases there were Category 2 changes.

Example 5.   This example is based on data published in Mathieu and Farr (1991). One purpose of the original study was to investigate the discriminant validity of measures of job satisfaction and organizational commitment. The data were collected from 194 bus drivers randomly sampled from a large midwestern city who completed surveys during paid working hours. Predictor variables included role strain, job scope, group processes, and job tension.

A comparison of the standardized parameter estimates for the three equivalent models is presented in Table 10.5. As noted with previous examples, there were changes in magnitude and significance of some of the paths in these models. For example, in Model SC with a path from satisfaction to commitment, neither of the parameters from role strain and job scope to commitment were statistically significant. However, when the direction of the pathway reversed in Model CS, both of the parameter estimates from role strain and job scope to commitment became significant (−.31, .29). There were also several changes in the magnitude of the parameter estimates across the models. For example, the estimates for paths from role strain and job scope to satisfaction were lower in Model CS than in the other two models. In sum, two out of eight sets of parameter estimates indicated a Category 1 change, whereas four other cases indicated a Category 2 change.

Example 6.   The data for this example came from research by Williams, Gavin, and Williams (1994). The sample consisted of 182 employees from various libraries, and the original research examined method effects in employee attitude research. We used role ambiguity, role conflict, role overload, leader member exchange, and job complexity as the predictor variables for job satisfaction and organizational commitment. Table 10.6 contains the standardized parameter estimates for the equivalent models. As previously cited, reversing the path between the two dependent variables changed both the magnitude, and for some paths, the significance of the estimates from the predictors to the dependent variables. For example, in Model SC, the parameter estimate of role overload to satisfaction is significant and has a value of −.31. In Model CS, the parameter between those two variables remains significant, but its value drops to −.22. Similarly, both leader member exchange and job complexity show patterns of changes in significance in moving from Model SC to Model CS. Specifically, these variables were significantly related to satisfaction in Model SC, but not in Model CS. Finally, the path from leader member exchange to commitment

TABLE 10.5
Standardized Parameter Estimates for Example 5 Equivalent Models

Exogenous Variables	Estimates of Paths to Satisfaction			Type of Change	Estimates of Paths to Commitment			Type of Change
	Model SC	Model CS	Model CD	Change	Model SC	Model CS	Model CD	Change
Rolestrain	-.48*	-.36*	-.48*	2	.01	-.31*	-.31*	1
Jobscope	.33*	.22*	.33*	2	.06	.29*	.29*	1
GroupProc	.06	-.01	.06		.15*	.18*	.18*	2
Jobtension	-.19*	-.13*	-.19*	2	-.03	-.16	-.16	

Note. Variables: Rolestrain = role strain (12 items selected from House, Schuler, & Levanoni, 1983; Jobscope = job scope (15 items drawn from Stone, 1974, and Sims, Szilagyi, & Keller, 1976); GroupProc = group processes (6 items adapted from Jones & James, 1979); Jobtension = job tension (7 items scale drawn from House & Rizzo, 1972).

Change categories: 1 = change in statistical significance; 2 = change in value of estimate ≥ 20%; 3 = change in direction of significant estimate.
*indicates significant values $p < .05$.

TABLE 10.6
Standardized Parameter Estimates for Example 6 Equivalent Models

Exogenous Variables	Estimates of Paths to Satisfaction			Type of Change	Estimates of Paths to Commitment			Type of Change
	Model SC	Model CS	Model CD	Change	Model SC	Model CS	Model CD	Change
RoleAmbiguity	.22	.06	.22		.02	.23	.23	
RoleConflict	-.08	-.02	-.08		.00	-.08	-.08	
RoleOverload	-.31*	-.22*	-.31*	2	.16	-.13	-.13	
Ldrmemex	.35*	.11	.35*	1	.01	.34*	.34*	
JobComplexity	.29*	.10	.29*	1	.00	.27	.27	1

Note. Variables: RoleAmbiguity = role ambiguity (from Rizzo et al., 1970); RoleConflict = role conflict (Rizzo et al., 1970); RoleOverload = role overload (3 items from Beehr, Walsh, & Taber, 1976); Ldrmemex = leader member exchange (8 items from Graen, Novak, & Sommerkamp, 1982); JobComplexity = job complexity (6 items from Sims et al., 1976).

Change categories: 1 = change in statistical significance; 2 = change in value of estimate ≥ 20%; 3 = change in direction of significant estimate.
*indicates significance $p < .05$.

was not significant in Model SC, but it was significant in Model CS. In sum, there were three Category 1 changes and one Category 2 change in the 10 sets of parameter estimates.

Example 7. This example is based on work by Lance (1991), who used a sample of 1870 employees in a telecommunications firm and examined job satisfaction, organizational commitment, and various precursors to voluntary turnover. Role stress, leader facilitation and support, coworker integration, job scope, and equity were predictor variables. As before, the results from the equivalent models indicate not only how significance and magnitude of parameters may change, but one variable indicated a change of direction when the causal paths were reversed. In Table 10.7, which compares the results from the three models, it can be seen that in Model SC, the parameter associated with role stress and satisfaction (−.32) decreased by 45% to −.22 in moving from Model SC to Model CS, whereas the parameter between role stress and commitment changed from −.10 to −.23. A similar shift is observable for job scope. The estimates for the effects of two of the predictors on satisfaction were not significant in Model SC, but were significant with Model CS. The estimated parameters associated with the variable equity indicated a directional shift. Finally, in Model SC the value of the parameter between equity and satisfaction is positive (.08, significant at $p < .05$); in Model CS the value has became negative (−.05, significant at $p < .05$). In sum, across the 10 sets of estimates, there were two Category 1 changes, five Category 2 changes, and one Category 3 change.

Example 8. This example drew upon Mathieu's (1991) study of 588 Army and Navy ROTC candidates, in which the antecedents of organizational commitment and job satisfaction were examined. The predictor variables included role strain, task characteristics, cohesiveness, and achievement motivation. As before, the equivalent models were developed by reversing a causal path between satisfaction and commitment, and also allowing the disturbance terms between those two variables to correlate freely. Table 10.8 displays the standardized parameter estimates of the three equivalent models. Again, both the magnitude and significance of the parameter estimates changed. For example, in the model that specified a path from satisfaction to commitment (Model SC), neither of the paths from role strain or cohesion to organizational commitment was significant. However, in the equivalent model that specified a path from commitment to satisfaction (Model CS), both of the paths to commitment were significant (−.26, −.09). Alternatively in Model SC, the estimated parameters from achievement to both satisfaction and commitment are significant; when the path is reversed in Model CS, the parameter from achievement to satisfaction drops becoming nonsignificant, and the parameter from

TABLE 10.7

Standardized Parameter Estimates for Example 7 Equivalent Models

Exogenous Variables	Estimates of Paths to Satisfaction			Type of Change	Estimates of Paths to Commitment			Type of Change
	Model SC	Model CS	Model CD	Change	Model SC	Model CS	Model CD	Change
RoleStress	-.32*	-.22*	-.32*	2	-.10*	-.23*	-.23*	2
LeaderFacilitate	-.03	-.04*	-.03	1	.04	.02	.02	
CoworkIntent	.01	-.04*	.01	1	.10*	.11*	.11*	
JobScope	.48*	.34*	.48*	2	.13*	.33*	.33*	2
Equity	.08*	-.05*	.08*	2,3	.25*	.28*	.28*	

Note. Variables: RoleStress = role stress (3 items from Rizzo, House, & Lirtzman, 1970; 3 items from James, Gent, Hater, & Coray, 1978; 3 items from Wanous, 1973); LeaderFacilitate = leader facilitation and support (4 items from James et al., 1978; 4 items from Jones & James, 1979; 8 items from Bowers & Seashore, 1966; 3 items from Lance, 1991); CoworkIntent = co-worker integration (3 items from Jones & James, 1979; one item from Sims et al., 1976; 6 items from Lance, 1991); JobScope = job scope (7 items adapted from James et al., 1978; and Sims et al., 1976); Equity = equity (7 items developed by Lance, 1991).

Change categories: 1 = change in statistical significance; 2 = change in value of estimate ≥ 20%; 3 = change in direction of significant estimate.

*indicates significance at $p < .05$.

295

TABLE 10.8
Standardized Parameter Estimates for Example 8 Equivalent Models

Exogenous Variables	Estimates of Paths to Satisfaction				Estimates of Paths to Commitment			
	Model SC	Model CS	Model CD	Type of Change	Model SC	Model CS	Model CD	Type of Change
Rolestrain	-.32*	-.18*	-.32*	2	-.06	-.26*	-.26*	1
Taskchr	.39*	.32*	.39*	2	-.13*	.12*	.12*	3
Cohesive	-.17*	-.13*	-.17*	2	.03	-.09*	-.09*	1
Achievmot	.21*	-.02	.21*	1	.29*	.42*	.42*	2

Note. Variables: Rolestrain = role strain (5 items adapted from House, Schuler, & Levanoni, 1983; 3 items from Abdel-Halim, 1978); Taskchr = task characteristics (19 items adapted from Sims et al., 1976; 4 items adapted from Jones & James, 1979); Cohesive = unit cohesion (6 items adapted from Moos, 1980); Achievmot = Achievement motivation (7 items based on Steers & Braunstein, 1976; additional items from Murray, 1938).

Change categories: 1 = change in statistical significance; 2 = change in value of estimate ≥ 20%; 3 = change in direction of significant estimate. *indicates significance $p < .05$.

achievement to commitment increases by 45% (from .29 to .42). In sum, in eight sets of parameter estimates, there were three examples of Category 1 changes, four examples of Category 2 changes, and one example of a Category 3 change.

Comparing of Changes in Other Parameters

The focus of the preceeding section was on the changes in a set of parameter estimates for paths common to a set of equivalent models (i.e., the paths whose specification did not change across the three models). However, a brief mention should be made of the parameter estimates for the paths whose specification did change to yield the three equivalent models. As was noted earlier, in Model SC, this path depicted a relationship from satisfaction to commitment, whereas in Model CS, this specification was changed to represent a path in the opposite direction (from commitment to satisfaction). Finally, in Model CD, this path was replaced by a correlation between the disturbance terms from the satisfaction and commitment equations.

The estimates for these three paths from the equivalent models across the six examples are presented in Table 10.9. All three estimates were statistically significant across the models from Examples 3 through 8. Also, in five of the six examples, the path from satisfaction to commitment had a larger value than the corresponding path from commitment to satisfaction. Finally, the correlations among the disturbance terms ranged from .16 to .52.

Summary of Changes Across Examples 3–8

The results in Tables 10.3 to 10.8 indicate further how changing the path in one part of a model (to yield alternative equivalent versions) impacts parameters in other parts of the model. These results were obtained across six different examples. Before proceeding, it is informative to summarize the changes we observed in our parameter estimates (see Table 10.10).

TABLE 10.9
Standardized Parameter Estimates Between Satisfaction and Commitment
for All Six Studies

	Example 3	Example 4	Example 5	Example 6	Example 7	Example 8
Model SC	.83*	.66*	.68*	.94*	.40*	.65*
Model CS	.71*	.42*	.38*	.71*	.45*	.54*
Model CD	.41*	.16*	.19*	.52*	.20*	.29*

Note. Model SC and Model CS show structural path values; Model CD shows the correlation between disturbance terms.

*indicates significant $p < .05$.

TABLE 10.10
Summary of Changes in Results for 29 Predictor Variables Across Studies

	Dependent Variable	
Type of Change	Satisfaction	Commitment
Change in significance	21%	35%
Change of 20% in magnitude	59%	24%
Change in direction, significant	3%	3%
Change in number of significant predictors	4 of 6 studies 2 with change > 1	5 of 6 studies 4 with change > 2

First we examine the Category 1 changes, which reflect instances where a parameter is statistically significant in one model, but not significant in one of the other two models. For the paths from the 29 predictors to job satisfaction, a Category 1 change occured in 21% of the cases. For the paths from the predictors to organizational commitment, a Category 1 change occurred in 35% of the cases. One implication of this pattern is that in four of the six examples, there was a change in the number of significant predictors of job satisfaction, and in five of the six examples there was also a change in the number of significant predictors of organizational commitment. For job satisfaction in two of the studies, the number of significant predictors changed by two or more, whereas for organizational commitment, this pattern was obtained in four of the six examples.

Additionally, we noted instances where a parameter estimate increased or decreased by more than 20% across the three models, and this type of change was labeled as Category 2. Category 2 changes occurred 59% of the time for paths linking the predictors to job satisfaction. Alternatively, Category 2 changes were found in 24% of the 29 paths linking predictors to organizational commitment. Finally, we did not find many instances where a parameter was significant in one model, and significant but of the opposite sign in the other models. This type of change was labeled as Category 3, and it was found in only 3% of the paths from the predictors to both job satisfaction and organizational commitment.

SELECTING FROM A SET OF EQUIVALENT MODELS

The results from all eight examples included in this chapter indicate the inference problems that challenge researchers selecting from among a set of equivalent models. Clearly, the choice of a specific model from among such a set of equivalent models can have important implications for the conclusions reached about all the relationships in the model. Estimates of these relationships were shown to vary across the three equivalent models examined, and changes of statistical significance and magnitude were common across the predictors included in the analyses. Thus, it is important to consider any criteria that can be used to help researchers in the model assessment process.

Nonstatistical approaches to this problem have appeared in the literature. Lee and Hershberger (1990) have discussed how knowledge of time precedence can be used to determine a better model among equivalent models. In some cases, researchers may have variables measured at different points in time. If so, this knowledge can be used to rule out some of the equivalent models as being untenable, since it is clear that effects must follow causes in time. Thus, an alternative model that includes a path from a predictor to a consequence, which has been measured before the predictor, may be rejected. The use of longitudinal designs to avoid equivalent model problems has also been discussed by MacCallum et al. (1993).

Alternatively, knowledge about the mediating nature of variables in a model may allow for equivalent models to be minimized by allowing for certain paths associated with direct effects to be set to zero. To understand how setting these paths to zero may eliminate some equivalent models from consideration, we can refer to the replacement rule introduced by Lee and Hershberger (1990). It was noted earlier that this rule can be applied in cases where the predictors of the source variable are the same as or include those of the effect variable. Knowledge of mediational processes may support the restriction to zero of one or more paths to the source variable, which would result in alternative models containing different specifications of the relationship between the effect and source variables no longer being equivalent to the first model.

In addition to these nonstatistical approaches, it has also been suggested that statistical information might be used to select a model from a set of equivalent models. Specifically, Jöreskog and Sörbom (1989) suggested that the values for the squared multiple correlations of equations from a set of equivalent models might be used to identify a preferred model. They presented an example with two dependent variables in a model, making specific reference to the sum of the R^2 values for the two equations. In their example, the sum for one model was .989, and .974 for the other model. Although this approach may have merit, there currently is no other information about how the values for R^2 vary among a set of equivalent models.

We have reported the R^2 values obtained from the two equations in our models for Examples 3–8 in Table 10.11. We also display the sum of the two values. In some of the examples the R^2 sum varied over the three equivalent models. For instance, with Model SC from Example 1, the R^2 sum was 1.28, and with Model CS, the sum was 1.23, whereas with Model CD, the value dropped to .94. In Example 4, the sum varied from 1.84 with Model SC to 1.37 with Model CD; the value for Model CS (1.43) was

TABLE 10.11
RSquare Values for Six Examples

	Rsquare SAT	Rsquare COM	Rsquare SUM
Example 3			
Model SC	0.51	0.77	1.28
Model CS	0.80	0.43	1.23
Model CD	0.51	0.43	0.94
Example 4			
Model SC	0.90	0.94	1.84
Model CS	0.82	0.61	1.43
Model CD	0.76	0.61	1.37
Example 5			
Model SC	0.72	0.63	1.35
Model CS	0.79	0.50	1.29
Model CD	0.72	0.50	1.22
Example 6			
Model SC	0.45	0.76	1.21
Model CS	0.82	0.27	1.09
Model CD	0.45	0.27	0.72
Example 7			
Model SC	0.55	0.64	1.19
Model CS	0.70	0.46	1.16
Model CD	0.55	0.46	1.10
Example 8			
Model SC	0.60	0.70	1.30
Model CS	0.62	0.68	1.30
Model CD	0.60	0.68	1.28

close to that of Model CD. Similarly, in Example 6, the range for the sum of R^2 was from 1.21 (Model SC) to .72 (Model CD), and the value for Model CS (1.09) fell in between these two values. In the other three examples (Examples 5,7, and 8), the difference between the sums of the R^2 values was not very large across the equivalent models.

The values in Table 10.11 indicate that there are differences in R^2 values for various equivalent models. However, as suggested by Parzen (1983), statisticians should be thinking to replace R^2 (the multiple correlation coefficient) by an informational measure of dependency, such as the complexity. Information-theoretic measures exhibit remarkable regularity in their significance levels across different sample sizes, as compared to the significance levels of R^2. This suggests that we should not use the values of R^2 or the R^2 sums in equivalent models to choose the best fitting equivalent models among a class of competing equivalent models, because these sums are not based on any theoretical grounds.

An alternative statistical approach that might have merit is based on recent developments in the area of goodness-of-fit indices. As noted in the introduction to this chapter, one of the defining features of equivalent models is that they yield identical predicted covariance matrices, which implies that these models will also have identical values for traditional goodness-of-fit indices that are based on a discrepancy between the predicted covariance and the sample covariance matrices. Also, since equivalent models typically (but not necessarily) will have the same number of parameters, these models will also have identical values with traditional parsimonious based fit indices (e.g., Williams & Holahan, 1994). However, a new approach to model assessment that shows promise for selecting from among equivalent models and is not affected by the aforementioned problems has recently been developed by Bozdogan (e.g., 1988).

COMPLEXITY AND SELECTION
AMONG EQUIVALENT MODELS

A new entropic statistical complexity criterion called ICOMP was recently developed by Bozdogan (1988, 1990a, 1990b, 1993, 1994a, 1994b, 1994c, in preparation-a, in preparation-b) for model selection in multivariate linear and nonlinear structural models. Analytic formulation of ICOMP takes the "spirit" of Akaike's (1973) classic AIC, but it is based on the generalization and utilization of an entropic covariance complexity index of a multivariate normal distribution in parametric estimation (Van Emden, 1971). The definition and mathematical details of the ICOMP complexity criterion are provided in Appendix A.

To investigate the utility of the complexity approach to model evaluation, we present the analyses on four of the previously discussed empirical examples. Specifically, complexity of IFIM (Inverse Fisher Information Matrix) values were obtained for the equivalent models for Examples 3–6, because only these examples were based on the analysis of a covariance matrix. The results of these supplementary analyses are provided in Table 10.12. The computations were all carried out using open architecture computational module developed in MATLAB (Bozdogan, in preparation-b). The modules can interface with results of LISREL output provided by the user.

An examination of Table 10.12 reveals that, based on the complexity of IFIM in Example 3, the Models SC, CS, and CD exhibit almost the same

TABLE 10.12
Model Evaluation Results of Examples 3–6 and Their Entropic
Complexities of the Estimated Inverse-Fisher Information Matrix (IFIM)

Examples	Models	$C_1\ (\mathcal{F}^{-1})$	95% ACI	$w = width\ of\ ACI$
	SC	30.4478*	(15.2737, 45.7214)	30.4478
Example 3	CS	30.4653	(15.2575, 45.6703)	30.4155
	CD	30.4725	(15.2611, 45.6839)	30.4228
	SC	60.5556	(40.2006, 80.9106)	40.7100
Example 4	CS	60.6384	(40.2556, 81.0213)	40.7657
	CD	59.3449*	(39.3969, 79.2930)	39.8961*
	SC	135.2279	(20.9902, 248.6662)	228.3509
Example 5	CS	134.8282*	(21.0031, 248.8184)	227.6760*
	CD	134.9107	(16.2208, 538.8432)	227.8153
	SC	277.5320	(16.2208, 538.8432)	522.6225
Example 6	CS	262.6715*	(15.3522, 509.9908)	494.6386*
	CD	277.6354	(16.2268, 539.0440)	522.8172

Note. *Indicates the minimum of the complexity of the estimated IFIM and the width w of the 95% approximate confidence interval of the complexity of IFIM to be the best fitting model.

fit. These are also seen in the same compact values of the width **w** of the 95% approximate confidence intervals (ACIs) of these complexity measures. We see that there is an overlap in 95% ACIs across these three models. So it is difficult to distinguish among these models in this example. However, Model SC seems to be the least complex one based on the minimum value of the complexity of IFIM. In Example 4, Model CD is the best fitting model among the Models SC and CS because the minimum of the complexity of IFIM occurs at Model CD. Also, we note that there is some overlap in the 95% ACIs between the Models SC and CS. In Example 5, the winner is Model CS, followed by the Model CD. Finally, in Example 6, the Model CS seems to be clearly the best fitting model based on its complexity value. The minimum width **w** of the 95% ACI of the complexity of IFIM certainly verifies this.

The aforementioned results demonstrate that the informational complexity of the estimated inverse-Fisher information matrix can be used to distinguish the equivalent models. As mentioned previously, because the equivalent models typically (but not necessarily) have the same number of parameters estimated within the model, it will not be possible for the researcher to distinguish the equivalent model structures based on the number of parameters only. It should be noted that the results based on complexity differ from those based on the sum of the squared multiple correlations. This finding along with the suggestion of Parzen (1983), indicate that the R^2 values from equivalent models should not be used in model selection with equivalent models.

In general, we obtain the complexity of each restriction imposed on the model provided that the parameter identifiability is satisfied, and study the significance and insignificance of the paths in the model. This helps to confirm and disconfirm substantive arguments, and carry out confirmatory as well as exploratory analysis of the data in a systematic fashion.

CONCLUSIONS

In this chapter, we studied the inference problems in equivalent structural equation models. Results from population and sample based models demonstrated that parameter values can vary dramatically among a set of equivalent models. Thus, the conclusions reached by a researcher can be greatly impacted by a failure to consider equivalent models. We also introduced a new criterion called *the information complexity* to assess the goodness of the equivalent models among a class of competing alternative models. Equivalent models occur in many practical applications, not just in SEM models. For example, we see equivalent models in multivariate time series analysis, in harmonic analysis in detecting signals, in multiple comparison procedures of multivariate data, in multisample cluster analysis, and in subset selection of variables in regression analysis, to mention a few. Equivalent models are special type of models that need attention and careful study. Unfortunately, to date, little attention has been focused on the inference problems in equivalent models. With this chapter, we hope to influence researchers so that they pay closer attention to inference problems in equivalent models.

Equivalent models will have identical values for traditional goodness-of-fit indices. In addition, because equivalent models typically (but not necessarily) will have the same number of parameters, these models will have identical values with the traditional parsimony fit indices. Therefore, we recommend that traditional fit indices not be used in testing the goodness-of-fit of equivalent models, on the grounds that we have no provision of distinguishing among the equivalent models based on the number of estimated parameters. For this reason, we propose the use of a novel informational complexity approach to assess the model fit among the equivalent models based on their complexities of the estimated inverse-Fisher information matrices. This approach requires minimal assumptions and measures the strength of the structure of an equivalent model. It represents relations such as similarity, dissimilarity, and higher order correlations within the model. Of course, if the variables show neither similarity nor dissimilarity, then the complexity becomes zero, and one should not use these new procedures because there is nothing to account for complexity. Although these results are promising, further extensive research needs to be carried out in the area of equivalent class of models with known structures to study the empirical performance of this new criterion.

APPENDIX A

Bozdogan (1990b) defines the concept of complexity and information theoretic measure of complexity of a multivariate distribution as follows:

Definition 1.1.   Complexity of a system (of any type) is a measure of the degree of interdependency between the whole system and a simple decomposition of its subsystems or parts.

Let C denote any real-valued measure of complexity of a System S. If S is a joined composition of Subsystems S_1 and S_2, and they both interact, then

$$C(S) = C(S_1 \otimes S_2) \leq C(S_1 \text{ and } S_2)\, C(S_1) + C(S_2). \tag{1}$$

Note that if there is no interaction between S_1 and S_2, then

$$C(S) = C(S_1 \otimes S_2) = C(S_1) + C(S_2), \tag{2}$$

where $\otimes$ denotes the Kronecker (or direct) product. Equation 1 is known as the axiom of joined composition of complexity. In this way, complexity of the overall System S is reduced to the sum of complexity of the interaction of the subcomponents of the system plus the sum of the complexities of their individual subcomponents.

Bozdogan (1990b) uses the joining axiom of complexity in Equation 1 as the basis to characterize the dependency structure of the subsystems with respect to the whole System S. To quantify these concepts, one only has to express the interactions in a mathematical definition. One accomplishes this by appealing to information theory.

To define the multivariate informational measure of dependence among the random variables $X_1, X_2, \ldots, X_p$ the following entropy identity is used:

$$
\begin{aligned}
I(X) &\equiv I(X_1, X_2, \ldots, X_p) \\
&\widetilde{=}\; \underbrace{H(X_1) + H(X_2) + \ldots + H(X_p)}_{\text{Marginal entropies}} - \underbrace{H(X_1, X_2, \ldots, X_p)}_{\text{Gobal or joint entropy}}.
\end{aligned}
\tag{3}
$$

This is also known as the expected mutual information or the information proper. Watanabe (1985) calls $I(X)$ the strength of the structure and a measure of interdependence.

Using Equation 3, when

$$X \sim N(\mu,\Sigma) \quad \text{(Multivariate Normal)}$$

Van Emden (1971) provides a reasonable initial definition of informational complexity of a covariance matrix Σ. This measure is given by

$$C_0(\Sigma) = 1/2 \sum_{j=1}^{p} \log(\sigma_j^2) - 1/2 \log|\Sigma|. \tag{4}$$

To improve upon $C_0(\Sigma)$, Bozdogan proposes to use the following:

Proposition 1.1. A maximal information theoretic measure of complexity of a covariance matrix Σ of a multivariate normal distribution is

$$\begin{aligned} C_1(\Sigma) &= \underset{T}{\text{Max}}\{H(X_1) + \ldots + H(X_p) - H(X_1, X_2, \ldots, X_p)\} \\ &= \frac{p}{2}\log\left[\frac{\text{tr}(\Sigma)}{p}\right] - \frac{1}{2}\log|\Sigma|, \end{aligned} \tag{5}$$

where the maximum is taken over orthonormal transformations T of the overall coordinate systems $X_1, \ldots, X_p$.

$C_1(\Sigma)$ measures both inequality among the variances and the contribution of the covariances in Σ. It is minimized with the minimum zero when all said random variables are independent. Otherwise, $C_1(\Sigma) > 0$. Large values of complexity indicate a high interaction between the variables, and low degree of complexity represents less interaction between the variables.

Thus, using the idea of the maximal informational covariance complexity measure $C_1(\Sigma)$ in (5) along with the additivity property of complexity of an overall system S given in Equation 1, Bozdogan introduces and develops a very general informational complexity (ICOMP) criterion to evaluate nearly any class of statistical models.

For example, for a general multivariate linear or nonlinear structural model defined by

$$\begin{aligned} \text{Statistical model} &= \frac{\text{signal}}{\underbrace{}} + \frac{\text{noise}}{\underbrace{}} \\ &= \text{deterministic} + \text{random} \\ &\quad\ \text{component} \quad\ \text{component,} \end{aligned} \tag{6}$$

ICOMP is designed to estimate a loss function:

$$\text{Loss} = \text{Lack of Fit} + \text{Lack of Parsimony} + \text{Profusion of Complexity} \tag{7}$$

in two ways, using the additivity property of information theory and the developments in Rissanen (1976) in his Final Estimation Criterion (*FEC*) in estimation and model identification problems, as well as Akaike's (1973) Information Criterion (AIC), and its analytical extensions given in Bozdoǧan (1987).

Approach 1.   Bozdogan uses the covariance matrix properties of the parameter estimates of a model starting from their finite sampling distributions. Using the joining axiom of complexity in (1) on the estimated covariance matrices, and after some work ICOMP is defined as

$$\text{ICOMP (Overall Model)} \qquad\qquad\qquad (8)$$
$$= -2\log L(\hat{\Theta}) + 2[C_1(\hat{\text{Cov}}(\hat{\Theta})) + C_1(\hat{\text{Cov}}(\hat{\varepsilon}))]$$
$$= -2\log L(\hat{\Theta}) + q\log\left[\frac{\text{tr}\,\hat{\Sigma}(\hat{\Theta})}{q}\right] - \log|\hat{\Sigma}(\hat{\Theta})| + n\log\left[\frac{\text{tr}\,\hat{\Sigma}(\varepsilon)}{n}\right] - \log|\hat{\Sigma}(\hat{\varepsilon})|,$$

where, C_1 denotes the maximal information complexity of a covariance matrix Σ of a multivariate normal distribution given in Equation 5.

We interpret this first approach to ICOMP as follows.

- The first term in ICOMP in Equation 8, measures the lack of fit (i.e., inference uncertainty),
- The second term measures the complexity of the covariance matrix of the parameter estimates of a model, and
- The third term measures the complexity of the covariance matrix of the model residuals.

Therefore using ICOMP with this approach, one can treat the errors to be correlated, because in general, there does not appear to be any easy way to include dependence. As the parameters of the model increases, so will the interaction between them increase. As a result, the second term of ICOMP will increase and will dominate the third term. On the other hand, as the errors become more correlated, so will the interactions among them be larger and the complexity of the covariance matrix of the errors increase. Consequently, it will dominate the second term. Hence, the sum of the last two terms in ICOMP will automatically take into account the number of parameters and the degrees of freedom by "trading-off" with the first term, which measures the lack of fit. So, comparing with AIC, the sum of the last two terms in ICOMP will replace the penalty term, two times the estimated parameters in the model of AIC, and more. Note that lack of parsimony and profusion of complexity is taken into account by the sum of the complexities, and they are not necessarily weighted equally due to the different dimensionalities of $\hat{\Theta}$ and $\hat{\varepsilon}$.

To cover the situation where the random error must be modeled as an independent and/or a dependent sequence, the following second approach is proposed.

Approach 2.   Bozdogan uses the estimated inverse-Fisher information matrix (IFIM) of the model by considering the entire parameter space of the model. In this case, ICOMP is defined as

$$\text{ICOMP(Overall Model)} = -2\log L(\hat{\Theta} + 2C_1(\hat{\mathcal{F}}^{-1}) \tag{9}$$

where

$$C_1(\hat{\mathcal{F}}^{-1}) = s/2\log[\text{trace}(\hat{\mathcal{F}}^{-1})/s] - 1/2\log|\hat{\mathcal{F}} \tag{10}$$

and where, $s = \dim(\hat{\mathcal{F}}^{-1}) = \text{rank}(\hat{\mathcal{F}}^{-1})$.

For more on the C_1 measure as a "scalar measure" of a nonsingular covariance matrix of a multivariate normal distribution, we refer the reader to the original work of Van Emden (1971). The C_1 measure also appears in Maklad and Nichols (1980, p. 82) with an incomplete discussion based on Van Emden's work in estimation. However, we further note that these authors abandoned the C_1 measure, and never used it in their problem (Bozdogan, 1990a).

The first component of ICOMP in Equation 9 measures the lack of fit of the model, and the second component measures the complexity of the estimated IFIM, which gives a scalar measure of the celebrated Cramér-Rao lower bound matrix of the model. Hence:

- ICOMP controls the risks of both insufficient and overparameterized models;
- It provides a criterion that has the virtue of judiciously balancing between lack of fit and the model complexity data adaptively;
- ICOMP removes from the researcher any need to consider the parameter dimension of a model explicitly and adjusts itself automatically for the sample size;
- A model with minimum ICOMP is chosen to be the best model among all possible competing alternative models.

The theoretical justification of this approach is that it combines all three ingredients of statistical modeling in Equation 7 based on the joining axiom of complexity of a system given in Equation 1. Also, it refines further the derivation of AIC, and represents a compromise between AIC and Rissanen's (1978, 1989) MDL, or CAIC of Bozdogan (1987, p. 358). It shows that Akaike (1973), in obtaining his AIC, goes to the asymptotic distribution of the quadratic form too quickly, which involves the Fisher information matrix (FIM) of the estimated parameters.

As is well known, the sampling distribution of the ML estimators is multivariate normally distributed with the covariance matrix being the IFIM. Instead of immediately passing to the asymptotic distribution of the parameter estimates, and if one uses the complexity of the finite sample estimate of IFIM of the multivariate distribution, one obtains ICOMP given above in the second approach. Indeed, if C_1(Est. IFIM) is divided by the numbers of estimated parameters across different competing alternative models, one can obtain the so-called the "magic number" or the "penalty per parameter" in information criteria, rather than fixing this at the critical value 2 as in AIC.

In what follows, we briefly develop ICOMP based on Bozdogan's (1991) work in structural equation models (SEM). Following Jöreskog & Sörbom (1989) in matrix notation, we define the full SEM by three equations:

Structural Model:

$$\underset{(rxr)}{\eta} = \underset{(rxr)}{\mathbf{B}} \underset{(rx1)}{\eta} + \underset{(rxs)}{\Gamma} \underset{(sx1)}{\xi} + \underset{(rx1)}{\zeta} \tag{11}$$

Measurement Model for y:

$$\underset{(px1)}{y} = \underset{(pxr)}{\Lambda_y} \underset{(rx1)}{\eta} + \underset{(px1)}{\varepsilon} \tag{12}$$

Measurement Model for x:

$$\underset{(qx1)}{x} = \underset{(qxs)}{\Lambda_x} \underset{(sx1)}{\xi} + \underset{(qx1)}{\delta} \tag{13}$$

with the usual assumptions.

To show the closed form analytical expression of ICOMP using the second approach in (9), we let $\hat{\Sigma}(\hat{\Theta})$ denote the maximum likelihood estimator (MLE) of the implied covariance matrix $\Sigma(\Theta)$ of the full SE model given by

$$\hat{\Sigma}(\hat{\theta}) = \begin{bmatrix} \hat{\Lambda}_y (\mathbf{I} - \hat{\mathbf{B}})^{-1} (\hat{\Gamma}\hat{\Phi}\hat{\Gamma}' + \hat{\Psi})(\mathbf{I} - \hat{\mathbf{B}}')^{-1}\hat{\Lambda}_y + \hat{\Theta}_\varepsilon & \hat{\Lambda}_y (\mathbf{I} - \hat{\mathbf{B}})^{-1}\hat{\Gamma}\hat{\Phi}\hat{\Lambda}'_x \\ \hat{\Lambda}_x\hat{\Phi}\hat{\Gamma}'(\mathbf{I} - \hat{\mathbf{B}}')^{-1}\hat{\Lambda}'_y & \hat{\Lambda}_x\hat{\Phi}\hat{\Lambda}'_x + \hat{\Theta}_g \end{bmatrix}. \tag{14}$$

Following the notation in Magnus (1988, p.169), Magnus and Neudecker (1988, p. 319), we give (see Bozdogan, 1991) the estimated inverse-Fisher information (IFIM) for the full SE model in the case of single sample defined by

$$\text{Est. } \mathcal{F}^{-1} = \hat{\mathcal{F}}^{-1} = \begin{bmatrix} \hat{\Sigma}(\hat{\theta}) & 0 \\ 0 & 2\mathbf{D}^+_{(p+q)} [\hat{\Sigma}(\hat{\theta}) \otimes \hat{\Sigma}(\hat{\theta})]\mathbf{D}^{+'}_{(p+q)} \end{bmatrix}. \tag{15}$$

In Equation 15 $\mathbf{D}_p$ is a unique $p^2 x 1/2p(p+1)$ duplication matrix which transforms $v(\mathbf{\Sigma})$ into $\text{vec}(\mathbf{\Sigma})$. $\text{Vec}(\mathbf{\Sigma})$ denotes the $1/2p(p+1)$-vector, which is obtained by eliminating all the supradiagonal elements of $\mathbf{\Sigma}$. $\text{Vec}(\mathbf{\Sigma})$ vectorizes a matrix by stacking the columns of $\mathbf{\Sigma}$ one underneath the other, and $\mathbf{D}^+_p$ is the Moore-Penrose inverse of the duplication matrix $\mathbf{D}_p$, and that $\mathbf{D}^+_p = (\mathbf{D'D_pD_p})^{-1}\mathbf{D_p}$.

Then, after some work (see Bozdogan, 1991, 1994b) information complexity ICOMP of the estimated IFIM for models with latent variable for single multivariate sample is given by

$$\text{ICOMP(SEM)} = -2\log L(\hat{\boldsymbol{\Theta}}) + s\log[\text{trace}(\hat{\mathcal{F}}^{-1})/s] - \log|\hat{\mathcal{F}}^{-1}|$$

$$= n(p+q)\log(2\pi) + n\log|\hat{\mathbf{\Sigma}}| + n \, \text{tr}\hat{\mathbf{\Sigma}}^{-1}S \Big\} \text{ (Lack of fit)}$$

$$+ \frac{(p+q)(p+q+3)}{2}\log\Big[\frac{\text{tr}(\hat{\mathbf{\Sigma}}) + 1/2\text{tr}(\hat{\mathbf{\Sigma}}^2) + 1/2(\text{tr}\hat{\mathbf{\Sigma}})^2 + \sum_{j=1}^{p+q}(\hat{\sigma}_{jj})^2}{1/2(p+q)(p+q+3)}\Big] \Big\} \text{ (Comp. of IFIM)},$$

$$+ (p+q+2)\log|\hat{\mathbf{\Sigma}}| - (p+q)\log(2), \qquad\qquad (16)$$

where $\text{tr}(\hat{\mathbf{\Sigma}}) = $ trace (estimated model covariance matrix), which measures the total variation, and $|\hat{\mathbf{\Sigma}}| = $ determinant (estimated model covariance matrix) which measures the generalized variance.

We note that in ICOMP(SEM), the effects of the parameter estimates and their accuracy are taken into account. Thus, counting and penalizing the number of parameters are eliminated in the model-fitting process and complexity is viewed not as the number of parameters in the model, but as the degree of interdependence among the components of the model. As we pointed out, $C_1(\mathcal{F}^{-1})$ in Equation 16, measures both the lack of parsimony and the profusion of complexity (i.e., interdependencies among the parameter estimates) of the model. It also gives us a scalar measure of the celebrated Cramér-Rao lower bound matrix of the model that measures the accuracy of the parameter estimates. By defining complexity in this way, ICOMP provides a more judicious penalty term than AIC and MDL (or CAIC). The lack of parsimony is automatically adjusted by $C_1(\mathcal{F}^{-1})$ across the competing alternative models as the parameter spaces of these models are constrained in the model fitting process.

It is because of this virtue of ICOMP that we use just the complexity part of IFIM to choose among the equivalent models, because equivalent models typically (but not necessarily) have the same number of parameters estimated within the model. Therefore, in equivalent models, just counting and penalizing the number of parameters does not distinguish the models, because these often have the same integer value with each of the equivalent models. One should bare in mind that the structure of equivalent models, or the structure of nonequivalent models, is not determined just by the number of its parameters only. In this sense, just counting and penalizing the number of parameters does not have the provision of taking into account the interdependencies among the parameter estimates in the estimated implied model covariance matrix as we alter the paths, or change the signs of some of the parameters as we validate our substantive models. In other words, the usual parsimony fit indices, or the noncentrality fit indices, and also AIC-type criteria, will all fall short for the estimation of the internal cohesion or description of the equivalent models.

Therefore, the general principle is that for a given level of accuracy, a simpler or a more parsimonious model with minimum complexity (i.e., in the sense of minimum variance) is preferable to a more complex one among the equivalent models to choose a good model structure.

To investigate the utility of the complexity approach to evaluate equivalent models, in this chapter, we propose to use

$$
\left.
\begin{array}{l}
C_1(\hat{\mathcal{F}}^{-1}) = \\[2ex]
\dfrac{(p+q)\,(p+q+3)}{2}\,\log\left[\dfrac{\operatorname{tr}(\hat{\Sigma}) + 1/2\operatorname{tr}(\hat{\Sigma}^2) + 1/2(\operatorname{tr}\hat{\Sigma})^2 + \sum\limits_{j=1}^{p+q}(\hat{\sigma}_{jj})^2}{1/2\,(p+q)\,(p+q+3)}\right] \\[3ex]
+ \ (p+q+2)\log|\hat{\Sigma}| - (p+q)\log(2),
\end{array}
\right\} \quad \text{(Comp. of IFIM)}
\tag{17}
$$

that is the second component of the ICOMP(SEM) defined in Equation 16, because the lack of fit term will be equal (or almost equal) in equivalent models. Since $C_1(^{-1})$ is a "scalar measure" of the estimated inverse-Fisher information matrix (IFIM), based on the results in Roger (1980, p. 174) and correcting the error, Bozdogan (1992) proposed a new $100(1-\alpha)\%$ approximate confidence interval (ACI) for the complexity of IFIM of the SE model given by

$$
C_1(\hat{\mathcal{F}}^{-1}) \ \pm \ z_{\alpha/2}\left[\frac{2(p+q)}{n}\,C(\hat{\mathcal{F}}^{-1})^2\right]^{1/2}
\tag{18}
$$

If we let **w** be the width of the ACI, then, say, for different SE models we can compute the $100(1-\alpha)\%$ ACI's and minimize the width **w** to choose the best fitting SE model. This approach is yet another approach to choose among the competing equivalent models.

Exploiting the block diagonality of the IFIM in Equation 15 for the SE model in Equations 11–13, we can also construct $100(1-\alpha)\%$ ACI's for the generalized variance of Cov $(\hat{\mu})$ and for the generalized variance of Cov $(v\hat{\Sigma})$), respectively. This will be useful in studying the stability of the parameter estimates especially in Monte Carlo experiments, because we know the true values of the mean vector μ and the implied model covariance matrix Σ.

ACKNOWLEDGMENTS

Special thanks to Margaret L. Williams, Mark B. Gavin and Sherry L. Magazine for their helpful comments on earlier drafts of this chapter, and to Julia Huffer and Carol Wood for their word processing support during the preparation of this chapter.

REFERENCES

Abdel-Halim, A. A. (1978). Employee affective response to organizational stress: Moderating effects of job characteristics. *Personnel Psychology, 31,* 561–579.

Adams, J. S. (1963). Toward an understanding of inequity. *Journal of Abnormal and Social Psychology, 67,* 422–436.

Akaike, H. (1973). *Information theory and an extension of the maximum likelihood principle.* In B. N. Petrov & F. Csaki (Eds.), *Second International Symposium on Information Theory* (pp. 267–281). Budapest: Academiai Kiado.

Anderson, J., & Gerbing, D. (1988). Structural equation modeling in practice: A review and recommended two-step approach. *Psychological Bulletin, 103,* 411–423.

Beehr, T., Walsh, J., & Taber, T. (1976). Relationship of stress to individually and organizationally valued states: Higher order needs as moderator. *Journal of Applied Psychology, 61,* 41–47.

Bentler, P. (1986). Structural modeling and Psychometrika: An historical perspective on growth and achievements. *Psychometrika, 51,* 35–51.

Bluedorn, A. C. (1982). A unified model of turnover from organizations. *Human Relations, 35,* 135–153.

Bollen, K., & Long, S. (1993). *Testing structural equation models.* Beverly Hills, CA: Sage.

Bowers, D. G., & Seashore, S. E. (1966). Predicting organizational effectiveness with a four-factor theory of leadership. *Administrative Science Quarterly, 11,* 238–263.

Bozdogan, H. (1987). Model selection and Akaike's Information Criterion (AIC): The general theory and its analytical extensions [Special issue]. *Psychometrika, 52*(3), 345–370.

Bozdogan, H. (1988). ICOMP: A new model selection criterion. In Hans H. Bock (Ed.), *Classification and related methods of data analysis* (pp. 599–608). Amsterdam: North-Holland.

Bozdogan, H. (1990a, December). *Multisample cluster analysis of the common principal component model in K groups using an entropic statistical complexity criterion.* Paper presented at the International Symposium on Theory and Practice of Classification, Puschino, Soviet Union.

Bozdogan, H. (1990b). On the information-based measure of covariance complexity and its application to the evaluation of multivariate linear models. *Communications in Statistics, Theory and Methods, 19*(1), 221–278.

Bozdogan, H. (1991, June). *A new information theoretic measure of complexity index for model evaluation in general structural equation models with latent variables.* Paper presented at the Symposium on Model Selection in Covariance Structures at the Joint Meetings of Psychometric Society and the Classification Society, Rutgers University, Newark, NJ.

Bozdogan, H. (1992). *A new approximate confidence interval (ACI) criterion for model selection.* Working paper.

Bozdogan, H. (1993). Choosing the number of component clusters in the mixture-model using a new informational complexity criterion of the inverse-Fisher information matrix. In O. Opitz, B. Lausen, & R. Klar (Eds.), *Studies in classification, data analysis, and knowledge organization* (pp. 40–54). Heidelberg: Springer-Verlag.

Bozdogan, H. (1994a, June). *Bayesian factor analysis model and choosing the number of factors using a new informational complexity criterion.* Paper presented at the Second Annual Meeting of the International Soceity for Bayesian Analysis, Alicante, Spain.

Bozdogan, H. (1994b). Mixture-model cluster analysis using model selection criteria and a new informational measure of complexity. In H. Bozdogan (Ed.), *Multivariate statistical modeling,* Vol. 2. *Proceedings of the First US/Japan Conference on the Frontiers of Statistical Modeling: An informational approach* (pp. 69–113). Dordrecht, Netherlands: Kluwer.

Bozdogan, H. (1994c, August). *Subset selection of predictors in Bayesian regression model using a new informational complexity criterion.* Paper presented at the ASA Meeting on Bayesian Statistics and Information Theory, Toronto, Canada.

Bozdogan, H. (in preparation-a). *Informational complexity and multivariate statistical modeling.*

Bozdogan, H. (in preparation-b). *Statistical modeling and model evaluation: A new informational approach.*

Cliff, N. (1983). Some cautions concerning the application of causal modeling methods. *Multivariate Behavioral Research, 18,* 115–126.

Cudek, R. (1989). Analysis of correlation matrices using covariance structure models. *Psychological Bulletin, 105,* 317–327.

Duncan, O. D. (1975). *Introduction to structural equation models.* New York: Academic.

Graen, G., Novak, M., & Sommerkamp, P. (1982). The effects of leader-member exchange and job design on productivity and attachment: Testing a dual attachment model. *Organizational Behavior and Human Performance, 30,* 109–131.

House, R. J., & Rizzo, J. R. (1972). Role conflict and role ambiguity as critical variables in a model of organizational behavior. *Organizational Behavior and Human Performance, 1,* 467–505.

House, R. J., Schuler, R. S., & Levanoni, E. (1983). Role conflict and role ambiguity scales: Reality or artifacts? *Journal of Applied Psychology, 68,* 334–337.

James, L. R., Gent, M. J., Hater, J. J., & Coray, K. E. (1978). Correlates of psychological influence: An illustration of the psychological climate approach to work environment perceptions. *Personnel Psychology, 32,* 563–588.

James, L. R., Mulaik, S., & Brett, J. (1982). *Causal analysis.* Beverly Hills, CA: Sage.

Jones, A. P., & James, L. R. (1979). Psychological climate: Dimensions and relationships of individual and aggregate work environment perceptions. *Organizational Behavior and Human Performance, 23,* 201–250.

Jöreskog, K. G., & Sörbom, D. (1989). *LISREL 7: A guide to the program and applications* (2nd ed.). Chicago: Statistical Package for the Social Sciences, Inc./McGraw Hill.

Lance, C. E. (1991). Evaluation of a structural model relating job satisfaction, organizational commitment, and precursors to voluntary turnover. *Multivariate Behavioral Research, 26,* 137–162.

Lee, S., & Hershberger, S. (1990). A simple rule for generating equivalent models in covariance structure modeling. *Multivariate Behavioral Research, 25,* 313–334.

MacCallum, R. (1986). Specification searches in covariance structure modeling. *Psychological Bulletin, 100,* 107–120.

MacCallum, R., Wegener, D., Uchino, B., & Fabrigar, L. (1993). The problem of equivalent models in applications of covariance structure analysis. *Psychological Bulletin, 114*, 185–199.

Magnus, J. R. (1988). *Linear structures*. New York: Oxford University Press.

Magnus, J. R., & Neudecker, H. (1988). *Matrix differential calculus with applications in statistics and econometrics*. New York: Wiley.

Maklad, M. S., & Nichols, T. (1980). A new approach to model structure discrimination. *IEEE Transactions on Systems, Man, and Cybernetics, SMC-10*(2), 78–84.

Mathieu, J. (1991). A cross-level non recursive model of the antecedents of organizational commitment and satisfaction. *Journal of Applied Psychology, 76*, 607–618.

Mathieu, J., & Farr, J. (1991). Further evidence for the discriminant validity of measures of organizational commitment, job involvement, and job satisfaction. *Journal of Applied Psychology, 76*, 123–133.

Mislevy, P. (1986). Recent developments in the factor analysis of categorical variables. *Journal of Educational Statistics, 11*, 3–31.

Moos, R. H. (1980). *Group environment scale*. Palo Alto, CA: Consulting Psychologists Press.

Mulaik, S., James, L., Van Alstine, J., Bennett, N., Lind, S., & Stilwell, C. (1989). An evaluation of goodness of fit indices for structural equation models. *Psychological Bulletin, 105*, 430–445.

Murray, H. J. (1938). *Explorations in personality*. New York: Oxford University Press.

Muthén, B., & Kaplan, D. (1992). A comparison of some methodologies for the factor analysis of non-normal Likert variables: A note on the size of the model. *British Journal of Mathematical and Statistical Psychology, 45*, 19–30.

Parzen, E. (1983). Time series identification by estimating information. In S. Karlin, T. Amemiya, & L. A. Goodman, *Studies in econometrics, time series, and multivariate statistics* (pp. 279–298). New York: Academic Press.

Podsakoff, P. M., Niehoff, B. P., MacKenzie, S. B., & Williams, M. L. (1993). Do substitutes for leadership really substitute for leadership? An empirical examination of Kerr and Jermier's situational leadership model. *Organizational Behavior and Human Decision Processes, 54*, 1–44.

Price, J. L., & Bluedorn, A. C. (1980). Test of a causal model of turnover from organizations. In D. Dunkerley & G. Salaman (Eds.), *International yearbook of organizational studies 1979*. London: Routeldge & Kegan Paul.

Rissanen, J. (1976). Minmax entropy estimation of models for vector processes. In R. K. Mehra & D. G. Lainiotis (Eds.), *System Identification* (pp. 97–119). New York: Academic Press.

Rissanen, J. (1978). Modeling by shortest data description. *Automatica, 14*, 465–471.

Rissanen, J. (1989). *Stochastic complexity in statistical inquiry*. Teaneck, NJ: World Scientific Publishing Company.

Rizzo, J. R., House, R. J., & Lirtzman, S. D. (1970). Role conflict and ambiguity in complex organizations. *Administrative Science Quarterly, 15*, 150–163.

Roger, G. S. (1980). *Matrix derivatives*. New York: Marcel Dekker.

Schriesheim, C. A. (1978). *Development, validation, and application of new leader behavior and expectancy research instruments*. Unpublished doctoral dissertation, The Ohio State University, Columbus.

Sims, H. R., Szilagyi, A. D., & Keller, P. T. (1976). The measurement of job characteristics. *Academy of Management Journal, 19*, 195–212.

Steers, R. M., & Braunstein, D. N. (1976). A behaviorally-based measure of manifest needs in work settings. *Journal of Vocational Behavior, 9*, 251–266.

Stelzl, I. (1986). Changing a causal hypothesis without changing the fit: Some rules for generating equivalent path models. *Multivariate Behavioral Research, 21*, 309–331.

Stone, E. F. (1974). *The moderating effect of work-related values on the job scope-job satisfaction relationship*. Unpublished doctoral dissertation, University of California at Irvine.

Van Emden, M. H. (1971). *An analysis of complexity*. Amsterdam: Mathematical Centre Tracts 35.

Wanous, J. P. (1973). Effects of a realistic job preview on job acceptance, job attitudes, and job survival. *Journal of Applied Psychology, 58*, 327–332.

Watanabe, S. (1985). *Pattern recognition: Human and mechanical*. New York: Wiley.

Williams, L. J., Gavin, M. B., & Williams, M. L. (1994, April). *Controlling for method effects in employee attitude research*. Paper presented at the 1994 annual meeting of the Society for Industrial and Organizational Psychology.

Williams, L. J., & Hazer, J. T. (1986). Antecedents and consequences of satisfaction and commitment in turnover models: A reanalysis using latent variable structural equation methods. *Journal of Applied Psychology, 71*, 219–231.

Williams, L. J., & Holahan, P. (1994). Parsimony-based fit indices for multiple-indicator models: Do they work? *Structural Equation Modeling, 1*, 161–189.

CHAPTER ELEVEN

An Evaluation of Incremental Fit Indices: A Clarification of Mathematical and Empirical Properties

Herbert W. Marsh
University of Western Sydney, Macarthur

John R. Balla
University of Sydney

Kit-Tai Hau
The Chinese University of Hong Kong

When evaluating the goodness of fit of structural equations models (SEMs), researchers rely in part on subjective indices of fit as well as a variety of other characteristics (for more extensive overviews of assessing goodness of fit, see Bentler, 1990; Bentler & Bonett, 1980; Bollen, 1989b; Browne & Cudeck, 1989; Cudeck & Browne, 1983; Gerbing & Anderson, 1993; Marsh, Balla, & McDonald, 1988; McDonald & Marsh, 1990; Tanaka, 1993). There are, however, a plethora of different indices with no consensus as to which are the best. Adding to this confusion, major statistical packages (e.g., LISREL8, EQS, CALIS: SAS) tend to be overinclusive in their default presentation of indices, automatically including some that are known to have undesirable properties. Because there is no "best" index, researchers are advised to use a variety of qualitatively different indices from different families of measures (Bollen & Long, 1993; Tanaka, 1993). Whereas there is no broadly agreed upon typology of indices, the family of incremental fit indices is one of the most popular.

Incremental fit indices appeal to researchers wanting an apparently straight-forward evaluation of the ability of a model to fit observed data that varies along a 0 to 1 scale and is easily understood. Bentler and Bonett (1980) popularized this approach and developed an index that seemed to satisfy these requirements. Subsequent research, however, indicated that the interpretation of incremental fit indices was more complicated than initially anticipated. The number of incremental indices proliferated, partly in response to real or apparent limitations in existing incremental fit indices, and more or less successful attempts to incorporate other desirable properties that evolved from this particularly active area of research. The usefulness of incremental fit indices was further hindered by the lack of standardization in the names assigned to the same index, including the independent rediscovery or simultaneous discovery of the same index by different researchers. The purposes of this chapter are to more clearly delineate the incremental fit indices in popular use and to evaluate these indices in relation to desirable criteria for these indices.

Our task has been simplified, perhaps, by Jöreskog and Sörbom's (1993) decision to include five incremental fit indices as the default output in their LISREL8 program. Because of LISREL's historical dominance in confirmatory factor analysis and structural equation modeling, we have used Jöreskog and Sörbom's selection as an operational definition of popular usage. There is, however, considerable similarity in the incremental indices included in the more popular of the growing number of packages that are challenging LISREL's dominance (e.g., EQS). For reasons that we discuss later in this chapter, we have added two additional indices—actually variations of indices provided by LISREL8. The seven incremental fit indices considered are defined in Table 11.1. In order to provide further clarification, key references to each index are presented along with most of the alternative labels that have been used in the literature. We begin the chapter with a brief historical overview of incremental fit indices.

INCREMENTAL FIT INDICES

Bentler and Bonett's (1980) Indices

The use of incremental fit indices was popularized by Bentler and Bonett (1980). Based in part on earlier work by Tucker and Lewis (1973), they argued that it was desirable to assess goodness of fit along a 0 to 1 continuum in which the zero-point reflects a baseline, or worst possible fit, and 1 reflects an optimum fit. They suggested that a *null model*, in which all the measured variables were posited to be mutually uncorrelated, provided an appropriate basis for defining the zero-point. Other researchers have argued that other more realistic models may provide a better baseline against which to evaluate target models (Marsh & Balla, 1994; Sobel & Bohrnstedt, 1986); these alternative baseline models are typically idiosyncratic to a particular application and have not been widely accepted.

Bentler and Bonett proposed two incremental fit indices: the Non-Normed Fit Index (NNFI) based on the work by Tucker and Lewis, and their new Normed Fit Index (NFI). The major distinction between these indices was that the NFI was strictly normed to fall on a 0 to 1 continuum,

TABLE 11.1
Seven Incremental Fit Indices: Alternative Labels and Definitions

Index	Other Labels	F'' of CHISQ	F'' of FF	F'' of NCP
Nonnormed Fit Index [NNFI] (Tucker & Lewis, 1973; Bentler & Bonnet, 1980)	TLI; χ^2/df12; rho; ρ; or ρ2; BEBOUC	$[\chi^2_o/df_o - \chi^2_t/df_t] / [\chi^2_o/df_o - 1.0]$	$(F_o/df_o\text{-}F_t/df_t) / (F_o/df_o\text{-}1/(n))$	$(d_o/df_o\text{-}d_t/df_t) / (d_o/df_o))$
Normed Tucker Lewis Index [NTLI] (this volume)	NTLI	$\text{Min}(\text{Max}(0, \text{NNFI}),1)$	$\text{Min}(\text{Max}(0, \text{NNFI}),1)$	$\text{Min}(\text{Max}(0, \text{NNFI}),1)$
Normed Fit Index [NFI] (Bentler & Bonnett, 1980)	BBI; χ^2-I1; Δ or Δ1; BEBONC	$(\chi^2_o - \chi^2_t) / (\chi^2_o)$	$(F_o\text{-}F_t)/(F_o)$	$(d_o\text{-}d_t)+(df_o\text{-}df_t)/n / (d_o+df_o/n)$
Relative Fit Index (RFI) (Bollen, 1986)	χ^2/df11; π1; RHO1	$[\chi^2_o/df_o - \chi^2_t/df_t] / [\chi^2_o/df_o]$	$(F_o/df_o\text{-}F_t/df_t) / (F_o/df_o)$	$(d_o/df_o)\text{-}d_t/df_t) / (d_o/df_o)$
Incremental Fit Index (IFI) (Bollen, 1989a)	χ^2-I2; Δ2; DELTA 2	$(\chi^2_o - \chi^2_t) / (\chi^2_o\text{-}df_t)$	$(F_o\text{-}F_t)/ (F_o\text{-}df_t/n)$	$(d_o\text{-}d_t)+[(df_o\text{-}df_t)/n / [d_o+(df_o\text{-}df_t)/n)]$
Relative Noncentrality Index (RNI) (McDonald & Marsh, 1990)	RNI, FI	$1 - [(\chi^2_t - df_t) / (\chi^2_o - df_o)]$	$(F_o\text{-}F_t)\text{-}(df_o\text{-}df_t)/n / F_o\text{-}(df_o)/n)$	$do\text{-}d_t)/d_o = 1\text{-}d_t/d_o$
Comparative Fit Index (CFI) Bentler (1990)	CFI	$1 - [\text{Max}(\chi^2_t - df_t),0 / \text{Max}(\chi^2_o - df_o,\chi^2_t - df_t,0)]$	$1 - [\text{Max}(nF_t\text{-}df_t,0) / (\text{Max}(nF_t\text{-}df_t,nF_o\text{-}df_o,0)]$	$1 - [(\text{Max}(d_t,0) / \text{Max}(d_o,0)]$

whereas the NNFI could fall outside of the 0 to 1 range due to sampling fluctuations. Although there are no absolute guidelines as to what values represent a good fit, Bentler and Bonett (1980) suggested that values greater than .90 may constitute an "acceptable" fit and this somewhat arbitrary "rule of thumb" has been widely applied. This guideline, as to what constitutes an apparently acceptable fit, seems to be an important aspect of the popularity of the incremental fit indices.

Despite the initial and continued popularity of the NFI, subsequent research (e.g., Bentler, 1990; Bollen, 1989b; Gerbing & Anderson, 1993; Marsh et al., 1988) demonstrated that NFI estimates are biased by sample size, a feature deemed to be undesirable for incremental fit indices. Whereas NFI is still widely used, it is typically not among the recommended indices in recent reviews (e.g., Bollen, 1989b; Bollen & Long, 1993; Gerbing & Anderson, 1993).

Bentler and Bonett (see also Bentler, 1990) preferred the NFI to the NNFI in particular because the NFI was "normed" (could only take on values between 0 and 1) in the sample whereas the NNFI was not. Although both NFI and the NNFI are strictly normed in the population, the NNFI can take on values outside this range due to sampling variability. They also noted that the variability of NNFI is greater than NFI. Bentler (1990, 1992) further emphasized this feature of being normed in the sample and the population in his subsequent research. However, McDonald and Marsh (1990) emphasized that the NNFI and NFI are qualitatively different in that the NNFI incorporates a correction for model complexity whereas the NFI does not. Because this feature of the NNFI is not widely recognized, this chapter will explore its implications beyond what has been considered in previous research.

Indices Proposed by Marsh, Balla, and McDonald (1988)

Marsh et al. (1988; see also Marsh & Balla, 1986; Gerbing & Anderson, 1993) noted that incremental fit indices can be expressed in one of two general forms that they called Type-1 and Type-2 incremental indices:

$$I1 = |I_t - I_o|/((\text{Max}(I_o, I_t)), \text{ which can be expressed as}$$
$$I1a = (I_o - I_t)/(I_o) \text{ or } I1b = (I_t - I_o)/(I_t) \tag{1}$$

$$I21 = |I_t - I_o|/E(I_t) - I_o, \text{ which can be expressed as}$$
$$I2a = (I_o - I_t)/(I_o - E(I_t)) \text{ or } I2b = (I_t - I_o)/(E(I_t) - I_o), \tag{2}$$

where I_o and I_t are values of a "stand alone" (nonincremental) index for an appropriately defined baseline model (typically a null model that assumes that all measured variables are uncorrelated) and the target model respectively, and $E(I_t)$ is the expected value for the stand alone index for a "true" target model that is correctly specified so that there is no misspecification. Variations of a and b are appropriate for stand alone indices in which poorer fits are reflected by larger values (e.g., χ^2), and by smaller values, respectively. Thus, for example, they evaluated the χ^2/df-I2, χ^2/df-I1, χ^2-I2, χ^2-I1 that are referred to here as the NNFI, Relative Fit Index (RFI), Incremental Fit Index (IFI), and NFI, respectively (see also Marsh & Balla, 1986).

Marsh et al. evaluated a wide variety of Type-1 and Type-2 incremental fit indices. In their Monte Carlo study, they considered 7 different sample sizes and a variety of models based on real and simulated data. Their results suggested that incremental Type-1 indices were normed in the sample but had values that were systematically related to sample size. In contrast, Type-2 indices were not normed and were not systematically related to sample size. These conclusions, however, were premature. In a trivial sense they were wrong in that some stand alone indices have expected values of 0 so that the Type-1 and Type-2 forms are equivalent. McDonald and Marsh (1990) subsequently evaluated the mathematical properties of a number of these fit indices by expressing them in terms of the population noncentrality parameter for a target model (δ_t), which is independent of N and can be estimated from sample data by d_t:

$$d_t = (\chi^2_t - df_t)/N. \tag{3}$$

Of particular relevance, they demonstrated that FFI2 and χ^2I2 are mathematically equivalent (i.e., substituting χ^2 for FF = $\chi^2 \times N$ into Equation 2 results in the same value) and should vary with N according to their mathematical form. This effect was not found by Marsh et al. (1988), due in part to the small number of replicates of each sample size and the nature of the data that were considered. However, McDonald and Marsh (1990; see also Marsh, 1995) demonstrated that FFI2 and χ^2I2, which is called IFI here, should be biased in finite samples. This is shown by the following expression where $E(\chi^2)$ for a true target model is the degrees of freedom for the model (df_t):

$$\begin{aligned}
IFI &= (\chi^2_o - \chi^2_t)/(\chi^2_o - df_t) \\
&= [(Nd_o + df_o) - (Nd_t + df_t)]/[(Nd_o + df_o) - df_t] \\
&= [(d_o - d_t) + (df_o - df_t)/N]/[d_o + (df_o - df_t)/N] \\
&= 1 - \{d_t/[d_o + (df_o - df_t)/N]\}
\end{aligned} \tag{4}$$

McDonald and Marsh (1990) noted that "it may be verified that this quantity approaches its asymptote from above, overestimating it in small samples" (p. 250). Inspection of Equation 4 also revealed that the overestimation tends to disappear as misspecification (δ_t) approaches zero.

The Type-1 and Type-2 forms of incremental fit indices proposed by Marsh et al. (1988) were a heuristic basis for generating a large number of different incremental indices, and many of the indices have subsequently been proposed by other researchers. However, subsequent research—particularly that by McDonald and Marsh (1990)—indicated that not all Type-2 indices are unbiased, thus undermining some of the usefulness of the Type-1 and Type-2 distinction.

Indices Proposed by Bollen (1986, 1989a, 1989b)

Bollen (1986, 1989b, 1990; Bollen & Long, 1993) has emphasized the usefulness of indices whose estimated values are unrelated or only weakly related to sample size and that provide a correction for model complexity. Bollen (1986) suggested that the NNFI was a function of sample size and proposed the RFI to correct this problem. McDonald and Marsh (1990), however, showed mathematically that the NNFI "should not exhibit any systematic relation to sample size" (p. 249), a conclusion that was consistent with Monte Carlo results (e.g., Anderson & Gerbing, 1984; Bentler, 1990; Bollen, 1989a, 1989b; Marsh, Balla, & McDonald, 1988). Marsh et al. (1988, Appendix 1; see also Marsh & Balla, 1986) also demonstrated that the RFI was a variation of their general form of Type-1 incremental indices based on the χ^2/df ratio. Values for RFI were shown to vary systematically with N in Monte Carlo research (Marsh et al., 1988) and by its mathematical form (McDonald & Marsh, 1990). The usefulness of RFI is undermined by the fact that it is biased by N (i.e., N is systematically related to the means of its sampling distribution).

Bollen (1989a, 1989b, 1990) subsequently proposed the IFI (which he called $\Delta 2$; see Table 11.1), a new fit index that was intended to correct this problem of sample size dependency and to provide a correction for degrees of freedom. Although derived independently by Bollen (see Bollen, 1990, footnote 1), Bollen actually rediscovered the Type-2 incremental fit index for the χ^2 that had been proposed several years earlier by Marsh and Balla (1986; Marsh et al., 1988). Whereas the IFI index should probably be attributed to Marsh and colleagues rather than to Bollen, a subsequent evaluation of the index by McDonald and Marsh (1990) suggested that the IFI is flawed and should not be considered further. If these claims are substantiated, then "credit" for a possibly discredited index may be of dubious value.

McDonald and Marsh (1990; Marsh, 1995; see also Equation 4) demonstrated that IFI should be biased by N according to its mathematical form and that the size of the bias should approach zero as misspecification approaches zero. More specifically, IFI should approach its asymptotic value from above (i.e., become systematically less positively biased for increasing Ns), but the size of the bias should decrease as the degree of misspecification approached zero. Bollen (1989a) and Bentler (1990) both demonstrated that the index was unbiased in Monte Carlo studies of a correctly specified ("true") model. However, because the index is not biased when there is no misspecification, these were not critical tests of IFI. Bentler also evaluated a slightly misspecified model and reported that IFI was relatively unrelated to N. Marsh (1995), however, noted that whereas the differences reported by Bentler were small, there appeared to be a systematic pattern of effects that was consistent with McDonald and Marsh's suggestions. Marsh (1995), expanding on observations by McDonald and Marsh (1990), also suggested that the nature of the penalty for model complexity in the IFI may be inappropriate. Hence, another purpose of this chapter is to evaluate these characteristics of the IFI, using a Monte Carlo study more specifically designed to consider these features than previous research.

Incremental Indices Based on Noncentrality

The most recently developed incremental fit indices are based on the noncentrality parameter (δ) from the noncentral chi-square distribution (e.g., Bentler, 1990; McDonald, 1989; McDonald & Marsh, 1990; Steiger & Lind, 1980) and its sample estimate (Equation 3). Bentler (1990) and McDonald and Marsh (1990) both emphasized that the noncentrality parameter reflects a natural measure of model misspecification. Two features of this research particularly relevant to this chapter are the expression of incremental fit indices in terms of the noncentrality parameter and the development of new incremental fit indices based specifically on noncentrality. Thus, for example, McDonald and Marsh (1990) derived expressions of NFI, NNFI, RFI, and IFI in terms of noncentrality, df, and sample size. In this form, they demonstrated that NNFI should be independent of sample size, whereas values for the other three indices should vary systematically with sample size. They also demonstrated that the critical difference between NNFI and NFI was not that the NFI is normed (i.e., is bounded by 0 and 1 in the sample) whereas NNFI was not. Rather, they argued that the more important distinction was that the NNFI is an unbiased estimate of a quantity that incorporates a correction for model complexity, whereas NFI is a biased estimate of a quantity that does not. (They also argued for the use of the label Tucker-Lewis Index [TLI] instead of NNFI, but we have used the NNFI label here to be consistent with notation used in major SEM statistical packages). McDonald and Marsh proposed RNI that provides an unbiased estimate of the asymptotic values estimated (with bias) by NFI and IFI. They concluded that researchers wanting to use a incremental fit index should logically choose between the RNI and the NNFI.

Working independently from a similar perspective, Bentler (1990) also emphasized the noncentrality parameter (in an article published in the same issue of Psychological Bulletin as the McDonald and Marsh study). Bentler (1990) initially proposed a new incremental fit index identical to the RNI, but showed that sample estimates of this index were not strictly bounded by 0 and 1. For this reason, he proposed a normed version of RNI, called CFI, in which values falling outside of the 0–1 range are truncated so that CFI is strictly bounded by 0 and 1 in samples as well as in the population (see Table 11.1). Bentler then noted that NFI, IFI, CFI, and RNI all have the same asymptotic limit, which differs from that of NNFI and RFI. Consistent with conclusions by McDonald and Marsh (1990), Bentler suggested that the NNFI reflects the relative reduction in noncentrality per degree of freedom so that "it does appear to have a parsimony rationale" (p. 241). Bentler argued that RNI was better behaved than NNFI in that (a) sampling fluctuations are greater for NNFI than RNI, (b) NNFI estimates are more likely to be negative, and (c) when NNFI exceeds 1, RNI will exceed 1 by a smaller amount. He then pointed out that the standard deviation of estimates for CFI must be less than or equal to that of RNI. This led Bentler to prefer CFI over RNI, and RNI over NNFI. The reasons for this preference of CFI and RNI over NNFI, however, did not seem to reflect that NNFI is a qualitatively different index from RNI and CFI. Bentler (1992) subsequently noted comments by McDonald and Marsh (1990) about NNFI, defending the use of the NNFI label instead of the one recommended by McDonald and Marsh. More importantly, recognizing the validity of concerns for parsimony, Bentler (1992) still contended that "in my current opinion, the NNFI is not as good as the CFI in measuring the quality of model fit" (p. 401) and that "I prefer not to mix the separate criteria of fit and model parsimony into a single index" (p. 401).

Bentler (1990) also demonstrated the behavior of NFI, NNFI, IFI, RNI, and CFI in a simulation study in which a true and slightly misspecified model was fit to the same data varying in sample size. He emphasized that the sample size effect was evident in NFI but not in any of the other indices. Consistent with previous research, he reported that the range of the NNFI (.570 to 1.355 for the true model with $N = 50$) was very large and that the within-cell SDs for NNFI values were consistently much larger than for the other indices. Focusing on results based on small samples ($N = 50$) with a true model, Bentler noted that the standard deviations (SDs) for CFI were smaller than for any of the other indices. However, the CFI SDs are expected to be substantially smaller for true models (where half the values of CFI would be expected to exceed 1.0 if the values were not truncated) and smaller sample sizes. Thus, for the slightly misspecified model the SDs for NFI and IFI tended to be as small or smaller than those for the CFI (particularly for $N > 50$), although the NNFI SDs were still substantially larger than for the other indices. Bentler also noted that for the slightly misspecified model, the NNFIs (mean = .892) were consistently lower than for the other indices (mean = .95). These results led Bentler to prefer CFI, noting however that its advantages were at the expense of a slight downward bias (due to the truncation of values greater than 1.0).

Population values of CFI and RNI are equal to each other and strictly bounded by 0 and 1. Whereas sample estimates of RNI can fall outside of a 0–1 range, corresponding values of CFI are assigned a value of 0 when RNI < 0 and a value of 1.0 when RNI > 1 (Table 11.1; see also discussion by Gerbing & Anderson, 1993; Goffin, 1993). In practice, this distinction is not very important because such extreme values are rare, values of RNI > 1 or CFI = 1 both lead to the conclusion that the fit is excellent, and values of RNI < 0 or CFI = 0 both lead to the conclusion that the fit is very poor. In a comparison of RNI and CFI, Goffin (1993) concluded that RNI may be preferable for purposes of model comparison, whereas CFI may be preferred with respect to efficiency of estimation. In Monte Carlo studies, however, the difference between CFI and RNI is particularly important when "true" models (i.e., $\delta_t = 0$) are considered. For such models, the expected value of RNI is 1.0 (i.e., approximately half the sample estimates will be above 1 and half below) and this value should not vary with N. The expected value of CFI, however, must be less than 1.0 for any finite N (because CFI is truncated not to exceed 1.0) and the size of this negative bias should be a systematically decreasing function of N. For this reason, it may be desirable to consider RNI in addition to, or instead of, CFI, at least for Monte Carlo studies in which a "true" model is fit to the data.

POSSIBLY DESIRABLE CHARACTERISTICS FOR INCREMENTAL INDICES

Different researchers have proposed a variety of desirable characteristics that may be useful for incremental fit indices and their evaluation. Consequently, we next discuss the most widely recommended of these criteria, including the effect of sample size, appropriate penalties for model complexity, and rewards for model parsimony, sampling fluctuations, and interpretable metrics.

Sample Size Independence

Researchers (e.g., Bollen, 1990; Bollen & Long, 1993; Gerbing & Anderson, 1993) have routinely proposed that a systematic relation between sample size and the values of an index of fit is undesirable, and this characteristic was evaluated in detail by Marsh et al.(1988) and McDonald and Marsh

(1990). Bollen (1990), attempting to clarify what is meant by sample size effect, distinguished between cases in which (a) N is associated with the means of the sampling distribution of an index (the effect of N emphasized by Marsh et al., 1988, and by Gerbing & Anderson, 1993), and (b) values calculated for an index vary as a function of N. The critical concern for purposes of this discussion is whether the expected value of an index varies systematically with N (Bollen's first case) and this is what we mean when we refer to a sample size effect or bias. Similarly, Bollen and Long (1993) recommended the use of indices "whose means of their sampling distribution are unrelated or only weakly related to the sample size" (p. 8), whereas Gerbing and Anderson (1993) suggested that an ideal fit index should be independent of sample size in that higher or lower values should not be obtained simply because the sample size is large or small.

Penalty for Model Complexity

Researchers have routinely recommended indices that control for model complexity and reward model parsimony (e.g., Bollen, 1989b, 1990; Bollen & Long, 1993; Bozdogan, 1987; Browne & Cudeck, 1989; Cudeck & Browne, 1983; Gerbing & Anderson, 1993; Marsh & Balla, 1994; Mulaik et al., 1989; Steiger & Lind, 1980; Tanaka, 1993; but for possibly alternative perspectives see Bentler, 1992; McDonald & Marsh, 1990; Marsh & Balla, 1994; Marsh & Hau, 1994). Marsh and Balla (1994), however, emphasized two very different perspectives of this issue which they referred to as (population) parsimony penalties and (sample) estimation penalties.

Penalties for (a lack of) parsimony, according to the distinction offered by Marsh and Balla (1994), do not vary with sample size and are intended to achieve a compromise between model parsimony and complexity at the population level. As noted by McDonald and Marsh (1990), such a compromise would be needed even if the population were known in that freeing enough parameters will still lead to a perfect fit. Although many alternative operationalizations of parsimony penalties are possible, one popular approach is the set of parsimony indices described by Mulaik et al. (1989; see also McDonald & Marsh, 1990). They recommended the use of a penalty that does not vary with N so that their parsimony indices are unbiased (so long as their parsimony correction is applied to indices that are unbiased). They proposed the parsimony ratio, the ratio of the degrees of freedom in the target model and the degrees of freedom in the null model (df_t/df_o), as an operationalization of model parsimony. In their implementation of this penalty they recommended that other indices—including incremental fit indices—should simply be multiplied by the parsimony ratio. Thus, for example, Jöreskog and Sörbom (1993) define the parsimony NFI (PNFI) as the product of the NFI and the parsimony ratio.

Marsh and Balla (1994) suggested that it would be more appropriate to define parsimony indices in terms of indices that did not vary with sample size and evaluated the PRNI based on the product of the parsimony ratio and the RNI. In their Monte Carlo study, however, they found that parsimony indices overpenalized model complexity in relation to criteria that they considered. Although we do not consider parsimony indices per se in this chapter, McDonald and Marsh (1990) demonstrated that the NNFI can be expressed as a function of the parsimony ratio, the noncentrality estimate of the target model, and the noncentrality estimate of the null model (see Table 11.1).

Estimation penalties, according to the Marsh and Balla (1994) distinction, are aimed at controlling for capitalizing on chance when fitting sample data. From this perspective, Cudeck and Browne (1983; Browne & Cudeck, 1989, 1993; Cudeck & Henly, 1991) claimed that under appropriate conditions a dependency on sample size may be appropriate. In particular, they argued that model complexity should be penalized more severely for small N where sampling fluctuations are likely to be greater. They supported this contention by showing that less complex models cross-validated better than more complex models when sample size was small, but that more complex models performed better when sample size was sufficiently large (see McDonald & Marsh, 1990, for further discussion). Based on this research, they proposed penalties for model complexity that were a function of sample size such that model complexity is more severely penalized at small N, moderately penalized for moderate N, and not penalized at all for a sufficiently large N. Although this type of penalty has not been incorporated into any of the incremental indices considered here, it is interesting to note that the negative sample size bias in NFI works in this fashion. At small N, the NFI is negatively biased. With increasing N, the size of the bias decreases and for a sufficiently large N it disappears. In contrast, McDonald and Marsh (1990; Marsh, 1994) claimed that the IFI is positively biased—not negatively biased—for small N and that the size of this positive bias decreases with increasing N. Hence, the direction—as well as the existence—of this sample size effect in IFI is particularly worrisome.

Consistent with these perspectives, Bollen (1989b, 1990; Bollen & Long, 1993), Gerbing and Anderson (1993), and others have argued that an appropriate adjustment for model complexity is a desirable feature. For this reason, it is appropriate to evaluate the incremental fit indices considered here in relation to this criterion. RNI, CFI, and NFI do not contain any penalty of model complexity. NNFI (and its normed counterpart NTLI first proposed here; see Table 11.1) and RFI do provide a penalty for model complexity, but this feature in the RFI is complicated by the sample size bias in this index. There remains some controversy about the nature and appropriateness of the penalty for model complexity in the IFI. Although Bollen (1989a, 1989b) claimed that the IFI adjusts for df and Gerbing and Anderson (1993) reported that this is an important strength of the index, Marsh (1995) and McDonald and Marsh (1990; see also Equation 4) claimed that the nature of this penalty was inappropriate. However, Marsh et al. (1988) found no support for this claim in their Monte Carlo study. Furthermore, Marsh (1995) cited no empirical support for this suggestion and apparently no appropriate Monte Carlo studies have been conducted to evaluate this aspect of the IFI. Hence, another purpose of this chapter is to provide a stronger test of the nature of the correction for df in the IFI.

Reliability of Estimation and an Interpretable Metric

Reliability of estimation (i.e., precision of estimation and a relative lack of sampling fluctuations) is an important characteristic of incremental fit indices that has not been given sufficient attention. In Monte Carlo studies, this feature is typically represented by the within-cell standard deviation of the estimates for a particular index. Based on this criterion, many researchers (e.g., Bentler, 1990; Bollen & Long, 1993; Gerbing & Anderson, 1993) recommended that the NNFI should be considered cautiously because of the apparent large sampling fluctuations found in simulation studies. The appropriateness of this approach rests in part on the implicit assumption that all the incremental fit indices vary along the same underlying metric (i.e., a 0 to 1 metric in which .90 reflects an acceptable fit).

The juxtaposition of concerns about sampling fluctuations and the underlying metric has not received adequate attention. Whereas estimation reliability is a desirable characteristic that is reflected in part by within-cell standard deviations, this is not a fully appropriate basis for evaluating the relative precision of estimation in different indices. If, for example, two indices vary along different metrics, then within-cell standard deviations are not comparable. Two trivial examples demonstrate some of our concerns: (a) if an index has a constant value (say, 1.0) for all correctly and incorrectly specified models, then it will have no within-cell variation; and (b) if an index is multiplied by a constant, then the within-cell standard deviation must vary accordingly. A more appropriate measure of reliability of estimation should reflect the relative sizes of within-cell variation compared to between-cell variation due to systematic differences in model misspecification. This situation is analogous to the estimation of reliability as a ratio of true score variance to total variance and not just (raw score) error variance. Whereas there are many ways in which this notion could be operationalized, one approach is to evaluate the proportion of variance due to systematic differences in model misspecification. Hence, no variation due to model misspecification is explained by an index with a constant value in Example a, and variance explained is not affected by multiplication by a constant in Example b. From this perspective, the minimum condition necessary for evaluating reliability of estimation is to test a variety different models that vary systematically in terms of model misspecification including, perhaps, a true model with no misspecification. Because most simulation studies have considered only true models and apparently none has evaluated some index of variance explained as an indication of reliability of estimation, conclusions based on this previous research must be evaluated cautiously. Alternative approaches to the comparison of relative sampling fluctuations are considered in this chapter.

REVIEW OF SIMULATION STUDIES

Gerbing and Anderson (1993) evaluated the design of Monte Carlo studies of goodness of fit indices and reviewed results from this research with the primary aim "to provide the substantive researcher with guidance regarding the choice of indices to use" (p. 40). Although Gerbing and Anderson did not limit their consideration to incremental fit indices, this family of measures was emphasized in their review and is the basis of discussion presented here. They reviewed the initial research by Bentler and Bonett (1980), the Marsh et al. (1988) classification of Type-1 and Type-2 indices, Bollen's (1986, 1989a, 1989b) indices, and the comparison of CFI and RNI indices. In their evaluation of fit indices, they emphasized sample size effects, appropriate corrections for model complexity, and distributional properties of fit indices. In their discussion of Monte Carlo studies, they emphasized that appropriate compromises between adequacy and manageability must be achieved in choosing the appropriate design to study the behavior of particular indices. Design characteristics considered by Gerbing and Anderson that are particularly important to our discussion include the number of replications for each cell of the design, the range of sample sizes (i.e., the number of cases within each replication), the range of models, and the consideration of true and false models. They recommended that at least 100 or more replications per cell in the design are needed to provide an accurate estimate of population values. Whereas most early simulation studies evaluated only true models in which data were generated by the model to be tested, they emphasized the need to evaluate incorrect models to test the sensitivity of indices to misspecification.

Early simulation studies reviewed by Gerbing and Anderson (1993) evaluated the ability of true models to fit data varying systematically in sample size (e.g., Anderson & Gerbing, 1984; Boomsma, 1982). Anderson and Gerbing (1984), the most comprehensive of these early studies, found that NFI was systematically affected by sample size whereas the NNFI was not, but that NNFI had much larger within-cell standard deviations. Gerbing and Anderson noted that these trends were replicated by Marsh et al. (1988), despite the use of only 10 replications per cell in that study. Gerbing and Anderson also reviewed Bollens's (1989a) research, indicating that IFI is relatively unaffected by sample size, and "an adjustment for the available df is provided, in that a model with fewer parameters to estimate will provide a higher DELTA2 [IFI] value than a model with more parameters to estimate" (p. 53). They concluded that IFI was better than NFI because it was free from the sample size bias and better than NNFI because it had considerably smaller standard errors. Gerbing and Anderson (1993) then evaluated recent developments in indices based on noncentrality discussed earlier, noting the similarity in the CFI and RNI indices independently developed by Bentler (1990) and McDonald and Marsh (1990), respectively. Based on their review, Gerbing and Anderson recommended two incremental fit indices, RNI (or its bounded counterpart CFI) and IFI. They also recommended that further Monte Carlo research was needed to study the behavior of misspecified models in which true paths were omitted and false paths were included. Their recommendation is also considered in this chapter.

Further Consideration of IFI

Gerbing and Anderson (1993) reviewed Marsh et al. (1988) and McDonald and Marsh (1990), but apparently did not realize that IFI had been previously proposed by Marsh et al. under a different name and further criticized by McDonald and Marsh. Based on their review of Monte Carlo studies, Gerbing and Anderson recommended the IFI because it was apparently unbiased and provided an apparently appropriate adjustment for df that penalized a lack of parsimony. However, the more critical evaluation of IFI offered by McDonald and Marsh suggests that Gerbing and Anderson's recommendation may have been premature. There seems to be an unresolved controversy about IFI reflecting suggestions by McDonald and Marsh (1990) and Marsh (1995), based on the mathematical form of the index and empirical results from Monte Carlo studies such as those reviewed by Gerbing and Anderson (1993). The resolution of this controversy requires a stronger Monte Carlo study in which sample sizes and the degree of misspecification in the approximating model are varied systematically over a wider range of values than considered in previous studies of this index, and in which there are enough replications particularly for small sample sizes where sampling fluctuations are larger. Furthermore, whereas most of this controversy has focused on conditions under which IFI is or is not related to sample size, Marsh (1995) argued that the correction for model complexity in the IFI is also inappropriate and opposite to the direction inferred by Gerbing and Anderson (1993) and others. Although these claims apparently run counter to implications offered elsewhere, there seems to be no relevant Monte Carlo studies of the behavior of this aspect of the IFI.

Further Consideration of NNFI

McDonald and Marsh (1990; see also Bentler, 1990) demonstrated that when the NNFI was expressed in terms of the noncentrality and the parsimony ratio (Equation 5), it became apparent that NNFI was qualitatively different from other incremental fit indices such as NFI and RNI. The NNFI, by its mathematical form (McDonald & Marsh, 1990) and on the basis of Monte Carlo results (Marsh & Balla, 1994), provides a parsimony correction—a penalty for model complexity.

$$
\begin{aligned}
NNFI &= [d_o/df_o - d_t/df_t]/[d_o/df_o] \\
&= 1 - [(d_t/df_t)/ (d_o/df_o)] \\
&= 1 - [(d_t/df_t) \times (df_o/d_o)] \\
&= 1 - [(d_t/d_o) \times (df_o/df_t)] \\
&= 1 - [(d_t/d_o)/PR]
\end{aligned}
\tag{5}
$$

where $PR = df_t/df_o$ is the parsimony ratio recommended by Mulaik et al. (1989).

Hence it is clear that NNFI incorporates the parsimony ratio recommended by Mulaik et al. (1989) and satisfies preferences by Bollen and Long (1993), Gerbing and Anderson (1993), and Tanaka (1993) for fit indices that control for model complexity by taking into account the degrees of freedom of a model. The form of this adjustment for df is appropriate in that model complexity is penalized. Marsh and Balla (1994; see also McDonald & Marsh, 1990) also discuss how the penalty function in the NNFI differs from that in other indices such as those discussed by Cudeck and Henly (1991) and by Mulaik et al. (1989).

Marsh (1995) suggested that this property of the NNFI may be particularly useful in tests of nested models (because the NNFI penalizes model complexity). Thus, for example, the inclusion of additional parameters (decreases in df_t) can result in a *lower* NNFI when the improvement in fit (decreases in d_t) is sufficiently small even though the RNI can never be smaller. Conversely, the NNFI rewards model parsimony. Thus, for example, the imposition of equality constraints to test the invariance of solutions over multiple groups may actually result in a higher NNFI even though the RNI can never be higher (e.g., Marsh & Byrne, 1993; Marsh, Byrne, & Craven, 1992). Similarly, a higher order factor model that is nested under the corresponding first-order measurement model can have a higher NNFI even though the RNI can never be higher. This feature of the NNFI provides one potentially useful decision rule (i.e., Accept the more parsimonious model if its NNFI is equal to or better than the less parsimonious model) for concluding that the difference between a more complex model and a more parsimonious model is not substantively important, an aspect of fit not captured by the RNI. Indeed, researchers typically interpret values of greater than .90 as "acceptable" for incremental fit indices like the RNI, but there appears to be no compelling rationale for this rule of thumb. Also, the RNI provides no objective decision rule for choosing between alternative models that result in RNIs greater than .9 but differ substantially in terms of parsimony. Whereas the application of the RNI decision rule logically leads to the selection of the least parsimonious model in a set of nested models, the NNFI may lead to the selection of a model with intermediate complexity. Because the nature of the penalty for model complexity embodied in the NNFI is not broadly recognized, there is a need for more research to evaluate this aspect of the NNFI-decision-rule.

The major criticism of the NNFI has been its large sampling fluctuations. However, interpretations of previous research must be made cautiously because of the apparently overly simplistic manner in which reliability of estimation has been assessed, and this concern will be an important focus of our discussion in the chapter. It is also apparent, however, that NNFI is extremely unstable in some situations. Thus, for example, Anderson and Gerbing (1984) reported extreme NNFIs far in excess of 1.0 when sample size very small. Inspection of the definition of NNFI (Table 11.1 and Equation 5) demonstrates that the index is undefined due to division by zero when $df_o = 0$ (i.e., the null model is able to fit the data) or $df_t = 0$ (i.e., the target model is the saturated model), and is likely to be very unstable in situations approximating these conditions. Whereas it would be extremely unlikely for population values of noncentrality to approach zero for the null model (i.e., for the null model to be "true"), this can happen for sample estimates based on small Ns (e.g., $N \leq 50$), and this apparently accounts for the extremely large values of NNFI reported in some simulation studies. A viable strategy to avoid such extreme values and associated problems with large sampling fluctuations is to develop a normed counterpart of the NNFI. This strategy is somewhat analogous to the comparison of RNI and its normed counterpart CFI. In the case of the NNFI, however, the advantages of a normed counterpart are likely to be much greater because extreme values of NNFI are apparently much more likely than those for RNI (Bentler, 1990). Thus, anyone preferring the normed CFI over the RNI, its unnormed counterpart, should also prefer the normed version of the NNFI over the unnormed version that has been so severely criticised for problems related to sampling fluctuations.

Following McDonald and Marsh's (1990) recommendation that the label Tucker-Lewis index (TLI) should be used instead of NNFI, a new index, the normed Tucker-Lewis index (NTLI) is defined according to the following rules:

1. If NNFI < 0 or $d_o \leq 0$ then NTLI = 0, but
2. If NNFI > 1 or $d_t \leq 0$ (including $df_t = 0$, and both d_t and $d_o \leq 0$) then NTLI = 1.0; otherwise
3. NTLI = NNFI,

where NNFI is defined as in Equation 5 and Table 11.1. (In order to emphasize more clearly which indices are merely normed versions of unnormed indices our preferred labels for NNFI, RNI, and their normed counter-parts would be TLI [instead of NNFI], NTLI, RNI, and NRNI [instead of CFI], but popular usage of the labels NNFI and CFI may not allow for such a logical nomenclature). Hence, NTLI is strictly normed for sample and population values, is defined when NNFI is undefined (i.e., $d_o = 0$ and for the saturated model with $df_t = 0$), and takes on its maximum value of 1.0 whenever $d_t \leq 0$. NTLI should have smaller within-cell SDs than NNFI, particularly when N is small, df_t approaches 0, or δ_o approaches 0. This smaller within-cell SD, however, is at the expense of a slight downward bias in NTLI that should be evident when δ_t approaches 0, particularly with small N.

A PRIORI PREDICTIONS FOR THE PRESENT ANALYSIS

In this section, we evaluate the behavior of the NFI, IFI, RFI, NNFI, NTLI, CFI, and RNI in a large Monte Carlo study. Based on a known population model used to generate simulated data (see Fig. 11.1), models are hypothesized that are true (i.e., misspecification is zero), over-specified (i.e., superfluous parameters known to be zero in the population are added), parsimonious (i.e., parameters known to be equal in the population are constrained to be equal), and misspecified to varying degrees (varying numbers of parameters known to be nonzero in the population are constrained to be zero). We include a wide range of different sample sizes (100 to 5,000) and include more replicates in cells where small samples sizes produce large sampling fluctuations (e.g., 1,000 replicates in cells with $N = 100$). For purposes of this analysis, we focus on the comparison of the RNI with the other incremental fit indices. This is appropriate because it is well established that the RNI is not systematically related to N and contains no penalty for model complexity (see McDonald & Marsh, 1990, and earlier discussion), thus providing a basis of comparison for the other indices in

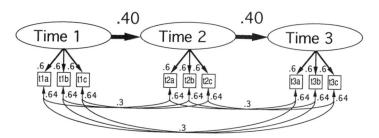

FIG. 11.1. Population generating model used to create the simulated data.

relation to these characteristics. Consistent with earlier discussion and previous research, it is predicted that:

1. RFI and NFI are positively related to sample size for all approximating models.

2. RNI and its normed counterpart, CFI, are identical for most cases, except for true models or nearly true models tested with small Ns where RNI will be greater than CFI (whenever RNI > 1) and CFI will be positively related to sample size. Whereas it is technically possible for RNI to be negative and thus smaller than CFI (e.g., when $d_o < 0$), simulated data considered here are unlikely to result in this occurrence.

3. NNFI and its normed counter-part, NTLI, are also identical for most cases. The most likely exceptions are: (a) true models or nearly true models tested with small Ns where NTLI will be smaller than NNFI (whenever NNFI > 1) and NTLI will be positively related to sample size; or (b) relatively unusual cases when the null model is able to fit the sample data due to sampling fluctuations so that NNFI is unstable or undefined.

4. RNI is relatively unrelated to sample size for all approximating models. For all true models with misspecification of zero, including those with invariance constraints and superfluous parameters, the mean value of RNI is 1.0. For misspecified models, the inclusion of superfluous parameters leads to higher RNIs whereas the imposition of equality constraints leads to lower RNIs (i.e., RNI rewards the inclusion of superfluous parameters and penalizes parsimony).

5. NNFI is relatively unrelated to sample size for all approximating models. For all true models with misspecification of zero, including those with invariance constraints and superfluous parameters, the mean value of NNFI is 1.0. For misspecified models, the inclusion of superfluous parameters leads to lower NNFIs whereas inequality constraints lead to higher NNFIs (i.e., NNFI penalizes the inclusion of superfluous parameters and rewards parsimony). Thus, in contrast to the RNI (and CFI), NNFI (and NTLI) provides an appropriate penalty for model complexity and reward for model parsimony.

6. IFI is relatively unrelated to sample size for all true approximating models, but IFI is negatively related to sample size for all misspecified approximating models. For all true approximating models, including those with invariance constraints and superfluous parameters, the mean value of IFI is 1.0. For misspecified models, the inclusion of superfluous parameters leads to increases in IFI that are as large or larger than those found with RNI (i.e., IFI rewards the inclusion of superfluous parameters as much or more than RNI). The imposition of equality constraints known to be true in the population leads to decreases in IFI that are as large or larger than those found with RNI (i.e., IFI penalizes parsimony as much or more than RNI).

In addition to these a priori predictions, we also consider research questions about the reliability of estimates in different incremental fit indices. In particular, as discussed earlier, we compare results based on the within-cell standard deviations (the traditional approach) and true score variation due to the level of model misspecification. More specifically, we compare results based on these alternative approaches to evaluate suggestions that NNFI has greater sampling variation than the other incremental fit indices and to extend this consideration to the new NTLI fix index.

METHODS

Analyses were conducted with the PC version of LISREL8 (Jöreskog & Sörbom, 1993) and the accompanying GENRAW procedure. A population covariance matrix was generated from a population model (Fig. 11.1) derived from a multiple-indicator simplex model (Marsh, 1993; see also Marsh & Hau, 1994). In this hypothetical model, a set of three indicators of a single latent variable is administered on each of three occasions. Each measured variable is substantially related to its latent variable (.6), but also has a substantial component of measurement error (.64). Residual covariances for the same measured variable administered on different occasions, autocorrelated errors, are moderate (.4). A population covariance matrix based on Fig. 11.1 was constructed with LISREL8 and a total of 100,000 cases were simulated from this population covariance matrix by GENRAW (see discussion of Monte Carlo studies with LISREL8 by Jöreskog & Sörbom, 1993).

In order to evaluate the effects of sample size, the 100,000 cases were divided into 1,000 replicates of $N = 100$ cases, 500 replicates of $N = 200$, 200 replicates of $N = 500$, 100 replicates of $N = 1000$, 50 replicates of $N = 2000$, and 20 replicates of $N = 5000$. By holding the total number of cases (sample size × number of replicates) constant across each sample size, the standard error of the mean for each cell of the design was more nearly equal than would be the case if the number of replicates was held constant. This is a particularly desirable feature in the evaluation of sample size effects because typically estimates based on small sample sizes are of particular interest, but the sampling variability of these estimates is systematically higher than those based on larger sample sizes when the number of replicates is held constant for all sample sizes.

In order to evaluate the effects of varying degrees of misspecification, four approximating models were fit to the data. Model 1 was a "true" model with no misspecification (all nonzero parameter estimates in the population generating model, Fig. 11.1, were freely estimated). Models 2, 3, and 4 differed from Model 1 in that one (Model 2), three (Model 3), or all nine (Model 4) of the nine nonzero correlated uniquenesses in the population were constrained to be zero in the approximating model. In order to evaluate the effects of invariance constraints known to be true in the population and superfluous parameters known to be zero in the population, three versions of each model were considered. In Version 1, no superfluous parameters or invariance constraints were considered. In Version 2, three additional correlated uniquenesses known to be zero in the population (the operation-alization of superfluous parameters considered here) were freely estimated. In Version 3, all nine uniquenesses that were known to be equal in the population were constrained to be equal (the operationalization of a more parsimonious model considered here). For purposes of this analysis we refer to the versions as *normal* (Version 1), *overfit* (Version 2), and *parsimonious* (Version 3). In summary, the analysis had 72 cells representing all combina-tions of 6 (sample sizes) × 4 (models) × 3 (versions).

As previously indicated, seven incremental indices (Table 11.1) were considered. The mean, standard deviation, and standard error were com-puted for all indices in each of the 72 cells of the study, excluding only the nonconverged solutions (see Gerbing & Anderson, 1987, 1993, for a rationale for this approach). Because a particular emphasis of the analysis was on the comparison of RNI with each of the other indices, difference scores were also summarized in which the values for each index was sub-tracted from RNI. In order to assess the relative size of the various effects and to provide a nominal test of statistical significance, a three-way ANOVA was conducted in which the effects of the six sample sizes, the four models, and the three versions were considered.

RESULTS AND DISCUSSION

Mean Values of the Incremental Fit Indices

CFI vs. RNI. The results are summarized in Tables 11.2 and 11.3 and in Fig. 11.2. CFI and RNI are identical in most cases. However, for all

TABLE 11.2

Goodness of Fit Indices: Correlations with Log Sample Size (r), Mean and Standard Error of the Mean for Each of the Twelve Cells (4 Models × 3 Versions; see Fig. 11.2)

Index	Version	Model 1			Model 2			Model 3			Model 4		
		r	Mean	SE	r	Mean	SE	r	Mean	SE	r	Mean	SE
RNI	1	.0074	.9997	.0004	-.0084	.9452	.0007	-.0272	.8068	.0010	-.0752	.5573	.0015
	2	-.0022	1.0000	.0003	-.0157	.9517	.0006	-.0474	.8333	.0009	-.0666	.5964	.0014
	3	.0479	.9984	.0005	.0303	.9384	.0007	.0173	.8012	.0011	.0129	.5472	.0016
NNFI	1	.0159	.9987	.0010	-.0084	.8841	.0015	-.0272	.6340	.0019	-.0752	.3624	.0021
	2	-.0022	1.0000	.0009	-.0157	.8757	.0016	-.0474	.6249	.0021	-.0666	.3396	.0023
	3	.0479	.9976	.0007	.0303	.9113	.0011	.0173	.7349	.0015	.0129	.5060	.0018
DNNFIRNI	1	.0180	-.0010	.0007	-.0084	-.0612	.0008	-.0272	-.1729	.0009	-.0753	-.1948	.0006
	2	-.0022	.0000	.0006	-.0157	-.0759	.0010	-.0474	-.2084	.0012	-.0666	-.2568	.0009
	3	.0479	-.0008	.0002	.0303	-.0271	.0003	.0173	-.0663	.0004	.0129	-.0412	.0001
IFI	1	.0080	.9997	.0004	-.0515	.9479	.0006	-.1189	.8151	.0010	-.1702	.5697	.0014
	2	-.0016	1.0000	.0003	-.0644	.9543	.0006	-.1478	.8416	.0009	-.1831	.6107	.0013
	3	.0485	.9985	.0005	.0048	.9401	.0007	-.0289	.8059	.0011	-.0114	.5508	.0016
DIFIRNI	1	.0006	.0000	.0000	-.5099	.0026	.0001	-.7652	.0083	.0001	-.8260	.0124	.0002
	2	.0095	.0000	.0000	-.4968	.0026	.0001	-.7511	.0083	.0001	-.8222	.0143	.0002
	3	-.0352	.0000	.0000	-.5346	.0018	.0000	-.7535	.0046	.0001	-.8095	.0036	.0000
RFI	1	.7298	.9137	.0012	.4968	.8084	.0016	.2828	.5798	.0018	.0900	.3314	.0019
	2	.7009	.9143	.0013	.4552	.8008	.0017	.2344	.5713	.0020	.0779	.3105	.0020
	3	.7782	.9122	.0012	.6377	.8333	.0013	.4467	.6721	.0015	.2798	.4630	.0017
DRFIRNI	1	.8536	-.0860	.0010	.7337	-.1368	.0011	.5789	-.2271	.0009	.5164	-.2258	.0005
	2	.8180	-.0857	.0011	.6515	-.1509	.0012	.4532	-.2620	.0011	.3490	-.2859	.0007
	3	.8973	-.0862	.0010	.8808	-.1051	.0009	.8626	-.1291	.0008	.8994	-.0842	.0005

(Continued)

TABLE 11.2
(Continued)

Index	Version	Model 1			Model 2			Model 3			Model 4		
		r	Mean	SE	r	Mean	SE	r	Mean	SE	r	Mean	SE
CFI	1	.2458	.9941	.0003	-.0018	.9450	.0007	-.0272	.8068	.0010	-.0752	.5573	.0015
	2	.2345	.9949	.0002	-.0083	.9514	.0006	-.0474	.8333	.0009	-.0666	.5964	.0014
	3	.2725	.9917	.0003	.0371	.9381	.0007	.0173	.8012	.0011	.0129	.5472	.0016
DCFIRNI	1	.2886	-.0057	.0002	.0813	-.0003	.0001	-.0063	.0000	.0000	-.0005	.0000	.0000
	2	.2931	-.0051	.0002	.0922	-.0003	.0001	-.0335	.0000	.0000	-.0157	.0000	.0000
	3	.2713	-.0067	.0003	.0717	-.0003	.0001	-.0299	.0000	.0000	-.0486	.0000	.0000
NFI	1	.7290	.9617	.0005	.4968	.9095	.0007	.2828	.7782	.0010	.0900	.5357	.0013
	2	.7009	.9691	.0005	.4552	.9225	.0006	.2344	.8095	.0009	.0779	.5786	.0012
	3	.7782	.9415	.0008	.6377	.8842	.0009	.4467	.7541	.0011	.2798	.5077	.0015
DNFIRNI	1	.8934	-.0380	.0004	.8880	-.0357	.0004	.8598	-.0286	.0003	.7816	-.0215	.0003
	2	.8927	-.0309	.0004	.8841	-.0291	.0003	.8491	-.0238	.0003	.7502	-.0178	.0003
	3	.8945	-.0569	.0007	.8924	-.0541	.0006	.8821	-.0471	.0006	.8576	-.0395	.0005
NTLI	1	.1935	.9861	.0008	-.0018	.8835	.0014	-.0272	.6340	.0019	-.0752	.3624	.0021
	2	.2345	.9858	.0006	-.0083	.8750	.0016	-.0474	.6249	.0021	-.0666	.3396	.0023
	3	.2725	.9876	.0005	.0371	.9109	.0010	.0173	.7349	.0015	.0129	.5060	.0018
DNTLIRNI	1	.2331	-.0136	.0006	.0044	-.0618	.0007	-.0272	-.1729	.0009	-.0753	-.1948	.0006
	2	.3871	-.0142	.0004	-.0033	-.0767	.0009	-.0474	-.2084	.0012	-.0667	-.2568	.0009
	3	.4550	-.0108	.0003	.0521	-.0275	.0003	.0173	-.0663	.0004	.0129	-.0412	.0001

Note. Considered here are seven goodness of fit indices (RNI, NNFI, IFI, CFI, RFI, NFI, NTLI) and six sets of difference scores determined by subtracting RNI from each index (DNNFIRNI, DIFIRNI, DRFIRNI, DCFIRNI, DNTLIRNI). Within each of the 12 combinations of model and version, the mean and standard error of each index was calculated and the fit indices were correlated with the log sample size. rs > .040 are statistically significant (p < .05, two-tailed).

TABLE 11.3
Variance (Sum of Squared Deviations) Attributable of Sample Size, Model, and Version for Six Indices

Source	DF	IFI	RNI	CFI	NNFI	RFI	NFI	NTLI
Size (S)	5	.233*	.016	.001	.059	18.780*	5.874*	.002
Model (M)	3	595.143*	623.147*	611.923*	1169.808*	978.035*	578.804*	1133.622*
Version (v)	2	2.994*	2.335*	2.401*	26.492*	22.252*	8.607*	27.192*
S × M	15	.231*	.039	.115*	.094	2.904*	.392*	.402*
S × V	10	.102*	.041	.044*	.104	.262*	.855*	.080
M × V	6	1.979*	1.445*	1.386*	19.119*	16.040*	1.200*	18.442*
S × M × V	30	.069	.019	.017	.039	.127	.013	.057
Explained	71	600.827*	627.088*	615.929*	1215.427*	1037.835*	595.736*	1179.491*
Residual	22327	37.183	40.345	39.137	106.954	87.912	33.252	101.737
Total	22398	638.009	667.433	655.065	1322.381	1125.747	628.988	1281.228
Variance Due to (eta)								
Residual		.241	.246	.244	.284	.279	.230	.282
Model		.966	.966	.966	.941	.932	.920	.941
M + V + MxV		.970	.969	.969	.959	.950	.967	.960

Note. Considered here are seven goodness of fit indices (RNI, NNFI, IFI, CFI, RFI, NFI, NTLI). Variance components were derived from a 6 (Sample Size) × 4 (Model) × 3 (Version) analysis of variance conducted separately for each index that also resulted in nominal tests of statistical significance for each effect.

*p < .01.

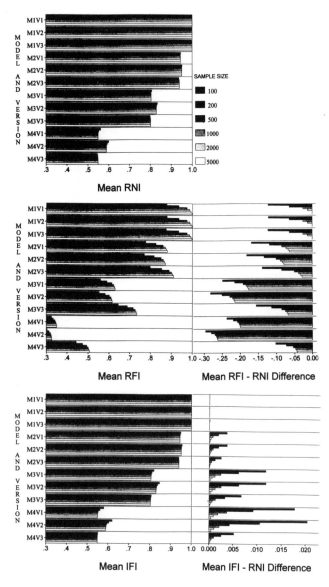

FIG. 11.2. *(Continued)*

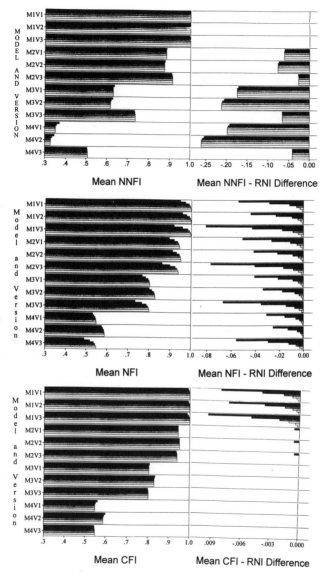

FIG. 11.2. *(Continued)*

339

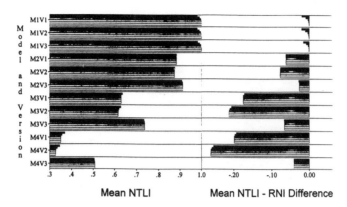

FIG. 11.2. Seven goodness-of-fit indices and differences from RNI as a function of model (M1-M4), version (V1-V3), and sample size. All seven indices are presented along the same (.30 to 1.0) scale. However, the scales for the difference scores vary with the range of the observed values and may not be directly comparable.

versions of Model 1 and, to a lesser extent, Model 2, CFI is systematically smaller than RNI and is positively related to sample size. Inspection of Fig. 11.2 shows that the difference between RNI and CFI occurs primarily when N is small. Consistent with earlier discussion and a priori predictions, these results reflect a systematic bias in CFI (due to the truncation of CFI so as not to exceed 1.0) when N is small and when the amount of misspecification in the model is small. In typical practice, the difference between RNI and CFI should be sufficiently small to be of no practical significance, but the RNI is apparently more appropriate for Monte Carlo studies in which true approximating models are considered. Because patterns of results based on the RNI and CFI are so similar, we emphasize the RNI in subsequent discussion.

NNFI vs. NTLI. NNFI and NTLI are identical in most cases. However, for all versions of Model 1 and, to a lesser extent, Model 2, NTLI is systematically smaller than NNFI and is positively related to sample size. Inspection of Fig. 11.2 and Table 11.1 shows that the difference occurs primarily when N is small. Consistent with earlier discussion and a priori predictions, these results reflect a systematic bias in NTLI (due to the truncation of NTLI to remain in the 0–1 range) when N is small and when the amount of misspecification in the model is small. Because of the nature of the simulated data, the sample sizes, and the approximating models considered here, the extreme values of NNFI discussed in the literature (e.g., Bentler, 1990; Gerbing & Anderson, 1993) were not evident. Hence, the potential advantages of the NTLI are likely to be much greater when conditions leading to extreme values of NNFI are present (e.g., $N < 100$,

d_o approaching 0, df_t approaching 0). Thus, the results do not provide a fully adequate basis to evaluate whether differences between NNFI and NTLI are sufficiently large to be of practical significance in typical practice. Because patterns of results based on the NNFI and NTLI are so similar, we emphasize the NNFI in subsequent discussion.

Sample Size Biases. The average values of RNI, NNFI, and IFI, consistent with a priori predictions, are approximately 1.0 for all versions of Model 1 (the true model with $\delta_t = 0$) and are relatively unrelated to N (Table 11.2). In contrast, the mean values of RFI and NFI are significantly less than 1.0 for all versions of Model 1 and are substantially related to sample size (Table 11.2, see also Fig. 11.2). For both RFI and NFI, the size of this sample size effect is systematically larger for the parsimonious Version 3 and slightly smaller for overfit Version 2 (with superfluous parameters known to be zero in the population). Because of this sample size bias, RFI and NFI should be used cautiously and are not recommended for routine use.

RNI and NNFI are relatively unrelated to sample size for all three versions of each of the models (Table 11.2 and Fig. 11.2). In contrast, there is a small but systematically negative correlation between N and IFI. The nature of this sample size effect in IFI varies systematically with the degree of misspecification and the version of the model. Whereas the effect is approximately zero when the approximating model is true (Model 1) and small when the degree of misspecification is small (Model 2), the size of the effect increases with the degree of misspecification. The nature of this effect is shown clearly in the RNI-IFI difference scores (Table 11.1 and Fig. 11.2). Except for Model 1 with no misspecification, IFI is systematically *larger* than RNI (i.e., the differences are positive) for all versions of each model considered here. The sizes of these differences are small. (However, note that the *x*-axis reflecting differences between RNI and other indices varies for each index so that RNI-IFI differences may "appear" larger than they actually are). Nevertheless, the RNI-IFI differences are substantially larger than the corresponding standard errors (see Table 11.2 where mean differences between IFI and RNI are at least 18 standard errors for all versions of misspecified Models 2, 3, and 4). The size of this difference increases with the degree of misspecification (going from Model 1 to Model 4), is slightly larger for the overfit Version 2 and smaller for the parsimonious Version 3.

RFI, NFI, and IFI all have systematic sample size effects, but the nature of these effects is quite different. For small sample sizes, NFI and RFI are more negatively biased (i.e., values are systematically lower than RNI). For sufficiently large sample sizes, the bias is negligible: RFI approximates the NNFI and NFI approximates RNI. In contrast to RFI and NFI, the IFI is positively biased (i.e., the values are systematically higher) for small sample sizes with misspecified models. For sufficiently large sample sizes IFI values approximate the RNI values. Although the size of the sample size effect for IFI is small, the nature and direction of the bias is worrisome. In particular, IFIs based on smaller Ns tend to be positively biased and this effect is larger for more misspecified models. Note that this is the opposite of the typical sample size bias (e.g., those in the NFI and RFI) that results in lower values—not higher values—for small Ns. Whereas the negative biases in NFI and RFI lead to more conservative evaluations of model fit when N is small, the positive bias in IFI leads to inflated evaluations of fit when N is small. For this reason, IFI should be used with caution and is not recommended for routine use.

Penalties For Model Complexity. NNFI, IFI, and RFI each claim to control appropriately for df—to penalized model complexity and to reward model parsimony—whereas RNI has no such control. In this respect, it is useful to compare the results of the RNI with each of the other indices. The nature of the penalty is clearly evident for the NNFI (and the NNFI-RNI differences). For all versions of Model 1, NNFI is approximately 1.0 and approximately equal to the RNI. This is consistent with the claim that the NNFI has no penalty for model complexity or reward for parsimony when the approximating model is a true model with no misspecification. For all versions of each of the other models, NNFI is systematically smaller than RNI (i.e., difference scores are negative). Furthermore, there is a systematic pattern of results for the three versions. For the overfit Version 2 (with superfluous parameters), NNFI is systematically smaller than for Version 1, reflecting the NNFI penalty for model complexity. For the parsimonious Version 3 (with 9 equality constraints), NNFI is systematically larger than for Version 1. This pattern reflects the NNFI reward for parsimony. Although the pattern of results for RFI is complicated by the large sample-size effect, the pattern is similar to that observed with the NNFI. For the largest sample sizes RFI and NNFI results are very similar, approximating their asymptotic behavior.

The pattern of results for the IFI (and the IFI-RNI differences) is dramatically different from those of the NNFI and RFI. In particular, whereas the NNFI and RFI are systematically smaller than the RNI for all misspecified models, IFI is systematically larger than the RNI for all misspecified models. Whereas the introduction of superfluous parameters in the overfit Version 2 leads to smaller NNFIs and RFIs (reflecting the penalty for model complexity), it results in larger IFIs (reflecting a reward for model complexity). Furthermore, this reward for model complexity in IFI is as large or larger than the corresponding effect in RNI. Whereas the invariance constraints in the parsimonious Version 3 lead to larger NNFIs and RFIs for all misspecified models (reflecting a reward for parsimony), these invariance constraints result in lower IFIs (reflecting a penalty for parsimony). Furthermore, this penalty for parsimony in the IFI is as large or larger than the corresponding effect in RNI. Hence, contrary to claims that IFI penalizes model complexity appropriately, these results show that the IFI penalty is in the opposite direction to what it should be. For this reason, IFI should be used with caution and is not recommended for routine use.

Reliability of Estimation and Sampling Fluctuations

An overly simplistic approach to evaluating sampling fluctuations is to inspect the within-cell standard deviations. Thus, for example, the standard errors (Table 11.2) and the SS-residuals (Table 11.3) for NNFI, NTLI, and RFI are substantially larger than those for NFI, IFI, RNI, and CFI. Also, NNFI and RNI have somewhat higher standard errors and SS-residuals than their normed counterparts, NTLI and CFI, respectively. However, this comparison is predicated on the assumption that the underlying metric for each of the indices is comparable. Inspection of the SS-totals for the different indices demonstrates that the variability of the NNFI, NTLI, and RFI are also substantially larger than the other indices, suggesting that at least these indices vary along a substantially different metric.

A better approach to evaluating sampling fluctuations is to compare standardized variance components instead of those associated with raw scores. Here, for example, we considered eta coefficients [(SS explained/SStotal)$^{1/2}$] in Table 11.3. Whereas NNFI, NTLI, and RFI still have marginally larger residual variance etas than the other indices, the differences are substantially smaller than observed with SS residual terms. We further suggest, however, that the eta associated with the residual variance may not be appropriate because some of the variance explained is due to undesirable sample size effects (a systematic bias) in some indices. Hence, a better basis for comparison is the variance associated with models that differ systematically in their level of misspecification (our operationalization of true score variance) or, perhaps, variance associated with differences in models and versions. A comparison of the etas for NNFI and RFI demonstrates this point. Whereas NNFI has a slightly larger residual eta than RFI (.284 vs. .279 in Table 11.3), part of the smaller RFI residual is due to the systematic sample size effect in this index. Thus, the corresponding etas for model and for the combined effects of model and version are larger for NNFI than for RFI. A similar pattern of results is evident in the comparison of NFI and RNI.

The most appropriate eta may depend on the intent of a particular index and the interpretation of other effects. Thus, for example, the NNFI, NTLI, and RFI provide appropriate penalties for model complexity and so it may be most appropriate to evaluate the combined effects of model and version (M + V + MxV in Table 11.3). In contrast, the IFI, RNI, CFI, and NFI provided no or inappropriate penalties for model complexity, and so the eta associated with model may be most appropriate. Based on these criteria, IFI, RNI, and CFI are all equivalent (etas of .966) and marginally better than NNFI and NTLI (etas of .959 and .960, respectively), whereas the performances of RFI (eta = .950) and particularly NFI (eta = .920) are somewhat poorer.

The critical substantive issue addressed by these analyses was to evaluate more thoroughly the claim that the sampling fluctuations for the NNFI (and NTLI) are substantially larger than those associated with other incremental fit indices. Whereas there appeared to be support for this claim based on the inappropriate comparison of within-cell standard deviations or the SS-residuals, there was almost no support for the claim based on more appropriate comparisons. Although the systematic effects in the NNFI and NTLI are marginally smaller than those for the RNI, CFI, and IFI, the differences are very small. Because these conclusions differ so much from those reported elsewhere (see Gerbing & Anderson, 1993), it is important to evaluate the generalizability of our conclusions. The approach used here requires that a number of different models varying systematically in misspecification be fit to the same data, but, as noted by Gerbing and Anderson, most studies have only evaluated true models. Hence, according to criteria used here, few studies have considered data appropriate for addressing the question. There are, however, limitations in the present analysis that may limit its generalizability. Inspection of the definitions of NNFI in Table 11.1 demonstrates that the index is undefined due to division by zero when $d_o = 0$ (i.e., the null model is able to fit the data) or $df_t = 0$ (i.e., the target model is the saturated model), and is likely to be very unstable in situations approximating these conditions. Neither of these conditions were likely in the present investigation because of the nature of the generating and approximating models and the minimum sample size of 100. Thus, we did not experience the extreme outliers for NNFI such as those reported by Gerbing and Anderson, and our results do not generalize to those situations where NNFI is likely to be most unstable and may be inappropriate. Whereas there is a need for more research into the behavior of NNFI in these situations, it seems that these are precisely the situations in which the advantages of NTLI over NNFI are likely to be the greatest.

The results of these analyses have potentially important methodological implications for the evaluation of sampling fluctuations in fit indices. In the same way that reliability cannot be evaluated by assessing raw score residual variance without reference to true score variance, it is inappropriate to evaluate sampling fluctuations by assessing within-cell standard deviations (or SS-residuals) without reference to variation due to systematic variation of model misspecification. The difference in the approaches can be substantial as shown by inspection of the NFI that was best according to the traditional approach (i.e., lowest SS-residuals) but worst according to criteria used here (i.e., lowest model eta). The important implication of these results, as suggested by Gerbing and Anderson, is that researchers need to pursue Monte Carlo studies that include true models and models varying systematically in level of misspecification. Although we have not pursued these implications fully in the present comparison, this seems to be a potentially important new area of research in which procedures such as generalizability theory can make a useful contribution. Furthermore, systematically pursuing the contribution of different sources of misspecification in various indices will contribute substantially to our understanding of the behavior of all goodness of fit indices.

SUMMARY AND IMPLICATIONS

There seems to be a growing consensus that goodness of fit is most appropriately evaluated with a variety of different perspectives. Hence, researchers are typically recommended to consider several qualitatively different indices with well-known properties to assess fit. Whereas no clearly defined typology of fit indices has been developed, incremental fit indices like those considered here have been used extensively since they were popularized by Bentler and Bonett (1980). Researchers have considered several broad criteria in evaluating incremental fit indices, such as the bias due to sample size, penalties of model complexity, rewards for model parsimony, and estimation reliability. Thus, it is important to critically evaluate incremental fit indices in relation to these criteria.

Evaluations of Each Incremental Fit Index

NFI and RFI. The NFI was proposed by Bentler and Bonett (1980) to provide an incremental fit index that varied on a 0 to 1 scale. Although heuristic, subsequent research showed that NFI was biased by N, a conclusion consistent with the results of this study. The RFI was developed, in part, in response to this problem with the NFI, but subsequent research and the present results show that it is also substantially biased by sample size. Hence, neither the NFI nor the RFI are recommended for routine use.

IFI. The IFI index has been claimed to be unbiased and to control for degrees of freedom. Whereas the results of various Monte Carlo studies seemed to support these conclusions (see review by Gerbing & Anderson, 1993), McDonald and Marsh's (1990) evaluation of mathematical properties of the index led them to question these conclusions. In the present analysis, a more detailed evaluation of the mathematical properties of IFI and the Monte Carlo results both indicate that: (a) IFI is positively biased for misspecified models and that the size of this bias is more positive for small N; (b) the adjustment for df is inappropriate in that it penalizes model parsimony and rewards model complexity; and (c) the inappropriate penalty for model parsimony and reward for model complexity is larger for small N. Marsh (1995) noted that previous Monte Carlo studies of the IFI based on true models did not provide a test of the claimed bias in the IFI. Whereas Bentler (1990) reported that IFI was relatively unrelated to sample size for a slightly misspecified model, Marsh (1995) suggested that a small trend consistent with the expected bias was evident in Bentler's results and that the bias would probably be larger if the model misspecification had been larger. It is interesting to note that values for CFI, NFI, IFI, RNI, and NNFI reported by Bentler (1990) are similar to those reported here with Model 2 (Table 11.2) where there was a small, marginally significant correlation between IFI and sample size. As predicted by Marsh (1995), the negative correlations are larger for Models 3 and 4 where model misspecification is larger. Whereas our empirical research and IFI's mathematical form suggest that the sizes of the effects of sample size and inappropriate penalties for model complexity may be small, the nature and direction of these effects are particularly worrisome. It is also interesting to note that the asymptotic value of the IFI and its behavior when N is large approximates the RNI that has no control for model complexity rather than that of the NNFI, NTLI, and RFI that do penalize model complexity and reward model parsimony. These undesirable properties of IFI summarized here demonstrate that this index has not achieved its intended goals or claims by its proponents. For these reasons the IFI is not recommended for routine use.

RNI. In the present comparison, the RNI was not systematically related to sample size, had mean values of approximately 1.0 for true approximating models and appropriately reflected systematic variation in model misspecification. In this respect, it was successful in relation to its intended goals. The only substantial limitation for this index, perhaps, is its failure to penalize appropriately for model complexity (i.e., RNIs were larger for overfit models with superfluous parameter estimates) and to reward model parsimony (i.e., RNIs were smaller for the parsimonious models that imposed equality constraints known to be true in the population). There is, however, room for disagreement on the interpretation of even this one apparent limitation. Whereas most researchers agree that penalties for model complexity and rewards for model parsimony are desirable, a few argue otherwise. Thus, for example, Bentler (1992) recognized the importance of this feature but preferred not to mix the separate characteristics of fit and parsimony in a single index. Marsh and Balla (1994) offered related advice in their discussion of model complexity penalties and sample estimation penalties. Because the RNI was well behaved in relation to its intended goals and most of the desirable criteria proposed here, we recommend the continued use of the RNI (or, perhaps, its normed counterpart, the CFI).

NNFI. In the present comparison, the NNFI was not systematically related to sample size, appropriately penalized model complexity, appropriately rewarded model parsimony, and systematically reflected differences in model misspecification. In this respect it was the most successful index in meeting the desirable criteria considered here. Previous research suggested that the NNFI had much larger sampling fluctuations than did the other incremental fit indices. We showed, however, that most of this research used inappropriate methods to assess sampling fluctuations, apparently invalidating many of these earlier conclusions. Using more appropriate methodology introduced in the present comparison, we showed that sampling fluctuations in the NNFI were similar to those in the other incremental fit indices. Although not the major focus of this chapter, this alternative methodology seems to provide a potentially important basis for future research. Nevertheless, we did specify particular situations in which the behavior of the NNFI was likely to be unstable and recommend that the index should be used cautiously when these conditions prevail. Particularly in these situations, researchers should consider the use of the NTLI. Except for this possible limitation that was not evident in our research and may not be typical in practice, the NNFI was the most successful index considered here in relation to the criteria typically used to evaluate incremental fit indices. For these reasons we recommend the routine use of the NNFI (or, perhaps, its normed counterpart, the NTLI).

NNFI vs. NTLI and RNI vs. CFI. The NNFI and NTLI, like RNI and CFI, are nearly equivalent and so the choice between the normed and unnormed versions of these indices is arbitrary in most situations. However, for true or approximately true models, CFI and NTLI are biased in that the mean of the sampling distribution is not 1 and the size of this bias is a systematically decreasing function of sample size. In the present comparison this bias was still evident but trivial in size for Model 2 that was only slightly misspecified. Because of these concerns, we recommend the RNI and NNFI instead of, or in addition to, the CFI and NTLI. Whereas the CFI and NTLI are intended to provide greater reliability of estimation, their advantages over their unnormed counterparts were negligible in the present investigation. Whereas the SS-residuals were somewhat smaller for the normed indices, our operationalization of true score variance (etas reflecting the effects of model or model and version) were nearly identical. We suspect, however, that there may be situations (e.g., δ_0 approaching zero and small N) where the advantages of the normed versions of these indices may be more evident. Logically, based on an inspection of the definitions of RNI and NNFI, and empirically, based on findings of extreme values for NNFI reported in previous research, the advantages of NTLI over NNFI should be more substantial than those of CFI over RNI. Hence, researchers who chose to use CFI instead of (or in addition to) RNI should be even more inclined to use NTLI instead of (or in addition to) NNFI. For these reasons, we recommend that researchers use NTLI and CFI as adjuncts to their unnormed counterparts, but that more research is needed in conditions in which the advantages of the normed versions of these indices are likely to be greatest.

Further Consideration of NNFI

NNFI has the longest history of any of the incremental fit index considered here. Ironically, it also seems to be the most misunderstood and inappropriately maligned. Bentler and Bonett (1980) favored their NFI over the NNFI in part because sample values of NFI were normed whereas those for NNFI were not. However, we are not fully convinced that being normed per se is all that desirable, because any strictly normed incremental index must also be biased. To the extent that there is value in being normed, as in the CFI and particularly the NTLI, it is because the norming process counteracts situations where indices are otherwise undefined or unstable. Furthermore, in the same way that Bentler (1990) operationally defined CFI to be the normed counterpart of the RNI, we operationally defined the NTLI to be the normed counterpart of the NNFI. Hence, as argued by McDonald and Marsh (1990), the critical distinction between the NFI and NNFI is that the NFI provides a biased estimate of a quantity that does not control for model complexity whereas the NNFI provides an unbiased estimate of a quantity that does. In retrospect, NNFI is a more useful index than NFI.

Bollen (1986) suggested that by its algebraic form the NNFI would be influenced by sample size and proposed the RFI which he argued should be independent of sample size. However, further clarification of the meaning of the sample size effect (e.g., Bollen, 1989b, 1990) and a growing body of empirical research showed that values of RFI are systematically related to N whereas those of NNFI are not. Although RFI and NNFI both provide an appropriate penalty for model complexity, NNFI is more useful than RFI according to the criteria specified here. Recognizing problems with the RFI, Bollen (1989a, 1989b) subsequently proposed the IFI that was intended to be relatively independent of sample size and to provide a correction for degrees of freedom. The design of the IFI and initial research led to its recommendation over the NNFI by a number of researchers, even though McDonald and Marsh (1990) claimed that their earlier version of this same index had potentially serious flaws. Our Monte Carlo results provided empirical support for the McDonald and Marsh claims, demonstrating that the IFI provided no control for model complexity, no reward for model parsimony, and is slightly biased by sample size. Hence the IFI is qualitatively different from the NNFI and weaker than the RNI that it more closely resembles. In retrospect, the appropriate credit for the IFI index or apparent discredit (Marsh & Balla, 1986; Marsh et al., 1988, or Bollen, 1989a, 1989b, 1990) may not be an important consideration, if our recommendation that the index not be routinely used is accepted.

A frequently expressed concern is that the NNFI is prone to extreme values resulting in large sampling fluctuations. However, such claims are typically based on comparisons of within-cell standard deviations or SS-residuals from studies that included only true models. Part of the reason for these differences is evident from an inspection of the mean values of NNFI and, for example, RNI (Table 11.2). Whereas both indices have values of about 1 for the true Model 1, NNFIs are progressively much lower than RNIs for increasingly misspecified models. Hence, it is evident that the metrics underlying the NNFI and RNI are qualitatively different so that within-cell standard deviations and SSresiduals based on raw scores are not comparable. Using a more appropriate approach to assessing the reliability of the various indices requires researchers to evaluate a series of models in which misspecification is systematically varied such as considered here. Whereas the SS-residuals observed here are substantially larger for the NNFI than the RNI, the etas associated with the effects of models and/or versions were nearly as high for NNFI as RNI. Although extreme values of NNFI, like those reported in some studies, may limit the generalizability of our results for conditions likely to produce such results, these conditions should also have deleterious results on RNI sampling fluctuations (although not so extreme as for NNFI). In these conditions, the CFI and particularly the NTLI are likely to perform substantially better than their nonnormed counterparts.

It is not generally recognized that NNFI incorporates a penalty for model complexity and a reward for model parsimony. The results of this study provide one example where the introduction of equality constraints resulted in higher NNFIs even though it led to lower RNIs. Similarly, the introduction of superfluous parameters led to poorer NNFIs even though there was an increase in RNIs. However, an important limitation of the present comparison and a direction for further research is to evaluate the generality of these empirical results. In particular, an important limitation of the present Monte Carlo study was that the added superfluous parameters were exactly equal to zero in the known population and the equality constraints were exactly true in the known population. In application, the population values of added parameters are unknown and never exactly equal to zero, whereas equality constraints are never exactly true (see Williams & Holahan, 1994). For these reasons, it is useful to examine the nature of the penalty for model complexity and the reward for model parsimony embodied in the NNFI. Inspection of the mathematical form of the NNFI (see Table 11.1) indicates that the χ^2_t/df_t is the only part of the equation that can vary when considering a given set of data (i.e., 1.0 is a constant and the null model is fixed so that χ^2_o/df_o is also a constant). Thus, the change in NNFI due to the introduction of invariance constraints or additional parameters is only a function of the resulting change in χ^2/df (i.e., $\chi_2^2/df_2 - \chi_1^2/df_1$ where χ_1^2/df_1 refers to the original model). If the change in χ^2/df is large relative to the χ^2/df for the original target model then NNFI decreases, and if the resulting change in χ^2/df is smaller than χ^2/df for the original model then NNFI increases. From this relation, several generalizations can be offered. Within the limits of sampling fluctuations:

1. The introduction of true constraints (e.g., constraining parameters to be equal that are equal in the population) should increase NNFI unless the original target model is also true, in which case the introduction of the invariance constraints should have no systematic effect. (This behavior is evident in Fig. 11.2.)

2. The introduction of superfluous parameters that have zero values in the population should decrease NNFI unless the original model is true, in which case it should have no systematic effect. (This behavior is evident in Fig. 11.2.)

3. The change in NNFI due to the introduction of any constraints to the original model will depend on the degree of misspecification in the original target model relative to the degree of misspecification introduced by the constraints. For any misspecified target model, the introduction of constraints should

    • increase NNFI if the degree of misspecification in the constraints is sufficiently small relative to the misspecification in the target model (i.e., $\chi_2^2/df_2 < \chi_1^2/df_1$),

    • decrease NNFI if the degree of misspecification in the constraints is sufficiently large (i.e., $\chi_2^2/df_2 > \chi_1^2/df_1$), or

    • have no systematic effect if misspecification in the constraints is the same as that in the original target model (i.e., $\chi_2^2/df_2 = \chi_1^2/df_1$).

4. The change in NNFI due to the addition of new parameters to the original model will depend on the degree of misspecification in the original target model and the degree of misspecification due to not

allowing the new parameters to be freely estimated. The rationale for this statement follows that from constraints in Item 3.

CHAPTER SUMMARY

The RNI and NNFI were both well behaved in the present comparison in that values of these indices were relatively unrelated to sample size. However, these two indices behaved differently in relation to the introduction of superfluous parameters and of equality constraints. RNI has no penalty for model complexity or reward for model parsimony, whereas NNFI penalizes complexity and rewards parsimony. In this respect, the two indices reflect qualitatively different, apparently complimentary characteristics. Based on these results, we recommend that researchers wanting to use incremental fit indices should consider both RNI (or perhaps its normed counterpart, CFI) and NNFI (or perhaps its normed counterpart, NTLI). The juxtaposition between the two should be particularly useful in the evaluation of a series of nested or partially nested models. The RNI provides an index of the change in fit due to the introduction of new parameters or constraints on the model, but will typically lead to the selection of the least parsimonious model within a nested sequence. Here the researcher must use a degree of subjectivity in determining whether the change in fit is justified in relation to the change in parsimony. The NNFI embodies a control for model complexity and a reward for parsimony such that the optimal NNFI may be achieved for a model of intermediate complexity. This juxtaposition of the two indices was clearly evident in the present comparison in that the introduction of superfluous parameters (Version 2 of each misspecified model) led to an increase in RNIs but a decrease in NNFIs, whereas the imposition of equality constraints (Version 3 of each misspecified model) led to a decrease in RNIs but an increase in NNFIs. Whereas these incremental indices may be useful in the evaluation of a single a priori model considered in isolation, we suggest that they will be even more useful in the evaluation of a series of viable alternative models, particularly if the set of alternative models are nested or partially nested.

It is important to emphasize that the recommendation of the RNI and NNFI does not preclude the use of other, nonincremental fit indices. Along with Bollen and Long (1993) and Gerbing and Anderson (1993), we recommend that researchers consider the most appropriate indices from different families of measures. It is, however, important to critically evaluate the alternative indices in different families of measures as we have done with the incremental indices. More generally, it is important to reiterate that subjective indices of fit like those considered here should be only one component in the overall evaluation of a model.

REFERENCES

Anderson, J. C., & Gerbing, D. W. (1984). The effect of sampling error on convergence, improper solutions, and goodness-of-fit indices for maximum likelihood confirmatory factor analysis. *Psychometrika, 49*, 155–173.

Bentler, P. M. (1990). Comparative fit indices in structural models. *Psychological Bulletin, 107*, 238–246.

Bentler, P. M. (1992). On the fit of models to covariances and methodology to the *Bulletin*. *Psychological Bulletin, 112*, 400–404.

Bentler, P. M., & Bonett, D. G. (1980). Significance tests and goodness of fit in the analysis of covariance structures. *Psychological Bulletin, 88*, 588–606.

Bollen, K. A. (1986). Sample size and Bentler and Bonetts nonnormed fit index. *Psychometrika, 51*, 375–377.

Bollen, K. A. (1989a). A new incremental fit index for general structural equation models. *Sociological Methods and Research, 17*, 303–316.

Bollen, K. A. (1989b). *Structural equations with latent variables*. New York: Wiley.

Bollen, K. A. (1990). Overall fit in covariance structure models: Two types of sample size effects. *Psychological Bulletin, 107*, 256–259.

Bollen, K. A., & Long, J. S. (1993). Introduction. In K. A. Bollen & J. S. Long (Eds.), *Testing structural equation models* (pp. 1–9). Newbury Park, CA: Sage.

Boomsma, A. (1982). The robustness of LISREL against small sample size in factor analysis models. In K. G. Jöreskog & H. Wold (Eds.), *Systems under indirect observation: Causality, structure, prediction* (Part 1, pp. 149–173). Amsterdam: North-Holland.

Bozdogan, H. (1987). Model selection and Akaike's information criterion (AIC): The general theory and its analytical extensions. *Psychometrika, 52*, 345–370.

Browne, M. W., & Cudeck, R. (1989). Single-sample cross-validation indices for covariance structures. *Multivariate Behavioral Research, 24*, 445–455.

Browne, M. W., & Cudeck, R. (1993). Alternative ways of assessing model fit. In K. A. Bollen & J. S. Long (Eds.), *Testing structural equation models* (pp. 136–162). Newbury Park, CA: Sage.

Cudeck, R., & Browne, M. W. (1983). Cross-validation of covariance structures. *Multivariate Behavioral Research, 18*, 147–167.

Cudeck, R., & Henly, S. J. (1991). Model selection in covariance structures analysis and the "problem" of sample size: A clarification. *Psychological Bulletin, 109*, 512–519.

Gerbing, D. W., & Anderson, J. C. (1987). Improper solutions in the analysis of covariance structures: Their interpretability and a comparison of alternative specifications. *Psychometrika, 52*, 99–111.

Gerbing, D. W., & Anderson, J. C. (1993). Monte Carlo evaluations of goodness-of-fit indices for structural equation models. In K. A. Bollen & J. S. Long (Eds.), *Testing structural equation models* (pp. 40–65). Newbury Park, CA: Sage.

Goffin, R. D. (1993). A comparison of two new indices for the assessment of fit of structural equation models. *Multivariate Behavioral Research, 28*, 205–214.

Jöreskog, K. G. (1993). Testing structural equation models. In K. A. Bollen & J. S. Long (Eds.), *Testing structural equation models* (pp. 294–316). Newbury Park, CA: Sage.

Jöreskog, K. G., & Sörbom, D. (1993). *LISREL 8: Structural equation modeling with the SIMPLIS command language*. Chicago: Scientific Software International.

Marsh, H. W. (1993). Covariance stability in multiwave panel studies: Comparison of simplex models and one-factor models. *Journal of Educational Measurement, 30*, 157–183.

Marsh, H. W. (1995). The $\Delta2$ and $\chi^2 I2$ fit indices for structural equation models: A brief note of clarification. *Structural Equation Modeling, 2*(3), 246–254.

Marsh, H. W., & Balla, J. R. (26 February, 1986). *Goodness-of-fit indices in confirmatory factor analysis: The effect of sample size.* (ERIC Document Reproduction Service No. ED 267 091).

Marsh, H. W., & Balla, J. R. (1994). Goodness-of-fit indices in confirmatory factor analysis: The effect of sample size and model complexity. *Quality & Quantity, 28,* 185–217.

Marsh, H. W., Balla, J. R., & McDonald, R. P. (1988). Goodness-of-fit indices in confirmatory factor analysis: The effect of sample size. *Psychological Bulletin, 102,* 391–410.

Marsh, H. W., & Byrne, B. M. (1993). Confirmatory factor analysis of multitrait–multimethod self-concept data: Between-group and within-group invariance constraints. *Multivariate Behavioral Research, 28,* 313–349.

Marsh, H. W., Byrne, B. M., & Craven, R. (1992). Overcoming problems in confirmatory factor analysis of MTMM data: The correlated uniqueness model and factorial invariance. *Multivariate Behavioral Research, 27,* 489–507.

Marsh, H. W., & Hau, K.-T. (1994). *Assessing goodness of fit: When parsimony is undesirable.* Unpublished manuscript.

McDonald, R. P. (1989). An index of goodness-of-fit based on noncentrality. *Journal of Classification, 6,* 97–103.

McDonald, R. P, & Marsh, H. W. (1990). Choosing a multivariate model: Noncentrality and goodness-of-fit. *Psychological Bulletin, 107,* 247–255.

Mulaik, S. A., James, L. R., Van Alstine, J., Bennett, N., Lind, S., & Stilwell, C. D. (1989). Evaluation of goodness-of-fit indices for structural equation models. *Psychological Bulletin, 105,* 430–445.

Sobel, M. E., & Bohrnstedt, G. W. (1986). Use of null models in evaluating the fit of covariance structure models. In N. B. Tuma (Ed.), *Sociological methodology 1985* (pp. 152–178). San Francisco: Jossey-Bass.

Steiger, J. (1990). Structure model evaluation and modification: An interval estimation approach. *Multivariate Behavioral Research, 25,* 173–180.

Steiger, J. H., & Lind, J. M. (May, 1980). *Statistically based tests for the number of common factors.* Paper presented at the Psychometrika Society Meeting, Iowa City.

Tanaka, J. S. (1993). Multifaceted conceptions of fit in structural equation models. In K. A. Bollen & J. S. Long (Eds.), *Testing structural equation models* (pp. 10–39). Newbury Park, CA: Sage.

Tucker, L. R., & Lewis, C. (1973). The reliability coefficient for maximum likelihood factor analysis. *Psychometrika, 38,* 1–10.

Williams, L. R., & Holahan, P. J. (1994). Parsimony-based fit indices for multiple-indicator models: Do they work? *Structural Equation Modeling, 2,* 161–189.

Author Index

356

AUTHOR INDEX

Bollen, K. A., 5, 6, 17, 53, 128, 156, 195,
196, 202, 203, 206, 208–212, 215,
217, 218, 222, 223, 225, 227–230,
232, 234, 235, 237, 240, 272, 276,
280, 311, 315, 317, 318, 320, 321,
324–328, 329, 348, 349, 351, 352
Bonett, D. G., 164, 194, 315–318, 327, 345,
348, 352
Boomsma, A., 202, 203, 210, 211, 225, 327,
352
Boos, D. D., 207, 226
Bowden, R. J., 228, 237, 240
Bowers, D. G., 295, 311
Bozdogan, H., 10, 53, 301, 304, 306–310,
311, 312, 324, 352
Bradway, K. P., 106, 121, 122
Bramble, W. J., 9, 19, 22, 23, 56
Brandt, D., 126, 157
Brannick, M. T., 14, 53
Braunstein, D. N., 296, 313
Brett, J., 280, 312
Brown, D., 164, 183, 194
Brown, R. L., 4, 5, 6, 229, 240, 244, 276
Browne, M. W., 9, 10, 14, 32, 33, 38, 42,
43, 50, 53, 56, 62–64, 87, 106, 109,
121, 209, 212, 216, 223, 225, 315,
324, 325, 352
Bryk, A. S., 3, 6, 89, 90, 106, 108, 120,
121, 126–128, 151, 156
Burchinall, M., 128, 156
Byrne, B. M., 329, 353

C

Caines, P. E., 162, 165, 194
Campbell, D. T., 2, 6, 7, 8, 14, 23, 32,
43–45, 54
Cattell, R. B., 112, 114, 123, 174, 194
Chatfield, C., 162, 194
Chatterjee, S., 200, 202, 203, 211, 225
Clark, L. A., 160, 194
Cleveland, W. W., 167, 194
Cliff, N., 1, 6, 279, 280, 311
Cohen, J., 91, 96, 121
Cohen, P., 91, 96, 121
Cole, N. S., 89, 124
Coleman, J. S., 109, 121
Coray, K. E., 295, 312
Corneal, S. E., 161, 184, 194
Cornwell, J. M., 229, 241
Craven, K., 329, 353

Cronbach, L. J., 91, 122
Cudeck, R., 9, 10, 32, 38, 54, 216, 225,
228, 240, 287, 311, 315, 324, 325,
329, 352
Curry, J., 244, 277

D

Dalgleish, L. I., 195, 225
DeGooijer, J. G., 177, 184, 194
DeLeeuw, J., 89, 90, 119, 122
Demmel, J., 28, 53
Dempster, A. P., 89, 90, 122, 273, 276
Dicken, C., 17, 53
Dickinson, T. L., 23, 25, 49, 54
Dielman, T. E., 121, 122
Dietz, T., 195, 225
Dijkstra, T., 212, 213, 224, 225
DiMatteo, M. R., 10, 55
Dongarra, J., 28, 53
Du Croz, J., 28, 53
Duncan, O. D., 280, 312
Duncan, D. B., 235, 237, 241
Durand, R. M., 196, 202, 206, 207, 211, 226
DuToit, S., 106, 109, 121
Duval, R. D., 196, 226

E

Efron, B., 4, 6, 195, 196, 201, 204–206,
224, 225
Eicker, F., 235, 240
Entwisle, B., 89, 123
Epanchin, A., 126, 157
Epstein, D., 127, 128, 149, 156

F

Fabrigar, L., 281, 282, 286, 313
Falkner, F., 107, 122
Farr, J., 291, 313
Finkbeiner, C., 244, 247, 276
Finn, J. D., 23, 54
Fishbein, M., 76, 85, 87, 88
Fiske, D. W., 2, 6, 7, 8, 14, 23, 32, 43–45,
54
Flamer, S., 12, 47, 54
Frey, R. S., 195, 225

Subject Index

About the Authors

Lynda Aiman-Smith is a doctoral student in Organizational Behavior and Human Resources at Purdue University. She has worked for many years in industry in production control, quality assurance, and as a manufacturing plant manager.

James L. Arbuckle is Associate Professor in the Psychology Department at Temple University. He does research in structural equation modeling.

John R. Balla is Senior Lecturer in the Faculty of Health Sciences at the University of Sydney in Australia. He received his PhD in Education from Macquarie University in 1989. His areas of interest include psychometrics, students' learning processes, the optimal use of information technology, evaluation, and the derivation of indicators of quality of various aspects of teaching, learning, and administration.

Peter M. Bentler is Professor of Psychology at the University of California, Los Angeles. His research deals with theoretical and statistical problems in psychometrics and multivariate analysis, especially structural equation models, as well as with personality and applied social psychology, especially drug use and abuse.

Kenneth A. Bollen is Professor of Sociology at the University of North Carolina at Chapel Hill. His major research interests are in sociometrics (especially structural equation modeling) and in international development. He is author of *Structural Equations With Latent Variables* (1989, NY: Wiley) and is co-editor with J. S. Long of *Testing Structural Equation Models* (1993, Newbury, CA: Sage).

Hamparsum Bozdogan is Associate Professor of Statistics and Adjunct Associate Professor of Mathematics at the University of Tennessee in Knoxville. He received his doctorate in Statistics from the Department of Mathematics at the University of Illinois in Chicago. He was on the faculty at the University of Virginia, and a Visiting Professor and Research Fellow at the Institute of Statistical Mathematics in Tokyo, Japan. He is an internationally renowned expert in the area of informational statistical modeling. He is the recipient of many distinguished awards, one of which is the prestigious Chancellor's 1993 Award for Research and Creative Achievement at the University of Tennessee in Knoxville. He is Editor of the three-volume Proceedings of the First U.S./Japan Conference on *Frontiers of Statistical Modeling: An Informational Approach.*

Sherry E. Corneal is Assistant Professor in the Department of Human Development and Family Studies at The Pennsylvania State University. Her research interests include single subject designs and stepfamily life.

Fumiaki Hamagami is a research associate at the L. L. Thurstone Psychometric Laboratory of the University of North Carolina at Chapel Hill. His research interests focus on individual differences in human cognitive abilities and structural equation models.

Kit-Tai Hau is Lecturer in the Faculty of Education at the Chinese University of Hong Kong. He received his PhD in Psychology from the University of Hong Kong in 1992. His areas of interest include developmental psychology, moral development, achievement motivation, causal attributions, and self-concept.

Scott L. Hershberger is Assistant Professor of Quantitative Psychology in the Department of Psychology at the University of Kansas. His research interests include structural equation modeling, psychometric theory, and developmental behavior genetics.

Karl G. Jöreskog is Professor of Multivariate Statistical Analysis at Uppsala University, Sweden. His main interests are in the theory and applications of structural equation models and other types of multivariate analysis, particularly their applications in the social and behavioral sciences. He is coauthor of *LISREL 7—A Guide to the Program and Applications* published by SPSS, 1989, and *LISREL 8: Structural Equation Modeling With the SIMPLIS Command Language* published by SSI, 1993.

George A. Marcoulides is Professor of Statistics at California State University, Fullerton, and Adjunct Professor at the University of California, Irvine. He is the recipient of the 1991 UCEA William J. Davis Memorial Award for outstanding scholarship. He is currently president-elect of the Western Decision Sciences Institute, Review Editor of *Structural Equation Modeling*, and Associate Editor of *The International Journal of Educational Management*. His research interests include generalizability theory and structural equation modeling.

Herbert W. Marsh is the Research Professor of Education at the University of Western Sydney-Macarthur in Australia. He received his PhD in psychology from UCLA in 1974. His research spans a broad array of methodological and substantive concerns (students' evaluations of teaching effectiveness, self-concept, school effectiveness, gender differences, sports psychology), and he has published widely in these areas. He is the author of psychological instruments including multidimensional measures of self-concept (the SDQs) and students' evaluations of university teaching (SEEQ).

John J. McArdle is a professor in the Department of Psychology at the University of Virginia. His research interests include structural equation modeling and individual differences.

Peter C. M. Molenaar graduated from the University of Utrecht, The Netherlands, in mathematical psychology, psychophysiology, and time series analysis. He is currently at the University of Amsterdam and The Pennsylvania State University. He has published in the following areas: state-space modeling of developmental processes, behavior genetics, and psychophysiological signal analysis. His current interests include nonlinear dynamical approaches to epigenetics and biophysics.

Aline G. Sayer is Assistant Professor of Human Development and an Associate of the Center for the Development and Health Research Methodology, both at The Pennsylvania State University. She received an EdD in Human Development from Harvard University and was recently a Postdoctoral Fellow in Psychiatry at Harvard Medical School. Her research interests include the integration of individual growth curve modeling and structural equation modeling, and the psychosocial and cognitive development of children with chronic illnesses.

Randall E. Schumacker is Associate Professor of Educational Research at the University of North Texas, where he teaches structural equation modeling, psychometric theories, and statistics. He received his doctorate in Educational Psychology from Southern Illinois University, where he specialized in measurement, statistics, and research methods. He is currently Editor of *Structural Equation Modeling* and on the editorial board of several measurement and statistics journals.

John B. Willett is a professor at the Harvard University Graduate School of Education, where he teaches courses in applied statistics and data analysis. His research interests focus on the development and explication of methods for the analysis of longitudinal data, including the use of covariance structure analysis in the measurement of change and the use of discrete-time survival analysis for investigating the occurrence and timing of critical events. Along with his colleague, Judy Singer, he was awarded the 1992 *Raymond B. Cattell Early Career Award* and the 1993 *Review of Research Award*, both given by the American Educational Research Association.

Larry J. Williams is Associate Professor and Jay Ross Young Faculty Scholar at the Krannert Graduate School of Management at Purdue University. He received his doctorate from the Indiana University School of Business in 1988. He is the Consulting Editor for the Research Methods and Analysis section of the *Journal of Management*, and is Co-Editor of the series, *Advances in Research Methods and Analysis for Organizational Studies*. His research interests include organizational behavior, method variance, and structural equation modeling techniques.

Werner Wothke is President of SmallWaters Corporation. He received his doctorate in methodology in behavioral sciences from the University of Chicago in 1984 and then served for 9 years as Vice President of Technical Operations at Scientific Software, Inc. In 1993, Dr. Wothke cofounded SmallWaters Corporation to publish and promote innovative statistical software. His research interests are in multivariate model building and statistical computing.

Fan Yang is a PhD student in statistics at Uppsala University working on a dissertation with nonlinear structural equation models.

Yiu-Fai Yung is Assistant Professor at the L. L. Thurstone Psychometric Laboratory of the University of North Carolina at Chapel Hill. He received his PhD in Psychology at UCLA in 1994, with his dissertation entitled *Finite Mixtures in Confirmatory Factor-Analytic Models*. His current research interests are subsampling methods and mixture models in structural equation modeling.